BRIEF THERAPY
AND MANAGED CARE

BRIEF THERAPY AND MANAGED CARE

Readings for Contemporary Practice

Michael F. Hoyt

Jossey-Bass Publishers · San Francisco

The opinions expressed herein are those of the author and do not necessarily reflect any official policies of Kaiser Permanente or any other organization.

The quote from Henry Stack Sullivan was reprinted with permission from *The Interpersonal Theory of Psychiatry.* Copyright © 1953 by W. W. Norton & Company.

The quote from Saul Feldman was reprinted with permission from *Managed Mental Health Services.* Copyright © 1992 by Charles C. Thomas, Publisher, Springfield, Illinois.

Excerpt from "Burnt Norton" in *Four Quartets,* copyright © 1943 by T. S. Eliot and renewed 1971 by Esme Valerie Eliot, reprinted by permission of Harcourt Brace & Company.

The lines from "stand with your lover on the ending earth—" are reprinted from *Complete Poems: 1904–1962* by E. E. Cummings, Edited by George J. Firmage, by permission of Liveright Publishing Corporation. Copyright © 1949, 1977, 1991 by the Trustees for the E. E. Cummings Trust.

Substantial discounts on bulk quantities of Jossey-Bass books are available to corporations, professional associations, and other organizations. For details and discount information, contact the special sales department at Jossey-Bass Inc., Publishers (415) 433-1740; Fax (415) 433-0499.

For sales outside the United States, please contact your local Paramount Publishing International office.

Manufactured in the United States of America on Lyons Falls Pathfinder Tradebook. This paper is acid-free and 100 percent totally chlorine-free.

Produced by *Publishing Professionals,* Eugene, Oregon.

Library of Congress Cataloging-in-Publication Data

Hoyt, Michael F.
    Brief therapy and managed care : readings for contemporary practice / Michael F. Hoyt.
        p.   cm. – (Jossey-Bass social and behavioral science series)
    Includes bibliographical references and index.
    ISBN 0-7879-0077-X
    1. Brief psychotherapy.   2. Managed mental health care.
I. Series.
RC480.55.H68   1995
616.89'14–dc20

94-44548

HB Printing   10 9 8 7 6 5 4 3 2 1   FIRST EDITION

Contents

———◆◆◆———

Contents

I think the development of psychiatric skill consists in very considerable measure of doing a lot with very little—making a rather precise move which has a high probability of achieving what you're attempting to achieve, with a minimum of time and words.

—*Harry Stack Sullivan (1954)*

Also worthy of evaluation, planning and thought by a therapist are the matters of time spent, of effective utilization of effort, and above all of the fullest possible utilization of the functional capacities and abilities and the experiential and acquisitional learnings of the patient. These should take precedence over the teachings of new ways in living which are developed from the therapist's possibly incomplete understanding of what may be right and serviceable to the individual concerned.

—*Milton H. Erickson (1980)*

My job as therapist is to be available as long as you need me; your job as patient is to make me obsolete as soon as possible.

—*Nicholas A. Cummings*

At some time or other the conscience of society will awake and remind it that the poor man should have just as much right to assistance for his mind as he now has to the life-saving help offered by surgery; and that the neuroses threaten public health no less than tuberculosis, and can be left as little as the latter to the impotent care of individual members of the community. When this happens, institutions or out-clinics will be started.

—*Sigmund Freud (1919a/1955)*

The Director of a managed-care company died and got up to heaven. At the Pearly Gates St. Peter met the director and said, "We have good news and we have bad news."
"What's the good news?" the Director asked.
"You can come in," replied St. Peter.
"And the bad news?"
"You can only stay for two days!"

—*Anonymous*

At its best, managed mental health can improve quality, reduce inappropriate utilization, control costs and protect mental health and substance abuse benefits from a society that has not infrequently been inclined to reduce them. It can also protect individuals, most of whom have benefit limitations, from using up benefits on unnecessary care and then not having any left when care is truly needed.

But at its worst, managed mental health can fall victim to greed, deprive people of services they really need, truncate the role of mental health providers and successfully cut costs but damage the quality of the clinician /patient relationship so central to the success of the therapeutic process.

Managed mental health is now a fact of life and will be increasingly so.

—*Saul Feldman (1992)*

Preface

❖

Psychotherapy in this day and age is being influenced and shaped by a series of sociocultural forces that originate outside of the consulting room. Economic pressures, the pace of life, the information explosion, and shifting goals and values all have an impact on what happens between therapist and patient, as do new clinical theories and techniques. Managed care—which emerged largely in response to the problem of runaway health care costs—is a broad and evolving attempt to regulate the utilization, site, and costs of services, and it is affecting both the practice of psychotherapy and the delivery of medical care in general. We should not simply capitulate or follow the latest fads, of course, but we should also not cling to the past, waging a retrograde battle for an economic yesteryear, at the expense of good reality testing. More than 100 million Americans are now covered by various forms of managed care, and the numbers are expanding rapidly.

The debate about health care delivery has too often focused more on issues of *cost* than *care*, although I am encouraged by recent discussions that give primacy to the idea of quality being the avenue to cost reduction rather than a benefit one tries to tack on after setting a (low) price. My hope is that we will continue to move toward a system of genuine managed *care*, not just managed costs. To do this we will need to enhance our clinical and administrative skills (work smarter, not just harder) and advocate on many levels (sociopolitical as well as individual, public as well as within our professional societies) for what we consider to be ethical, humane, and clinically appropriate services. I share the following view expressed by Arthur Ashe in his eloquent memoir, *Days of Grace:*

> I believe that there are five essential pillars to support the health and well-being of every individual. The first is unhindered access to physicians [and other clinicians] who will render primary care, listen to and advise the patient, and follow up with treatments in a professional manner. The second is the availability of medicines, treatments, and other therapies. The third is the support of family and friends. The fourth is the determination of the patient to make himself or herself better, to take charge of his or her well-being in cooperation with others. The fifth essential pillar is health insurance, because few people can bear the cost of a serious illness without falling irretrievably into debt. Take away any of those five pillars, I believe, and the structure of individual health and welfare starts to collapse [Ashe and Rampersad, 1993, pp. 245–246].

My primary professional interest is in improving the *efficacy* of psychotherapy, in *doing what works* to assist the persons who seek our help in ways that are the most respectful, most effective, most efficient, and least harmful. This volume presents some of my own attempts in those directions. It is a collection of writings about brief therapy and managed care (many of which have been previously published as book chapters and journal articles) that is, by necessity, incomplete and very much (I hope!) a work in progress. The first two chapters discuss some of the specific features involved in the conduct of therapy within the context of managed care. The emphasis is on efficiency, outcomes, and accountability, managed-care organizations preferring providers who work with clients to target and achieve specific treatment goals. Chapters Three through Six focus on issues especially relevant to practice within health maintenance organizations (HMOs), a service-delivery model that is particularly well suited for improving quality while containing costs and that can be expected to play an increasingly prominent role in health care reform. Chapters Seven through Twelve describe and illustrate—using numerous case examples—several models of brief psychotherapy. Chapters

Thirteen through Eighteen examine various issues that can facilitate or impede efficient treatment. Chapter Nineteen describes diagnostic issues for so-called personality disorders, organizing some of the problematic ways clients typically get "stuck" that may suggest opportunities for "second order" interventions. Chapter Twenty reviews the current field of brief psychotherapies and presents extended case illustrations of several major approaches. Notes are collected at the end of each chapter. All citations in the text are collected in the References section at the end of the book, and a supplemental bibliography is provided in the For Further Reading section; this is followed by a section entitled Directories for Training, Publications, Professional Associations, and Managed-Care Organizations.

Looking in my crystal ball toward the future of managed mental health care as we move toward the meta-goals of universal access, increased effectiveness, and benefits preservation, I see twelve likely trends:

1. More outcomes measurement, particularly assessment of resolution of the presenting complaint and determination of patient satisfaction
2. More treatment planning and more attention to differential therapeutics and the integration of techniques drawn from varying theoretical backgrounds, asking, What would be the best approach with this patient with this problem in this setting at this time?
3. Greater involvement of mental health services in primary care, based on fuller recognition of the connection between physical and mental well-being, following from the many studies that demonstrate that unnecessary medical utilization is reduced when emotional and psychological issues are addressed professionally
4. Increasingly organized, vertically integrated systems of care
5. Fewer and larger managed-care companies
6. More group practices and fewer solo practitioners
7. More care provided by masters-level clinicians, psychiatric nurses, and various certified counselors, in keeping with the managed-care cost-saving principle of having the least

expensive workers do most of the labor

8. More group therapy, including more psychoeducational programs on a variety of topics (e.g., stress reduction, parenting skills, communication training), which will require administrative and financial support to make group referrals available and attractive

9. Much less inpatient care, with what there is mostly emphasizing rapid stabilization and return to the community as soon as possible

10. Greater reliance on computer technology, with its information processing and research advantages as well as attendant risks to confidentiality

11. Less utilization review, at least in the outpatient arena, as education, certification, and credentialing of efficient preferred providers moves forward

12. More emphasis on constructive therapies, ones that are future oriented, collaborative, and based on patients' competencies and resources

Decisions about what services will and will not be covered under managed health care need to be made on rational and moral grounds and clearly spelled out. Those who ultimately control the system are the purchasers of health care, not the managed-care companies that apply the benefit packages that were negotiated and purchased. Will we be able to educate and persuade purchasers—including the public—to pay for the resources that are required? We will need to work in a collaborative, four-way partnership—provider, patient, manager, and purchaser—if we are to do the right thing and get the job done. I believe that the worst phase of the shift to managed care is over; we will need to work together to ensure that the best is yet to come. We need to move toward managed *care*, not just managed *costs*. Gandhi, when he was once asked, "What do you think of Western civilization?" replied, "It would be a good idea!" I submit that *true managed care*—arrangements to regulate the costs, site, and utilization of services in an ethical and clinically appropriate manner—would be a good idea, too. We need to meet this challenge, as clinicians and as citizens.

It is especially important that we mental health professionals stay open to new possibilities and not engage in the internecine battles of "my theory versus yours." This is not to say that we should suspend critical thinking. Quite the opposite. It can be very helpful to have a consistent theoretical perspective, but constructive thinking and the search for what works best often stop when individuals line up into "schools" and only listen to the other side long enough to prepare a rebuttal. Each person is a unique case. As Milton H. Erickson (Zeig, 1980, p. 104) said: "And I do wish that Rogerian therapists, Gestalt therapists, transactional therapists, group analysts, and all the other off-spring of various theories would recognize that not one of them really recognizes that psychotherapy for person #1 is not psychotherapy for person #2." Or, as John Weakland (Hoyt, 1994d, p. 39) has put it, "Stay curious."

My own development has taken me through many of the major systems of psychotherapy, and I keep going forward and recycling back to new things. When asked about my theoretical orientation, I usually reply that I don't quite know, though if pushed, nowadays I'll finally say something like, "Constructive therapy . . . helping people see how they're putting their story together and how they might do it in a way that gets them more of what they want." I like that.

It is a daunting task to attempt acknowledging one's gratitudes. Where did I learn that? Did they tell me, did I tell them, or did it come out of our conversation together? I would like to thank the many patients and clients, colleagues, consultants, authors and readers, workshop attendees and directors, teachers and students, editors and publishers, friends, and others who have influenced me—and will continue to do so—whether they (or I) know it or not. I would be particularly remiss if I did not explicitly thank Kaiser Permanente Health Plan for its long-term support, Jossey-Bass Publishers and Becky McGovern for their interest, and my family for the ground and the sky.

Mill Valley, California Michael F. Hoyt
February 1995

To Ruth

Who Always Manages to Care

The Author

———◆◆———

MICHAEL F. HOYT received his Ph.D. (1976) in psychology from Yale University. He is the director of Adult Psychiatric Services at the Kaiser Permanente Medical Center in Hayward, California, and serves on the clinical faculty at the University of California, San Francisco. Widely published on brief therapy and related topics, Hoyt is the author of approximately one hundred articles and book chapters and is the coeditor of *The First Session in Brief Therapy* (1992) and editor of *Constructive Therapies*, Vol. 1 (1994) and Vol. 2 (in press). A multitheoretical thinker and expert clinician, he is an internationally respected lecturer and workshop presenter. He resides with his wife and son in Mill Valley, California.

BRIEF THERAPY
AND MANAGED CARE

CHAPTER ONE

Characteristics of Psychotherapy Under Managed Health Care

Psychotherapy under managed care involves arrangements that regulate the utilization, site, and costs of services; the nature and length of mental health treatment is determined partially by parties (insurers and reviewers) other than the clinician and patient/client. Brief (or short-term) therapy, which is the backbone of such arrangements, is defined not by a particular number of sessions but rather by the intention of helping patients make changes in thoughts, feelings, and actions in order to move toward or reach a particular goal as time-efficiently as possible. The key is to be "time sensitive" (Budman and Gurman, 1988), to make the most of each session. Traditionally, therapy has been a long, ongoing process during which therapist and patient gradually "worked through" layers of material. The new emphasis is on pragmatism and cost-effectiveness. Consistent with the values of managed care and health maintenance, the emphasis is more on patient strengths and resources rather than looking for underlying pathology (O'Hanlon and Weiner-Davis, 1989). The goals of brief therapy are essentially symptom relief and increased function. Specific "impairments" (Goodman, Brown, and Deitz, 1992) or target symptoms are identified, and treatment addresses their amelioration or repair. Personal development can also result, but it is usually not the primary goal.

Therapists are being asked to help patients identify and achieve a particular attainable goal in a relatively brief period

Note: Reprinted, with changes, from Hoyt, M. F. "Characteristics of Psychotherapy Under Managed Healthcare." *Behavioral Healthcare Tomorrow,* 1994, *3* (5), 59–62. Used by permission of the publisher.

of time. This may be an uncomfortable shift for therapists more accustomed to open-ended treatment, but there are sound clinical and public health reasons for practicing time-sensitive therapy.

Values and Meta-Goals of Managed Care

There is an ecological aspect to managed behavioral health care. Time is a limited resource, and we need to use it wisely. Brief therapy techniques and the managed-care movement support the shift from the value of giving a lot of care to a few patients to treating a population—offering some care to many people.

There are three interrelated "meta-goals" for managed care (Freeman and Leggett, 1992):

1. *Increasing access* so that more patients can have services, with universal access being the ideal. This meets social and humanitarian goals.
2. *Increasing effectiveness* by finding out what works and doing more of what works. Accurate outcomes assessment is essential.
3. *Preserving benefits* and maintaining mental health coverage by demonstrating that what is done is clinically useful. This helps patients and supports therapists' continued livelihoods.

Barriers and Resistances to Brief Therapy

The following are common assumptions—which may operate outside of awareness—that often interfere with therapists practicing in the most efficient way possible:

- The belief that "more therapy is better," even though research does not bear this out.
- Overvaluation of insight and extensive exploration of past-present links at the expense of other therapeutic modalities, such as guidance, suggestion, skill training, reassurance, and practical problem solving.

- The confusion of therapists' and patients' interests, the former often wanting to explore broadly while the latter often wants the most succinct treatment to relieve a particular problem.
- Theoretical obligations that can become self-fulfilling prophecies, like the frequent therapist belief that alliances must develop slowly and that unconscious meanings and psychosocial developments need to be "deeply" probed. In practice, brief therapy requires a great deal of focus, selectivity, and activity on the part of both the therapist and the patient.
- Money and other incentives, such as the pleasures of intimate conversation and friendship, that may make it difficult to terminate treatment. A fee-for-service model gives incentives to prolong treatment, sometimes unnecessarily.
- Countertransference problems, including the therapist's need to be needed and difficulties saying goodbye.
- The burdens of paperwork and expected—and sometimes veridical—hassles with insurance forms and reviewers when opening a new case.
- Reactance to perceived encroachments upon professional autonomy, the sense that no one should dictate our treatments or oversee our practices. Resistance to brief therapy may occur because we don't want to be told we have to work briefly—even if it helps!

Key Phases in Brief Therapy

Each treatment, as well as each session, has five synergistic phases. Attention to the specific tasks associated with each phase helps make treatment more time-efficient, a particularly important consideration when—as is usually the case under managed care—the number of sessions is preset or at least restricted and closely monitored.

1. *Pre-treatment.* In this phase, the therapist helps patients prepare for the first session when they make the appointment, asking them to give some thought to what they want to accomplish. The therapist might pose the "Skeleton Key" question, developed by de Shazer (1985): "Between now

and when we meet, I would like you to notice the things that happen to you that you would like to keep happening in the future. This will help me find out more about your goals and what you're up to." The therapist may also ask patients to think about how they expect therapy to help them, and how long they expect it to take.

2. *Beginning phase.* In the first session, as well as the first portion of each subsequent session, certain tasks need to be accomplished: developing an alliance; defining the purpose of the meeting; orienting the patient regarding how to use therapy; presenting an opportunity for the expression of thoughts, feelings, and behavior; mutually formulating a focus and achievable goals; making (initial) treatment interventions and seeing the response; and discussing confidentiality, fees, and future appointments. As my colleagues Simon Budman and Steven Friedman and I have written in *The First Session in Brief Therapy* (1992), it is important to introduce novelty, since more of the same does not make a change. Mental imagery, role playing, and other techniques can help the patient begin to have a glimpse of the possible. It engenders hope and helps patients see that they can make a change. It is also important, in each session, to check on progress since the last contact and to amplify that which helps the patient move in the desired direction.

3. *Middle phase.* This is the time of "working through"—increasing awareness ("making the unconscious conscious") and also applying the lessons of therapy outside of the office. This is also a time to make sure that the right problem is being addressed, to monitor progress and refine the focus as needed. Therapy becomes unnecessarily long when switching from problem to problem without completing work on one topic. If a patient brings up another serious matter, the therapist and patient must prioritize. Covering too many subjects at once diminishes the clarity and thrust needed to resolve any of the problems. As the old saying has it, "If you're too well rounded, you're not pointed in any direction."

4. *End phase.* Toward the end of treatment, as in each session, termination becomes a central issue. Termination simply means extracting the therapist from the successful equation. "You've been doing well with me. How will you continue to do well without me?" Often patients will respond to the termination phase matter-of-factly: the work has been accomplished, and they're ready to move on. It is important for the therapist to avoid making more (or less) of ending than is appropriate and supportive of the work completed. If the patient is feeling disappointed that therapy is not ongoing and continuous, that should be acknowledged; it also may be useful to confront all or nothing thinking such as, "Why bother going to therapy if I can't have all I want?" or the notion that therapy is ineffective if it doesn't solve all of the patient's problems quickly. Help the patient see that just as he or she may have started to make changes between the time they made the appointment and came for the first session (Weiner-Davis, de Shazer, and Gingerich, 1987), many changes may occur after the formal ending of therapy. It is important to realize that while treatment may be brief, the benefit may be long-term.

5. *Follow-through.* Tasks that patients are assigned between sessions connect one session to another. Frequently, a process will be set in motion or amplified but not completely resolved during a session or course of treatment. Both the therapist and the patient may need to live with a certain amount of suspense, and it's helpful to schedule follow-ups by phone, questionnaire, or in person. The patient and therapist may both benefit by knowing that follow-up contact is possible.

Key Characteristics of Managed Mental Health Care

Cutting across various administrative systems and specific brief-therapy approaches are several principles that characterize treatment in HMOs and other managed-care systems (Austad and Berman, 1991). As seen in Table 1.1, these summarize much of what constitutes effective brief psychotherapy.

**Table 1.1. Eight Characteristics
of Managed Behavioral Health Care.**

Features	Comments
1. Specific problem solving.	Why has the patient come to therapy now? Identification with patient of achievable, measurable goals.
2. Rapid response and early intervention.	Therapy begins right away, engaging the patient as soon as possible, including amplifying useful pre-treatment progress.
3. Clear definition of patient and therapist responsibilities, with an emphasis on patient competencies, resources, and involvement.	The therapist structures treatment contacts, conducts particular interventions, and involves significant others as needed. The patient is encouraged to participate actively, including doing "homework assignments" and making behavioral changes outside of therapy sessions.
4. Time is used flexibly and creatively.	The length, frequency, and timing of sessions vary according to patient needs, with the ideal being the most parsimonious intervention likely to have positive effects in a given situation.
5. Interdisciplinary cooperation.	Medical and psychological involvement blends into a more holistic view of the patient. Allied health professionals may be used as indicated, as may appropriate psychopharmacology.
6. Multiple formats and modalities.	Individual, group, and/or marital/family therapy may be used in sequential or concurrent combinations, and participation in various community resources (including self-help, twelve-step, and support groups) may be vigorously encouraged.
7. Intermittent treatment or a "family practitioner" model.	The idea of a once-and-for-all "cure" gives way to a more realistic view that patients can return for "serial" or "distributed" treatment as needed, often focused around developmental issues throughout the life cycle. The therapist-patient relationship may be long term although frequently abeyant.

**Table 1.1. Eight Characteristics
of Managed Behavioral Health Care,** *Cont'd.*

Features	Comments
8. Results orientation and accountability.	Is treatment helping? Outcomes measurement helps define what works best. Utilization review and quality assurance function as complementary procedures, efficacious relief of symptoms being in the best interests of the patient and the company.

Source: Hoyt, M. F. (1994a, p. 61). Reprinted by permission of the publisher.

Judicious Use of Time

Therapists working in managed care would do well to not always use the maximum number of authorized sessions. For patients, time is then available to schedule follow-ups or is placed "in the bank" for future use. For therapists, it is important in building a relationship with a managed-care company for the organization to see that the therapist is judicious, not simply trying to use every session that can be had. Later, when there is a case where the therapist feels that additional sessions are required, he or she can refer back to those times when treatment finished early so that the clinician can develop a reputation as flexible and not as someone who always treats to the benefit limit.

It is also important that therapists not give in to the temptation to "up-code"—that is, to describe the patient's condition as worse than it is in order to get more sessions authorized. Even if well-intended, this is insurance fraud. It is appropriate to advocate for the patient within the contract that the provider, the patient, and the company have, but it is important not to distort information. To do otherwise not only is dishonest and unethical but also deprives the company of accurate information needed to make correct determinations of how many sessions are usually required.

When Brief Therapy Is Not Enough

While brief therapy is the backbone of managed care, there are times when, for various reasons, a patient is not able to resolve his or her problems within a brief period of time. When this is the case, it may be appropriate to request additional sessions. When doing so, it is especially important to communicate clearly with utilization review case managers. The request for additional sessions is much more efficient and likely to produce the desired result if the clinician is well-organized, focused, and professional; information like diagnosis, current clinical assessment, particular difficulties and proposed treatments, and a specific number of additional sessions with supporting rationale should be well thought out before contacting the company. If a request is denied, it is highly recommended that an appeal be made promptly in writing, both to increase the chance of the additional sessions being authorized and to carefully document one's efforts if the appeal is also denied. Among the challenges facing the managed-care field is the design of benefits packages that will provide appropriate services for patients requiring longer-term or continuous care.

The Need for Education

Making the optimal use of limited time and resources while providing high-quality professional services requires special skills and orientation. Graduate schools and professional schools generally have not yet adapted their curricula to teach the methods of assessment, time-sensitive therapy, and case management required by behavioral health care programs (Austad, Sherman, and Holstein, 1993; Bennett, 1994; Blackwell and Schmidt, 1992; Budman and Armstrong, 1992; Sabin and Borus, 1992). Continuing education is an important part of quality assurance, with workshops, conferences, consultation, and professional publications all playing important roles. Clinicians and managed-care companies are increasingly coming to realize the importance of specific training for the provision of more efficient and satisfying services, and it can be expected that graduate and professional schools that are interested in equipping their students for the realities of contemporary practice will soon begin to emphasize the requisite skills for working under the auspices of managed care.

CHAPTER TWO

Twenty-Five Questions to Ask Before Joining a Managed-Care Organization

There are also other issues that need to be addressed, such as avoiding incentive systems that represent a conflict of interest, carrying adequate malpractice coverage, and observing all applicable laws, regulations, and ethical guidelines.
—Anthony Broskowski (1991)

Provider manuals for specific organizations contain important information regarding policies and procedures that should be carefully reviewed and understood. It is strongly advised that a qualified health care business attorney be consulted before signing any contract, since joining a managed-care plan may involve legally binding obligations. Colleagues, groups, and professional associations may at times find it advantageous to share legal expenses, particularly if the alternative is to find the truth behind Mark Twain's adage, "Only a fool has himself for a lawyer." I emphasize the importance of sound legal counsel to protect our clients, ourselves, and our various professions during these times of rapidly changing laws, rules, regulations, and ethical standards. What applies in one jurisdiction or for one professional discipline, or at one point in time, may not apply elsewhere or at another time. The following questions and answers regarding various practical, legal, and ethical issues are offered to organize some general principles worthy of further evaluation in specific situations. Particularly useful resources in-

Note: Epigraph reprinted with permission of the publisher from Broskowski, A. "Current Mental Health Care Environments: Why Managed Care Is Necessary." *Professional Psychology: Research and Practice,* 1991, *22,* 6–14.

clude Austad and Berman, 1991; Browning and Browning, 1993;
Broskowski, 1991; Cummings, 1991b; Feldman, 1992; Feldman
and Fitzpatrick, 1992; Freeman and Leggett, 1992; German,
1994; Giles, 1993; Gottlieb, 1992; Haas and Cummings, 1994;
Langman-Dorwart and Harris, 1992; Lowman and Resnick,
1994; Newman and Bricklin, 1991; Poynter, 1994; the journal
Psychotherapy Finances; Sharfstein, 1992; Small, 1992; Sterman,
1993; Winegar, 1992; and Winegar and Bistline, 1994. For additional references, see the Managed Care/HMO Practice list-
ings in the For Further Reading section at the end of this book.

1. *Is it necessary to join managed-care organizations? Is managed
   behavioral health care a good career option for all practitioners?*
   While it is important to get on networks and panels if you
   are going to get involved, before rushing out to join a
   managed-care company, ask yourself the following questions: Why am I doing this? What's my motivation?
   Where am I in my practice: building? maintaining? near-
   ing retirement? How do I feel about managed care and
   its emphasis on time-sensitive, outcomes-oriented treatment and case management and review? Managed care
   covers approximately 100 million Americans and is rapidly expanding. If its strong orientation toward arrangements to regulate the cost, site, and utilization of services
   in a highly efficient and cost-effective manner are contrary
   to your values and ways of working, and you don't feel
   willing or able to adapt and successfully utilize the necessary skills and orientation, it may be best to find ways of
   practicing that bypass involvement with managed care.
   This will be a shrinking portion of the mental health market, but some practitioners will be needed to serve patients
   who are out-of-pocket (non-insurance) payers.

2. *Who does best in the managed-care field?* In addition to having a clear preference for brief therapy and efficient case
   management, providers who thrive in a managed-care
   environment are those who are good at organizing, implementing, and networking; who are comfortable with
   a fair degree of uncertainty and risk; who are good at

customer relations (patient, referral source, and case reviewer); and who have good administrative, business, and information-management skills.

3. *Are there warning signals of which companies to avoid?* In addition to formal complaints that may be researched through professional associations, state insurance commissioners, and better business bureaus, it is useful to ask colleagues about their experiences with particular companies. Because the field is evolving so rapidly, it is important to determine the specific nature and currency of any complaint; a bad reputation may be based on an isolated incident, while the policies, procedures, and personnel of the company have long since changed for the better. Additional warning signals might include unqualified reviewers, cumbersome and intrusive paperwork, inappropriate discharges, the absence of clear review criteria and appeals processes, inappropriate short-term models for high-risk patients, and the punishing of providers who appropriately challenge reviews.

4. *How does one find the best companies in a particular area?* At first, most companies were open and solicited clinicians to become providers for them. Now they are much more selective and sometimes indicate that they are closed—that they have all the providers they can use. Word-of-mouth networking is a good way to get up-to-date local information. Major employers have personnel or human resource departments that can tell you which companies they contract with for mental health services. Again, insurance commissioners and professional associations can be helpful. Use the information provided in the Directories for Training, Publications, Professional Associations, and Managed-Care Organizations section at the end of this book; the newsletters and journals listed are also valuable resources, and they often carry advertising for upcoming workshops and conferences of particular relevance to managed-care professionals. For more information, one can also contact the national association for health maintenance organizations (HMOs), preferred provider organizations (PPOs),

and employee assistance programs (EAPs) for a directory of companies in your area.

5. *How does one get on board? What are they looking for?* In the area of marketing yourself to managed care, four particularly valuable references are Browning and Browning (1993), Poynter (1994), *Psychotherapy Finances,* and Winegar and Bistline (1994). Contact companies directly, writing to a particular person. Do your homework; don't address your letter to "Dear Sir or Madam." Let them know your strengths and interests, including any other managed-care experience as well as particular training or expertise, licensure, and memberships in relevant clinical societies or professional associations. Point out any other special capabilities, activities, and skills that might make you particularly attractive, such as involvement in a multidisciplinary group with twenty-four-hour emergency coverage, extended office hours and convenient locations, home visit and mobile crisis capacity, knowledge of different languages or subpopulations, and so on. Having a market niche can be advantageous. Specialties with time-sensitive treatment for eating disorders, affective disorders, traumatic stress and abuse victims, crisis intervention, child and family problems, dual diagnoses, workplace issues, somatoform disorders, and chronically and severely disturbed persons are often preferred. Descriptions of your typical treatment profile and approach, with some details about diagnoses and average numbers of sessions, show that you pay attention to information management and accountability. Cognitive-behavioral and solution-focused/ solution-oriented psychotherapeutic approaches are usually most compatible with the managed-care emphasis on cost containment. Having a psychodynamic theoretical orientation is not the kiss of death, but since the emphasis is strongly towards specific outcomes, it is important to have an orientation toward focused results. Of course, if this is not a characteristic and comfortable modus operandi, it should not be misrepresented. Not only would it be unethical to be less than honest, but a serious mismatch may

result. The goal-directed problem-solving work that will be expected requires specific skill and commitment, if not enthusiasm.

6. *Does getting on a panel assure that I'll get referrals? How do I stay on board and do well?* A company might not continue to require your services if they downsize (e.g., lose a big contract and thus not need as many providers) or if your practice patterns don't fit their profile expectations (e.g., your treatments take longer or are less successful than those of colleagues involved in similar cases). A successful ongoing relationship with a managed-care organization involves developing a good working alliance with the company and being courteous, punctual, and professional. One needs to be knowledgeable about benefits and aligned with managed-care values (see Chapter Four); demonstrate good clinical skills and achieve obtainable symptom-reduction outcomes and discharges in a reasonable time frame; promptly provide good treatment plans, progress updates, discharge reports, and related documentation; and actively attend to constructive suggestions, customer (patient, purchaser, company) satisfaction, and continuous quality improvement. Browning and Browning (1993) and Poynter (1994) detail many ways to achieve these vital objectives.

7. *What if a company says it is "full" or "closed"?* Companies can only use a certain number of providers, since the company only covers a certain number of potential patients. If a company says it is full, stay in touch, checking back regularly. An informational get-acquainted interview may be possible to arrange. Don't be unprofessionally pushy, but do show entrepreneurial initiative. Make a case why (particular skills, availability in hours, geographic location) you should be included even though the panel is officially "closed." Having an office in an area underserved by clinicians can be helpful. You may be able to get on a panel if a patient you are treating under one coverage moves to coverage by the closed panel, if it can be documented that your skills and continuity of care are required.

A human resource department or EAP can request that
you be included. A physician referring a patient for psychological services can request your services specifically.

8. *Who takes the risk?* In traditional arrangements, the insurer
took the financial risks. In some managed-care systems,
some of the risk is shifted to the patient, with increasing
co-payments. The risk may also be shifted on to the
provider, as in capitated HMO arrangements where payment is fixed and the company is at risk to provide all
contracted-for services. Some companies may also shift
some of the financial risk on to provider-clinicians by withholding some percentage of fees until the end of the year
and only distributing them once claims have been reviewed and certain profit levels have been achieved. All
regular clinical responsibilities—such as providing competent treatment, maintaining clinical records, making Tara-
soff and child/elder protective service reports—are still in
place, and providers should maintain their own professional liability insurance.

9. *How much does the plan intrude into the patient-provider relationship?* In traditional practice, privacy was total. In managed care, by definition, the company has a say-so. How
controlling is it? Is the emphasis more on "managed" or
on "care"? Is it more important to get patients out than
to get them well? How will you balance your relationship
with the patient and your relationship with the company?
Clinicians would be wise to avoid companies whose case
review practices seem destructive to successful treatment.

10. *What provisions exist for exceptions to the rules?* Some companies are flexible and will let you substitute benefits, with
the patient's informed consent. For example, a greater
number of group therapy sessions may be had in lieu of
individual sessions. In some instances, with careful assessment and cogent discussion, you and the patient may be
allowed to convert inpatient coverage to outpatient coverage to avoid the necessity of hospitalization—if this seems
likely to be beneficial. Of course, once the benefits are
authorized and used, they are gone, so that inpatient care

may not be insured if it was converted and spent as additional outpatient visits.

11. *What if patient needs should exceed plan benefits?* Many plans will allow you to continue seeing the patient if his or her needs extend beyond the benefit limit, but the contract may prohibit you from ever raising your fees beyond the initial "preferred provider" rate. Some companies may help you find another therapist for the patient. It is very important to recognize that once you accept a patient, he or she is yours until you can appropriately terminate treatment or transfer their care. You cannot stop seeing someone just because they have no money or the company refuses to pay, any more than an emergency room can turn away an indigent patient appearing with a medical emergency. Not every problem has to be resolved, of course, but even an evaluation appointment may obligate us to care for the patient until he or she is reasonably stable and/or another professional actively assumes responsibility. Patient abandonment is a major ethical breach, and legal cases have found clinicians to be liable if they stop treatment because a managed-care company wouldn't authorize payment. In critical situations, responsible decisions have to be made on clinical grounds, not fiscal ones. The law in this area is still very much under development, so clinicians are best advised to act conservatively, i.e., to assume they are at least partially responsible. This underscores the importance of the timely filing of written appeals for any cases you believe are being denied services that should be authorized per contract.

12. *Does the plan provide assistance or training to help the provider achieve treatment goals?* Good companies are increasingly providing training as part of their quality assurance or continuous quality improvement efforts, bringing special speakers in-house and/or encouraging attendance at professional workshops by negotiating discounts for their providers. Good companies want to support their clinicians' efficiency; they may provide treatment protocols and selected literature reviews. They may also, when needed,

help locate specialists for referrals. Competency is an ethical issue, and providers should be sure they are skilled with a particular problem (e.g., posttraumatic stress disorder, anorexia) they may be asked to treat—or decline the case.

13. *Does the plan minimize economic incentives to provide or deny certain services?* Some plans have built-in incentives for certain types of treatment. For example, a plan may offer incentives or pressures to hospitalize, especially if the plan is affiliated with a psychiatric hospital. There may be a "perverse" incentive situation, such as when a patient gets 100 percent of inpatient services covered but only 50 percent of outpatient services, tempting the clinician to hospitalize a patient (though it may be clinically unnecessary) in order to get payment for treatment. This form of "upcoding" (describing the patient as worse than he or she actually is in order to get additional payment) should be avoided, even if well intended. Providers in these settings should lobby for alternatives when appropriate. Professionals who function as evaluators or utilization reviewers also need to be wary of the conflict of interest that may develop if the reviewer is paid ("incented") to deny services. Persons in such roles should be salaried, so as not to make their decisions too sensitive to the finances of any particular case. The Utilization Review Accreditation Commission (see the Directories for Training, Publications, Professional Associations, and Managed-Care Organizations section) provides standards and ethical guidelines for reviewers.

14. *Are there ways in which the plan is open to provider input?* Will you be viewed as merely a technician or as a professional whose input is valued? Does the plan welcome feedback? How? Does the plan have a provider panel?

15. *Do plans clearly inform their policyholders of the limits of benefits?* Does the plan let people know what is covered and what isn't? Some companies contractually specify that they don't pay for psychological testing, treatment of primary personality disorders, marital therapy, and/or certain treat-

ments that they consider "experimental." Don't get caught in the middle, lest you later get blamed for a misinterpretation. It is best to refer the patient back to their benefits department for clarification, and to chart that you did so.

16. *What are the basic elements of information that a company will want about a patient?* While each company may have its particular questions and format for an initial report, authorization request, or treatment plan, most require that the following basic information be provided accurately and concisely: (1) a brief description of the patient, including any relevant personal and family psychiatric history and previous treatments; (2) the presenting complaint, impairments, and diagnoses; (3) the goals, methods, and objectives of the proposed treatment; (4) a description of how progress will be assessed; and (5) justification for the level of treatment (e.g., why not more intensive or less intensive). Good treatment plans generally do the following: (1) address specific symptoms and impairments (behaviorally described and measured) supporting "medical necessity," (2) estimate the duration of treatment, and (3) include the utilization of collateral treatments, consultations, and community support when appropriate (e.g., medical referrals, school counselors, parenting classes, Alcoholics Anonymous, and so on).

17. *What is an* impairment? In their excellent book, *Managing Managed Care: A Mental Health Practitioner's Survival Guide,* Goodman, Brown, and Deitz (1992, p. 31) say: *"Impairment* describes a worsening, lessening, weakening, damaging, or reduction in ability to function and, in turn, anticipates a potential for repair, improvement, enhancement, and strengthening. . . . [They] signal the appropriateness for treatment and frame the documentation and communication of not only the treatment plan but also the patient's response to treatment interventions. . . . Impairments are the reasons why a patient requires treatment. They are not the reason(s) for the presence of the disorder, nor are they the disorder itself. Rather, they are observable, objectifiable manifestations that necessitate and justify care."

In short, impairments (such as suicidal thoughts, dysphoric mood, alcohol abuse, insomnia, rage reactions, agitation, hallucinations, social isolation, and so on) may be thought of as the "target symptoms" that treatment is intended to improve or eliminate.

18. *What is the managed-care organization's definition of* medical necessity (*or* clinical necessity)? These terms generally refer to situations where the individual's level of functioning interferes with or disrupts community living to the extent that without treatment services the individual would be unable to maintain residence, engage in productive activities and daily responsibilities, maintain a social support system, and remain healthy. Essentially, the idea is that treatment is required to maintain a level of functioning and to avoid an acute exacerbation (that would then require a more intensive level of care). It should be noted that some companies may contractually apply a different standard, restricting services only to those situations where there is a "significant likelihood of improvement through relatively brief therapy." In instances where "maintenance" or "chronic support" are not covered benefits, alternative arrangements will need to be made for the continuous care requirements of selected clients.

19. *What are some frequent treatment planning problems?* Discussions with many utilization reviewers and managed-care providers indicate that plans often get questioned or disapproved because of the following: (1) inadequate assessment and diagnosis; (2) vagueness and lack of a clear connection between diagnoses, impairments, and specific proposed treatments; (3) insufficiently individualized plans that sound like a page from a book or a typical computer profile rather than an approach with a particular human being; (4) overly ambitious conception; (5) unnecessary seeking of further problems; (6) failure to review plans with the patient and to get his or her assent; and (7) lack of compliance with the managed-care organization's recommended protocols and preferred programs. It seems wise to cultivate a respectful, non-adversarial relationship

with a particular utilization reviewer at the managed-care organization. Remembering that the person on the other end of the phone or fax line has a job to do and trying to make his or her job easier by being organized and attending to the specific information that is needed will do a lot to avoid these kinds of problems.

20. *What is the plan's approach to payment?* Most plans will agree to pay a set amount per session. How are claims submitted? How often will you get paid? What is the turnaround time for claims? (Some states now require companies to pay interest on accounts after thirty days.) What if they are contested? Most plans prohibit clinicians from charging patients more than the plan pays, and may require you to hold the patient harmless if the company does not authorize payment. EAP arrangements often require the therapist to refer the patient to another provider if treatment cannot be completed in the allotted number of sessions. Other arrangements may allow the therapist to continue with a patient beyond the authorized number of sessions but with the restriction that rates can never be raised beyond what was originally charged when treatment was covered by the managed-care contract. Are co-payments involved, and if so, how are they handled (e.g., does the clinician collect them)? What are the reimbursement arrangements for missed sessions? If non-covered services are indicated (e.g., psychological testing), will the plan allow you to charge the patient, and if so, how much? In considering payment, it is important to recognize the increased overhead that may be involved in working with managed-care organizations: paperwork, time on the phone, faxing, and so forth. Overall, one should be careful not to accept too low a fee, since it may lead to counter-transference difficulties that can compromise the quality of patient care. A fee that seems professionally insulting may be a first signal of a lack of collegial respect and may also indicate that the company will be inappropriately parsimonious in other important areas (such as the number of authorized sessions or the availability of support staff).

21. *What are some common reasons for payments being delayed?* Claims reviewers respond unfavorably to the following: (1) an incorrect member or group identification number; (2) a missing diagnosis; (3) a wrong procedure code; (4) a sloppy or illegible claim form; (5) incorrect itemization of fees; (6) missing or incorrect service dates; (7) an incomplete treatment planning, progress, or closing report; (8) a missing license number; (9) claims submitted to the wrong address or office; (10) claims with no provider signature; and (11) a missing taxpayer number.

22. *How financially stable is the insurer?* If you are going to put all (or most) of your eggs in one basket, you want it to be durable. This is important, because if a plan goes broke, therapists are usually not allowed to bill the patient directly because of the "hold harmless" clause in many contracts that may specify no one can be required to pay for claims the company rejects. Companies may come and go; one company went bankrupt while owing therapists millions. Developments can sometimes be tracked in industry newsletters (see the Directories for Training, Publications, Professional Associations, and Managed-Care Organizations section). A bad reputation, seeming lack of office staff, and long payment delays can be cautionary signals.

23. *What is the protocol for emergency treatment?* Does the plan clearly instruct you on how to deal with emergencies? Are certain inpatient facilities to be used? What are the procedures for getting treatment authorization outside of regular business hours? It is especially important that these matters be clarified in advance, since emergency situations can require prompt (and potentially expensive) actions.

24. *What are the provisions for terminating or interrupting my obligations?* What notification is required to discontinue a relationship with a particular managed-care company? Contracts often call for thirty-, sixty-, or ninety-day notification. Can patients already being seen continue with a given therapist if the therapist severs her or his relationship with Company X? When a therapist goes on vacation or

has a full caseload, how should she or he let the company know not to make referrals? Again, these issues should be clarified before a difficult situation arises.

25. *How is confidentiality protected?* What information is required for authorization and payment? Following the basic principle of informed consent, patients should know and understand the content of such information and agree to its release. Clinicians should be accurate and circumspect in reporting data. Is it clear that the information provided to the managed-care company will not go beyond the company, or is the patient consenting to have information re-released to other agencies or data bases? Does the company clearly describe and adhere to practices for protecting confidentiality? The documentation required by managed care for payment does not replace the obligation therapists may have to create, maintain, and protect the privacy of their own professional records.

CHAPTER THREE

Psychotherapy in a Staff-Model HMO: Providing and Assuring Quality Care in the Future

with Carol Shaw Austad

At some time or other the conscience of society will awake and remind it that the poor man should have just as much right to assistance for his mind as he now has to the life-saving help offered by surgery; and that the neuroses threaten public health no less than tuberculosis, and can be left as little as the latter to the impotent care of individual members of the community. When this happens, institutions or out-clinics will be started.

–Sigmund Freud (1919a/1955)

The expansion of health maintenance organizations (HMOs) and the current controversies regarding managed health care involve major developments in the present and future field of psychotherapy (Austad and Berman, 1991; Austad, DeStefano, and Kisch, 1988; Austad and Hoyt, 1992; Berkman, Bassos, and Post, 1988; Budman, 1985; Cheifetz and Salloway, 1984; Cummings, 1986, 1988; DeLeon, Uyeda, and Welch, 1985; Goldensohn, 1977; Kiesler and Morton, 1988; Kisch and Aus-

Note: Reprinted, with changes, from Hoyt, M. F., and Austad, C. S. "Psychotherapy in a Staff-Model HMO: Providing and Assuring Quality Care in the Future." *Psychotherapy,* 1992, *29,* 119–129. Used by permission of the coauthor and the publisher.

Epigraph reprinted from Freud, S. "Lines of Advance in Psycho-Analytic Therapy." In J. Strachey (ed.), *The Standard Edition of the Complete Psychological Works of Sigmund Freud.* Vol. 17. Copyright 1955 by Hogarth Press. Used by permission of the publisher. (Originally published 1919.)

tad, 1988; Shulman, 1988). The focus of this chapter is on the future practice of psychotherapy services within *staff-* or *group-model* HMOs, which were the first large-scale forms of prepaid insurance (Bennett, 1988) and which by history have best demonstrated the capacity for providing and assuring compre- hensive quality care. Some of the advantages that accrue from the staff- and group-model organizational structure will be discussed.

Staff- and group-model HMOs can be essentially identical in terms of their organization for provision of services, involving a (usually full-time) staff of in-house clinicians serving a prepaid membership population. Not only may these clinicians be salaried—as in the staff model—but, in the group model, clinicians may also be owners (or partners) and thus be at risk financially for the comprehensive services covered in the HMO-member contract. Staff- and group-model HMOs are the same in having a closed panel of providers, but it should be recognized that all HMOs are not the same in quality of services. One should not assume an HMO uniformity anymore than one would assume that all patients or all therapists are equivalent (Kiesler, 1966). The potential advantages of HMOs, such as the provision of mental health services to a wider client base and the better integration of psychological and medical services, cannot be fairly assessed until one first separates the wheat from the chaff. In this chapter we will discuss the future of *good* HMO therapy. Therapy in a staff- or group-model HMO is not a panacea. The traditional HMO model was developed to provide services as needed to a basically functional (note: *health maintenance*) population, and significant adaptations will be required to meet the needs of those persons who are more chronically troubled or persistently ill. The HMO has its limits and problems, as will be discussed, but it also has its values.

Most psychotherapists, unless they have just awakened from a decade-long coma, have more than just noticed that the field is evolving rapidly. If we want clinical and ethical factors to carry weight, not just fiscal considerations (what Berman [1992, p. 43] calls the "economic juggernaut"), it will behoove concerned mental health professionals—both HMO therapists and private practitioners—to understand how psychotherapy may be practiced in an HMO and to join in determining what would best serve our patients and our profession.

In recent years the number of HMOs in the United States has grown exponentially (Bennett, 1988; Zimet, 1989). More than thirty million Americans are now covered by HMO prepayment plans (Relman, 1990). In the San Francisco Bay area, where Kaiser Permanente, the nation's largest HMO, originated, more than 28 percent of the population is now enrolled in Kaiser (Kramon, 1989). By attracting so many subscribers, good HMOs may provide potential mental health services to many people who otherwise would not receive treatment. This is suggested by the finding (Bittker, 1985) that per capita use of outpatient HMO mental health services is better than twice the rate for fee-for-service systems. This same pattern has been well documented for pediatric care (Szilagyi and others, 1990; Torphy, Campbell, and Davis, 1988; Valdez and others, 1989; see also Moreno, 1989)—more people come to the doctor if they have prepaid coverage than if they pay stiff fees for each visit. By contractually delimiting psychiatric services to "crisis intervention and brief therapy" (frequently defined as up to twenty sessions for conditions likely to show significant improvement in a short-term format), HMOs are de facto mandating the expansion of forms of brief therapy while, by implication, leaving long-term therapy to other practitioners. As Lange and others (1988, p. 455) have noted, "HMOs are playing an important role in expanding the client base for outpatient services . . . psychotherapy is no longer a resource for the privileged minority."

Because the staff- or group-model HMO are both in essence closed systems providing comprehensive services, patients being treated in such settings potentially get better follow-up than people in independent private practice. If HMO patients are not helped, they may return to their medical doctor and/or to the same psychiatry department (Bennett and Wisneski, 1979; Budman, Feldman, and Bennett, 1979). The incentive in a closed system is thus to provide mental health services, both to help patients *and* to avoid unnecessary medical and emergency room visits. Both motivations, to serve patients and to contain costs, can be addressed simultaneously. They are no more mutually exclusive than the ideas that the fee-for-service practitioner can both serve patients' interests and charge for each service. In a well-run staff-model HMO, there are no incentives for a nonpsychiatric doctor to hold on to a patient. Patients can usually self-refer to mental health services. HMO-type systems that operate by avoiding or curtailing needed and contracted-for services should not be tolerated.

The Brief Treatment Orientation of Good HMO Therapy

The essence of good HMO therapy is that it is *short-term, eclectic,* and *effective.* Psychotherapy when well practiced in an HMO is not just an abbreviated, miniaturized, or truncated version of long-term therapy. The goals of most therapy in an HMO are more circumscribed (symptom relief, return to function) than those of most long-term treatment. Thus, therapists who prefer longer-term work or pursue different goals need not view the HMO as a rival. The essential belief of the effective short-term therapist is that people can change in the moment, that with skillful assistance they can begin immediately to make beneficial movement. A short-term therapy "credo" might include the following working assumptions (see Chapter Eight), as summarized by Hoyt, Rosenbaum, and Talmon (1992, pp. 61–62):

1. View each session as a whole, potentially complete in itself.
2. The power is in the patient. Never underestimate your patient's strength.
3. This is it. All you have is now. Play it where it lies.
4. Therapy starts before the first session and will continue long after it.
5. The natural process of life is the main force of change.
6. You don't have to know everything in order to be effective.
7. You don't have to rush or reinvent the wheel.
8. More is not necessarily better. Better is better. A small step can make a big difference.

9. Helping people as quickly as possible is practical and ethical. It will encourage patients to return for help if they have other problems and will also allow therapists to spend more time with patients who require longer treatments.

Much of psychotherapy, not just in HMOs, is moving toward being more focused, goal oriented, and shorter term (Garfield and Bergin, 1986; Zeig, 1987). Although some clinicians may not like this move because they feel it isn't "real therapy" or that it can't help patients, there is considerable evidence to suggest otherwise. Others know that short-term therapy can be helpful but still don't like it, because it's not familiar or not cozy or threatens their lucrative practice.

To enjoy practicing effective brief therapy, which is the mainstay of HMO work, the therapist must first confront and overcome a series of potential barriers or resistances (see Chapter Seventeen): the belief that "more is better"; the overvaluation of insight and analysis at the expense of other therapeutic avenues; the brief treatment demand for greater therapist activity and focality; the confusion of the therapist's interests with those of the patient; financial payoffs; and countertransference and other problems with termination, including the need to be needed and difficulties saying good-bye.

The assumptions of the long-term therapist can often become self-fulfilling prophecies. There is an alternative set of assumptions that guides most short-term work: the belief that focused interventions can set into motion a whole system of changes; the belief that many patients can rapidly form a good working alliance and that generalized regression should be avoided; and the belief that focusing and time limits increase and intensify the work accomplished and that gains are consolidated throughout the treatment and continue long after the end of formal therapy contact.

Essential Characteristics of HMO Therapy

While there are many different forms of brief therapy, the following principles cut across various systems and specific technical approaches and extend beyond the single parameter of "short-term" to characterize what Austad, DeStefano, and Kisch (1988; Austad and Berman, 1991) have called *HMO therapy*. These trends are likely to continue as HMOs and managed care expand in the future.

1. *Rapid setting of clearly defined goals with an orientation toward brief therapy and specific problem solving.* This stimulates the development and application of *differential therapeutics* (Frances, Clarkin, and Perry, 1984), the effort to implement specific treatments for specific problems rather than taking a broad, exploratory approach. The HMO therapist needs to achieve a rapid, accurate assessment and to arrive at a clear, specific formulation of an effective treatment plan, one that will guide both psychosocial and pharmacological interventions as needed (Bittker and George, 1980). In many cases assessment and intervention are intertwined, with test interventions used to clarify the assessment.

2. *Crisis intervention preparedness, so that problems can be dealt with before they get entrenched or produce avalanches of secondary problems.*[1] The HMO therapist often has generous organizational support to help in handling crises. In staff- and group-model HMOs a referral can be as simple as a walk to a different part of the building. The availability of urgent-visit programs, emergency services, coordinated follow-through appointments, temporary holding environments, and extensive medical backup are essential HMO features for preventing or limiting unnecessary exacerbations of acute mental health problems (Bittker and George, 1980; Budman and Gurman, 1988; Cummings, 1988). HMO therapists are trained to think quickly, rapidly develop a working alliance, and diagnose and intervene on short notice.

3. *Clear definition of patient and therapist responsibilities, with an explicit understanding (often described as a "contract") of the purpose, schedule, and duration of treatment.* An atmosphere is fostered in which the patient assumes much of the responsibility for the work of therapy, including active involvement in bringing relevant material to the sessions,

carrying out homework assignments, and implementing behavioral changes outside of the therapy sessions. The therapist is authoritative and prudently active, utilizing various clinical skills to assist the patient in a positive, productive direction. The therapist is responsible for structuring therapeutic contacts, recommending and conducting particular interventions, and involving significant other people as needed.

4. *Time used flexibly and creatively.* For example, appointments need not occur on a once-a-week basis or last for the conventional fifty minutes (Chapter Seven; Talmon, Hoyt, and Rosenbaum, 1990). The frequency, length, and timing of treatment varies according to patient needs, with the paramount consideration being to use the "least intensive, least expensive, least intrusive" intervention that would be appropriate in a given situation (Bennett, 1986; Bennett and Wisneski, 1979; Bonstedt and Baird, 1979). Programmatic forms of intervention—such as therapy groups, psychoeducation, and community resources—are important components of HMO mental health treatment (Boaz, 1988), along with family interventions, self-help groups, and partial hospitalization.

5. *Interdisciplinary cooperation, including the use of concurrent psychotherapy and psychopharmacology when indicated.* Staff-model HMO practice involves close contact between medical and nonmedical mental health providers, allowing for a ready integration of their respective skills. Some primary-care physicians are also well educated about caring for patients with mental health problems (including initiating and maintaining patients on psychotropic medications) when they have consultative support from mental health professionals (Kisch and Austad, 1988). Similarly, emergency-room personnel can handle many frontline crises with appropriate psychological backup and guidance. In the context of a primary care (HMO) medical setting, there is a blending of medical and psychological involvement, which encourages a balanced, holistic view of the patient (Meier, 1981; Patrick, Coleman, Eagle, and Nelson, 1978).

6. *Use of multiple formats and modalities.* Treatments may also involve concurrent or sequential combinations of individual, group, and/or family therapy. Frequent referrals to community resources are made (Schneider-Braus, 1987). Participation in various twelve-step, self-help, and support groups is vigorously encouraged when it is appropriate.

7. *A "family practitioner" model that replaces the notion of definitive once-and-for-all "cure" with the idea that patients can return for intermittent treatment throughout the life cycle* (Cummings, 1986, 1990). There is "interrupted continuity" (Morrill, 1978), the patient having a series of brief treatment episodes over long periods of the life span (Anderson, 1981). The intermittent model of therapy assumes that as soon as the patient no longer needs treatment, the therapist will recede into the background of the patient's life until needed again. The therapist-patient relationship is long-term although frequently abeyant. The patient trusts that the therapist (or HMO) can be called upon as needed and that he or she will provide efficient, effective, and least intrusive therapeutic interventions. The therapist encourages autonomy and independence rather than regression and dependence.

8. *Utilization review to monitor and ensure that services are being delivered in the most cost-effective manner possible.* HMO therapists recognize the practical necessity of such reviews for purposes of cost containment. Ideally, both patients and therapists carry a sense of social responsibility to use the HMO resources in a caring way (Adler, 1963; Spoerl, 1974), appreciating that there are other HMO members waiting for psychotherapeutic services. *Utilization review* is distinct from *quality assurance* (Chestnut, Wilson, Wright, and Zemlich, 1987), which assesses what care the patient received. The two procedures can be complementary but can also engender conflicts of interest. As in the field of psychotherapy private practice, there is a clear need for standards and regulations in the emerging field of managed-care mental health services.

HMO Flexibility to Meet Diverse Needs

Life cycle developmental issues often play a key role in determining why a patient seeks treatment now (Bennett, 1983, 1984; Budman and Gurman, 1988; Cummings, 1977; Cummings and VandenBos, 1979; Meresman, 1983). Many times these problems are best dealt with in a group setting (Goulding, 1987; Zimet, 1979), and one of the influences of HMOs on psychotherapy practice has been a veritable renaissance and proliferation of group therapies (Budman and Bennett, 1983; Budman and Gurman, 1988; Donovan, Bennett, and McElroy, 1981; Folkers and Steefel, 1991; Lonergan, 1985; see Chapter Five), many with circumstance-of-life themes focusing on emancipating adolescents, harried mothers, couples' communication skills, young adults, older adults, divorce and separation, and the bereaved. Other, more generic groups may also be useful as well as ones with such specific themes as assertiveness training, adult children of alcoholics, persons recovering from childhood sexual abuse, anger management, chemical dependency early recovery and graduation groups, chemical dependency spouse groups, gay men's issues, minority women's issues, and so on. HMO group therapy is viable and diverse, recognizing and serving different patient needs. Groups are an important part of HMO practice not only because of their possible cost-effectiveness but also because of their intrinsic power. People learn from one another, they diminish isolation, and they often find that they can give as well as get help. Groups can provide a powerful experience for appropriately selected and prepared people. Therapists interested in group therapy will find HMOs a congenial setting, and HMO therapists will find group treatment to be a valuable option in their treatment planning. Especially within staff-model HMO settings, group therapies can be expected to continue development and expansion.

Short-term psychodynamic psychotherapy is one useful approach to treatment with a portion of patients, but there are many other approaches that go under such theoretical rubrics as cognitive-behavioral, multimodal, interpersonal, transactional analytic, family systems, strategic interactional, and Ericksonian.

In many instances, one or more of these may be the treatment(s) of choice. A number of authors working within HMO settings have described the advantages of clinical techniques based on principles of family systems theory and brief strategic therapy (Chubb, 1983; Friedman, 1988; Kempler, 1985; Kreilkamp, 1989; Rosenbaum, 1990; Talmon, 1990). Consistent with the HMO therapy principles of emphasizing strengths and seeking solutions rather than focusing on weaknesses and interminable problems are family systems approaches that use such methods as reframing, positive connotation, and paradoxical intention. Some treatment models that have been developed within the HMO context are described by Austad and Hoyt (1992).

Effective therapy requires a variety of perspectives (Gustafson, 1986; see Chapters Seven and Twenty) lest one impose the same "solution" on all problems. After all, if all one has is a hammer, everything begins to look like a nail. Herein lies an advantage for a staff- or group-model HMO: because no one therapist can be expert at everything, a good staff collectively should have practitioners who are able to offer a variety of skills, so that patients can be referred to someone with the differential expertise to meet their needs and so that individual therapists can do what they are good at and enjoy rather than trying to be everything to everyone.

Therapists who are traditionally trained or have a long-term orientation but who are working part-time for an HMO or other managed-care program will have to adjust their perspective, pace, goals—and ultimately, methods—if they are to be effective within the parameters and exigencies of managed care. If they are working independently, they may also lack ready access to some of the resources that help make good HMOs effective (such as therapy groups, peer consultation, and specialized continuing education programs) and/or may be less willing to make referrals to other colleagues with particular skills.

In the future, HMOs may be expected to expand as training sites as managed care continues to grow. A staff-model HMO can bring together clinicians with a panoply of skills to exchange. HMOs also provide an excellent setting for various types of psychotherapy research, because there are many patients available and relatively specified and rapid outcomes (Koss and Butcher, 1986). Examples of psychotherapy research within HMOs include development of patient assessment instruments (Budman and others, 1987; Horowitz Rosenbaum, and Wilner, 1988; Leary, 1957); outcome studies of time-limited individual versus group psychotherapy (Budman and others, 1988; Shapiro, Sank, Shaffer, and Donovan, 1982); the effects of psychotherapy on medical utilization (Budman, Demby, and Feldstein, 1984a, 1984b; Cummings and Follette, 1976; Follette and Cummings, 1967; Holden and Blose, 1987); preventive family counseling based on infant temperament assessment (Cameron, Hansen, and Rosen, 1990; Cameron and Rice, 1986); and the development of specialized treatment methodologies (Austad and Hoyt, 1992; Hoyt, Rosenbaum, and Talmon, 1992; Talmon, 1990).

The Utility of a Growth-Oriented Problem-Solving Approach

The good HMO therapist is results oriented. He or she learns to select and prepare patients for brief therapy; he or she interviews with the goal of identifying the patient's strengths and adaptive capacities and finding the way or opening for the patient to access and utilize his or her abilities; and he or she strives to be parsimonious while promoting continuing growth and the possibility of later return to therapy should it be indicated. The HMO therapist recognizes the patient's drive toward health and his or her resourcefulness, while also valuing the input of natural helpers and "co-therapists" who can be utilized in groups and family therapy.

The goal of the HMO therapist is to become unnecessary quickly and to help the patient get "unstuck" and then to move on. Dramatic and profound changes can occur rapidly, to be sure, but the HMO therapist does not usually conceptualize the treatment in terms of a "definitive restructuring of character." The medical model of "cure" becomes less useful than an approach toward growth, problem solving, and enhanced coping skills. The good HMO therapist knows both that a great deal can be accomplished at once and that with some assistance people can do a lot on their own. There are also a multiplicity of ways to do and get therapy: for example, in addition to individual, group, family, and marital therapy, many people benefit enormously from psychoeducational approaches such as parenting classes, stress-reduction workshops, and recommended readings.

HMOs work best when they function along a public-health model (Caplan, 1964), emphasizing prevention, early detection, prompt referral, and effective intervention (Brooks, 1983; Friedman, 1988; Tulkin and Weinstein, 1980). They are designed to provide necessary and sufficient treatment for many people rather than a great deal of unnecessary treatment for a few. The economic realities of insurance plans, including HMO structures, circumscribe long-term therapy for most folks, even if they want it. Arguments for HMO provision of long-term psychotherapy (Karon, 1992; Wright, 1992) are economically unrealistic and simply don't recognize that most patients want brief treatment and find it useful and sufficient. The real choice is not between long-term therapy versus short-term therapy but, rather, realistic and practical short-term therapy versus no therapy (Cummings, 1977; Kovacs, 1982).

Some Lessons from Research and Practice

Most good treatments, however, need not go the maximum number of sessions, usually twenty, that are provided for in an HMO contract. Boaz (1988, pp. 36–39) gives a good example of how a patient may confuse *more* with *better* treatment, citing the case of a woman who went to her HMO demanding referral to an "agoraphobia clinic" for twenty sessions, when what was actually needed—and what was provided—were marital therapy and parenting classes to resolve the primary areas of her conflict and stress. This also illustrates the importance of attending to the interpersonal context of symptoms, rather than attempting specialized treatment without reference to current life stresses.

Many people are helped relatively quickly. As Koss and Butcher (1986, p. 662) have concluded from their extensive review of the literature:

Most psychotherapeutic contacts, whether by plan or by premature termination, are brief, lasting less than eight sessions. In recent years, partly because of design, brief psychotherapy has become a treatment of choice. Comparative studies of brief and unlimited therapies show essentially no differences in results. Consequently, brief therapy results in a great saving of available clinical time and can reach more people in need of treatment. It is quite likely that brief therapies will be more widely utilized in the future if government health plans and private insurance companies cover the costs of psychotherapy. Such insurance coverage would likely be limited to relatively few sessions.

How many sessions are enough? This is a highly complicated question, of course, with many interactive factors to be considered (DeLeon, Uyeda, and Welch, 1985; Newman and Howard, 1986). There is no "magic number," although there is a range or consensus in the clinical literature regarding what constitutes brief therapy. Wolberg (1965b, p. 140), for example, refers to "short-term treatment . . . up to 20 treatment sessions." Mann (1973) has developed his model of time-limited psychotherapy within a twelve-session framework. For Wells (1982, p. 99), "short-term treatment comprises three or four sessions up to a maximum of fifteen interviews." Budman and Gurman (1988) point out that the essence of planned brief therapy is not simply a specific number of sessions but rather that the participants are "time sensitive," aware of the value and pressure of passing time. They also note that most therapy ends briefly, usually by default rather than design, so that "virtually every major review of the efficiency of various individual therapies . . . has been an unacknowledged review of time-unlimited brief therapy" (p. 7).

In addition to Koss and Butcher's (1986) conclusion quoted earlier, three other large-scale reviews are especially relevant. In one, Smith, Glass, and Miller (1980) conducted a meta-analysis of almost four hundred psychotherapy outcome studies involving more than 25,000 patients and control subjects and found psychotherapy to be effective with the mean length of treatments being approximately seventeen sessions. In another meta-analysis of outcome studies, with a mean treatment length of about seven sessions, Shapiro and Shapiro (1982) also found therapy to be effective. In a more recent meta-analytic study, Howard, Kopta, Kraus, and Orlinsky (1986) examined data based on over 2,400 patients covering a period of thirty years of research. They found that by eight sessions approximately 50 percent of patients were measurably improved and that approximately 75 percent were improved by twenty-six sessions. Given these findings (and despite the methodological limitations noted by Phillips [1988]), it would seem reasonable to speculate that most change in psychotherapy occurs relatively quickly, within the period usually considered to be brief treatment.[2]

Although any conclusions might seem premature, it is important to note that the Smith, Glass, and Miller (1980) and Howard, Kopta, Kraus, and Orlinsky (1986) investigations were based on data sets almost exclusively drawn from original studies of long-term or at least open-ended therapies. Most of the original studies were not of *planned* short-term treatments. The results would thus seem to imply that most of what is accomplished in *long*-term therapy is accomplished relatively quickly. These results could be interpreted more as providing a challenge for long-term therapists to justify the length of their prolonged treatments than as an indication that the HMO-based short-term therapists should extend their brief work!

Problems and Limitations of HMO Psychotherapy

Although much psychotherapeutic work can be done relatively briefly, there are situations, such as those involving patients with severe character problems and other long-term or chronic disorders, where the limits of brief (or any) psychotherapy are apparent. In these situations, professional caregivers are at high risk for potential guilt: What are we going to do for the people who need more? Should we feel guilty that we cannot be everything for everyone? Just as there is a potential for patients to form an institutional transference (Reider, 1953), there is also the danger of clinicians engaging in *institutional countertransference,* the overassumption of responsibility in response to patients' neediness and dependency on the institution.

When HMO therapists and trainees begin to feel as if "Mother HMO should take endless care of her children," it will be important to recall that professional activity is based on a contractual relationship, that patients have bought a form of health coverage that specifies the limits of what will be provided. We can certainly be concerned about the plight of some patients and can make efforts to help them find appropriate care, but it would be grandiose to think that we can offer a panacea for all mental health problems. As a nation we are facing a crisis in the cost of health services, and there are no easy answers. Like all conscientious practitioners, HMO therapists struggle to find financially viable ways to treat those patients (the "chronics") who need long-term or ongoing care.

Doing brief therapy with most patients may help make longer-term treatment available for those patients who most require it, with innovative intermittent treatment, brief intensive treatment, and group therapies also being helpful. In addition to ethical and humanistic concerns, group- and staff-model HMO therapists know that the HMO is accountable (at risk) for the comprehensive health costs of its members and also know that there is a strong tendency for untreated psychological problems to result in excessive medical (including emergency room) services. As Shectman (1986) has said, necessity sometimes proves to be the mother of intervention.

In addition to the transferences and countertransferences that all psychotherapeutic work can entail, working within an HMO institution can engender other, more specific problems. Patients who do not understand the benefits and limits of their HMO mental health coverage may feel deprived when they are not given certain hoped-for (but uncontracted) services. This calls attention to the importance of truth in packaging to minimize misunderstandings (Boaz, 1988; Practice Directorate 1988b). Other managed-care–specific patient reactions may involve concerns about confidentiality and the role of the third party (the HMO) in the patient-therapist relationship, as well as feeling "forced" by the focality and time limits of treatment.

There are also various therapist problems specific to working in an HMO, including conflicts about being a salaried employee, problems with authority, discomfort with the frequent exposure of one's work to peers and quality control, and impingements on one's self-esteem if one thinks working for an HMO is second rate compared to independent private practice (Goldensohn, 1977; Goldensohn and Haar, 1974; Kisch and Makover, 1990; Lange and others, 1988). Some therapists find focused treatment frustrating and restrictive and view "symptom relief" and "return to function" as second-rate goals, even though these are the reasons most patients seek treatment and despite the fact that experience has shown that in many cases personality changes also occur in goal-oriented HMO therapy (Bennett and Wisneski, 1979). It is interesting to note that one survey of HMO therapists (Lange and others, 1988, p. 462) found "uniformly high ratings given HMOs by the providers who work for them," although not surprisingly some providers felt their clinical load was too great. A second survey (Austad, 1989) has confirmed the generally positive experience of therapists working within an HMO.

Professional Responsibilities and Quality Assurance

HMO therapy, like all therapy, can be done well or poorly, and abuses are possible. Because the incentive is toward efficiency (Bennett, 1988; Boaz, 1988; Kaplan, 1989; Kramon, 1989; Nelson, 1987), care must be taken to assure that treatment is brief and effective, not just brief. Just as the fee-for-service practitioner must guard against the temptation to rationalize unnecessary prolongations of treatment, the HMO therapist must guard against the tendency to *undertreat.* Institutionalized forces that encourage utilization review and promote rapid turnover of patients need to be balanced against professional standards and values. *Quality assurance* is the watchword here, and good HMOs are well equipped to provide such assurances, because group practices are convenient settings for peer review meeting, difficult-case seminars, continuing education presentations, and the like. This may more easily be accomplished with a full-time in-house staff rather than a scattered collection of independent part-time providers. This is an advantage of a staff or group model, a centrally organized structure of providers whose professional activity is enhanced and supported by a common culture dedicated to technical innovation and interdisciplinary cooperation to expand the delivery of efficient mental health services (Budman, Feldman, and Bennett, 1979; Bittker and Idzorek, 1978; Spoerl, 1974; Tulkin and Frank, 1985). Unfortunately, the "monetarization" of HMOs has brought a rash of upstart managed-care programs that are not organized to promote the qualities that make good HMOs succeed. Some may be poorly equipped and unmotivated to provide the mental health services they have promised, suffering from misstaffing, underfinancing, and mismanagement. As Bennett (1988, pp. 1546–1547) has observed:

> Currently there is a trend toward open systems composed of mental health professionals geographically remote from each other and engaged in office practices that include fee-for-service patients as well as those belonging to one or more HMOs. . . . This configuration offers little opportunity to develop the cultures associated with closed systems or to educate providers who may be poorly prepared by standard training programs for the demands of prepaid practice. Those involved for primarily economic reasons are more likely to view each other as competitors than as collaborators. Lacking the support and incentive to be innovative, they are likely to use abbreviated traditional methods instead, especially individual forms of psychotherapy. Lacking internal mechanisms to maintain cost-effective patterns of care, IPAs [independent practice associations] must rely on benefit constraints and checks of provider behavior. These are often retrospective and can be intrusive, even adversarial. . . . Control, rather than education, alliance, and collaboration, is the dominant theme.

HMO practitioners should avoid the painful conflict-of-interest situation wherein their decision regarding the continuation of services impacts in a direct, one-to-one way on their income or status within their organization. Salaries should not be made too sensitive to the specifics of individual cases (Practice Directorate, 1988a, pp. 6–7; 1989) lest the HMO therapist be seen as someone who is paid to withhold treatment, a kind of mirror of the private practitioner who sometimes is seen as someone cultivating and harvesting the benefits of unnecessary patient dependency (Haley, 1969; Minsky, 1987).

In summary, HMOs are not the perfect solution for providing mental health care for everyone, but quality HMOs are making valuable contributions by developing effective brief therapies and providing mental health services to many patients who otherwise would go without. The expanding influence of HMOs in the foreseeable future seems certain. Let us conclude by quoting from an important article by Zimet (1989, p. 708) on this very theme: "The battle to preserve the past is already over; the health care revolution is upon us. We need to put forward great effort to help shape a process that will provide good care for our patients and a place for psychology in a system that today is almost exclusively physician oriented. Psychology cannot meet its social responsibility of advocacy for humane and cost-effective services in the public and private sector by taking a conservative *status quo* position."

Notes

1. It should be noted that there is not a clear line between crisis intervention, which aims to put out the fire and restore the preexisting equilibrium, and so-called "real psychotherapy," which aims to make enduring personality changes. (These two positions are nicely summarized by Malan [1976a].) In actual practice, so-called "crisis patients" oftentimes make genuine, lasting changes as a result of their therapeutic experience.

2. Qualitatively different changes may be possible in long-term therapy (Schafer, 1973), but these may go beyond what HMOs contract to do: treat and attempt to ameliorate specific psychiatric symptoms. Even if long-term therapy were to produce additional changes, it is still questionable whether the further gains would be commensurate with the added time and expense (Appelbaum, 1975).

CHAPTER FOUR

Promoting HMO Values and a Culture of Quality: Doing the Right Thing in a Staff-Model HMO Mental Health Department

Good things cost less than bad ones.

–Italian proverb

"Doing the right thing" in the world of managed mental health care requires innovation, collaboration, and efficiency in the service of three interrelated values or meta-goals: benefits preservation, enhanced clinical effectiveness, and increased access to services (Freeman and Leggett, 1992). What is at stake is whether patients will continue to receive mental health services, the kinds and qualities of services that will be provided, and who will provide them. Our "customers" are more and more both our patients and the large purchasers of health care that direct patients to us. When the goals of meeting the needs of patients, supporting the success of partners, and maintaining a humane work environment–to borrow appreciatively from a vision statement of Group Health Cooperative of Puget Sound–are reflected in day-to-day decisions and practices, the HMO mental health service can provide high-quality, cost-sensitive, integrated, and comprehensive patient care.[1] This idea of collaborative partnership is supported by processes that promote identification with HMO values and goals.

Note: Reprinted, with changes, from Hoyt, M. F. "Promoting HMO Values and a Culture of Quality: Doing the Right Thing in a Staff-Model HMO Mental-Health Department." *HMO Practice,* 1994, *8,* 122–126. Used by permission of the publisher.

Promoting HMO Values in the Staff Model

How can we promote working in the cooperative, innovative, and efficient manner that is a legacy of the staff-model HMO cultures of the 1970s and 1980s,[2] fostering what Schneider-Braus (1992) has called "an alignment of values between the professional caregivers and the insuring organization"? The following is a description of some of the ways the staff-model HMO outpatient psychiatric clinic at the Kaiser Permanente Medical Center in Hayward, California, has been able to promote HMO values and a culture dedicated to quality. As Berwick, Baker, and Kramer (1992) have commented, managed-care organizations are still in the early phases of total quality management (TQM), too often relying on measurement and surveillance at the expense of "other essential quality management methods such as emphasizing process improvement, decreasing individual incentives, focusing on customer requirements, innovating, benchmarking, and reducing costs through quality improvement." Perhaps the following seven guidelines, as simple as they are, will be useful.

1. *Hire good people.* Even though there is the adage from Deming (1986) that 85 percent of the problem is management, start by carefully hiring good people who share a pro-HMO vision. Be highly selective. It is better to do it right the first time than to spend a lot of energy, effort, and money on remediation. Intelligence, energy, and kindness are basics; demonstrated skills in short-term therapies and case management, an enthusiasm for HMO practice, and an affinity for teamwork should also be prerequisites.

2. *Create a user-friendly environment.* "Drive out fear" is the way Deming put it. It has long been known in psychology that rewards work better than punishment if sustained productivity, creativity, loyalty, and positive interpersonal relations are the goal. In his classic paper, Berwick (1989) contrasted "Inspecting for Bad Apples" with "Promoting Continuous Improvement." His opening image (p. 53) bears repeating:

Imagine two assembly lines, monitored by two foremen.

Foreman 1 walks the line, watching carefully. "I can see you all," he warns. "I have the means to measure your work, and I will do so. I will find those among you who are unprepared or unwilling to do your jobs, and when I do there will be consequences. There are many workers available for these jobs, and you can be replaced."

Foreman 2 walks a different line, and he too watches. "I am here to help you if I can," he says. "We are in this together for the long haul. You and I have a common interest in a job well done. I know that most of you are trying very hard, but sometimes things can go wrong. My job is to notice opportunities for improvement—skills that could be shared, lessons from the past, or experiments to try together—and to give you the means to do your work even better than you do now. I want to help the average ones among you, not just the exceptional few at either end of the spectrum of competence."

Which line works better? Which is more likely to do the job well in the long run? Where would you rather work?

It is important that from the top down, management fosters an atmosphere where people feel safe, where learning and improvement can take place. Staff need to feel that identifying problems will be welcome, not punished or just accepted or tolerated. When problems are discussed, the emphasis is on *what*, not *who*, focusing on technical problems or systems glitches rather than on people. To emphasize the value of teamwork, the ticklish question of merit evaluation pay in a staff- or group-model HMO may be best dealt with by distributing monies equally—like the World Series, where if you were on the team all year, you get a full share.

3. *Be multicultural and multitheoretical.* The staff-model HMO benefits by having personnel of varying backgrounds, races, and ethnicities. Not only does this resemble society, but a broader range of perspectives can be brought to bear as we serve an increasingly multicultural population. It serves to keep one aware not to develop a "one way"

or monolithic approach (Gonzales, Biever, and Gardner, 1994). It is also useful for the staff-model HMO to include clinicians with a range of theoretical and technical abilities, offering more opportunities for matching patients' needs with clinicians' skills. Since staff can be hired to specialize in doing a lot of what they are good at and enjoy, this in-house referral network is a great advantage in "doing the right thing." In contrast, practitioners in solo (independent) practice may be much less likely to refer.

4. *Empower staff and build a culture.* People tend to live up (or down) to expectations, so it is best to treat carefully selected professionals like professionals (not like co-dependents). Within the parameters of the department, staff should control their own schedules, determine their treatments, and support one another's achievements. Staff members may be asked to struggle with difficult decisions, such as which services to intensify or which groups to offer (or discontinue) and may be involved in determining and collecting the necessary information to make such decisions. Recalling that Donabedian (1988) defines *quality* as "The extent to which care provided is expected to achieve the most favorable balance of risks and benefits," providers need to discuss how they perceive outcomes and procedures and how they will weigh them—a discussion that promotes a shared vision. What's a reasonable outcome? What does the patient want? What is possible? What will we have to give up? Should we do X or Y? Patients with recurring service needs, such as those with chronic depression, personality disorders, and/or dissatisfying marital relationships (Bennett and Wisneski, 1979; Bonstedt, 1991; Kisch, 1992; Robinson, 1991; Strosahl, 1991) often inspire these discussions. Rotating committee memberships, including the committee charged with matters of quality development, helps promote a "culture" for the committee and department. The Harvard Community Health Plan's mental health redesign project (Abrams, 1993) is an excellent large-scale example of management and clinical partnership. Taking the time to have the mission come

directly from the staff helps avoid morale problems, burn-out, and passive resistance that can reduce productivity (Schneider-Braus, 1992; Savitz, 1992).

The very process of holding regular staff meetings promotes the development of a group identity and common culture dedicated to getting the job done through technical innovation and cooperation. Treatment discussions reinforce an HMO therapy philosophy as they focus around such key questions as, Why has the patient sought therapy? What are the goals of treatment? What skills and resources do the patient (and therapist) have that can be utilized therapeutically? (Budman, Friedman, and Hoyt, 1992; Budman and Gurman, 1988; Hoyt, 1994b).

Clinicians like to learn, and staff-model HMOs are especially conducive settings for difficult case conferences, peer review meetings, hallway and lunchtime consultations, and continuing education presentations. Working as cotherapists in group therapy provides clinicians with further opportunities to learn from one another and to develop collegial solidarity, and offers a variety of clinical advantages such as relationship modeling, binocular vision, and continuity of care when one therapist is absent (see Chapter Five). When new members join our staff at Kaiser-Hayward, after a careful selection process, they undergo a six-month period of intensive proctoring that not only focuses on monitoring for assurance of quality standards but also serves as a time of acculturation as they "learn the ropes" while attending regular meetings and working closely with different staff.

The strengthening of a group culture and loyalty to HMO values is also fostered by providing a nurturing and caring environment for staff, one that demonstrates a commitment to enhanced health and reduced stress. Offering facilities for noontime exercise, providing lunch food at least once a week so that staff are encouraged to eat and talk together, funding team-building off-site conferences, and recognizing birthdays and various happy and sad major life events are all additional ways to promote group cohesion, quality improvement, and productivity.

5. *Provide training and encourage research.* It is remarkable how little orientation and training in brief therapy most clinicians have, even those working in managed-care settings (Budman and Armstrong, 1992). Again, as Deming (1986) said, "Everyone doing his best is not the answer. Everyone is doing his best . . . there must be consistency of understanding and of effort. There is no substitute for knowledge." In other words, the idea is to work smarter, not just harder. Intelligently designed systems and specific training for HMO practice—both for mental health specialists and primary-care providers—will advance productivity and reduce staff turnover (Budman and Armstrong, 1992; Feldman, 1992; Sabin, 1991, 1992; Sabin and Borus, 1992). HMO mental health departments that allow experienced clinicians to teach trainees and younger colleagues help prepare for future health care reforms while enhancing staff satisfaction.

It is becoming increasingly important to learn about and meet the special mental health needs of various subpopulations, which involves addressing issues of cultural diversity as well as the problems of elderly members, the chronically distressed, the dually diagnosed (psychiatric and substance abuse problems), and the medically complicated. HMOs that encourage clinical research (e.g., studies of innovative intake and screening procedures, treatment methods, and outcomes assessment) will be rewarded by the benefits of what is learned as well as by the invigoration of staff. Providing opportunities for intellectual growth helps organizations keep good people (Herman, 1991).

6. *Demonstrate a commitment to quality.* It is important to have the department head demonstrate a true interest in quality improvement by dedicating time, personnel, and dollars to quality enhancement endeavors. Having the mental health department headed by an active clinician helps assure attention to professional matters and ethics—not just finances—when difficult decisions have to be made.

Leading from the front, working hard, and dealing with the kinds of problems and dilemmas others are asked to face are the actions of a good role model and give clinician-managers legitimacy. Informal opinion leaders may also exercise considerable influence on practice patterns (Lomas and others, 1991), and a core of articulate and energetic clinicians can provide the right "starter" or impetus to grow a productive HMO therapy culture. And again, entrusting each person with responsibility for the success of the enterprise makes everyone a self-manager and draws from the collective best.

It can be very useful to establish various indicators of care (such as completion of diagnoses on intake evaluations, regular monitoring of blood levels for patients treated with lithium carbonate, and the timely scheduling of outpatient follow-ups for patients discharged from inpatient treatment) in order to identify systems and procedures requiring improvement. Morbidity and mortality reviews can yield vital information that will help prevent avoidable recurrences; these rare but troubling instances of bad outcomes also provide an important opportunity for management to demonstrate a supportive and nonpunitive attitude that can encourage subsequent quality improvement discussions.

In general, we need data to tell us what works and what doesn't work. Special attention should be paid, I think, to assessing two outcome factors: (1) how well patients feel they have achieved their treatment goals, and (2) patient satisfaction. Recognizing that we are also increasingly partners with employer-purchasers, employee assistance programs (EAPs), and primary-care medical providers suggests that regular assessment and utilization of feedback should be extended to these consumers as well. We need to constantly make ourselves an integral and invaluable part of the overall HMO enterprise. Our skills in promoting treatment adherence, communicating with difficult patients, and managing cases with significant psychosocial components should all be extended and visible. Closer collaboration between primary care and mental health specialists in the areas of prevention, early detection, and ongoing treatment will help meet the HMO ideal of enhanced quality through comprehensive, integrated services (Cummings, 1991a; Martin, 1994; Strosahl, 1994).

7. *Face marketplace realities.* HMO therapists may also become more involved in quality improvements by realizing that there is competition out there trying to replace them. The possibilities of "carve-outs" and "unbundling" of mental health services will require HMO staff-model clinicians to be increasingly innovative and efficient to remain competitive (Strosahl and Quirk, 1994). Remembering Peter Drucker's statement (1991, p. 228; see also Bowles and Hammond, 1991) that "Quality in a product or service is not what the supplier puts in. It is what the customer gets out and is willing to pay for," research methods such as surveys and focus groups can also be used to identify what mental health outcomes and treatment processes are most valued by customers and what factors produce the best member satisfaction. *Benefits preservation* translates into continued livelihood and security for providers.

Improving Quality: What Is the Alternative?

The importance of quality care has been eloquently described by Donabedian (1978): "We have granted the health professions access to the most secret and sensitive places in ourselves, and entrusted them to matters that touch on our well-being, happiness, and survival. In return, we have expected the professions to govern themselves so strictly that we need have no fear of exploitation or incompetence" (p. 856). In addition to the challenges of mental health care in general, to achieve a high level of quality HMO staff-model therapists may have to contend with specific problems related to conflicts about being a salaried employee, rapid case turnover and restriction to focused goals, and discomfort with the frequent exposure of their work to peers and quality assessment procedures (Goldensohn, 1977; Goldensohn and Haar, 1974; Kisch and Makover, 1990; Lange and others, 1988). Caseload demands can be heavy—underscoring the importance of maintaining adequate staffing ratios to keep up with the fast pace and many clinical responsibilities that HMO work involves. Since the goal of continuous quality improvement is win-win-win-win (patient-clinician-HMO-purchasers), it is important that providers thoroughly understand such procedures and that they do not perceive them as a method to "squeeze" more and more out of already overburdened workers (as may happen particularly when standards are externally imposed and continually raised), lest the frontline clinician respond in a manner similar to a horse that is resisting having its cinch tightened further.

These cautions notwithstanding, it is clear that we who work in HMOs need to work smarter, continually improving our quality. What is the alternative to "doing the right thing"? Let us answer with these lines from Shakespeare's *Julius Caesar* (IV, iii, lines 217–223[3]):

> There is a tide in the affairs of men,
> Which, taken at the flood, leads on to fortune;
> Omitted, all the voyage of their life
> Is bound in shallows and in miseries.
> On such a full sea are we now afloat,
> And we must take the current when it serves,
> Or lose our ventures.

Notes

1. The Joint Commission for the Accreditation of Healthcare Organizations (JCAHO, 1993) has described "doing the right thing" in terms of the performance dimensions of efficacy and appropriateness and doing the right thing *well* in terms of availability, timeliness, effectiveness, continuity, safety, efficiency, and respect and caring.

2. As Bennett (1988; see also Austad and Berman, 1991; Austad and Hoyt, 1992; see Chapter Three) has written: "Through the 1970s and early 1980s the staff or group model HMO became a distinct form of psychiatric prac-

tice, characterized by a culture common to most programs. Attracted by the spirit and ideals of the movement and its expanding commitment to mental health care, professionals working in HMOs had to reconcile traditional models of care with the constraints and opportunities of the setting. . . . Members joined HMOs voluntarily and had some awareness of their advantages and disadvantages. This favored alliance with staff seeking to be innovative rather than traditional. Second, staff were also self-selected, attracted to the settings for reasons other than necessity, e.g., the opportunity to provide population-based, single-class care, the chance to be innovative, and the excitement associated with a reform movement. All were challenged to contain costs while maintaining excellence" (p. 1546).

3. This passage served as an epigraph to a system-wide conference held by the Kaiser Permanente Northern California Region Departments of Psychiatry in Oakland, California, on November 17–18, 1992.

CHAPTER FIVE

———◆◆◆———

Group Psychotherapy
in an HMO

Where group formation developed, neurosis tended to diminish,
at times even to disappear.
                                    —Sigmund Freud (1921/1955)

One of the influences of HMOs on the practice of psychotherapy has been a veritable renaissance and proliferation of innovative group therapies, especially various forms of short-term
and crisis groups. Such groups are often the treatment of choice
for patients seeking mental health services, if patients are properly selected and prepared. Well-run groups offer a powerful
way for patients to gain support and resolve problems. Diverse
needs can be recognized and served as patients learn from one
another, diminish isolation, and find that they can give as well
as receive help.

   Groups are sometimes an efficient modality for delivering
a particular form of treatment (e.g., cognitive therapy for depression), while in other instances, the group process itself is
the treatment. Group therapy is also a cost-sensitive treatment
option for those more impaired patients who may require continuing support to maintain their otherwise tenuous psychosocial level of functioning. Groups are an important part of HMO
psychotherapy because of their clinical utility, not simply be-

Note: Reprinted, with changes, from Hoyt, M. F. "Group Psychotherapy in
an HMO." *HMO Practice,* 1993, 7, 129–132. Used by permission of the publisher.
   Epigraph reprinted from Freud, S. "Group Psychology and the Analysis
of the Ego." In J. Strachey (ed.), *The Standard Edition of the Complete Psychological
Works of Sigmund Freud.* Vol. 18. Copyright 1955 by Hogarth Press. Used by
permission of the publisher. (Originally published 1921.)

cause of their possible cost-effectiveness, since there is no cost conservation without treatment efficacy (Kaplan, 1989).

The therapeutic purposes of short-term groups have been summarized by Klein (1985, p. 312): "These typically include: (1) the amelioration of distress (i.e., the reduction of symptomatic discomfort); (2) prompt re-establishment of the patient's previous emotional equilibrium; (3) promoting efficient use of the patient's resources (e.g., increasing the patient's sense of control or mastery, emphasizing adaptation, or providing cognitive restructuring, aiding behavioral change, self-help, and social effectiveness); (4) developing the patient's understanding of his current disturbance and increasing coping skills for the future."

This chapter has three main topics: (1) factors common to all modes of short-term group therapy, (2) different models of short-term groups practiced in an HMO context, and (3) the relationship of HMO structures to the use of group therapy. As will be seen, many forms of group therapy reflect the HMO and managed-care emphasis on problem solving, crisis-intervention preparedness, clear definition of patient and therapist responsibilities, flexible and creative use of time, interdisciplinary cooperative treatments, use of multiple formats and modalities, intermittent treatment throughout the life cycle, and quality assurance and utilization review procedures (Mac Kenzie, 1994; see Chapter Three).

Important Factors in Effective Short-Term Group Therapy

Short-term therapy groups typically pass through a series of overlapping phases or stages: (1) starting, (2) early therapy, (3) middle of the group, (4) late therapy, (5) termination, and, if scheduled, (6) an often useful six-to-twelve-month follow-up meeting. It is crucial, if short-term group treatment is to be effective, that therapists recognize and attend satisfactorily to the various tasks and challenges that each stage presents. As numerous clinicians and writers (Budman and Gurman, 1988; Garvin, 1990; MacKenzie, 1990, 1994; McKay and Paleg, 1992; Piper, 1991; Poey, 1985) have observed, there are six overlapping elements common to different modes of effective short-term group therapy:

1. *Brief time limits.* Group participation may range from one or a few meetings to the limits of patients' HMO coverage. Therapy duration is relative to the problem. That is, treatment should be *time sensitive* (Budman and Gurman, 1988), meaning effective and efficient; limited resources are rationed and allotted in such a manner as to make optimal use of them. Time limits can be used to promote work and "getting down to business." In closed groups (where all members start and stop together), time is usually more important; similarly, in groups having *loss* as a focus, time and termination will be more salient. Work in crisis groups is usually done in one to six meetings, while groups with life cycle developmental themes often last twelve to twenty sessions. Patients with rigid and enduring personality problems or chronic mental illness may require more ongoing or longer treatments. While caution needs to be exercised that group programs don't become havens for unnecessary chronic utilizers of mental health services, HMO plans that do not exclude chronic patients have found longer-term groups to be useful, e.g., at Harvard Community Health Plan (HCHP), eighteen-month groups for personality-disordered patients (Budman, 1989), and continuing-care groups for chronically mentally ill patients (Bennett and Wisneski, 1979). These extended treatments are still time sensitive in that they make the optimal use of limited resources.

2. *Patient homogeneity.* Short-term therapy groups usually work better if there is a unifying theme, such as a common situation, lifestyle, or psychiatric problem. Patients who are likely to present serious management problems—such as those who are actively suicidal, homicidal, psychotic, or abusing alcohol or drugs—will need special attention and are usually best referred to specialized programs (e.g., alcohol treatment) or at least stabilized before entering group therapy. Similarly, short-term group therapy may not be indicated for persons unlikely to participate pro-

ductively because of major characterological difficulties, including those persons who are excessively self-centered, disruptive, or suspicious.

3. *Focality of treatment.* The goal of therapy is explicit and delimited, such as helping members handle a particular crisis, coping successfully with an adult developmental task, or helping married couples to improve their communication. Overly general goals, such as changing personality or character restructuring, are avoided.

4. *Rapid group cohesion.* Group cohesiveness is akin to the therapeutic alliance in individual treatment (Yalom, 1985). A quickly developed sense of trust, empathy, and bondedness is often enhanced by the therapist helping patients recognize their similarities and ways they are working together on a common group task. Rapid cohesion is often facilitated by patient homogeneity.

5. *Here-and-now orientation.* The focus is primarily on patients' current life situation and patterns, including examining the patients' ways of relating within the group, rather than spending extensive time on historical review.

6. *Therapist activity.* Leaders are active, clear, and direct in helping members stick to the group task and accomplish their individual goals (Dies, 1985). Transference and authority issues may arise and are dealt with, but they are not characteristically the central focus of successful short-term groups (Budman and Bennett, 1983; Lonergan, 1985).

These six treatment factors underscore the importance of selecting and preparing patients for group work—in the referral process, in pre-treatment contact, and in the beginning portion of the group experience itself. It is important that the referring person believe the group is the treatment of choice (Goulding, 1987) and conveys this positively. If one says apologetically, "Well, we have a group we could put you in," the patient usually might as well not be referred—the message is that this is the "booby prize." Pre-group contact with the group leader is very helpful—either face-to-face, on the phone, or even by letter.

What do you want to accomplish? What do you want to change? What are your goals? How do you want to function differently? are questions that help patients sharpen their purpose and recognize their responsibility and role in achieving their treatment goals (Goulding and Goulding, 1979).

An interesting and very useful innovation is the "pre-group workshop" that Budman and his colleagues (Budman and Gurman, 1988; Budman and others, 1981) have developed at HCHP. Prospective group members, eight to fifteen in number, attend a ninety-minute session. Members pair up and introduce themselves and then introduce each other to the larger group. The group then forms subgroups and performs a task related to the overall theme of the prospective group (e.g., role playing a situation that he or she wishes had been handled differently, with other members supplying alternative solutions). The leader then summarizes what has occurred, answers questions, and asks participants to consider whether they wish to join the group (which usually starts one to two weeks later). Since "the best predictor of group behavior is group behavior" (Budman, Bennett, and Wisneski, 1981), this experience provides leaders with much useful information, including the identification of potential pitfalls and individuals not yet ready for group work. It gives patients a better basis on which to make an informed decision regarding future participation, and it also helps to shape desirable group behavior skills and to teach patients to invest their energies in improvements rather than complaints. While it might seem like a lot of preparation, studies (Budman and others, 1981; Budman, Bennett, and Wisneski, 1981; Piper and Perrault, 1989) have shown that this kind of preliminary work results in reduction of subsequent dropouts, a critical factor in short-term groups when quick cohesion and "hitting the decks running" is so important.

Four Models of Short-Term Group Therapy in HMOs

According to Folkers and Steefel (1991) there are several basic models for group therapy that are particularly well suited to time-limited work and consistent with HMO therapy values that emphasize enhanced coping skills, new learnings, and growth. Four will be discussed here, but these are not completely discrete or mutually exclusive; hybrids are quite frequent.

Experiential Model

These modified forms of "classic" group therapy help people become more aware of themselves, their own social behavior, and the social interactions of others. Patients and groups typically move through stages of inclusion, conflict, affection, and termination. In an HMO, an experiential group is neither a posh life-enrichment exercise nor a treatment for severely disturbed patients; rather, it is a "safety zone" that allows members to personally regroup. Folkers and Steefel (1991) give HMO examples of experiential groups for couples with relationship problems, patients who have recently left inpatient settings, and socially awkward men. From our experience at Kaiser-Hayward, other useful groups that might be considered essentially experiential would be those for adult children of alcoholics, co-dependents, or adults who were molested as children. Additional experiential groups include various interpersonal-problems groups, men's groups, women's groups, and others addressing problems confronted by specific populations—such as a gay men's group or a minority women's group.

Psychoeducational Model

Folkers and Steefel (1991) indicate that a psychoeducational group "is used for teaching skills pertaining to a specified topic within a therapeutic setting. These groups are structured around a planned agenda in order to reach pre-established goals in a limited period of time" (p. 52). Cognitive-behavioral methods fit especially well into psychoeducational group approaches, with depression treatment and stress reduction being valuable examples. Groups for anger management, assertiveness training, and phobia and panic management are additional examples from our Kaiser-Hayward experience, as are groups for the treatment of chronic pain, chemical dependency early recovery, and chemical dependency graduate groups. Psychoeducational groups for new parents, for couples' communication skills, and for persons coping with physical illness (Lonergan, 1981; Rosenbaum, 1983) are also helpful. Groups for chronically mentally ill patients and medication groups provide patients with the destigmatizing experience of universality, promote education, support, and problem solving; and relieve clinicians of some of the tedium of repetitive individual work (Folkers and Steefel, 1991).

Crisis Intervention Model

Crisis intervention groups provide quick intervention while someone is acutely distressed following a specific stress event, in order to support reconstitution of coping skills. Emotional ventilation, normalization, and group support are basic therapeutic factors. Crisis groups usually meet one to two times per week and often accomplish their work in one to six sessions. Examples are (1) groups set up to help potentially traumatized persons after a specific event, such as a critical incident debriefing session for a particularly distressed paramedic team, a discussion group for parents upset by news of a kidnapping or some other violent act, or the Kaiser-Hayward crisis group preparation following the October 1989 Loma Prieta earthquake; and (2) a weekly open crisis group, to which patients may be referred after initial assessment. In crisis groups, therapists work very actively to promote problem solving, counter regression, and provide a "safety net," if necessary, while additional treatment planning is done and put into action. The crisis group, like other forms of group therapy, can also be an adjunct to other ongoing treatment. Therapist activities in crisis groups are very much focused on encouraging patients in their mutual support and reality-based problem solving (Allgeyer, 1973; Donovan, Bennett and McElroy, 1981; Imber and Evanczuk, 1990).

Developmental Stage Model

This model, which has its theoretical roots in Erik Erikson's (1963, 1968) psychosocial-stages-of-development formulations, was introduced as a concept by Zimet (1979). He noted that there are developmental tasks, "problems in everyday life rather than those emanating from psychopathology," that "we must master in order to grow successfully, to mature and to develop into effective and fulfilled human beings" (p. 2). Grouping together individuals facing similar life cycle tasks creates

> a setting where it is possible to find out that others experience similar feelings and similar problems [and] . . . where there is a natural system and where the setting is oriented to solving problems. . . . [These groups] would direct themselves to such areas as identity development, adolescent social skills, sex role development and intimacy, vocational decision making for young adults, generativity and childbirth, parenting, the empty nest stage, unmet career expectations, and the many adaptations required in old age. . . . I am not advocating the elimination of groups dealing with psychopathology, but it is my strong belief that the availability of short term, developmental task . . . groups will reduce significantly the need for traditional psychotherapy, be it individual or group [pp. 6–7].

Much of the theoretical and practical application of an adult developmental model of short-term group psychotherapy has been done at Harvard Community Health Plan. Briefly, they conceptualize most patients' presentations not as forms of major psychiatric illnesses but rather as manifestations of "assorted problems in living, including those which occur more or less predictably (and normatively) at the nodal points in adult development" (Budman and Bennett, 1983, p. 142). Treatment groups are "interpersonally oriented rather than symptom oriented. This means that rather than emphasizing, for example, the depression or anxiety experienced by those dealing with strained relationships, it is the nature of those relationships *themselves* that is examined. The interpersonal environment of the group is uniquely suited to the examination of such issues" (Budman and Gurman, 1988, p. 252). They see the following three frequent nodes for brief developmental groups:

1. *Young adult (twenties through mid-thirties)*, with the overrid-

ing theme of achieving intimacy away from the family of origin.

2. *Midlife (thirty-five through fifty)*, with common themes of reassessment of accomplishments and failures, recognition of mortality and limited time, coping with aging parents and growing children, compromises, and new beginnings.

3. *Late midlife (fifty and older)*, with frequent themes of life beginning to draw to a close, involving bodily deterioration, declining powers, economic problems, intergenerational conflicts, and loss of significant others. (See Austad and Henault [1989] for a discussion of an elderly women's group within an HMO.) Pooling of collective experience and wisdom plus connections with new people in the group (during a time of frequent loss of sustaining relationships) are especially valuable.

The Kaiser-Hayward Group Therapy Program has found all of these groups to be important parts of our comprehensive treatment program. Developmental groups designed to aid life cycle "passages" have included a young adults (emancipation) group, a new parents group, a separation-divorce group, a bereavement group, and an older adults group.

Group Therapy and HMO Structures

HMOs and various forms of managed care now provide mental health services to more than 100 million Americans, and indications are that the managed-care movement will continue to expand. Surveys (Goldman, 1988; Shadle and Christianson, 1988) suggest that more than 70 percent of HMO mental health patients receive individual psychotherapy, with group therapy alone being utilized in less than 15 percent of cases (the remainder are combined modalities, such as individual plus marital or family therapy). Group treatment has shown itself to be a clinically and administratively useful format, however, and higher percentages of HMO patients are treated in groups where there is an organized and supported group program available. Budman and Bennett (1983), for example, estimate that approximately 25 to 30 percent of treatment is done in groups at HCHP; Roller, Schnell, and Welsch (1982), then of Group Health Cooperative of Puget Sound, estimated 27 percent of their overall visits were for group therapy; and at Kaiser-Hayward we conduct several groups each day and see approximately 25 percent of post-intake patients in group formats. These figures are all quite consistent with what Boaz (1988) recommends for a well-run HMO mental health department.

This brings up two important points about group treatment and the structure of HMO services. First, in-house group- or staff-model HMOs will be particularly conducive to group therapy (Folkers and Steefel, 1991) since clinicians who are centrally located and cooperatively aligned are more likely to know about and refer to one another's groups. Clinicians in independent practice association (IPA) or preferred-provider organization (PPO)-style HMOs tend to be more scattered geographically and more likely to operate in a traditional one-on-one private practice model (Bennett, 1988). This pattern is borne out by two surveys of HMO treatment modalities (Altman and Goldstein, 1988; Shadle and Christianson, 1988) that found group therapy to be much more frequent in group models versus IPA models.

Utilization of appropriate therapy groups can be encouraged by a benefits structure that differentiates between group and individual treatment (e.g., a lower co-payment for groups or counting group sessions as half visits) as well as by rewarding therapists who do cost-effective groups (e.g., with somewhat reduced caseloads). Recognizing the benefits of treating patients at 2 P.M. rather than 2 A.M., HMOs that are "at risk" for the comprehensive care of their patients may be able to reduce unnecessary medical and emergency-room visits and psychiatric hospitalizations by designing incentives to encourage patients (such as those with chronic depression, recurring psychosis, somaticizers, and those with certain personality disorders) who may need ongoing or regular support to attend long-term maintenance groups.

A second important point is that to provide high quality and appropriate service, group therapy in HMOs requires a group therapy *program*, not just a haphazard potpourri of groups started here and there when too many patients back up the system. It is important that group therapy be part of a comprehensive and integrated full-service program including individual, group, couple, and family therapy as well as psychopharmacology options and appropriate inpatient services when indicated. A programmatic group therapy approach requires a group psychotherapy coordinator (Folkers and Steefel, 1991; Roller, Schnell, and Welsch, 1982). There needs to be a vision of the clinic's overall treatment plan and careful assessment of which groups are needed, along with ongoing administrative and continuing education support. Therapists need to value and like doing group treatment, since, as Roller, Schnell, and Welsch (1982) have said, "An unwilling group leader can be no more successful than an unwilling group patient" (p. 8).

HMO therapists also have to be careful that the rapid turnover of patients in short-term groups does not result in therapist "burnout" and loss of therapeutic commitment (Imber and Evanczuk, 1990). Co-therapy (Roller and Nelson, 1991) can be quite useful for educating and motivating therapists to do group work as well as for providing such unique advantages as binocular (dual-perspective) vision, morale enhancement, relationship modeling, and treatment continuity when one therapist is unavailable; but a co-therapy arrangement may greatly reduce the possible cost-effectiveness of therapy groups (Boaz, 1988; Donovan, Bennett, and McElroy, 1981). Whether led by one therapist or two, group therapy can be a valuable part of an HMO mental health service. Systematic research is needed, however, to provide specific data on the efficacy of different types of groups.

In summary, HMOs are providing fertile contexts for the development of innovative short-term group therapies. Therapists are typically active, promoting focality and group cohesion within time limits to help patients achieve greater self-empowerment by reducing distress, accessing and sharing psychological resources, and developing skills that facilitate maturational processes. Patients may use therapy—whether it be group, individual, marital, or family–during periods of stress and transition, and may return for intermittent treatment at different life cycle junctures (Cummings, 1990; Kisch and Makover, 1990). Ongoing "maintenance" or continuous care groups for more severely and chronically impaired patients may also be increas- ingly used as managed mental health care expands to serve more of the population in the future.

To be an effective group therapist requires specialized training and a high level of skill and energy. In staff- and group-model HMOs, where clinicians have chosen to work with their colleagues in a group setting, therapists may be especially inclined toward group therapy, noting the value of teamwork and of social interaction with other people coping with problems. Clinicians interested in group therapy ought to be interested in HMOs. Clinicians interested in HMOs ought to be interested in group therapy.

CHAPTER SIX

Teaching and Learning Short-Term Psychotherapy Within an HMO

Learning to practice short-term psychotherapy in an HMO involves the development of both a positive attitude toward brief treatment and the acquisition of specific clinical skills. Psychotherapy training within an HMO mental health service helps trainees acquire these professional skills by providing them with the following learning experiences:

1. The relatively rapid turnover of patients ensures that a greater number will be seen than if only a few were accepted and followed for a long period of time. The shifting caseload results in valuable exposure to more people, problems, diagnoses, and treatment options.
2. Trainees are exposed to the multiplicity of perspectives that a good HMO staff offers. Co-therapy, peer review, hallway consultations, and case study seminars are easily available and provide highly valuable learning situations. Trainees can benefit from the extended intensive experience of a co-therapy partnership as well as from the variety of viewpoints that can be brought to bear as a case is discussed during a staff meeting.
3. Institutional resources and support such as videotape equipment, one-way mirrored observation rooms, and hired con-

Note: Reprinted and condensed from Hoyt, M. F. "Teaching and Learning Short-Term Psychotherapy Within an HMO." In C. S. Austad and W. H. Berman (eds.), *Psychotherapy in Managed Health Care: The Optimal Use of Time and Resources.* Copyright 1991 by American Psychological Association. Used by permission of the publisher.

sultants are frequently available in some HMOs. It is important that HMO therapists, both trainees and experienced staff, not let the immediate need for direct service so preoccupy them that they neglect their own needs for support, consultation, and professional development.

4. Training and working within an HMO structure promotes the inculcation of HMO therapy values and beliefs. Observing successful outcomes in individual cases as well as seeing the system successfully serve the needs of a large and diverse catchment population helps trainees and staff appreciate the necessity and utility of brief therapy.

There are also potential disadvantages to learning psychotherapy in an HMO. The rapid turnover of cases tends to overemphasize quick assessment and rapid intervention and to minimize opportunities for more prolonged working through and attention to termination. The pressures of patient selection and the initial phases of treatment (including crisis services) allow comparatively little time for detailed case study. A trainee who is not yet comfortable working time-sensitively with a diversity of patients may feel overwhelmed or put upon by the pressure of his or her caseload. This suggests that developing clinicians should have experience with diverse approaches and/or settings to round out their HMO therapy training. Even if one prefers brief or short-term therapy, some supervised exposure to good long-term treatment—which may not be available within the HMO setting—will help a therapist to appreciate both the power and the limitations of short-term work.

Parallel Processes Between Therapy and Supervision: Phase-Specific Tasks and Resistances

Aspects of the patient-therapist relationship may be repeated in the therapist-supervisor relationship (Alonso and Rutan, 1988; Dasberg and Winokur, 1984; Ekstein and Wallerstein, 1972; Hess, 1980; Zalcman and Cornell, 1983). This may enhance a trainee's empathy for his or her patient while allowing the supervisor to demonstrate effective treatment techniques in the method of supervision (Frances and Clarkin, 1981b), a desirable situation in which development of the trainee depends in part upon modeling and identification with the supervisor. This is a potentially powerful learning situation but one that is also subtle and subject to distortions and abuse. Analogous to the interactions between patients and therapists, trainees and supervisors may enter into games and transactions that have more to do with gratifying desires for superiority or dependency than with promoting learning and change (Hawthorne, 1975; Kadushin, 1968). Any of these resistances may be manifested at any point in the course of learning and teaching brief therapy. Even if trainee and supervisor have good intentions, there may be a tendency in the supervision situation to enact in parallel process certain resistances that may be particularly related to the issues and strains of the specific phase of patient-therapist treatment in progress.

The *beginning phase* of supervision parallels the initial processes of therapist and patient evolving a working relationship, forming a treatment focus, and establishing the patient's recognition of his or her responsibility for making changes. At this time, the supervisor must be especially careful to foster the trainee's budding sense of competency. The supervisor must support nascent efforts toward selective focusing, confrontation, and rapport building. Supervisors need to avoid being overly critical or dazzling trainees with their knowledge and technical skill lest they demoralize them or promote excessive dependency rather than inspire hope and effort. The supervisor teaches the trainee how to use supervision, and depending on the trainee's level of skill and experience, the supervisor and trainee will have to select one or two major foci to emphasize in supervision. The old saying, "If you're too well rounded, you're not pointed in any direction" cautions against a possible pitfall in both therapy and supervision. As in the treatment contract, it may be helpful to have the trainee set specific goals for each session and for his or her overall supervision (Barnes, 1977; Berne, 1972; Goulding and Goulding, 1978, 1979).[1]

The *middle phase* of supervision parallels the patient-therapist work of enhancing the patient's sense of autonomy, refining the focus, and working through both within the transference and in relationships outside of therapy. At this stage, the trainee's presentation may become unfocused and may lack specificity and purpose. The supervisor may be tempted to take over, to change the focus radically (without sufficient reason), and/or to pursue topics closer to his or her interests than those of the trainee. The urge to diffuse the treatment may parallel the therapist-patient situation. The emergence of resistance or negative feelings toward the supervisor, who inevitably cannot give the trainee all that is desired (just as the trainee cannot totally satisfy the patient), needs to be handled tactfully. Calling attention to the parallel process may be instructive, although the supervisor has to be especially careful not to be critical or make blaming comments (e.g., "You're just like your patient!"). Constructive handling of the trainee-supervisor relationship during the beginning phase will lay the groundwork for the successful confrontation of tensions during the middle phase.

In the *end phase* of supervision, termination is the issue. Just as the therapist may be experiencing feelings of incompleteness, or guilt, or both, and the urge to extend therapy and somehow "rescue" the patient, the supervisor may experience similar sentiments. He or she may desire to continue supervision beyond the cutoff date, may feel unrealistically that he or she has not done an adequate job, or may try to cram unassimilable amounts of clinical lore and wisdom into the last supervision meetings. The trainee, not feeling "totally educated" and competent, may invite and welcome these eleventh-hour desperations. However, it is better for therapist and supervisor to learn about countertransference through the experience rather than through enactment.[2]

Conclusion

Interest in short-term therapy has increased tremendously in recent years, and the basic belief of the effective brief therapist that significant and enduring changes can be facilitated quickly through skilled intervention has been increasingly borne out by both systematic research and individual experience. Clinicians need to be willing and able to practice effective brief therapy if the needs of more than a handful of patients are to be served. This reality, which is the backbone of HMO therapy, provides the mandate (Cummings, 1986; Kovacs, 1982) for the expanded teaching and learning of brief therapy (Clarkin, Frances, Taintor, and Warburg, 1980). A wide variety of specific theoretical and technical approaches have been developed, and much can be learned by reading, attending conferences and workshops, observation, and autodidacticism. The pressures and problems inherent in doing psychotherapy are quite pervasive, however, and we all are subject, from time to time, to developing counterproductive patterns or blind spots. Therapists who find themselves repeatedly stuck or at a loss may benefit from consultation with a trusted peer or with a professionally skilled supervisor. Good supervision, like good therapy, pays for itself many times over.

Notes

1. The *selection phase* involves choosing patients for therapy who are likely to be successful (Malan, 1976a; Sifneos, 1987) and who do not have major contraindications or impediments. This can create an interesting dilemma, since those patients who are most suitable for short-term treatment (possessing high motivation for personal change, psychological mindedness, responsiveness to trial interventions, etc.) are also those who make the most desirable long-term patients. On the one hand, working with more responsive, relatively less difficult patients is important both for trainees who are developing their short-term skills and confidence, and for more experienced staff who need to have a satisfying mixture of cases. On the other hand, however, a manifestation of therapist resistance in this phase of brief therapy is the temptation to keep patients in therapy longer than is necessary. Unjustified treatment extension is both poor management of limited resources and unethical, so therapists and supervisors must guard against the temptation to extend treatment for the attractive at the expense of the less fortunate.

2. There are situations where we have to face the limits of brief (or any) psychotherapy. Then we, as professional caregivers, may experience a strong twinge of guilt: What are we going to do for the people who need more? Should we feel guilty that we cannot be everything to everyone? Just as patients can form an institutional transference (Reider, 1953), clinicians can engage in *institutional countertransference* by overassuming responsibility in response to patients' neediness and dependency on the institution. Professional activity is contractually based, it should be remembered; at times it may be appropriate and necessary to advocate for the full allocation or expansion of what is covered contractually.

CHAPTER SEVEN

On Time in Brief Therapy

Again and again I have had the impression that we have made too little theoretical use of this fact, established beyond any doubt, of the unalterability by time of the repressed. This seems to offer an approach to the most profound discoveries. Nor, unfortunately, have I myself made any progress here.
—Sigmund Freud (1933/1955)

My interest has been to convince you that you must assume responsibility for being here, in this marvelous world, in this marvelous desert, in this marvelous time. I wanted to convince you that you must learn to make every act count, since you are going to be here for only a short while; in fact, too short for witnessing all the marvels of it.
—Don Juan (Castaneda, 1972)

Time is of the essence in brief psychotherapy. The message, by definition, is *brevity*: do it now, no time to waste, be efficient, seize the moment, be here now, get on with it. At core, brief therapy is defined more by an attitude than by the specific number of treatment sessions. The brief therapist operates with

Note: Reprinted, with changes, from Hoyt, M. F. "On Time in Brief Therapy." In R. A. Wells and V. J. Giannetti (eds.), *Handbook of the Brief Psychotherapies.* Copyright 1950 by Plenum. Used by permission of the publisher.

First epigraph reprinted with permission from Freud, S. "The Unconscious: New Introductory Lectures." In J. Strachey (ed.), *The Standard Edition of the Complete Psychological Works of Sigmund Freud.* Vol. 22. Copyright 1955 by Hogarth Press.

Second epigraph reprinted by permission of the author, Carlos Castaneda, and the author's representative, Tracy Kramer, Toltec Artists, Inc., 183 North Martel Ave., Suite 220, Los Angeles, CA 90036. First published in *Journey to Ixtlan* (copyright 1972).

the belief and expectation that change can occur *in the moment*, that the patient has within himself or herself the power to be different or to remain the same (Goulding and Goulding, 1978, 1979). With skillful assistance, the patient will recognize his or her response-ability and thus move from being a victim to a creator of his or her psychological reality (Hoyt, 1977; Schafer, 1973; Kaiser, 1965).

Aspects of time underlie brief treatment across a variety of specific theoretical and technical approaches. My purpose here is to highlight a few of the connections between time and brief therapy, with the hope that heightened awareness of the temporal dimension can help therapists to construct and conduct more satisfying and parsimonious (brief and effective) treatments. What follows is not presented as an all-encompassing review or definitive statement; it calls attention to a few lines of inquiry and is intended to stimulate thought and experimentation.[1]

The Brief Therapist's Basic Attitude Toward Time

Time is both a medium and a perspective, and psychotherapies vary in their orientation toward time (Melges, 1982). Psychoanalysis seeks to produce change primarily by directing the patient's awareness toward the past and its persistence in the present—this is the principle Freud (1914) described in his essay, "Remembering, Repeating, and Working Through." Gestalt therapy (Perls, Hefferline, and Goodman, 1951; Perls, 1969; Naranjo, 1970), cognitive therapy (Beck, 1976; Emery and Campbell, 1986), and much of the family therapy movement (Guerin, 1976; Gurman and Kniskern, 1981; Budman, 1981) seek change by focusing on the patient's present experiencing and modes of conduct. There are also methods of treatment, such as the Gouldings' (1978, 1979) redecision therapy, de Shazer's (1985) "Crystal Ball Technique," and Melges' (1982) future-oriented therapy, that seek change by having patients actively imagine successful outcomes and their paths to them.

Effective brief therapy may look to the past or the future

for clues about where the patient is "stuck" and what experience might be needed for him or her to get "unstuck," but the brief therapist knows that only in the present can the patient make a change. Excessive concern outside of the present is counterproductive. The patient may engage in various security operations to remain the same (Gustafson, 1986), especially if he or she feels, as Melges (1982) describes it, that control over the future has been lost. The patient who wants to un-do or turn back time interferes with coping in the present (Mann, 1973). Secrets (Hoyt, 1978), obsessions (Hoyt, 1987a), remorse (Hoyt, 1983), and various reality distortions may be clung to in an attempt to avoid movement into a threatening present and future. The therapist will help the patient by assisting him or her to endure and control the present while approaching the future.

Elsewhere (Chapter Seventeen; also see Budman and Gurman, 1983, 1988) I have contrasted the temporal attitude of brief versus long-term (psychodynamic) therapists:

> Long-term therapy is based on a number of theoretical assumptions that presuppose that treatment must take a long time to be effective: the belief that pathogenic early experiences inevitably must be slowly and fully uncovered; the belief that rapport and therapist-patient alliance must form gradually; the belief that the patient must be allowed to regress and that transference takes a long time to develop and should not be interpreted too early; and the belief that the consolidation of gains requires a lengthy period of working through. . . . These theoretical assumptions—which may become self-fulfilling prophecies—are not necessarily always true, and may at times be held as quasi-intellectual resistances to short-term therapy. An alternative set of assumptions suggests that short-term treatment can be effective: the belief that focused interventions can set into motion a whole system of changes; the belief that selected patients can rapidly form a good working alliance and that early transference interpretations can strengthen the alliance; the belief that generalized regression should be avoided and that regression should be restricted as much as possible to the focal area; and the belief that a time limit increases and intensifies the work accomplished, that gains are consolidated throughout the treatment. . . . The

differences in these two sets of working assumptions highlight the technical methods that characterize effective short-term work: an explicit understanding that treatment will not be prolonged or "timeless," greater therapist activity and early transference interpretation, selective attention to a central dynamic focus, maintenance of a strong adult-to-adult therapeutic alliance and avoidance of generalized regression, and early attention to termination as part of the working-through process [pp. 97–98].

There are a series of beliefs or myths that are sources of resistance against short-term therapy, factors that are often permeated with therapists' assumptions and anxieties regarding time:

(a) the belief that "more is better," often held despite the lack of any evidence justifying the greater expense of long-term or open-ended treatment; (b) the myth of the "pure gold" of analysis, the overvaluation of insight and misassumption that change and growth require "deep" examination of an individual's unconscious and psychohistory; (c) the confusion of patients' interests with therapists' interests, the tendency of therapists to seek and perfectionistically treat putative complexes rather than attend directly to patients' complaints and stated treatment goals; (d) the demand for hard work, the need for the brief therapist to be active, intensely alert, selectively focused, intuitive, and risk taking; (e) financial pressures, the temptation to hold on to that which is profitable and dependable; and (f) countertransference and termination problems, the need to be needed and difficulties of saying goodbye [Hoyt, 1987b, p. 408].

Therapists accustomed to doing long-term or open-ended work will have to suspend or adjust their assumptions about the perspective and pace of treatment if they are to do effective brief therapy. The pursuit of a perfectionistic "cure" through the persistent probing of pathology will need to shift, if one is to work in a "time-sensitive" manner (Budman and Gurman, 1988), to a pragmatic and parsimonious promotion of patients' strengths and sources vis-a-vis the presenting problem.

The Structure of Brief Therapy

Brief psychotherapy (as well as other, more prolonged or open-ended treatments) can be conceptualized to have a structure of sequenced phases, as shown in Figure 7.1. In actual practice, of course, the phases blend into one another rather than being so discretely organized. The structure tends to be epigenetic or pyramidal, each phase building on the prior so that successful work in one is a precondition for the next, e.g., there is a need for rapport and focusing before working through, and termination will not be meaningful unless connection and work have preceded. There is often an interesting parallel between the microcosm and the macrocosm: the structure of each individual session resembles the structure of the overall course of treatment.[2] There is also often a parallel process (Dasberg and Winokur, 1984; see Chapter Six), observable in supervision, wherein brief therapy students/trainees move through the same sequence of phases as do their patients.

Figure 7.1. The Structure of Brief Therapy.

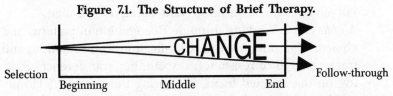

Source: Hoyt (1991, p. 118). Used by permission of the publisher.

1. *Pre-treatment selection criteria.* How well does the patient fit the indications for likely success in brief therapy (high motivation for personal change, circumscribed chief complaint, psychological-mindedness, history of beneficial relationships, responsiveness to trial interventions) as described by Sifneos (1979), Malan (1976a, 1976b) and others? Is the patient likely to be a spontaneous improver, nonresponder, or negative responder (exclusion criteria that Frances and Clarkin [1981a] suggest make no therapy the treatment of choice)? Are contraindications or major impediments present (marked inability to tolerate anxiety, guilt, or depression; active psychosis or threat of suicide;

active alcohol or drug abuse)? Change often begins with recognition of the problem and a decision to seek therapy, even before the first treatment contact occurs.

2. *Beginning phase.* Making contact. Forming rapport and a working alliance. Letting the patient know how to use treatment. Confronting resistance and negative transference. Taking history and complaint. Why therapy now? Finding a psychological focus, making a treatment contract. Getting the patient's agreement to change. Setting parameters, including the time allotted for each session, the frequency, and the short-term duration. Beginning and ending the session on time, a first encounter with therapeutic time limits. "The battle for structure" and "the battle for initiative" (Whitaker, in Napier and Whitaker, 1978), in which the patient attempts to dictate the parameters of treatment (where, when, and who attends) while trying to get the therapist to set the theme and take responsibility (what and why) for the work. Giving an initial task or homework assignment to increase the patient's active involvement and to promote and accelerate change.

3. *Middle phase.* Working through. Recognition of patterns and choices regarding options. Clarification, confrontation, and interpretation of resistance, discounting, transference. Staying on the selected focus, "honoring the contract." Homework, behavioral directives and anchors for change. Awareness that time is limited, that treatment will end soon.

4. *End phase.* Termination. Continued work on the central focus (the "contract") plus awareness of the impending end of therapist-patient contact. Arousal of dependency and underlying separation-individuation issues, with possible recrudescence of symptoms. Mourning. Countertransference pulls to avoid ending, to "rescue" the patient, to cram "extra" work into the last session or two (Hoyt and Farrell, 1984; Chapter Eighteen). Alternatively, a possibly "flat" last session as participants prematurely detach to avoid a genuine ending. Discussion of continuing change, maintaining gains, and possible backsliding or "self-sabotage" (Hoyt, 1986). Letting the patient know that a return to

treatment is possible (unless the therapist wants for specific reasons to strongly emphasize the separation, as in Mann's [1973] model of time-limited psychotherapy), and sometimes inviting a later follow-up or "check-in" appointment or contact, which may attenuate the emotional impact of termination while implying the therapist's continuing interest in the patient's life and progress.

5. *Follow-through.* Continuation of psychological work and change beyond the formal ending date of therapist-patient contact. Internalization of favorable aspects of the treatment: "If I give you a fish, you can eat a meal. If I teach you how to fish, you can feed yourself forever." In short-term therapy, much more than in longer-term treatments, change processes may be initiated or set into motion without being completely worked through during the course of actual patient-therapist contact (Horowitz and Hoyt, 1979; Shectman, 1986). Recognition of differences between treatment goals and life goals (Ticho, 1972), the fact that the consolidation of some benefits of treatment can only occur with lived time. This points to the need for long-term follow-up if therapeutic outcomes are to be thoroughly assessed (Bergin and Lambert, 1978; Butcher and Kolotkin, 1979; Cross, Sheehan, and Khan, 1982). Possible patient return to treatment or "checking in for a booster." The possibility of *serial* or *intermittent* short-term therapy—encouraged by quick success for one problem, a patient later seeks treatment for another (Cummings, 1977, 1990; Cummings and VandenBos, 1979; Budman and Gurman, 1983, 1988; Bennett, 1983, 1984).

Issues of time may attend each of the five phases. Does the patient have a problem pertaining directly to time (e.g., unresolved mourning, anniversary reactions, procrastination, anxiety about the future, a feeling of hopelessness about the future, and impulsiveness)? Does he or she seek an "instant cure" to avoid contact and vulnerability, or does the patient seek "timeless" (open-ended or long-term) treatment to avoid change and maintain dependency? Do sessions begin and end on time? If not, because of whom? Is time "squeezed" or "squandered"? Does change occur? How does the patient respond to the impending termination of treatment: How does the therapist respond? Many of these points are amplified in the following section.

Six Practical Issues
Regarding Time and Therapeutic Technique

"Fourth-dimension" decisions about the length of treatment and the length of each session, and how this is discussed and determined with the patient, do much to shape the content and course of the therapeutic work.

1. Duration of Contact

The essence of short-term therapy is an attitude that change is possible and expected now rather than later. There is no magic number of sessions that makes therapy brief—any figure would be arbitrary. Therapy should be as short as possible, and what is possible is determined partially by the expectations and beliefs of therapist and patient. I am reminded of an experience I had several years ago when I visited the Short-Term Therapy Seminar at the renowned Tavistock Clinic in London (Malan, 1976a, 1976b). Cases were presented and I was asked to comment, which I did with some trepidation. We got into a discussion about length of treatment. I indicated that at the clinic where I was then working we generally saw patients for twelve sessions, a number that followed Mann's (1973) time-limited psychotherapy model and allowed for a good research design (Horowitz and others, 1984b). "Here at the Tavistock we allow trainees thirty-five to forty sessions. It allows for wasting time and making mistakes," I was told. "Well, in America we're more efficient," I responded. "We find that we can waste time and make mistakes in twelve sessions!"

How many sessions constitute brief therapy? The above notwithstanding, there is a range or consensus in the literature. Short-term or brief therapy is often arbitrarily defined as twenty sessions or less. Wolberg (1965b, p. 140), for example, refers to "short-term treatment . . . up to 20 treatment sessions." Various insurance plans and health maintenance organizations (HMOs) often provide for "brief treatment up to 20 sessions." As mentioned above, Mann (1973; Mann and Goldman, 1982) and Horowitz (1976; Horowitz and others, 1984b) have reported successful psychodynamic treatments within a twelve-session framework. For Wells (1982, p. 99), "Short-term treatment comprises three or four sessions up to a maximum of fifteen interviews." There is also a growing literature on *single-session psychotherapy* (Malan, Heath, Bacal, and Balfour, 1975; Bloom, 1981; Rockwell and Pinkerton, 1982; Talmon, 1990; Chapters Eight and Nine), a maximally brief treatment approach that colleagues and I have been exploring with encouraging results. It should also be noted that for some people no therapy may be the treatment of choice; people who would get better if left untreated, those who do not respond to treatment, and those who get worse with treatment should not be in psychotherapy (Frances and Clarkin, 1981a).

There are a variety of ways to establish explicitly the planned brief duration of short-term therapy. One can either speak generally of meeting "for a few times" or "for a month or two," or one can indicate the exact end point at the beginning of treatment either by setting a specific number of sessions ("We'll meet six times") or an end date ("We'll meet weekly through November 7"). In any arrangement, there is the question of what to do about missed sessions. I prefer to count them as missed, not to "make them up." If the patient has been making progress but the desired goal has not yet been reached, I may sometimes negotiate for future sessions, as Wells (1982, p. 200) recommends. Generally, however, one has to be careful not to fall into the trap of simply adding "an extra session" (or two, or three . . .) unless extraordinary circumstances (e.g., a suicidal crisis or unforeseeable emergency) require it, since doing so threatens to undermine the integrity of the initial short-term agreement and violates the basic existential truth of time limits: "For psychotherapy to enable an individual to come to terms with the meaning of his existence, he must come to grips with the reality of nonexistence. Psychotherapy is true to this quest insofar as it is a process of termination rather than consolidation of relationship and proliferation of time" (C. Goldberg, 1975, p. 342).

The therapist can opt not to predetermine the number of sessions but to state, "We'll be meeting about half a dozen times" or "We'll only be meeting a few times" and set the termination date as the work draws to completion. In keeping with the idea that "brief" means "no more than necessary," it is interesting to note that two sessions held six months apart might be considered more brief than a twelve-week treatment consisting of one or more sessions per week.

Scheduling sessions weekly is probably the most common practice, although more frequent meetings can be arranged to intensify treatment, gain momentum, or provide needed support; or less frequently, to attenuate the transference or to allow time for homework and change (Selvini-Palazzoli, Boscolo, Cecchin, and Prata, 1978). Sessions may be spread out at the end of treatment for a gradual ending, with the probable effect of decreasing the impact of termination. A follow-up session can be arranged for several months later, to help maintain gains, encourage internalization, and assess continued developments. Therapists should be aware that altering the framework of treatment has effects (Langs, 1979), and they should consider what purpose (and whose needs) are being served with any temporal arrangement or modification.

When treatment ends, patients can be encouraged to return if needed (and may be helped by exploring what would indicate returning) but often benefit by being counseled to resist returning too quickly so that they can weather some ups and downs and realize their strength. I also prefer to let patients know that they could return for the same problem or a different problem, and that they could either contact me or seek a different therapist if desired. In my opinion, someone returning to psychotherapy does not necessarily indicate failure or "unresolved pathological transference" anymore than someone returning to the same restaurant indicates a "failure" the first time they were there.

2. Duration of Treatment Sessions

Most short-term or brief therapists work in conventional "fifty-minute hours," probably because of convenience and habit. This seems to allow a comfortable amount of time for most therapists and patients to make contact, get (or resume) a focus and contract, engage in exploration and working through, and end the session. (Again, note the parallel between the structure of individual sessions and the overall course of treatment—see Figure 7.1.) There is nothing sacrosanct about fifty-minute sessions, however, and it is worth considering alternatives. Two well known and highly effective brief therapists, Robert and Mary Goulding (1978, 1979), like to conduct redecision therapy sessions for twenty minutes. Others, often working in understaffed public or private settings, see patients for five- to thirty-minute sessions and need to make therapeutic impact quickly (Barten, 1965; Castelnuovo-Tedesco, 1986; Dreiblatt and Weatherly, 1965; Singh, 1982; Zirkle, 1961). The idea of fifty-minute consultations occurring over many meetings is essentially a middle-class notion (Wells, 1982), and persons of different socioeconomic backgrounds may not share this time perspective and may need to see valuable results quickly if subsequent sessions are to occur. Therapists experimenting with single-session therapies (Bloom, 1981; Rockwell and Pinkerton, 1982; Talmon, 1990; Chapters Eight and Nine) sometimes find it helpful to have ninety minutes or two hours for the treatment contact in order to have time to assess, prepare, and complete a substantial intervention. Certain kinds of intense work, such as "re-grief" (Volkan, 1975) or "grief resolution" (Melges, 1982) therapy, can be done in relatively few sessions, but each session may last for a couple of hours. Couples and family brief therapists may also find it helpful to have more time per session to deal with the complexities of multiple persons. Would the reader consider a single marathon session, such as the ten-hour treatment reported by Berenbaum (1969) to be a prolonged brief therapy or a brief prolonged therapy?

3. Conveying the Time Limit to the Patient

Explicit indication by the therapist that "we will only be meeting X times" or "a few times" or "until November," or stating that "you have the ability to deal with this pretty quickly if we get right down to work," conveys the message that the patient has the capacity and opportunity to use brief treatment advantageously. It is also honest and ethical in that it lets the patient know the therapist's intentions so that he or she can decide whether or not to engage in treatment. Offering brief therapy apologetically, by saying something such as, "The clinic will only let me see you five times, but we'll see what we can do," is obviously demoralizing and counterproductive. Clinicians' attitudes toward the value of brief therapy may influence how they communicate with brief therapy patients (Sifneos, 1981; Burlingame and Behrman, 1987; Johnson and Gelso, 1980), and this communication may contribute to a self-fulfilling prophecy. As John D. Rockefeller reputedly said: "Whether a man thinks he is going to be a success or a failure, he is probably right!"

A time-limited framework often creates a sense of urgency that helps to foster a rapid and deep involvement. Like the proverbial meeting of strangers on a train, the safety of knowing that the end is clearly defined and in sight sometimes permits short-term therapy patients to become quickly and intensely engaged in treatment (Stierlin, 1968). The operation of "Parkinson's Law" in psychotherapy—work expands or contracts to fill the time available for it—was observed by Appelbaum (1975; see also Appelbaum and Holzman, 1967; Mann, 1973; Rank, 1945; Wells, 1982), who advocates setting the end point at the beginning of brief therapy to stimulate the patient's will and to counteract passive, timeless waiting for change. This method, of forcing the patient to confront issues of separation by setting a termination date, was first reported by Freud (1918) in his case of the Wolf Man. It is also interesting that Freud, "the father of psychoanalysis," can rightfully be considered the first brief therapist in that many of his early cases (Breuer and Freud, [1893–95] 1955) only lasted from a single session to a couple of months.

In setting a time limit or conveying the idea of "a few sessions" or "a couple of months," the brief therapist does not need to appear arbitrary or ruthless. Indeed, the therapist should believe genuinely that he or she is able to render professional assistance in the time offered, and should be willing to discuss the recommendation with the patient. Iatrogenic resistance is minimized if therapy is a cooperative, bipersonal venture. Following the principle of informed consent, initial assessment should include asking patients what bothers them, what they want and how long they think it will take to accomplish, and discussing with them their ideas and reasons. Patients' beliefs and goals merit due respect, to be sure, but they may be inaccurate or colored by their pathology, e.g., many patients with "borderline personality" structures hope for a magically quick cure, while "dependent" patients are almost always sure that they will need to be seen "for a long time." When told that, say, twelve sessions of therapy are recommended, most patients will respond, "That many?" (June and Smith, 1983; Pekarik and Wierzbicki, 1986). Nowadays, most people (except, perhaps, mental health professionals!) seek and expect rapid results, a trend consonant with both economic realities and the "do it now" ethic of our "instant society" of high-speed computers, drive-thru fast food, "one-minute managers" (Blanchard and Johnson, 1982), and thirty-minute TV dramas. Even the popularization of digital clocks and timing devices may affect the conceptualization of temporal experience, as the cyclical nature of the sweep of the analog clock is replaced by the dizzying blur of the digital display. How right Bob Dylan was back in 1963 when he told us, "The times they are a-changin'"!

4. Selecting the Time Limit

As Wells (1982) has noted, the setting of time limits in brief treatment is far from an exact science. Experienced short-term therapists seem to rely primarily on "clinical judgment" or "intuition" when deciding whether a particular patient will be offered, say, ten sessions, rather than eight or twelve sessions. It is generally agreed among brief therapists that the expectation of success should be conveyed with firm confidence. But how does one decide how many sessions?

Sometimes the number is determined by external factors, such as a research design or agency policy, or by the patient's preference, ability to pay, or expected time to be available. Therapists should not automatically accede to such constraints—sometimes they are put forward as reality resistances that can be modified. If the therapist does not feel that successful treatment is likely in the amount of time being considered, he or she should so advise the patient and refer him or her elsewhere or suggest that the patient delay treatment until a more propitious time.

Inexperienced practitioners often set too *long* a time limit (e.g., fifteen to twenty sessions) and thus lose the structuring effect that a shorter time limit (six to eight sessions) might provide. It is also important, of course, especially while learning to work briefly, not to err too far in the other direction, setting time limits that are unrealistically brief, which might result in treatments that are frantically rushed and incomplete rather than pleasantly urgent and efficient. Factors that need to be taken into consideration include what the patient wishes to change in the treatment, his or her motivation and apparent abilities (and weaknesses), the therapist's level of skillfulness and sense that rapid change is possible, and the "friendliness" (supportiveness and malleability) of the circumstance the patient is confronting.

A fixed (typically twelve-session) time limit is useful if the therapist wants to engage the patient in a process (Mann, 1973; Mann and Goldman, 1982) that will restimulate, via the transference, unresolved mourning and other separation-dependency issues. The reactivation of latent maladaptive cognitive-affective schemata (Horowitz and others, 1984a, 1984b) permits their reworking, even if, as Westen (1986) has questioned, the twelve-session limit may not allow enough time for a fundamental internalization of the therapist as a replacement for previous and less benign figures. A "dozen sessions" does seem to offer enough time, if skillfully handled, for a meaningful engagement and mourning process to take place.

Perry (1987; see also Frances, Clarkin, and Perry, 1984; Budman and Gurman, 1983, 1988) provides a useful discussion of factors that tend to increase versus decrease the duration of psychotherapeutic treatment. He notes that therapy tends to be shorter under the following conditions: the diagnosis focuses on acute symptoms, there is a precipitating stress, treatment goals are limited, premorbid functioning was good, the patient expects brief therapy and believes that change should occur quickly, the patient has limited time and money, the therapist takes an actively directive approach and is not easily available for sessions, the goal or treatment is reparation or return to function, techniques are more behavioral or directive than "exploratory," and the identified patient is a minor or senior and a family or marital format is used.

This is not to say that brief therapy should necessarily avoid stirring up affect or uncovering painful material. As Malan (1976a) and others have written, the evidence suggests that "radical" techniques that "go to the root" can produce lasting benefit with brief, focused therapy.

During the initial assessment the therapist has to estimate the patient's capacity for work and integration when selecting the time limit. It is probably better to err slightly on the cautious side, since it is easier and more reassuring to declare the job done "ahead of schedule" and to stop earlier than planned rather than have to extend or prolong a treatment. Wolberg's recommendation (1965b, p. 140) is wise: "The best strategy, in my opinion, is to assume that every patient, irrespective of diagnosis, will respond to short-term treatment unless he proves himself refractory to it. If the therapist approaches each patient with the idea of doing as much as he can for him . . . he will give the patient an opportunity to take advantage of short-term treatment to the limit of his potential. If this fails, he can always then resort to prolonged therapy."

What is most important in selecting a length of treatment is attention to the needs of the particular patient at the particular time (de la Torre, 1978). "Fixed duration" should not be a Procrustean bed, with some patients fitting nicely while others are needlessly stretched or cut short. Flexibility and a genuine belief that lasting change can occur rapidly are paramount. Therapists should also know their own personal strengths and weaknesses but should not impose their preferences or predilections in the name of "policy" or "style." In this connection it is worth noting that Brodaty (1983) reviewed the brief therapy literature and concluded that the rigidity of a therapy timetable seems to be based more on the character of the therapist than on any theoretical evidence.

Generally speaking, the exact time limit is of less importance than the increased awareness of patient and therapist that there is a time limit. The element of time can be highlighted from the very first contact with the patient by referring to the treatment being "brief" or "time-limited." This will help convey the basic attitude and expectation of brief therapy, that change can occur within the moment. Some ways that this emphasis can be accomplished during sessions are described in the next section.

5. The Language of Time Limits

The brief therapist and patient should both be aware that time is limited, not endless, and that *now* is the time to move forward. (As Shectman [1986, p. 521] has put it, "Necessity is thus becoming not only the mother of invention but of intervention as well.") Setting a time limit or agreeing to meet "just a few times" helps instill this awareness. The language that therapists use during sessions can reinforce (or un-do) the therapeutic impact or thrust of time limit-setting.

Eric Berne (1961, 1972), the originator of transactional analysis, would ask himself before each session, "What can I do to cure this patient today?" Single-session "cure" did not always result, of course, but the question focused therapist and patient on making rapid changes. Goulding and Goulding (1978, 1979) have developed Berne's concept of *contractual therapy* and ask patients, as they begin each treatment session, "What are you willing to change today?" In this one brilliant sentence the key elements of brief therapy all occur. Here they are, spelled out:

What (specificity, target, focus)

are (active verb, present tense)

you (self as agent, intrapsychic focus, personal functioning)

willing (choice, responsibility, initiative)

to change (alter, not just "work on" or "explore")

today (now, in the moment)

? (inquiry, open field, therapist receptive but not insistent)

The effective brief therapist often includes references to time limits in setting the focus or contract with the patient. Consider, for example, this statement made to a bereaved and betrayed widow at the beginning of a twelve-session time-limited therapy:

Therapist: Let's have an agreement that we might meet, say, a dozen times, and keep our focus pretty much on what your husband's passing and what this affair meant in your life, and who you are now and how that is affecting it, and who you can be in the next few years, and not spend a lot of time talking about other problems (Hoyt, 1979a, pp. 211–212).

Time can also be used as a resistance (Appelbaum, 1975). Stalling, to avoid the present and the future, will need to be confronted and given up for therapy to progress. Consider these two interchanges:

Patient: Let me ask you a question in a roundabout fashion.

Therapist: You want to duck it slowly? (Mann, 1973, p. 37).

Therapist: You tell me, I mean look, we have spent fifteen minutes, you tell me what we've accomplished?

Patient: My goodness, many people come to psychiatrists for years on end . . .

T: Uh huh.

P: . . . and ah . . .

T: So what you say is this, that we have to come for years until we understand.

P: No, I, I hope not (Davanloo, 1986, pp. 119–120).

Some other statements made with similar purpose might include:

T: You seem to be filling our time together with small talk rather than confronting the problem that brought you here.

T: With all the serious problems you mentioned before, I'm wondering why you are spending so much time talking about X.

T: We're already halfway through our six sessions. You're going to have to really get going to get this worked out. What do you want to change today?

T: I'm not willing to keep meeting if you're going to waste time. Do you want to work?

Therapists sometimes convey the message that problems with a long history will necessarily require a long time to resolve, as in these statements by a therapist from transcripts of a hundred-plus-session marital therapy (Fanshel, 1971): "And I really think [*sighing*] we ought to allow ourselves more time for this because it's only going to make trouble" (p. 108) and "if it's a *long* story, it's a *long time* getting out in the open" (p. 287, italics in original). Sometimes long-term treatment is desired and necessary (as certain patients undergo self-exploration and characterological change, or to help them weather a difficult life passage or maintain a tenuous psychosocial adjustment), but the therapist should also have the theoretical ability, practical skill, and interest to consolidate a protracted story line into a treatable central issue. One might begin to do this by asking:

Therapist: What's most important is not how far back this goes, but how much further you're going to continue to do it. Are you willing to look at your part in it right now?

Once therapy gets under way it sometimes continues, week after week, simply because the time is reserved and appointments scheduled. As I learned from Carl Whitaker (personal communication), the patient's initiative and involvement can be strengthened by asking occasionally:

Therapist: Do you want to keep the appointment next week? We could cancel it if you don't want to work.

There are other brief therapists, such as Cummings (1977) and Austin and Inderbitzin (1983), who also advocate letting patients set appointments for when they are willing to work.

The language of brief therapy also gains therapeutic impact by being present-centered. Psychotherapy is more likely to be effective if the patient has a here-and-now experience rather than just a there-and-then explanation. Experience results in genuine learning and growth, whereas explanation or information simply leads to recognition. This is why the well-timed psychodynamic transference interpretation can be so powerful: it brings the patient into the present. Malan (1976b), for example, found the use of transference interpretations to be positively correlated with successful outcomes in short-term dynamic psychotherapy. Similarly, data (Hoyt, 1980; Hoyt, Xenakis, Marmar, and Horowitz, 1983) indicate that short-term dynamic therapy sessions are judged to be particularly "good" when the activities of therapist and patient emphasize the patient's expression of thoughts and feelings and the collaborative exploration of the meaning of this expression in terms of the patient's self-concept, reactions to the therapist, and links between past and present.

Mental imagery can serve the same purpose: it brings the patient's outside world into the therapist's office and increases the likelihood that a range of meaningful emotions will be experienced (Hoyt, 1986). This is consistent with what Whitaker and Malone (1953, p. 204) contend: "Any technique which succeeds in equating in the patient all time, whether past or future, with the present time, seems to have validity." William James

(1890, p. 293) recognized the same thing: "Each world whilst it is attended to is real after its own fashion."[3] Brief therapists who are skillful in using mental imagery (see Singer [1974] for a good overview of methods and Shorr [1972, 1974] and Goulding [1985] for some particularly creative applications) will be able to help patients rapidly generate therapeutic experiences. Gestalt therapists and redecision therapists (Goulding and Goulding, 1978, 1979), for example, know that it is often much more effective for producing change to have people talk *with* their introjects in the present, via double-chair work, rather than having them talk *about* them in the past tense. It is also helpful, both generally and when doing imagery work, to attend to patients' rate of speech. Sometimes patients will slow down or speed up to avoid particular images, feelings, or a "loss of control" that might actually be a step into the warded-off present.

There are a number of quotations and pithy statements about time that I have found to be helpful, when judiciously shared with patients, for heightening the existential impact of brief therapy. The "zingers" include: "Killing time isn't murder. Killing time is suicide" (William James); "If you don't change directions, you'll wind up where you're heading" (Old Chinese saying); "If not you, who? If not now, when?" (Rabbi Hillel); "Teach us to number our days that we may get us a heart of wisdom" (Moses, Psalm 90:12); "Brevity is the soul of wit" (Shakespeare, *Hamlet*, II, ii, 90); "There is no time like the present"; "You don't have to change, but you know what happened to the dinosaurs . . ."; "Growing old isn't bad, when you consider the alternative" (Maurice Chevalier); "Well, no one lives forever. But even if you believe in reincarnation, there is still the question: Is there life *before* death?"

Once I consulted with a man, about to turn forty, who complained that he was feeling old, that life was rushing by despite his increasingly "Type A" freneticism. He also complained of difficulty making commitments. I asked him to be specific: What commitment?

Patient: Well, my girlfriend wants to get married, but I'm not sure.

Therapist: How long have you been together?

P: Eight years.

T: Oh, I see. Well, you certainly don't want to rush into it. Why don't you wait to see how she handles menopause and retirement. You certainly don't want to get stuck with a crotchety old lady, do you?

He laughed, first at my gentle mockery, then harder, at himself. "It is crazy, isn't it?" he said. I tried to keep a straight face, but added, "Well, I don't know. You can't tell what's going to happen in the future." Many months later he telephoned to let me know that he had gotten married and was happy. He offered thanks for "bringing me to my senses." I told him I was glad to hear that he was happy, but that the credit was his because "you're the one who got the joke."

6. When Does Most Change Occur in Psychotherapy?

It is now well documented that change does occur in psychotherapy. Perhaps the most impressive study is that of Smith, Glass, and Miller (1980), who performed a meta-analysis of almost four hundred controlled psychotherapy outcome studies involving more than twenty-five thousand patients and control subjects. Their conclusive finding was that patients who received psychotherapy did better on various outcome measures than 75 percent of those persons who remained untreated, demonstrating the benefits of psychotherapy. Of special interest was the fact that the mean length of these effective treatments was approximately seventeen sessions. Howard, Kopta, Kraus, and Orlinsky (1986) found that 75 percent of patients show improvement within twenty-six sessions. Along the same vein, the Vanderbilt Psychotherapy Research Project (Strupp, 1980a–d; Strupp and Binder, 1984; Gomes-Schwartz, 1978; Hartley and Strupp, 1983; see also Frieswyk and others, 1986) found overall outcome to be predictable in time-limited dynamic psychotherapy from aspects of the first three interviews, a finding that jibes with the common experience of therapists that one often can tell pretty quickly if a case is going to "go anywhere." Several studies have found significant changes to occur after one session, and although Howard and others (1986) do find a positive correlation between number of sessions and amount of improvement in their meta-analysis of studies (they suggest twenty-six sessions as a practical limit), there is no research evidence (Butcher and Koss, 1978; Luborsky, Singer, and Luborsky, 1975; Meltzoff and Kornreich, 1970) that long-term therapy produces more changes than short-term therapy. Given these findings, it seems reasonable to speculate that most change in psychotherapy occurs relatively quickly, within the period of time usually considered to be brief treatment. Additional changes sometimes may occur in longer-term treatments, and there may be different criteria for assessing these changes, but there may also be diminishing returns as one approaches a psychotherapeutic asymptote. This was recognized by Appelbaum (1975), a psychoanalyst impressed by his experiences with brief therapy, who noted that even if long-term treatment were to produce some added gains, it would be questionable whether these gains would often be commensurate with the added expenditure of time and money. Appelbaum's (1975) observation of "Parkinson's Law" in psychotherapy is worth repeating: work often expands or contracts to fill the time available for it.

Three Models of Brief Therapy
That Explicitly Address Issues of Time

Time plays a role in all psychotherapies and particularly in those therapies that are planned to be brief or time limited. Some forms of short-term therapy are even more explicitly time oriented in that they deliberately address aspects of the patient's temporal experience as a central feature of the treatment. In this section I highlight three of these approaches.

Mann's Time-Limited Psychotherapy

This is a psychodynamic-existential model (Mann 1973; Mann and Goldman, 1982) built on the theory that the experience of time has central meaning in our psychological development. Mann (p. 25) believes that "in this kind of time-limited psychotherapy, mastery of separation anxiety becomes the model for the mastery of other neurotic anxieties, albeit in a somewhat derived manner. Failures in mastery of this basic anxiety must influence both the future course in life of the individual as well as the adaptive means he employs, more or less successfully." The reworking of the separation-individuation phase, according to Mann, is manifested in four universal conflict situations:

1. Independence versus dependence
2. Activity versus passivity
3. Adequate self-esteem versus diminished or loss of self-esteem
4. Unresolved or delayed grief

Mann believes that therapy should focus on the "present and chronically endured pain" of the patient's self. He posits, "All short forms of psychotherapy, whether their practitioners know it or not, revive the horror of time. . . . One way of understanding the failure to give time central significance . . . lies in the will to deny the horror of time by the therapists themselves" (Mann, 1973, pp. 10–11).[4]

He describes his approach clearly:

My method of time-limited psychotherapy includes more than the use of twelve sessions with the termination date known from the start of the first therapy session and the importance of the termination phase in rekindling the affective state that brought the patient for help. Of equal importance is the selection of a central issue, extracted out of the patient's history, which includes the elements of time, affects, and the image of the self; invariably a negative self-image. The goal of treatment in the twelve sessions becomes one of reducing as much as possible the negative self-image. The time restriction and the adherence of the therapist to this kind of central issue result in a telescoping of events and a heightened affective state that makes for an intense in vivo experience [1984, p. 207].

Mann delineates three phases of treatment, each lasting approximately four sessions. In the first trimester, a positive transference emerges as the patient experiences the unconscious fantasy of endless nurturance. This gives way to the more ambivalent affect of the second phase, wherein the therapist frustrates the patient by sticking to a focus and not gratifying the patient's desire for unending contact. Finally, in the last third of treatment, the patient deals constructively with the termination of therapy and reworks previous experiences of loss. Schwartz and Bernard (1981) have reported some empirical evidence to support this three-stage model; Westen (1986) has questioned it on theoretical grounds; and Hatcher, Huebner, and Zakin (1986) have reported data suggesting that for many therapists the central focus of time-limited psychotherapy tends to undergo significant revisions across the course of treatment.

In addition to Mann's (1973; Mann and Goldman, 1982) own case reports, an extended example is provided in Chapter Twelve (see also Leon, 1987), describing the termination work across a twelve-session time-limited psychotherapy conducted with a sixty-nine-year-old woman five months after the death of her husband. The initial setting of the twelve-session time limit has already been described above. The following quotations, taken from the therapist's remarks across the latter half of the twelve sessions, convey some of the unfolding emphasis on a reworking of the mourning/separation/self-esteem theme that was central to this treatment. There was much more work done than these few comments convey, of course, although they may portray some of the typical activity of a therapist working within this particular short-term model:

Therapist: Well, it sounds as if you're doing pretty well. You joke about a postgraduate course. I think that you're thinking about the fact that we will be ending pretty soon.

T: We are going to have five more meetings. From some of the things you've said, I imagine that you are beginning to have some feelings about the fact that we are going to end, and this is going to be another person that you have come to know and trust, and then it's going to end.

T: You said you don't feel sad now?

T: You look at your watch a lot.

T: A minute ago you cried when we talked about separating, and then you kind of quickly talked about going back East.

T: I think that as things come to an end over time we'll miss this relationship, but also it can remind you of other times when you've been involved with someone or cared about someone.

T: It sounds like you're saying that you don't want to get too attached.

T: Just because I'm the doctor and you're the patient doesn't mean you have to put up with me. There are times when I'm wrong and you want to stand up for yourself.

T: And the fact that you are getting a lot from this relationship may make it difficult for you to let yourself sometimes be annoyed with me or be angry with me.

T: I imagine your getting involved in that relationship with him has changed your feelings about ending therapy here, having someone else you're talking to.

T: What are your feelings about ending, terminating?

T: I understand that you'll take some things away with you, but there is also the reality that we will stop seeing each other, that it will end.

T: It's good that you see the difference between our relationship and what you had with M. You depended on him so much.

T: Have you thought much about our finishing?

T: Talking about his death and that time seems fitting, since we are almost at the end of our relationship.

T: It has been very good for me, too. I've not only been helpful, but I have also gained something personally from spending time with you.

T: I think you *took* it back, and I helped you.

This case had a very favorable outcome, documented with long-term follow-up. The patient's age raises an interesting point: "The successful outcome again demonstrates the value of psychotherapy with older persons. Her age also may be relevant in regard to our emphasis on temporal experience. With advanced age and the realistic awareness of the finitude of life, time may be experienced differently and may in some ways take on more value (Scott-Maxwell, 1968). The utility of a time-limited model thus would make sense both theoretically and practically with geriatric patients" (Hoyt, 1979a, p. 217).

Melges' Future-Oriented Psychotherapy

Melges' (1972, 1982) approach conceptualizes time distortions as altering consciousness and impairing reality testing. He posits that a person's inner sense of the future influences the present, a model that provides "a framework for focusing psychiatric treatment on time and the future. The restoration of control over the personal future can be accomplished through the correction of time distortions and the harmonization of future images, plans of action, and emotions. The restoration of control over the future is the key to interrupting psychopathological spirals" (Melges, 1982, p. xxi).

Melges' cybernetic model is that "psychopathological spirals occur when problems with sequence, rate, and temporal perspective disrupt the normal interplay between future images, plans of action, and emotions" (1982, p. 49). Table 7.1 indicates a hierarchy of time problems, with the most severe at the top.

Melges describes a number of methods for assessing patients' time sense and provides a brilliant exposition of the biopsychosocial treatment of time distortions, including the use of medication and hospitalization, psychodynamic therapy, transactional analysis, cognitive therapy, hypnosis, and family therapy. By focusing on the temporal aspects of the patient's functioning, particularly the patient's impaired future sense, Melges often is able to achieve significant improvements with brief treatment.[5,6]

Table 7.1. Different Problems with Time and the Personal Future in Psychiatric Disorders.

Time Problem	Personal Future	Psychiatric Disorder
1. Time disorientation	Confused	Organic brain disease
2. Temporal disintegration of sequences	Fragmented	Schizophrenic disorders
3. Rate and rhythm problems:		
Increased rate	Over-expanded	Mania
Decreased rate	Blocked	Depression
4. Temporal perspective problems:		
Over-focus on future	Threatened	Paranoid disorders
Over-focus on past	Dreaded (uncertain)	Anxiety disorders
Over-focus on present	Disregarded	Antisocial personality
5. Desynchronized transactions	Ambivalent	Adjustment disorders

Source: Melges (1982, p. 28), *Time and the Inner Future: A Temporal Approach to Psychiatric Disorders,* © 1982 by John Wiley & Sons, Inc. Reprinted by permission of the publisher.

Seeman (1976) illustrates through a case example how much of the disordered reality testing and thought process of a schizophrenic can be understood as manifestations of a defective time sense. Pathognomonic experiences regarding permanence versus change, unidirectionality versus bidirectionality, periodicity, simultaneity, duration, continuity versus atomicity, uncontrollable inevitability, sequencing versus causality or intentionality, clairvoyance, "marking time" and "doing time," and confusions of past, present, and future are all seen as reflections of disturbances underlying perceptual-cognitive schemata. Seeman describes a therapeutic approach that "can be viewed as a form of cognitive repair focused on the perception, interpretation, and integration of the sense of time" (p. 193), noting that a treatment explicitly directed toward a schizophrenic patient's cognitive-temporal organization helps to structure the patient's experience while defocusing from affect that might otherwise become too intense and stormy. Seeman sees this psychotherapy of time sense as also being consistent with the use of anti-psychotic medications that aim to "damp down affects but remove interferences with perceptual and cognitive functioning" (p. 194). Her case example is not short-term treatment, but her principles may be applicable to brief therapy, as Melges (1982) demonstrates.

Lesse (1971) has also used the term future-oriented psychotherapy to describe a treatment approach. He uses the term in a more global sense, not basing his therapy (which is essentially psychodynamic) on a theory of time, but rather providing a "prophylactic" function by guiding patients over a relatively brief number of sessions to consider their role in the future in order to prepare for the impending stresses and challenges. Lesse sees such a futurological perspective as especially valuable because "the ever accelerating rate of change that characterizes our society makes it necessary that the psychotherapy patient have a general idea of what his or her role is likely to be in the world of tomorrow" (p. 192).

Berne's Transactional Analysis and Goulding and Goulding's Redecision Therapy

The description of Berne's (1961, 1972) model of human development, intrapsychic organization, and interpersonal dynamics goes far beyond the scope of this exposition (see Woollams and Brown, 1978). There are three elements of Berne's work, however, that pertain directly to time and brief therapy.

Contractual Therapy. Berne favored the explication of specific, obtainable goals in treatment, ones that could be conceptualized in a manner such that they could be accomplished and recognized. He wanted patients to set their own treatment goals and to recognize their ability to make changes rapidly. "What can I do to cure this patient today?" was a question that Berne liked to ask himself before sessions.

Time Structuring. Berne theorized that patients early in life form a life plan or *script* that guides much of their subsequent course. He felt that scripts could be recognized and discarded or changed. To avoid the pain of boredom, people need to structure time. Essentially, there are six possible ways to structure time: withdrawal, ritual, pastime, activity, rackets/games, and intimacy. Since humans apportion their energy among these six alternatives and some are more satisfying and growthful than others, understanding of these concepts will reveal a great deal about a person's psychological way of being in the world. Woollams and Brown (1978, p. 91) explain the psychotherapeutic significance of this: "Analyzing a client's time structuring provides information about how she exchanges strokes, which in turn tells us how she maintains her script decisions. Helping the client understand and change how she structures her time provides new ways for her to give and get the kinds of strokes which her Free Child wants and needs. Invariably, as clients change their ways of structuring time and exchanging strokes, they need to work through the feelings connected with giving up their old patterns and relating in new ways."

Script Time. The script concept was central to Berne's later (1972) thinking. He saw that many people organize their life plan in terms of an approach to time: "Winning or losing, the script is a way to structure the time between the first Hello at mother's breast and the last Good-by at the grave. This life time is emptied and filled by not doing and doing; by never doing, always doing, not doing before, not doing after, doing over and over, and doing until there is nothing left to do. This gives rise to 'Never,' and 'Always,' 'Until' and 'After,' 'Over and Over,' and 'Open-Ended' scripts" (Berne, 1972, p. 205).

Brief therapists who wish to help patients make major changes quickly may find it helpful to recognize and focus directly on modifying basic aspects of temporal perspective such as script time orientations.

A patient in her late thirties complained of procrastination and feeling stagnant. She was bright and articulate but doing a job that lacked excitement for her. She had a number of years earlier left her marriage for another man, but that had not worked out, and now she was without a partner or likely prospects. Despite her efforts to be "rational" and "positive," she obsessed, looked sad, and sighed unhappily. The therapist, trying to gain ingress to the patient's deeper feelings, asked if there were any scene she could think of that expressed her situation (see Hoyt, 1986). "Yes," she responded almost immediately. "Did you see the film *Superman*? It's like the scene where he flies backward and stops time! God, I wish I could do that!" With tears in her eyes she described the scene where the hero flies backwards around the earth so quickly that time is somehow reversed, thus allowing him to intervene in something that had already happened.[7] This image opened wide the patient's regret for mistakes past and her attempts to avoid risks and stave off future misfortunes.

Robert and Mary Goulding (1978, 1979) have provided a major contribution by combining the theory of transactional analysis (Berne, 1961, 1972) with Gestalt techniques plus their own unique innovations. Their approach is built on the basic theory that as children people often make key life decisions (such as Don't Feel, Don't Think, Don't Be Close, Don't Grow Up, Don't Be Important, Don't Enjoy, or Don't Be) in order to survive or adapt to perceived and often veridical parental pressures. In treatment, the patient reenters and reexperiences the pathogenic scene as a child, via imagery and Gestalt work, and with the encouragement and support of the therapist makes a *re*decision that frees the patient from the pernicious injunction that he or she had earlier accepted. This here-and-now work involves a powerful combination of affect and insight, with support and behavioral anchors maintaining the gains achieved.

Oftentimes patients recognize in redecision therapy that they have been trying magically to change the past or control the future. An example would be the man who, after reliving an early scene, was asked by the redecision therapist to experiment with saying to his imagined father, "I'm going to stay angry at you until you treat me differently when I was six!" Hearing himself tilt absurdly against a long-gone windmill, he laughed, recognized his "craziness," and claimed his freedom.

Like the Zen monk who finds himself seeking permission from another for what only he can control (Hoyt, 1979b, 1985a), the patient suddenly realizes that "it's all in my mind, and I control my mind!" This is the basic truth behind the title of Mary Goulding's (1985) book, *Who's Been Living in Your Head?* Another well-known TA/Gestalt therapist, James (1985), has also suggested the possibility of rapid change through the title of one of her books, *It's Never Too Late to Be Happy.*

Motivated patients sometimes make a forceful redecision within a single session. The following case example occurred recently in my office:

> The patient was a thirty-seven-year-old married woman. She came for an initial appointment complaining of "insecurity, anxiety, and low-self-esteem." She reported that she was married to a man with strong macho tendencies, who sometimes verbally abused her. She also reported being bored and dissatisfied with her job, a teacher's aide in a school. She spoke in a mild, self-effacing way. Remarkably, she revealed that she was a licensed attorney, that she had graduated from a major law school and had passed the bar on her first attempt. She had then married and had children, however, and had only practiced law part-time for a short while before staying home with the kids and then returning to work as a teacher's aide.
>
> She again described herself as insecure and said that she "couldn't do anything right." The therapist asked her to repeat that phrase, which she did, and he then asked where she had heard it as a child. The patient then reported that her mother had been a very disturbed, highly critical woman, one whose irrational beliefs, fears, and occasional behaviors suggested schizophrenia. Indeed, the patient's mother had been hospitalized in mental institutions on and off throughout her childhood. The father had divorced her mother and left the family. What a remarkable accomplishment for this patient, to have done so well given such a rough start: she had married, mothered two children, and had become an attorney. The therapist complimented her success. "I know," she replied, "but I still hear my mother telling me how I can't do anything right." She gave several examples of things her mother would irrationally criticize.

At this juncture the therapist decided that talking about the problem would not generate a strong enough experience to produce genuine change in this bright woman. He announced that he wanted to meet the patient's mother. When she responded that "Mother would never agree to come here," the therapist said, "I want to meet the woman you carry around in your head. Do an experiment. Change seats. In that seat, be your mother. "Hi, Mother, what's your name?" The therapist then proceeded to interview "Mother" for about fifteen minutes. At first the patient was hesitant, but she quickly got into the part. She even surprised herself with the richness of her characterization of Mom: her gestures, her words, her easy flow of irrational ideas. Mom felt daughter (the patient) was always wrong, wouldn't go to her house or hold her children because they might have germs on them, felt it was "just wrong" for a girl to go to college or work with men, thought law school was because the patient had not done well in college, and kept insisting that all her children were "exactly the same." The therapist listened respectfully and then added, "I'm not a lawyer, so I'm not defending her, but I've heard that you have to be very smart to even get into that law school, and even smarter to graduate." Mom didn't know that. The therapist also commented that he could see how much Mom wanted to love all her children and that it must be hard to see that in some ways they were different from one another. (Mom had even given them all the same middle name.) After a bit, the therapist thanked Mom, asked her if she would be willing to come back sometime "if we need to hear from you," and had the patient resume her own chair in the office.

The patient was stirred up by the experience. She stared at the now empty chair where "Mom" had been, shook her head, and said, "I didn't realize how crazy Mom actually is." The therapist then said to her, "Do this: Say 'I *am* an attorney. I got into law school and I graduated,' and see how it feels." She said it once, with hesitation, then repeated it with conviction and added: "I *am* an attorney. I'm smart. I got into law school, I graduated, and I passed the bar on my first try!" She was sitting up straight and alert, confident and strong. The therapist noted the change, saying, "Do you feel how different you are? You look stronger, more attractive. I feel that now I'm sitting here with a professional woman, not the scared daughter of your crazy mother."

The patient understood but attempted to discount her change. She remarked, "It's a role that I'm good at playing."

The therapist nodded and said, "I think that you're right, except that you've got it 100 percent reversed. *This* is the real you, and you were playing a role to get along with your mother—you know, like they say, putting a bushel over your light. You were playing dumb so Mother wouldn't get upset or be threatened. Smart people can play dumb. This is the real you, not what she said." He gestured toward the empty seat "Mom" had occupied.

The patient looked transformed. She was grasping a basic truth and liking its feel. "You're right. I am smart. I am. I *am* an attorney, and I can be a damn good one, too. I'm not going to buy into Mom's crazy ideas anymore."

The therapist complimented her on her insight and awareness. They talked briefly about how she could start using her confidence and intelligence. She was full of good ideas. When asked if she wanted another appointment, she said, "Not now. I can handle what I have to do. I'm an intelligent woman. I'll be making calls to get my career back on track."

This interaction took no more than one hour, from start to finish, an example of effective single-session psychotherapy. It was useful to have the patient vividly see how unhealthy her mother's messages were and to help the patient make a new decision about her own competency and importance. This was an application of the redecision model of therapy, although it was not technically a full redecision since the patient did not make her new decision while actively in the Child ego state. Still, reinforcing the patient's strengths and helping her to sort out her true self from an archaic pathological introject allowed her to rapidly make the change in self-image necessary for her to get unstuck and resume movement in her life.

"Yes"[8]

As Yogi Berra once replied (Pepe, 1988) when asked what time it was, "Do you mean now?" Time is of the essence, in therapy and in life. To be intimate one must be, literally, "in-time-mate." Brief psychotherapy is true to this quest insofar as it calls for participants to "be here now." This is the message of this chapter, as indicated by its title, "On Time in Brief Therapy."

Notes

1. The broad topic of the study of time, which has fascinated me for years, goes far beyond the scope of this chapter. The literature is vast, with poets, philosophers, scientists, and that amalgam of the three–psychologists–all contributing richly. The reader interested in the psychological perspective should not miss the books by Boscolo and Bertrando (1993), Fraser (1966, 1975), Mann (1973), Melges (1982), and Hartocollis (1983). Other useful references that will lead in many directions include the following: Becker (1973), Berne (1972), Bonaparte (1941), Boorstin (1985), Cooper and Erickson (1959), Cottle and Klineberg (1974), Doob (1971), Dunne (1973), Fraisse (1963), Freud (1914, 1916, 1917, 1933, 1937), Gorman and Wesman (1977), Grudin (1982), Heidegger ([1927] 1962), May, Angel, and Ellenberger (1958), Minkowski ([1933] 1970), Nannum (1972), Naranjo (1970), Ornstein (1969), Piaget ([1927] 1969), Pollack (1971), Priestly (1968), Schilder (1936), Spitz (1972), Tart (1969), von Franz (1978), and Wallace and Rabin (1960).

2. Gustafson (1986, p. 279) has independently made the same observation: "Just as the entire course of a brief therapy may be seen as having its opening, middle and end game, any particular session may be seen as the microcosm of such thinking. The opening is concerned with where to take hold. The middle is for getting different illuminations of this focus. The end provides a concluding punctuation. Condense, widen, and condense again. Exposition, development and recapitulation."

3. As St. Augustine observed in his *Confessions* (quoted in Boscolo and Bertrando, 1993, p. 34): "What is by now evident and clear is that neither future nor past exists, and it is inexact language to speak of three times–past, present,

and future. Perhaps it would be exact to say: there are three times, a present of things past, a present of things present, a present of things to come. In the soul there are these three aspects of time, and I do not see them anywhere else. The present considering the past is the memory, the present considering the future is expectation."

Recognition of the present-centered construction of all time may have also inspired T. S. Eliot's "Burnt Norton," which begins with the famous lines (1943, p. 13):

> Time present and time past
> Are both perhaps present in time future,
> And time future contained in time past.

4. Mann's concern with the "horror of time" resonates with the depiction of the ancient Greek god of time, Chronos, who would eat his children. In the *Metamorphoses* (Book xv, line 234), Ovid (Cumberlage, 1953, p. 371) speaks of "Time, the devourer of all things." A similar image is provided in Indian mythology, where Kali (the feminine form of the Sanscrit word *kala*, meaning "time") is depicted as gruesome, with her tongue out ready to lick up the world (von Franz, 1978, illustration and caption 29).

For many adults, there is a reversal in the sense of directionality of time, usually in middle age (Neugarten and Datan, 1974). As children and youngsters, we measure time as time lived since birth. Sometime in adulthood—a profound moment of truth—we begin to experience time as time left to live. This is our mortality, the recognition of the finiteness of our being, an awareness that is often thrust upon us by a personal existential crisis, such as an illness, the death of a friend or parent (Malinak, Hoyt, and Patterson, 1979), the birth of a child, or beginning to work (Sarason, Sarason, and Cowden, 1975). Psychotherapy can help one constructively recognize the importance of living every moment. In this spirit, Castaneda (1987, p. 262) has Don Juan advise: "If you think about life in terms of hours instead of years, our lives are immensely long. Even if you think in terms of days, life is still interminable."

5. A related analysis is provided by Thomson (1983), who illustrates how overabsorption with either the future, the present, or the past can result in respective excesses of fear, anger, or sadness. From a psychoanalytic perspective, Hartocollis (1983) draws similar parallels between future versus past time orientation and anxiety versus depressive affects.

6. "Time therapy" is a fourth-dimensional meta-therapy that provides a form of hierarchical control over what occurs in three-dimensional space. Linear, unidirectional time is a Western invention, and time was not so neatly regularized before Galileo invented the mechanical clock (Boorstin, 1985). I think that the Church was so able to organize and dominate Europe partially by the ringing of bells to mark the hours. Uniform time structure was thus institutionalized, the assertion of a common external structure permitting more precisely coordinated social functions and profoundly influencing the patterning of consciousness.

7. This is an old motif, done one better: Zeus once held the sun back so as to spend a longer night with a lover.

8. See Cavafy (1981) regarding the consequences of saying "Yes" or "No" when one meets the moment.

Acknowledgements. I am grateful to Richard Wells for inviting me to write this chapter and for his many helpful suggestions. Additional thanks to Sidney Blatt, who long ago encouraged my study of the psychology of time; and to Bob and Mary Goulding, who have greatly expanded my appreciation of the therapeutic possibilities of the present. Finally, love and kisses to Alexander Lillard Hoyt (born May 18, 1987), who has changed my experience of past, present, and future time forever.

CHAPTER EIGHT

The Challenge of Single-Session Therapies: Creating Pivotal Moments

with Robert Rosenbaum and Moshe Talmon

He felt a faint shiver, a matutinal coolness and sobriety which told him that the hour had come, that from now on there could be no more hesitating or lingering. This peculiar feeling, which he was wont to call "awakening," was familiar to him from other decisive moments of his life. It was both vitalizing and painful, mingling a sense of farewell and of setting out on new adventures, shaking him deep down in his unconscious mind like a spring storm. . . . A line of verse suddenly sprang into his mind:

In all beginnings dwells a magic force
For guarding us and helping us to live . . .
So be it, heart: bid farewell without end!
                                                    —Herman Hesse (1943)

Note: Reprinted, with changes, from Rosenbaum, R., Hoyt, M. F., and Talmon, M. "The Challenge of Single-Session Therapies: Creating Pivotal Moments." In R. A. Wells and V. J. Giannetti (eds.), *Handbook of the Brief Psychotherapies.* Copyright 1990 by Plenum. Used by permission of the coauthors and the publisher.

Robert Rosenbaum, Ph.D., is a staff psychologist in the Department of Psychiatry, Kaiser Permanente Medical Center, Hayward, California. Moshe Talmon, Ph.D., is in private practice in Tel Aviv, Israel.

Support for this project was partially provided by the Sidney Garfield Memorial Fund (Michael F. Hoyt, Principal Investigator), administered by the Kaiser Foundation Research Institute.

The psychotherapeutic facilitation of "decisive moments of life," such as that described above, is not necessarily a function of treatment duration. Even a single session of therapy can sometimes provide a pivotal moment, invoking the "magic force dwelling in beginnings" that guards us and helps us to live.

Accounts of profound changes occurring in one session of therapy have existed at least since Freud's meeting with Katarina (Breuer and Freud, [1893–95] 1955) and his cure of Gustav Mahler's sexual problem on a single long walk (Bloom, 1981). Therapists as diverse as Davanloo (1986), Erickson (Haley, 1973), Winnicott (1971b), and Sullivan (Gustafson and Dichter, 1983; Gustafson, 1986) have all reported anecdotal single-session therapy successes, and studies (Kogan, 1957; Spoerl, 1975; Cummings and Follette, 1976; Bloom, 1981) have indicated that in most outpatient settings, single-session encounters—whether planned or not—are extremely common. Within our own psychiatric clinic, part of a large health maintenance organization, approximately 30 percent of our clients are seen for only a single session, despite having prepaid coverage entitling them to additional sessions if indicated.

There are a number of reasons a therapist and a client may meet only once. Sometimes a referral to another practitioner is made; sometimes a second appointment is scheduled but the client chooses not to come back despite the therapist's advice. However, there are also many occasions where the therapist and client mutually agree that enough has been accomplished in the single session so there is no immediate need for further sessions. This chapter will focus on the issues involved in planning for and successfully conducting these intentional single-session therapies (SSTs).[1]

Much as recognizing one's mortality can "concentrate the mind" and intensify our appreciation of life, so an awareness that the first therapeutic session with a client may be the last can heighten our involvement and efficacy with the client. Many therapists almost automatically regard clients who come in for but a single session as "dropouts," "premature terminations," or "treatment failures." Often, however, if these clients are seen on follow-up they show impressive gains. Change may occur more rapidly than many therapists expect. Even without psychotherapy, psychological difficulties have a spontaneous remission rate of around 40 percent (Lambert, 1986). Research evidence has been accumulating indicating that some patients make significant life changes facilitated by a single therapeutic encounter (Malan, Heath, Bacal, and Balfour, 1975; Cummings and Follette, 1976; Rockwell and Pinkerton, 1982; Bloom, 1981; Hoyt, Rosenbaum, and Talmon, 1992; Talmon, Hoyt, and Rosenbaum, 1990; Talmon, 1990; see also Chapter Nine) and that this may occur rather more frequently than might be expected. Other than mental health professionals and selected character pathologies, who make up the bulk of the people in psychoanalysis and other long-term therapies, the average client wants change "yesterday" and expects just a few sessions of therapy will do the job (Garfield and Wolpin, 1963; Garfield, 1978). "Yesterday" may not be possible (although often clients appear at their first session having already made important changes), but the therapist needs to be ready for changes "today."

Therapy is an ongoing process that persists after sessions end (R. Rosenbaum, 1983) and is independent of treatment duration (Shectman, 1986). Clients often display a vivid sense of the therapeutic encounter long after it has terminated, even when only a single session has taken place. Consider the following example taken from a follow-up interview two and a half years after a single psychotherapeutic session:

> My first [and only] interview here was like having to do a very complex algebraic problem, and somebody sits down with you and tells you how to work it out and get the answer. I didn't realize that my feelings were quite so strong and that my father was there behind things. Since that time I have been able to see it. This has helped. . . . The interview . . . made a tremendous impression on me. . . . [It] upset me, not because someone told me something I didn't want to know, but I felt as if I had been *run over*. You know, if you have a small accident, you feel sort of shaky afterwards [Malan, Heath, Bacal, and Balfour, 1975, p. 121, italics in the original].

Therapist Resistances to Single-Session Therapies (SSTs)

Planning for the possibility of an SST may enhance the efficacy of the initial encounter, whether further sessions are held or not. Many therapists, however, have difficulties accepting the fact that change can occur in a single session. Sifneos (1987, p. 88) has stated the problem succinctly:

> We should do all we can to spot these individuals who have a potential to resolve their problems rapidly. One of the difficulties, however, is the incredible speed with which changes can take place in these patients. Psychiatrists who have been trained to believe that psychological reactions take a long time to be modified become suspicious when they see such speedy resolutions and tend to undermine the patient's confidence by implying that they represent a "flight into health" or a "counterphobic reaction," or doubt that the positive results will be maintained. On the contrary, the role of the therapist should be to encourage such patients to do their own problem solving and not to urge them to accept long-term psychotherapy instead.

While some caution in approaching SST is wise, denying the existence of meaningful SSTs with automatic emotional intensity and rigid closed-mindedness may be evidence of a kind of resistance. Such resistances are often due not to reasoned disagreement with the *content* of the idea but rather to a need to maintain a consistent professional identity or personal self-image (Rosenbaum, 1988a). It is easy to form a syllogism: Long-term therapy is good therapy; I am a long-term therapist; therefore I am a good therapist. We become attached to certain ways of doing things, and these procedures then become a statement about ourselves. To be willing to entertain the idea that clients can change even in a single session, we must be willing to entertain changes in our images of ourselves as therapists.

Therapist resistances to brief therapy in general are detailed in Chapter Seventeen (see also Winokur and Dasberg [1983]). They include the following erroneous beliefs and barriers:

1. For therapy to be effective, "deep" character changes must be accomplished.
2. "More is better."
3. It is important to develop a therapeutic alliance cautiously; working relationships are fragile and hard to come by.
4. Client resistance is inevitable.
5. Countertransference to termination, including therapists' "need to be needed."
6. Brief therapy is hard work and requires special brilliance on the part of the therapist.
7. Confusion of the patient's interests with those of the therapist.
8. Economics and other payoffs.

Parsimony is part of the art of therapy; a single pithy sentence has more impact than a five-minute lecture. Wagner is "more" but not necessarily "better" than Mozart. Should our patients meander, in fear of losing their wits, we may find it helpful to recall, with Hamlet (II, ii, 90), that the soul of wit is brevity. Although a consumer society such as ours tends to promulgate the idea that "more is better," it is our responsibility to bear in mind that more is not better; *better* is better.

In therapy, the idea that "more is better" is often expressed as the belief that "deeper is better," and "inner truth" is superior to "mere, superficial" appearance. In fact, however, our inner selves are *less* individualistic than our surface appearances (Arendt, 1978). Inside, we are all more human than otherwise (Sullivan, 1954). Individual distinctiveness and psychological identity are matters of qualitative "surface" details creating differing styles (Rosenbaum, 1988a; Shapiro, 1965; see Chapter Nineteen); it is precisely these specific individual details as they are expressed in the here and now that successful SSTs must address. Freed from the idea that change can only occur through the alteration of "deep" structures, we can identify the small idiosyncratic perturbations that lead to large differences. The following story sometimes instills hope in patients who worry about having "deep-seated" problems:

Imagine if you had an old car which began to stall out on you. You don't know it, but while driving along a country road, some insects flew into your carburetor and blocked proper airflow. If you didn't know what was wrong, you might turn your engine over again and again, and in the process burn out your starter. Now it would really have a problem starting up! If you took it to a mechanic who said, "Your car's pretty old, it's at a stage in its life cycle where we're going to have to do an engine overhaul," you might be inclined to believe that mechanic, and let yourself in for a lot of unnecessary expense. All this could have been avoided by simply removing the fly in the ointment. After repairing the problem, you might prevent future recurrences by re-designing your entire engine, removing its carburetor and using fuel injection. You could get equally effective results, however, by installing a cheap plastic shield on your front hood to catch insects before they get to the engine.

Even when short treatments don't result in lasting "character changes," SSTs may help a person resolve an immediate problem. Therapists need not feel they have failed if further treatment is needed in the future. This kind of "life cycle psychotherapy" (R. Rosenbaum, 1983; Bennett, 1984; Budman and Gurman, 1988; Cummings, 1990) capitalizes on the fact that different kinds of therapeutic interventions may be appropriate to different life circumstances. It is not just that the content of a person's concerns changes at different stages of the life cycle: the style with which the client approaches problems also changes. Contrast, for example, the urgency of the adolescent with the caution of the middle-aged in dealing with an "identity crisis." The former may need to be slowed down supportively in therapy; the latter may need to be urged on through confrontation. One needs reins; the other, spurs.

Rather than keeping a person in psychotherapy for many years, during which the therapist accompanies the client on their journey through life, SSTs and other brief therapies provide what is needed when it is needed (Ticho, 1972). Doing so meets the client at their view of the world (Lankton and Lankton, 1983) in an empathic fashion that helps build rapport and a therapeutic alliance rapidly (Mann, 1973; Mann and Goldman, 1982) while reducing resistance. We find we can often get whatever work needs to be done accomplished in SSTs before untoward "resistance" arises, especially if we meet the patient in his or her framework of understanding and establish a mutually agreed upon treatment contract (Berne, 1972; Polster and Polster, 1976; Goulding and Goulding, 1978, 1979). If strong resistance does arise, we either utilize it strategically (Haley, 1977) or make it the focus of psychodynamic confrontation and interpretation (Davanloo, 1986). We conceptualize resistance as one more part of the change process: all stability is maintained through change, and all change is maintained through stability (Keeney, 1983). To be effective in an SST format, then, the therapist needs "the wit and deftness to 'work the opposing currents'" (Gustafson, 1987, p. 413).

Opening to the Possibilities of a Single Session

Before exploring specific technical questions, in order to "be alert to the possibility" that SSTs are helpful, we may need to acknowledge the possibility that people can change in the moment, and that change may occur through sudden discontinuous shifts of being. This is not to say we should deny that many people change gradually. We have no desire to create a psychotherapeutic schism paralleling those Buddhist disputes over the virtues of sudden, as opposed to gradual, enlightenment (Suzuki, 1956). We must, however, be alert to the possibility of the proverbial "bolt from the blue." Even though we often think of nature as existing continuously and changing in gradual increments, recent geological evidence suggests that the world has changed not only through gradual evolution but also through "punctuated evolution" where sudden discrete events such as meteorite strikes cause long-term changes (Gould, 1980).

One of the authors (Rosenbaum) was trained in short-term psychotherapy but still had his doubts about SSTs. He was walking in the mountains one day, indulging his doubts on the subject: "Perhaps some change can occur in a single session, but surely not *significant* change. Lasting change requires the gradual processes that mold mountains: time, slow erosion, wind and rain sculpting the face of the stone over and over again." At that point, the trail turned around a bend. A huge avalanche chute came into sight. Half of a mountain, seemingly, had slid down into the valley last winter, changing both mountain and valley forever, all in the course of less than thirty seconds.

The human experience is also sometimes marked by such quantum shifts in being. All our lives begin with a discrete event: birth, which provides a model for the emergence of truly new beginnings (Arendt, 1978; Hoyt, 1977; Rank, [1914] 1964, [1929] 1973), where something that was previously only imagined becomes tangible and fully present. There is a gestation period prior to birth, but compared to the life that will follow it, the actual birth process is short. Furthermore, in most cases the birth process proceeds more or less naturally, without undue intervention by medical professionals. The therapist who is interested in doing SSTs can take a lesson from this. Clients come to us at different stages in the gestation process of changing; some of them will require a certain amount of waiting and preparation before giving birth, but others will be virtually fully dilated. Wherever the client may be in the birth process, it is seldom our task to "do something" to create change; rather, our role is more similar to that of the midwife, who attends the process, eases the transition, and provides a helping hand in case anything gets temporarily stuck. This was well recognized by Berne (1966, p. 63):

> The patient has a built-in drive to health, mental as well as physical. His mental development and emotional development have been obstructed, and the therapist has only to remove the obstructions for the patient to grow naturally in his own direction. . . . The therapist does not cure anyone, he only treats him to the best of his ability, being careful not to injure and waiting for nature to take its healing course. . . . Hence in practice "curing the patient" means "getting the patient ready for the cure to happen today." . . . When the patient recovers, the therapist should be able to say, "My treatment helped nature."

Indications for Promoting Single-Session Therapies

As Rockwell and Pinkerton (1982, p. 39) have written, "The therapist must be alert to the possibility [of SST occurring], must assess quickly when s/he has a [potential SST] case in hand, set the process in motion, and determine a satisfactory stopping point." Recognizing when a patient may benefit from SST involves a number of factors:

1. What is the patient's motivation and expectation? Clinical experience and research (Pekarik and Wierzbicki, 1986) have shown the single best predictor of therapy duration is the patient's expectation of the likely number of sessions necessary.

2. What is the focus? What specifically does the patient want to accomplish? Can the therapist and patient formulate the problem in a concise manner? What (if any) is the patient's "hidden agenda"?

3. Is the patient's difficulty best conceived in terms of intrapsychic, characterological, interpersonal, or systemic processes (Gustafson, 1986)? What precisely triggers the patient's pain? What will allow the therapist access to that painful state, and what will provide a route out of the pain (Gustafson, 1987)?

4. What solutions have been attempted in the past? Which have been successful, and which ineffectual? Can something that proved helpful in the past prove helpful once again? (Don't reinvent the wheel!) What technical approach(es) will be most helpful: educational, behavioral, cognitive, psychodynamic, interpersonal, strategic, systemic, and so on?

5. Are there contraindications for SST, such as psychotic, suicidal, or assaultive risks? Is there an opportunity for other treatment approaches and/or additional sessions to be used if needed?

6. Timing and pacing: is the desired change possible now, or do other things need to happen first? Are the goals realistic, or do they reflect overly large expectations on the part of the client and/or the therapist?

In summary, the therapist asks, Where does the patient get stuck? What is needed for him or her to get unstuck? How can I, as a therapist, facilitate the patient's change process?

Basic Heuristic and Technical Principles for SST

Keeping these general ideas in mind, we can now discuss some aspects of how the therapist should conduct him- or herself in performing SSTs. Bloom (1981) has made the following helpful concrete recommendations:

1. Identify a focal problem.
2. Do not underestimate clients' strengths.
3. Be prudently active.
4. Explore, then present interpretations tentatively.
5. Encourage the expression of affect.
6. Use the interview to start a problem-solving process.
7. Keep track of time.
8. Do not be overambitious.
9. Keep factual questions to a minimum.
10. Do not be overly concerned about the precipitating event.
11. Avoid detours.
12. Do not overestimate a client's self-awareness (i.e., don't ignore stating the obvious).

In addition to these excellent specific suggestions, we have found certain heuristics particularly helpful in facilitating the SST process. One may or may not express all these attitudes in specific statements to the client, but it is essential that the spirit of the overall SST stance permeate the therapeutic encounter. We discuss each of these below, with illustrative case material. (The therapist for each case is indicated in brackets at the end of the case material.)

Expect Change

People are not unvarying beings but rather, like every stable phenomenon, changing all the time. In order to maintain stability, it is necessary to make constant small adjustments and changes: to steer a sailboat in a constant direction, you must constantly trim your sails and move your rudder. In therapy, the client has taken a new, temporary passenger (the therapist) into the boat; this will change the ballast of the boat and require the client to adjust the sails and pull on the rudder, thus increasing the probability of a change of course. The therapist need not explore theories of celestial navigation to help a client who is sailing in circles; if you move the rudder, pull on the sheets, or lean over the side of the boat, it is rather likely a change in direction will occur.

The effective SST therapist's attitude is that not only is change inevitable but in fact it is *already* happening, though the client may not have noticed yet. In hypnosis, for example, it is common to say to a patient, "I don't know if you've noticed *yet* how deeply you've begun to go into trance . . . how your rate of breathing is different *now*." The hypnotherapist takes an inevitable phenomenon (the fluctuation in the rate of respiration) and then punctuates it as a sign of something else (the beginning of trance), which ratifies and creates the phenomenon it purportedly is describing. Use of the word *yet* allows patients the freedom to experience the new phenomenon any way they want but has a strongly implied suggestion that if they haven't noticed up until now, they will in the future.

The client's first visit to the therapist presents a similar situation. As soon as the client considers entering therapy, the change process has already started; an aspect of his or her experience is being thought of as troublesome and changeable. The client's problem is being presented in a novel context: the very act of coming to the therapist makes a change for the client, so the therapist's job becomes helping the client pursue the change profitably. The therapist does not structure the therapy to continue *until* change occurs, since change is *already* occurring. Therapy focuses and amplifies the ongoing change process.

In terms of specific techniques to create an expectation of change, it is best to begin at the first therapeutic contact. Early in the meeting, we say something like the following: "We've found a large number of our clients can benefit from a single visit here. Of course, if you need more therapy, we can provide it. But I want to let you know that I'm willing to work hard with you today to help you resolve your problem quickly, perhaps even in this single visit, as long as you are ready to start doing something different or whatever's necessary."

We find this message contains a number of efficacious elements. In the first sentence, it immediately lets the patient know that change is possible. At the same time, we leave the door open to not change (by temporizing with "perhaps" and by making more therapy potentially available); this seems to minimize resistance and dependent passive-aggression and also helps clients feel any changes they make are made autonomously rather than coerced. Telling the client that we're willing to work hard with them is evidence of our sincerity and helps build an alliance. Finally, we let the patient know that change is in their hands– they must be an active participant. We purposely keep the kind of participation vague: "something different or whatever's necessary" provides an illusion of alternatives (Lankton and Lankton, 1983) in that it allows almost anything the patient does to be helpful, but it does not give the client the option of doing nothing.

Other similar messages include: What are you willing to change today? (Goulding and Goulding, 1978, 1979), What will you be doing differently when you don't come here anymore? and, We've scheduled plenty of time today so we can sit here and keep working until we get this thing dealt with. Sometimes it helps to emphasize growth by speaking with the client about what he or she wants to "accomplish" or "create" in therapy, rather than "change" or "improve." [2] All of these messages highlight client autonomy and response-ability by emphasizing that it is what the *client* does (rather than what is done to them by the therapist) that is crucial. Asking, What do you want to change today? orients the client to the present and future, and creates an expectation of change by talking about *when*, not *if*, change happens.

It is often helpful to have an explicit "contract," an agreed upon, operationally defined goal that is attainable. Unspecified or overly vague goals (such as "to be more open" or "to know myself better") may keep therapy unfocused and promote interminable treatment.

> A woman sought therapy wanting to "sort out my thoughts" about whether to continue at a certain job or to seek a different position. In one session, a semi-structured "motivational balance-sheet procedure" (Hoyt and Janis, 1975) was used to help her weigh the instrumental and emotional implications of her options. Within an hour she came to her decision, which she recognized as what she had thought she wanted to do. Her choice now felt more "solid," however, and she ended by saying that she had gotten what she had come for, and that she would call again if she needed help in the future [Hoyt].

In some situations, clients have difficulty specifying a clear goal. In those cases, using the session to help the client clarify their goals can be quite helpful. However, there are times when despite both parties' best efforts, therapy goals remain vague. The therapist may then elect to help the client by seeding suggestions for nonspecific change, with the idea that *any* alteration in the patient's system will result in new and potentially useful directions for the client.

> A woman in her mid-thirties, when asked what she wanted to accomplish, began her therapy session by handing the therapist a ten-page, single-spaced, typed narrative describing her early life history, unhappiness at still being single, being blocked creatively, feeling unappreciated at her low-paying job, and feeling embarrassed that she was still financially and emotionally dependent on her parents. She had been seeing another therapist for over a year, but that relationship had become attenuated (without actually terminating) due to the therapist's illness. She presented in an overcontrolled ruminative manner, with very tangential thinking, anxious mood, and depressed affect.
>
> Repeated attempts to establish a focus failed. The patient tended to obsess about whether to stay or leave her current job, but this was tied to so many issues regarding her self-

worth and conflicts about being independent that a "balance-sheet" approach such as the one described in the case above seemed unlikely to be effective. The patient felt torn between her "common sense" and her "feelings" and tended to feel alternately grandiose about her "inner, hidden abilities" and deflated at her lack of accomplishments and acknowledgment by others.

The therapist noticed the patient wore a pretty crystal on a necklace, and the patient described how she used crystals for meditation. She pulled out a variety of crystals from her purse. The therapist decided to use hypnosis to indirectly further treatment goals (Wolberg, 1980) and had the patient choose two crystals "of differing character" and hold one in each hand. A trance was induced by having her focus on the different sensations in each hand, where one crystal "could be thought of as hard, but ordinary, common sense," while the other "feels like it gives brilliance, healing, and comfort." The patient was then asked to combine the two inside herself; she then reported strong sensations of strength and energy with accompanying imagery. She was then given suggestions that she would be able to use this experience in the near future, together with posthypnotic cues for regaining the sensations when needed. After arousing from the trance, she was given an assignment: either to submit one of the stories she had already written for publication or to create something new.

By the end of the session, her rumination had given place to curiosity and mild excitement. On follow-up she was markedly less depressed, was less conflicted about her job, and had written some new children's stories she was attempting to get illustrated and published [Rosenbaum].

It is also important, at the end of the session, to leave the client with the idea that change will occur. Thus when we close the session, we mention we will be contacting the patient to find out *what* has changed and *how* he or she has progressed (rather than *whether* there has been any improvement).

A young woman, employed as a hair stylist, was seen about a year after she had been struck by a drunk driver in an automobile accident. She had retreated from social activities, feeling ashamed about the scarring on her legs. She experienced nightmares and intrusive thoughts about the accident and struggled to suppress displaced rage by becoming quite passive. She had continued her work but was feeling angry at her boss for not appreciating what she was going through.

The session utilized hypnotic trance for abreaction of her anger and indirect suggestions that reframed the scarring as a "badge of experience." At the end of the session, she mentioned that the anniversary date of the accident was approaching. I gave her the open-ended suggestion that "sometime soon, you'll notice a difference in the way you're feeling or thinking. . . . I'm not sure exactly what the difference will be: perhaps you'll find yourself having more thoughts about the accident in preparation to letting go of it when the anniversary comes; or perhaps you'll find yourself having fewer thoughts shortly after the anniversary. You may notice a difference in your dreams, or maybe just a general feeling of the beginnings of relief. You know how you don't notice your hair getting longer, and then one day, all at once, you say, 'My hair's grown!' This may be sort of like that. Or you can enjoy the changes when you notice a particularly nice job your hands have done on a customer."

On follow-up the patient reported a number of improvements in her symptoms and a general increase in well-being. Note that the above suggestions were given when the patient was no longer in a formal trance. As should be clear from the wide variety of approaches illustrated by our clinical vignettes, we do not feel hypnosis is a necessary component of SSTs. What is necessary is to help alert patients to change in general while allowing them to pick and choose which changes will occur [Rosenbaum].

View Each Encounter as a Whole, Complete in Itself

Bion (1967, 1977) suggested the therapist enter each session "without desire, memory, or understanding" so that each interaction would have "no history and no future." This "is a matter of approaching each hour with the openness . . . which will best serve therapist and patient in the pursuit of the unknown" (Langs, 1979). Such an attitude allows the therapist to seize the moment while fostering creativity and new learning.

By definition, effective single-session therapists do not have separate sessions for the gathering of information and history taking, the formulation and communication of a diagnosis, and then the "therapy proper." Rather, the problem must be elicited and its resolution derived in one meeting. Each move by the therapist, together with the client's response, includes both a probe for information (about each other, the problem, and so on) and an intervention requiring a response, providing feedback for succeeding interactions. Treatment begins when the client first telephones in and continues through the final words of the leave taking. The attitude for successful SSTs was succinctly stated by Berne (quoted by Goulding, Goulding, and Silverthorn, 1983, p. 67), who said that, before each session, "I ask myself what I can do this day, so that all patients are cured this day."

> A patient complained of people not liking him but not knowing why. As he sat down in the therapist's office he commented, "I guess you're a psychologist because you couldn't get into medical school, huh?" and smiled. The therapist stopped him, saying, "What effect do you think it had on me to start our meeting with that comment?" The patient said he didn't understand. The therapist decided to go along with the patient's ploy of innocence (avoiding the discussion of whether or not it was "unconscious") by explaining that sometimes a person has an interpersonal style that annoys other people without his or her realizing it, but that once they know about it, then they are responsible for what they do. He repeated the comment and asked the patient if there were other times the patient could think of when his "jokes" might have been misunderstood. The patient quickly learned about his counterproductive behavior and began to modify it [Hoyt].

Don't Rush or Try to Be Brilliant

It may seem paradoxical to advise practitioners of SST not to act too quickly, but sometimes it is helpful to remember the saying, "Don't just do something—sit there!" Too often therapists jump at the first bit of material they feel competent to comment on, rather than surveying the situation and picking carefully where to exercise their expertise. The tendency to find quick solutions to problems can have the effect of perpetuating or even creating problems (Watzlawick, Weakland, and Fisch, 1974). We agree with Sullivan (1954, p. 224) that therapeutic skill sometimes consists of "making a rather precise move which has a high probability of achieving what you're attempting to achieve, with a minimum of time and words," but we also agree with Spoerl (1975) that SSTs often succeed without heroic measures, by providing needed reassurance, catharsis, and problem solving.

If a therapist goes into a session thinking he or she must do something extraordinary or brilliant to make a change, it decreases the chance that change will occur, for it denies the client's autonomy. Trying too hard to be brilliant often is counterproductive; polishing a surface too much can scratch and dull its sheen. The therapist need only facilitate the *client's* natural tendency to keep changing. The therapist does not attack a client's problems or sculpt a client to fit an idea; rather, as stated above, the therapist is akin to a midwife attending a birth. Overly eager therapists would do well to remember to let the patients do the work, simply guiding and helping them to keep moving. It is counterproductive for therapists to do for patients what they can do for themselves; better to assist the patient to "stretch" a bit past their usual stopping point.[3]

SST may engender a sense of pleasant urgency, but it is important for the therapist and patient not to feel desperately rushed. Each session has its unique qualities, including pace, and enough time needs to be allotted to do the job well. Effective sessions can sometimes be accomplished relatively quickly, although scheduling ninety minutes or two hours can be helpful to allow enough time for a complete, impactful meeting.

A sixty-year-old woman was referred by her physician, who had successfully treated her breast cancer two years before. Since that time, however, she had become chronically anxious, fearful of a recurrence, and hypervigilant about all aches and pains. She had never been to a therapist before and was skeptical about the psychotherapeutic enterprise. The therapist, on hearing the presenting complaint, and noting the patient's apparent minimal psychological-mindedness and motivation for insight, quickly made a decision to treat the somatic preoccupations with hypnosis, a technique he had found useful in similar cases. The patient "rambled," however, and for a time he was unable to get a word in edgewise either to establish the treatment focus or to initiate trance.

In her ramblings, the patient mentioned that her elderly mother was living with her. The therapist asked how that was for the patient, and the patient related how she had been taking care of her mother since she (the patient) was fourteen years old, when her mother had ejected her alcoholic husband from the home. A simple question from the therapist, inquiring about the patient's father, elicited a tearful response. The patient described how much she had cared for her father and how hard it had been to see him die on skid row shortly after the divorce. She had been her father's favorite. She had been angry at her mother for leaving her father but had never expressed these feelings. Instead, she had gone to great lengths to take care of her mother, at considerable self-sacrifice. The patient would not go out by herself because the mother would demand to be taken along. The patient had many things she wanted to do, especially travel with her husband who was due to retire, but feared that, obligated to her mother, she might die or become ill before she had the opportunity.

The patient felt guilty about her resentment of her mother and hid the feelings; she was fearful that admitting to her anger would cause her to take actions that would be overly hurtful to her mother. It became clear she had never had the opportunity to discuss these feelings before with anyone, including her husband. The therapist gave her permission and encouraged her, commenting, "You have the right to figure this out." The remainder of the session involved working through, in affective imagery and detailed planning, how the patient could carve space for herself and deal with her mother in a fashion that was both assertive and caring.

In all of this, the therapist's interventions were minimal as the patient used the opportunity to think through her situation in a way that had not been available to her previously. At the end of the session, the patient stated, "You mean, I have to look out for myself more." She presented her immediate plan: instead of going directly from the session to pick up her mother, she would take a little time for herself. On follow-up, the patient had worked out a viable arrangement to allow her the freedom to engage in some of the activities she had wished for while still taking appropriate care of her mother. The anxiety symptoms had remitted.

If the therapist had jumped in with hypnosis too soon, the patient might have achieved some symptom relief but would have been denied a significant experience of autonomy and growth. By waiting, the therapist provided an opportunity for the patient to "ramble" herself free [Rosenbaum].

Emphasize Abilities and Strengths Rather Than Pathology

It is important to ask, How can this client create a solution? rather than stopping at, How does this patient create this problem? Faced with a client in pain, overwhelmed by his or her problems, diagnostic labels may seem to leap out at the clinician; it is easy to overlook client efforts at adaptation and coping. All too often, "assessment" means a lengthy description of all the manifestations and sources of illness, with at best a short sentence or two cursorily depicting "ego strengths" or "support networks." On a more profound level, we must realize that the distinction between healthy and pathological behavior is itself problematic.

Drawing distinctions is the first step in any assessment process, and the kinds of distinctions one makes help determine the range of intervention options that can be perceived (Bateson, 1979). If you focus on distinguishing between pathological and healthy behavior, you will then devote much of your time to seeing pathology. Therapists should attempt to avoid creating diagnostic labels that create patients (Szasz, 1970). To the extent that we try to find a formulation of the *problem*, we will be looking for problems rather than solutions, and the formulation—whether it be psychodynamic, psychiatric, behavioral, or systemic—will tend to foster pathology by highlighting difficulties. In contrast, to the extent that we try to find past successes and present client resources, we will be fostering flexibility and health. The kind of data one collects helps create the "reality" being investigated, which in turn influences the kind of data one looks for. Even the terms *patient* or *client* may have important implications (see Chapters Thirteen and Fourteen), connoting certain assumptions regarding dependency and respon- sibility in psychotherapy. Potential dangers (suicidal risk, alcohol or drug abuse, psychosis) should not be overlooked, of course, but neither should potential strengths.

The SST therapist looks for the information necessary to help the client make a change, rather than focusing on pathology. The focus is on finding solutions, not problems (de Shazer, 1985, 1988; O'Hanlon and Weiner-Davis, 1989). One way of doing this is to find skills the client already has that he or she can use. Therapists have listed a variety of ways of doing this: by looking for past client successes, by finding something the client already is doing that would be useful to do more of, or by looking for "exceptions to the rule" of the problem. Positive connotation and reframing look for the health-seeking intent in problematic behavior (Selvini-Palazzoli et al., 1978); the therapist must recognize that clients make the best choices for themselves at the moment, given the resources and circumstances they perceive as available to them (Lankton and Lankton, 1983).

All of these techniques presuppose that the therapist has a strong belief that the power is in the client (Goulding and Goulding, 1978, 1979), that ultimately the client knows himself or herself more than the therapist does, and that the therapist's task is to facilitate the client's finding his or her own solution. Whether stated explicitly or not, this therapist attitude encourages client autonomy and refuses to buy into the idea that clients are not in control of their lives. Since clients often come into treatment feeling like victims controlled by other persons, this affirmation of their ability to make a difference in their experience is itself helpful, countering the sense of powerlessness that results in client's feeling "stuck." Helping people feel autonomous rather than victimized is itself salutary and serves as a precondition for many further changes. Sometimes the therapist can facilitate a single-session ceremony or ritual that will mark a passage and help the patient to reclaim his or her sense of self-determination. The therapist may use a preliminary consultation to set the stage for the single-session intervention.

A woman in her late twenties mentioned a series of problems and then said, "What's really bothering me is something I've carried as a secret for years. My father molested me for a long time, when I was in my late teens." She described a situation of terrible abuse and exploitation, and she made the connection between the sexual abuse and her subsequent low self-esteem and various personal problems. She had made repeated attempts as an adult to confront her father and discuss what had happened and her feelings about it, but each time he rebuffed and mocked her. In fact, he continued to make occasional attempts to exploit her, promising to loan her money but then withholding the loan unless she gave him sexual "favors."

"I'm tired of this shit," the patient exclaimed. "I want to put it behind me and be done with it. I want to get him and what he did out of my life, once and for all!"

At this point the therapist, who had listened sympathetically, suggested she needed a way of divorcing her father and breaking the bond. What was needed was something that would make the break total and permanent *for her.* "Some people might want to say certain words, or burn a picture, or do whatever would mean to them they were free and done with him. You need to create a personal ceremony, one that will let you be free all the way through your mind and your soul. Spend some time really thinking about what you want to do, and bring it in. We'll meet in a week, OK?"

A week later the patient arrived with her husband, a portable stereo tape player, and an envelope. She looked nervous but indicated she was ready. The therapist gave a brief speech like a clergyman at a wedding but instead expounded on the significance of divorce ("an ending, a separating, one voice becoming two from this day on"). He then, as master of ceremonies, nodded to the patient to proceed, only occasionally directing, setting the pace, pausing for emphasis and heightened impact.

An extraordinary experience unfolded. The patient read aloud a several-page account of her betrayal and outrage, giving witness to what she had never before dared to reveal. While she read, taped music played—song lyrics about love and betrayal poignantly coordinated with her reading. Several times she paused, overcome with emotion, and then she would continue. At the end of her reading she produced a photograph of her father, along with a lighter. The therapist held the picture with scissors while she lit it. Eerily, the father's face was the last portion to burn. The ashes fell into the office trash can, a glass of water was poured over the ashes, and (for good measure and to the delight of all) the therapist spit into the ashes. The patient and her husband laughed. She said she felt "free," reached into the envelope, and pulled out several copies of a printed "Decree of Divorce" she had written and had professionally printed. It declared her "No longer the daughter of X except through biology." She signed each copy, as did her husband and then the therapist. Happy music was played. She explained that one copy was for her, to be displayed at home next to her graduation diplomas, another copy was for her sister, a third was to be sent to her father (the last time she would contact him, she said), and the last copy was for the therapist (who was honored to accept it).

The mood in the room was exceptionally positive, a marked contrast to her state earlier in the hour and at the initial consultation. Before closing the ceremony, however, the therapist asked her to close her eyes and to get a vivid picture of herself when she was a little girl, before "all the bad things happened." When she indicated having a clear image he asked her to keep that image and "now also see yourself as you are now, a strong, grown-up woman." When she got that image, he continued: "Now I want you to do two more things. First, notice that you're now grown-up, no longer a little girl, no longer vulnerable. You're strong now, adult, and able to take care of yourself. And now, in your mind's picture, see the grown-up you bend over and pick up the little girl and hold her close and lovingly, and in a nice way, the little girl just sort of blends into you and your arms are around yourself. And you know that she is safe inside of you and that you will always protect her."

Tears ran down the patient's cheeks. She opened her eyes. Her face looked beatific. She laughed freely, looked around, and hugged her husband. After a couple of minutes of celebrating and the clients expressing their appreciation, the session ended. No further treatment was sought [Hoyt].

Recognize That Life, Not Therapy, Is the Great Teacher

While SST therapists view each encounter as complete in itself, they do not regard it as completely fulfilling, a cure-all or final solution. Therapists who perform SSTs are neither megalomaniacs nor magicians. Rather, SST therapists believe that what happens in the therapy session can provide the *impetus* for the client to begin making significant changes in his or her daily life, outside the session. The purpose of SST is to help clients access healthful experiences in both their inner lives and their daily interactions with others that they may have overlooked. We therefore often give assignments to be performed after the SST meeting, which are designed to introduce some new element into a client's usual routine.

A young couple came in who described themselves as happily married. Over the past year, however, the husband had developed severe complex partial seizures. As part of the seizures, he had suffered a transient psychosis from which he was now recovered. However, he had residual obsessional symptoms, most prominently intrusive suicidal thoughts that he had no intention of acting on but that he would mention to his wife. She was anxious and depressed—quite tearful—and both fearful of his seizures (which he was having every other day) and concerned about his obsessional thoughts. She coped with the situation by emotionally smothering her husband, worrying about his seizures and trying to "take care of him." The more she did this, the more he told her of any symptoms, and the worse the situation became.

The therapist praised how much the couple cared for and took care of each other but worried out loud that the wife's hovering might prove draining to her or occasionally irritating to her husband. The therapist also shared his concern that the wife would feel guilty and depressed if, trying to pull back, she felt she was not helping enough.

The therapist then gave the couple a paradoxical assignment, in which the husband was to pretend to have minor seizures several times a day, while the wife was to guess whether the seizure was genuine or not, helping out if it were genuine and ignoring it if it had been initiated on purpose by the husband. They were told this would help the husband learn more about the signs and symptoms of his seizures while giving the wife an opportunity to learn when she should and shouldn't worry.

On follow-up, the couple said they had practiced the assignment faithfully for about a week but then had found it "silly," since the husband's obsessional thoughts had virtually vanished and his seizures had markedly decreased. The wife was no longer tearful, and she discussed detaching from her husband's condition enough to establish some independent plans for herself (such as attending school). These gains were maintained at follow-up one year after the intervention.

Talking about the seizures and the couple's relationship within the session was useful, but it was important to give the clients something different to do to alter their interactions in everyday life [Rosenbaum].

Focus on Pivot Chords

In music, the pivot chord is an ambiguous chord that contains notes common to more than one key and so can imply several possible "directions" to the music and facilitate the transition from one key to another. An important task of the SST therapist is to construe the client's difficulty in such a way that it can function as a pivot chord for change. The therapist can be helpful by putting the symptom into a larger pattern in which the problem contains the seeds of new directions for the client.

In the case of the couple just described, the occurrence of seizures acts as a pivot that allows the couple to achieve greater differentiation, rather than as an occasion for helplessness and smothering. In another case described in Chapter Seven, an insecure attorney who feels she is "dumb" is told that "smart people can play dumb." This transforms the patient's experience of herself as dumb into a pivot; "dumbness" becomes evidence of being smart. Sullivan provided a classic example when he was able to highlight a stifled housewife's strength in her presenting complaint: "[H]er feeling of helplessness to get going in the morning rather encourages me than otherwise. Has she never heard of a woman who preferred something else to domestic preoccupation?" (quoted by Gustafson, 1986, p. 47).

Psychotherapy involves a reframing of the clients' experience of themselves and their world (Frank, 1973). The task for any kind of reframing, of course, is to simultaneously meet the client at his or her view of the world, so he or she feels understood and validated, while at the same time offering a new perspective. All therapies face the challenge of joining and empathizing with the patient's attitude while trying to change it. The therapist wants to initiate some element of doubt or openness to alternative meanings in the patient's worldview without denying the client's experience or confronting it in a way that leads to a battle over which view of the experience is "right." In the behavioral therapies this may go under the rubric of "orientation and the correction of misconceptions" (Wolpe, 1973); in psychodynamic therapies it is accomplished by means of "interpretations." Strategic therapies offer many varieties of reframing, ranging from "positive connotation" (Selvini-Palazzoli, Boscola, Cecchin, and Prata, 1978) to "splitting the symptom" (Lankton and Lankton, 1983).

The therapist focuses on that portion of the client's problem that has sufficient ambiguity to be reconstrued as a bridge to new behaviors and experiences. The technique chosen is not as important as the attitude the therapist adopts: the therapist can convey the central experience of reframing—namely, joining with the client even while introducing doubt and the possibility of viewing events differently—by as simple a means as raising the eyebrows while maintaining a sympathetic facial expression.

A couple came in for treatment bitterly divided and distant from each other. They didn't even argue anymore, since they couldn't resolve a particular issue: their seven-year-old son slept in bed with his mother, while the husband slept on the couch. This had continued for years, ever since the child had

had nightmares as a three-year-old. The husband wanted the boy out, but while the mother complained of lack of sleep and regretted the growing distance from her husband, she felt she could not be a "bad mother" and, for "selfish" reasons, subject her son to the "rejection" she felt sending him to his own bed would entail. She also worried she would not be able to deal with the "loss" of her last child.

The therapist praised the woman for her motherly concern. He sighed and noted sadly how it was a parent's job to give their children the strength to cope with the inevitable losses and griefs of life. Tolerating the loneliness of his own bed was important practice for this. The therapist suggested it was the mother's painful duty to teach her child how to be on his own. At least, though, when her son slept in his own bed through the night, they could both value their morning snuggles more highly, when her son would come all that distance from his room to be with her. "Absence does make the heart grow fonder."

The woman quickly seized on this reframing as a "cross she would have to bear" to be a good mother. She and her husband were able to devise a two-week transition period for their son. On follow-up, the adults were in one bed, having both more arguments and more love-making, while the boy was enjoying his own room. The wife was delighted, and said: "This is great. I never knew this is what God meant bedtime to be for" [Rosenbaum].

Pivots are particularly useful when clients are troubled by ego-dystonic affects they regard as shameful, destructive, or otherwise "wrong." Many patients come in with symptoms related to unsuccessful attempts to ban all anger from their lives. For patients phobic about anger, the following story often proves helpful:

You know about Alfred Nobel, the inventor of dynamite? He woke up one morning to read his own obituary. Another man named Nobel had died, and a newspaper editor, thinking it was Alfred Nobel, had penned a piece in which he severely excoriated Nobel, condemning him as a creator of misery and destruction because of the explosive qualities of dynamite. Nobel was so upset by the article he used part of his fortune to establish the Nobel Peace Prize.

The interesting thing about all this is that the European editor had it all wrong. Americans in the 1800s greeted dynamite as the answer to their prayers. You see, Americans were just then trying to explore and settle the West, but it was very difficult cutting roads through hills with pickaxes, or blowing up tree stumps and boulders in farm fields with gunpowder, the only extant explosive at the time. Dynamite allowed you to control the amount and the direction of the explosive charge quite effectively, and so it enabled Americans to build the railroads and highways that could connect people from distant places and bring people together.

Now, dynamite is a very safe substance generally, except in one instance. If you store it in a shed and never attend to it, over the years the active ingredients slowly leak out and leach into the surrounding soil. When that happens, dropping something on the soil or walking on it can result in an unplanned, destructive explosion. It's important to use dynamite constructively, setting it off usefully rather than letting it just sit around.

That's just the way it is . . . usually, to make something, you have to tear something else up first. The trick is to use the power creatively. Of course, we've known that ever since taming fire for our uses [Rosenbaum].

Appreciate That "Big Problems" Don't Always Require "Big Solutions"

It is often useful to consider the possibility that symptoms may not be part of a person's psychological "essence" but instead may represent a response to some kind of intrusion, much as we get physiological symptoms when our body is invaded by a virus. Such symptoms do not represent pathology but rather a healthy attempt by our body to restore normal functioning.

A psychological symptom may fulfill a purpose in an individual or family negotiating a stage in the family life cycle (Carter and McGoldrick, 1980), of course, but sometimes it may be helpful to think of a symptom as having been introduced by a chance fluctuation that became more fixed as people put excessive unproductive energy into solving it. The meanings peo-

ple assign to a symptom may be self-fulfilling and contribute
to their difficulties, so calling something a "random glitch" is
less likely to make a person feel stuck than calling it a "problem
whose deeper meaning we will have to gradually uncover and
work through."

We know small changes can have large effects: a small addition to a radioactive pile can achieve a critical mass with a
self-sustaining chain reaction. In a similar way, any small change
in a client's life can lead to exposure to new life circumstances,
which will lead to new client reactions, which will lead to new
life circumstances, and so forth. The advantages of adopting
the attitude that a small change is sufficient are threefold: (1) it
takes the pressure off both therapist and client, so that neither
one stumbles in the process of trying too hard; (2) a client is
more likely to be undaunted and thus willing to make a (small)
change; and finally, (3) any kind of movement may suffice to
ignite hope in the client.

Consider the following excerpt from an interview with a
patient one year after an SST, quoted verbatim:

Patient: I remember at the time I came in I was feeling overwhelmed—the kids were getting under my skin. I had been a
twenty-four-hour-a-day mother for five years. I felt I was isolated, the only mother with such problems.

P: I remember the session well. . . . I took your suggestion
[making an appointment with herself, away from home]. Every
month I make two appointments with myself of two hours each.
I get my nails done, meet with a friend in a cafe, and we chat
about everything except the kids. If I feel the kids are getting
under my skin, I take a walk or switch to some other activity.

I realized nobody can be a twenty-four-hour-a-day mother.
We all need time and space.

When I stopped feeling the kids were getting under my
skin, I started feeling better as a mother. That freed me to take
care of other parts of myself; like, I started paying more attention to taking care of my looks. That led me to start feeling

better about myself. And that seems to have made my marriage better.

Therapist: You see how the little things make a big difference? [Talmon].

A corollary to the idea that big problems don't always require big solutions is that some patients can only tolerate a small change. In such cases, more would be less. Frequently, SSTs provide such patients with a positive, nonthreatening experience that can also set the stage for additional therapy should it be needed.

> A very intense and outspoken woman arrived complaining bitterly of mistreatment by her current boyfriend. Employers and past lovers were also all described as abusive. She rapidly displayed many strong affects and said that she needed answers *now,* that she didn't have the patience to spend weeks talking about her problems. The therapist complimented her on her direct, no-nonsense approach and her obvious emotional honesty and commitment to being treated fairly. They then discussed the patient's situation and her possible courses of action. The therapist also indicated to her that more sessions might be useful, if she wanted. She declined, saying the meeting had been very helpful, but "I don't like to get dependent on anyone." The therapist said, "Fine. Not now. But if you sometime want another session, call me" [Hoyt].

Use Termination Constructively

Termination is about the structure of memory and the realization of implications. In order to make a single session of therapy complete in itself, it must contain a fitting ending. This requires that SST therapists confront their countertransferences to termination: the disappointment of not being able to prolong what is pleasurable, having to leave some things incomplete, and experiencing loss. Too many therapists are not well trained in the art of termination, and they have particular difficulties in this critical phase of treatment.

Many therapists think of termination almost exclusively in terms of the content of the themes that emerge and therefore focus on issues of loss, longing, and incompleteness. In addition to thematic content, though, termination has processive and structural aspects as well (Rosenbaum, 1988b), and these often come to the fore in the context of SSTs. Our understanding of the meaning of an event includes not only what actually occurred (the realized implications) but also what might have happened but did not. In SST, as in any psychotherapy, patients present problematic patterns; these patterns may have many possible repercussions, outcomes, and pathways, but the client tends to expect certain outcomes and therefore repeats patterns unsuccessfully in a particular way. The therapy process, when successful, results in the realization of some new subset of the possible pathways implicit in the patient's repertoire. There are always important alternative implications that might have occurred in a relationship but did not appear. As Sampson and Weiss have noted (Sampson, 1976), if a patient expects certain responses from a therapist (e.g., to be criticized for being autonomous), and if the therapist "passes the test" by avoiding enactment of the feared response, patients may experience a sense that it is safe to continue their "unconscious plan" for growth. What did not happen becomes the mutative experience. However, the therapist cannot "pass the test" before completing it; only when the therapy is ended can the patient review what occurred and what did not and then realize that none of the expected, dreaded consequences have transpired. As long as the therapy is ongoing, even when the therapist passes test after test, until termination is completed successfully, the patient may wait for the other shoe to fall. The therapy must end in order for what did not happen to have meaning; this is the *processive* aspect of termination.

The *structural* aspect of termination refers to the architectonic sequence in which therapeutic events are organized in time: what happened when. Because therapy, like most human experience, is quintessentially temporal, it involves endings and thus invokes memory. Memory is a key to our experience of time, and the structure of sequences of events influences how they will be remembered. The effects of context, primacy and recency, distinctiveness, interference, and priming and depth of encoding all play critical roles (Cermak and Craik, 1979). Saying something at the beginning and then again at the end of a session is very different from saying the same thing several times in the middle of the session; the former will be much more likely to be remembered than the latter. Termination, by creating an ending point, punctuates experience and so structures how we remember and interpret what has occurred, both within the therapy session and in the passage of our lives.

Beginnings cannot be understood without endings; it is only after you have completed a journey that you can look back on the route you have traveled and put it in proper perspective. Termination allows both client and therapist to achieve a retrospective understanding of the therapy process. Understanding what did happen and what did not can give new implications to what can happen in the future as well as to what problems need not be repeated any more.

There is a paradox in remembrance: memory is an *immediate,* present-time experience that recalls the past and in so doing can affect our actions in the future. The SST therapist, by highlighting certain events and deemphasizing others, attempts to help the client focus on what will be useful while letting go of whatever needs to be left behind. In terminating the session, the SST therapist may help a client remember to remember, forget to remember, remember to forget, or forget to forget.

When concluding an SST, we may first ask the client if he or she feels that enough has been accomplished in the session to help him or her move on. If the answer is yes, we may ask for a description of what it was, to encourage lexical encoding, storage, and recall of a useful lesson. At other times, we may prefer to have the client leave with a more diffuse sense that "something" changed or will change soon. In all cases, we let clients know we will remain available on an as-needed basis. We encourage them, however, to take some time on their own (usually one to three months) to consolidate their gains. We also express a genuine interest in how things turn out for them; we may ask them to give us a follow-up phone report in a month or two or let them know we might call them in a few months to see how they've been progressing.

Sometimes an SST may conclude relatively uneventfully, with a mutual sense of the work being finished and "all wrapped up." At other times, it is best to stop dramatically after an important piece of work has been partially accomplished but before all of its ramifications are specifically spelled out. Since we tend to work over "unfinished business" (Perls, 1969) or uncompleted tasks more than completed ones (Zeigarnik, 1938), ending an SST in this fashion allows the patient to continue the work of the therapy on his or her own, realizing the unrealized implications in ensuing weeks and months.

The degree of closure appropriate to a termination covers a wide range, and it is influenced by the extent to which the therapy was seeking resolution of some issue or attempting to open up new possibilities (Rosenbaum, 1988b). Some clients will need to put the therapist behind them and get on with their lives; others will need to recall the therapist or some words of the therapist with a high degree of vividness. Since some of our SST clients will in the future seek further therapy, it is important to structure the termination in such a way that a decision for more treatment will be seen by the patient as an opportunity for further growth rather than as an indicator of failure. Whether the termination turns out to be for just a few weeks or forever, though, it still involves saying goodbye to the client, and all goodbyes have some degree of both grief and healing, sorrow and hope.

A young married couple sought consultation complaining of "communication problems." He referred to his stresses at work, financial frustrations, and sexual dissatisfaction with the marriage. She felt depressed and unable to connect with her husband, worried he would abandon her, and wondered if she should return to her parents' house. They looked reasonably healthy and neither had any previous psychiatric contact, but both now sat avoiding the other's eyes and appeared depressed. The room grew unpleasantly quiet.

"You look like someone died," the therapist observed aloud. "What happened?"

Previously unmentioned, a painful story was told: a mid-trimester pregnancy had miscarried the year before. The couple had tried to bury their grief over the unborn child and had pulled back from one another to avoid the sadness that closeness brought (see Leon, 1987). An hour spent talking, crying, and hugging "unstuck" the grieving/healing process. No further professional psychotherapeutic intervention was needed [Hoyt].

(No) Conclusion

Clients often come to psychotherapy having failed to resolve some problem because they have not yet accessed and used all their resources. In a similar fashion, clinicians can fail if they do not make use of all the resources at their disposal. Therapists have accumulated an enormous fount of knowledge and range of techniques, the product of nearly a century of work in psychiatry and psychology, plus many centuries' knowledge of human nature afforded by art, philosophy, religion, and common sense. Approaching each meeting as a potential successful SST has convinced us that it is possible to be very helpful with many clients quite quickly so long as we are willing to take an integrated approach to the psychotherapeutic endeavor. When we have attempted to restrict ourselves to the perspectives and techniques of a single therapeutic school, however, or when we have attempted to develop a single theoretical approach to SST, we have had markedly poorer results.

Ideally, therapists should be well-trained and skillful with a variety of approaches and techniques, so that they can apply what will be best for a particular client at a particular time. Even if one is theoretically orthodox, the skillful therapist can be *technically* eclectic (Lazarus, 1987; Rubin, 1986) lest every patient be forced into the Procrustean bed of a pet approach or be rejected as "resistant" or "unfit." Often the adherence to a particular therapeutic school does more to cement the personality and identity of the therapist than to resolve problems for the patient (Rosenbaum, 1988a). Therapists need not be "hostages to their early training rigidities" (Wolberg, 1987; Lamb, 1988), and may benefit from an ability to view cases in more than one way, with multiple descriptions. As Bateson (1979) noted, it takes two eyes, each with a slightly different perspective, to provide us with depth vision.

Single-session therapies ultimately work, as any therapy works, by mirroring within the therapy the real-life dilemmas and paradoxes our clients confront. In SST the choices we make as therapists are necessarily based on incomplete information. This, however, is a condition of life, rather than of SST: we cannot anticipate all the consequences of our actions until our lives are over and complete (Arendt, 1978). This is what makes Hesse's (1943) Magister Ludi, in the epigraph at the beginning of this chapter, describe "decisive moments of life" as both "vitalizing *and* painful" (our italics). The necessity to act, without being able to fully anticipate all the consequences of action, creates a mingled "sense of farewell and of setting out on new adventures." Our effort in SST is to create awakenings, a sense that there need be "no more hesitating or lingering." We seek "beginnings [in which] dwells a magic force," whose magic is intrinsic to the very brevity of the intense, mutative moment, in which dwells the experience that the time for change is now:

>   time time time time time

>   —how fortunate are you and i, whose home
>   is timelessness: we who have wandered down
>   from fragrant mountains of eternal now

>   to frolic in such mysteries as birth
>   and death a day (or maybe even less)
>   (e. e. cummings, "stand with your lover
>   on the ending earth—")

Notes

1. Some patients may be better off without *any* treatment. As Frances and Clarkin (1981a) point out, patients who are nonresponders, negative responders, and spontaneous improvers don't need therapy and may, in fact, incur needless expense and/or be harmed if treatment is attempted.

Other patients may require one session for evaluation and referral for medication or other nonpsychotherapy services (e.g., legal, vocational, financial, or spiritual counseling).

2. Sometimes the SST therapist, faced with a truly insoluble problem, can be helpful by acknowledging the impossibility of change. By aiding the client to cease useless or compulsive attempts to solve the impossible, the client may attain a measure of equanimity and acceptance by letting go of further treatment and attempts at "cure."

3. Single-session interventions in supervision may help therapists resolve transference-countertransference impasses involving the overassumption of responsibility and caretaking (see Chapter Eighteen; Hoyt and Farrell, 1984).

CHAPTER NINE

———◆———

Single-Session Solutions

Hey, man, grab the reins!
                                                    —Kenny Levey

When given a choice, a sizeable number of patients may elect a single treatment session and find it useful. This is suggested by the many anecdotal reports of successful one-visit treatments scattered throughout the literature (Hoyt, Rosenbaum, and Talmon, 1992; Chapter Eight); by the finding that single-session therapy—one visit without further contacts—is de facto the modal or most common length of treatment, generally occurring in 20 to 50 percent of cases (Baekeland and Lundwall, 1975; Bloom, 1992b; Talmon, 1990; Wierzbicki and Pekarik, 1993); and by the findings of three more systematic studies of the effectiveness of single-session therapy (SST):

1. Medical utilization was found to be reduced 60 percent over five-year follow-up after a single session of psychotherapy in a study done at the Kaiser Permanente Health Plan (the nation's largest health maintenance organization) by Follette and Cummings (1967). A second study (Cummings and Follette, 1976) found the benefits of SST still in effect after eight years and concluded that decreased medical utilization was due to a reduction in physical symptoms related to emotional stress.[1]
2. Significant symptom improvements years later were noted by Malan, Heath, Bacal, and Balfour (1975) in 51 percent of "untreated" patients who had only an intake

interview (which served to increase their insight and sense of personal responsibility) conducted at the Tavistock Clinic in London, and half of those patients were also judged to have made important personality modifications.

3. Patients and therapists agreed that a single treatment visit had been sufficient in 58.6 percent (thirty-four of fifty-eight) of attempted SSTs in another study conducted at Kaiser Permanente by Hoyt, Rosenbaum, and Talmon (reported in Talmon, 1990). The other patients continued meeting with their therapists. On three- to twelve-month follow-ups, 88 percent of the SST-only patients reported either "much improvement" or "improvement" in their presenting symptoms since the session, and 65 percent also reported other positive "ripple" effects, figures that were slightly (and statistically insignificantly) higher than those for the twenty-four patients seen more than once.

A single session may occur by plan or design, when patient and therapist mutually agree to stop after one session; or by default, usually when the patient does not continue (Hoyt, Rosenbaum, and Talmon, 1992; Talmon, 1990). The term *planned SST* (or *deliberate SST*) can refer to any one-visit treatment that is intended to be potentially complete unto itself—the psychological work may go on long past the session, but the session itself is conceived as a "total experience" with a beginning, middle, and end. Planned SST involves the willingness of therapist and patient to engage in a therapeutic experience such that additional treatment sessions may not be required or sought. There is no single theory, method, or goal for successful SST. The search is for a conceptualization that will allow a viable and efficient solution. Considering what the patient wants and asking how the patient is "stuck" and what is needed for him/her/them to be "unstuck" can lead in many directions. The therapist needs to be versatile, innovative and pragmatic, asking, What would help this patient today?

Attitudes, Indications, and General Guidelines for SST

Single-session treatments should be as varied as the patients and what they come to accomplish. The goal is not a "quick fix" or some mystical "cure" but rather a search for new learnings, enhanced coping, and growth; a chance for the patient to make a useful shift or pivot. Some people may need reassurance or confrontation; they may need to look at something deeply or to shift perspective. They may need to remember to remember, forget to remember, remember to forget, or forget to forget. As Talmon (1993, p. 112) has put it, it may be useful "to include, exclude, or conclude differently." In each case, the intention should be to help the patient to find/create an experience and answer—to build a solution—that works for him or her. The goal is not for therapy to take a single session; the goal is to make the most of each session and for treatment to end as soon as patient and therapist feel ready to carry on. Most effective single-session therapy is actually not time-limited therapy—it is open-ended, and the patient gets what is needed and elects to stop after one visit.

One should set out to do time-sensitive therapy (Budman and Gurman, 1988; Budman, Hoyt, and Friedman, 1992), attempting to assist the patient as efficiently as possible. Needing multiple sessions does not mean there has been an "SST failure." Many patients will require more than one visit to accomplish what is needed, for a variety of reasons: there is a lack of achievable goals or no solution is available; more time is needed to learn, relearn, let go, or work through; the patient is trying to change someone else; the steps being attempted are too big; reality is too unfriendly, etc.[2] What is most important is to make the most of each session, to use the patient's and therapist's skills to move toward an obtainable goal. It is also important to recognize that all of the work may not be accomplished or completed during the single session. The patient may get information and encouragement that helps get him or her "unstuck" or back "on track" (Walter and Peller, 1994). Indeed, patients will often acquire or access skills during the treatment meeting that they will then need to practice and apply if effective SST is to occur. A single therapy session may also be part of "intermittent treatment" (Budman, 1990; Cummings, 1990) with the provision of help in a single-session encounter encouraging patients to return later as needed. The potential quick utility of treatment may also promote referrals, thus supporting the fiscal viability of SST for fee-for-service practitioners while meeting the treatment needs of a larger population.

While there is no single theory or method for successful SST, a constructive, competency-based perspective is apparent in the following summaries based on the outpatient studies done by two psychologist colleagues and myself (see Chapter Eight; Hoyt, 1993b; Hoyt and Talmon, 1990; Hoyt, Rosenbaum, and Talmon, 1992; Rosenbaum, 1990, 1993; Talmon, 1990, 1993; Talmon, Hoyt, and Rosenbaum, 1990; Talmon, Rosenbaum, Hoyt, and Short, 1990) as well as those of earlier workers in this area (Bloom, 1981, 1992b; Spoerl, 1975; Rockwell and Pinkerton, 1982).

Attitudes such as the following are conducive to the possibility of successful SST:

1. View each session as a whole, potentially complete in itself. Expect change.
2. The power is in the patient. Never underestimate your patient's strength.
3. This is it. All you have is now.
4. The therapeutic process starts before the first session, and will continue long after it.
5. The natural process of life is the main force of change.
6. You don't have to know everything in order to be effective.
7. You don't have to rush or reinvent the wheel.
8. More is not necessarily better. Better is better. A small step can make a big difference.
9. Helping people as quickly as possible is practical and ethical. It will encourage patients to return for help if they have other problems and will also allow therapists to spend more time with patients who require longer treatments.

Those most likely to benefit from SST include:

1. Patients who come to solve a specific problem for which a solution is in their control.
2. Patients who essentially need reassurance that their reaction to a troubling situation is normal.
3. Patients seen with significant others or family members who can serve as natural supports and 'co-therapists.'
4. Patients who can identify (perhaps with the therapist's assistance) helpful solutions, past successes, and exceptions to the problem.
5. Patients who have a particularly 'stuck' feeling (e.g., anger, guilt, grief) toward a past event.
6. Patients who come for evaluation and need referral for medical examinations or other nonpsychotherapy services (e.g., legal, vocational, financial, or religious counseling).
7. Patients who are likely to be better off without any treatment, such as "spontaneous improvers," nonresponders, and those likely to have a "negative therapeutic reaction" (Frances and Clarkin, 1981a).
8. Patients faced with a truly insoluble situation. It will help to recast goals in terms that can be productively addressed.

Those for whom SST is less likely to be adequate and beneficial include:

1. Patients who might require inpatient psychiatric care, such as suicidal or psychotic persons.
2. Patients suffering from conditions that suggest strong biological or chemical components, such as schizophrenia, manic-depression, alcohol or drug addiction, or panic disorder.
3. Patients who request long-term therapy up front, including those who are anticipating and have prepared for prolonged self-exploration.
4. Patients who need ongoing support to work through (and escape) the effects of childhood and/or adult abuse.

5. Patients with longstanding eating disorders or severe obsessive-compulsive problems.
6. Patients with chronic pain syndromes and somatoform disorders.

Creative application of the following clinical guidelines facilitates SST:

1. Seed change through induction and preparation. Engage the patient via a pre-session phone call or letter encouraging a focus on goals and the collection of useful information about competencies, past successes, and exceptions to the problem. Ask, for example, the "Skeleton Key Question" of de Shazer [1985, p. 137]: "Between now and when we meet, I would like you to observe, so you can describe to me, what happens that you want to continue to have happen".

2. Develop an alliance and co-create obtainable treatment goals.[3] When getting started, inquire about change since pretreatment contact and amplify accordingly (see Weiner-Davis, de Shazer, and Gingerich, 1987). Introduce the possibility of one session being adequate, and recruit the patient's cooperation.

3. Allow enough time. Most of us work in the fifty-minute hour, which is usually adequate; but consider scheduling a longer session to allow for a complete process or intervention.[4]

4. Focus on "pivot chords," ambiguities that may facilitate transitions into different directions. Look for ways of meeting the patient in his or her worldview while at the same time offering a new perspective—reframing introduces the possibility of seeing and/or acting differently.

5. Go slow and look for patients' strengths.

6. Practice solutions experientially. Rehearsing desired outcomes provides a "glimpse of the future," teaches and reinforces useful skills, and inspires enthusiasm and movement.

7. Consider taking a time-out. A break or pause during a

session allows time to think, consult, focus, prepare, punctuate.

8. Allow time for last-minute issues. "Eleventh-hour" questions should be asked at about six o'clock, to allow time for inclusion or prioritization. Unaddressed issues may impede a sense of the session being complete and satisfactory.

9. Give feedback. Information should be provided that enhances the patient's understanding and sense of self-mastery. Tasks or "homework" may be developed that will continue therapeutic work.

10. Leave the door open. The decision to stop is usually best left to the patient.

Experiences in Single-Session Therapy

More of the same does not produce change. As the old saying has it: "If you don't change directions, you'll wind up where you're heading." Effective therapy involves breaking a pattern, doing something different (de Shazer, 1991b; Yapko, 1992). In successful brief therapy cases, including SSTs, something new happens early on (Budman, Friedman, and Hoyt, 1992). A powerful ingredient of most successful single-session treatments is a *new experience* in which the patient passes through his or her habitual, self-limiting patterns of thinking, feeling, and acting. This may be subtle or dramatic, disconfirming counterproductive expectations that were being used to hold him- or herself back and resulting in the patient having a sense of increased freedom and hope. There is a change in the patient's "viewing and doing" (O'Hanlon and Weiner-Davis, 1989; Cade and O'Hanlon, 1993). Reframing helps to change "meaning" and to increase perceived options, and practicing a desired outcome in session allows patient and therapist to experience success directly or recognize and correct impediments during a "dry run" rehearsal. A counterproductive "trance" may be loosened or disrupted (Wolinsky, 1991). In successful SSTs, in different ways, the patient has a new and salutary experience. The patient may achieve some insight into or awareness of a counterproductive pattern, a vision of how he or she is getting stuck, but that is not all. The patient also experiences himself or herself as different—there is a change in the story they are constructing and that is constructing/constricting them. This may occur via a mental-imagery exercise in which the patient has the experience of functioning in the desired way; or via a persistent confrontation of defenses until there is a breakthrough into true and deeper feelings; or via a guided transaction, ritual ceremony, or a behavioral rehearsal in which he/she/they actually act/think/feel differently; or via a problem-solving exercise in which a useful solution is thought out and practiced experientially. Whatever the method, the new experience is powerful and undeniable, promoting growth, change, and a shift toward new directions.

The following examples illustrate the narrative shift that frequently occurs in effective SST. (Unless otherwise indicated, the author was the therapist in each example.)

Example One

A young woman arrived complaining of "panic attacks" and states of great anxiety. When asked, she was vague but noted that her worst attacks occurred after seeing her sister. She was hazy on details, but persistent confrontation of her defenses (including her helplessness, vagueness, and weepiness) plus appeals to her desire to feel better and not render the therapist "useless"—all techniques best illustrated by the work of Davanloo (1980; Zois, 1992) and other proponents of intensive short-term dynamic psychotherapy—resulted in her becoming more engaged and active. Disallowing her typical defenses first engendered annoyance and then anger toward the therapist, who worked actively to help the patient acknowledge these feelings. When this was accomplished, and when the therapist did not retaliate or attack the patient, she then brought forward and experienced her anger toward her sister and others who had disappointed her. Her "de-repression" of anger and hurt resulted in her having both the insight and the corrective emotional experience of expressing herself without triggering damaging retribution. Her in-session experience led her to change her personal story, to "re-vision" herself as someone who could express anger and be assertive. On follow-up she described more comfort with self-assertiveness and reported having had no further panic attacks.[5]

Example Two

The redecision therapy model of Goulding and Goulding (1978, 1979) draws on transactional analysis (TA) theory and Gestalt techniques plus the Gouldings' own innovations to rapidly generate powerful and potentially life-changing therapeutic experiences. In the case of "Anne" presented in their professional training videotape, *Redecision Therapy* (1988), we see them work with a woman troubled by feelings of incompetency. Rather than working within a psychodynamic transference model, in which the therapist becomes the participant-observer "object," here the patient is encouraged to do two-chair Gestalt work. In a second chair she undergoes a "Parent Interview" (McNeel, 1976) in which she "becomes" her father (extrojecting the introject, if you will) and then engages in a power dialogue with him in which she, in essence, experiences and realizes the futility of trying to remain an incompetent child to please her father. Her therapeutic impasse is resolved as she externalizes and disengages from her sense of incompetency. Back in her adult self after the exercise, she processes the experience to gain further insight and a sense of autonomy and self-mastery.

Example Three

Chronic nightmares in twenty-three patients were successfully treated with one session of desensitization or rehearsal instruction, with seven-month follow-up, according to a recent report by Kellner, Neidhardt, Krakow, and Pathak (1992). Half the patients were instructed to practice progressive relaxation while imagining the nightmare, while the other patients were instructed to write down a recent nightmare, change it and write down the modified version, and rehearse the changed nightmare in imagery while in a relaxed state. In both conditions, patients were seen once and were to practice at home; skills and direction were provided in the therapy session, with the patient responsible for applying the task. On follow-up, the two methods were both successful and no one had worsened, whereas in a quasi-control group less change had occurred and two patients had actually worsened. Again, we see that the pattern is altered, that the patients have a new experience, in this instance relaxation and/or a more favorable ending. In clinical practice I have found it useful to present the two treatment conditions to patients and to have them choose the one they think most likely to work for them—a method that promotes their "buy in" and follow-through. As one might expect, most prefer the more active choice in which they get to enhance their sense of instrumentality by doing something positive—authoring a new ending.

Example Four

A widower in his late sixties was referred by his internist, who was concerned about the patient's "depression." Less than a year before, the patient's wife had died while undergoing cardiac surgery. He blamed himself for her death, noting that he had advocated she have surgery to restore her capacities for activities that he sought (e.g., sex, travel). Alas, she had not survived the operation, and he was suffering from heavy doses of "survivor's guilt." A long, quiet talk enabled him to see that sometimes bad things happen to good people, and that he, too, was a victim—a grieving survivor. Feeling relieved of his guilt, he was able to shift to the more constructive tasks of missing his wife and moving forward in his life. In a somewhat related case reported in his instructive book, *Single Session Solutions,* Talmon (1993, pp. 1–4) describes helping a guiltful man by first acknowledging the client's feelings and then facilitating and activating the positive traits that are submerged. He recognizes and reframes the man's depression: "You are feeling this way because you are a very caring, loving, and responsible husband and father. Your depression is your way of expressing to your family your regrets and sorrow for causing the accident." He then goes on to help the client build a better solution, saying: "Now that you have taken full responsibility for causing the accident you are ready today to go back to your regular self . . . I am sure you want to find a renewed way to show them your positive feelings."

Example Five

A couple complained of communication difficulties and unhappiness. Before they could launch into a long and mutually demoralizing diatribe, I interrupted them with the "Miracle Question" (de Shazer, 1988, p. 5): "Suppose tonight, while you're sleeping, a miracle happens and the problems that brought you here are resolved. Tomorrow, when you wake up, how would you notice that the miracle had occurred?" It took some prompting and probing, I promise you, but then the miracle did occur: they began to talk about good times, past and future; they began to see each other again as sources of light, not darkness; they laughed and rekindled hope. To help them shift from a problem-saturated story (White and Epston, 1990) to a more hopeful, solution-oriented narrative (Hudson and O'Hanlon, 1992; Weiner-Davis, 1992), I pursued my questioning, getting details and encouraging specific plans for fun and pleasure while cautioning, "Not so fast. Just two steps at a time." At the end of the meeting they were feeling good, had skills and plans ready, and did not think another appointment would be necessary but agreed to call back as needed.

Example Six

A woman was seriously contemplating a divorce and wanted to "check out" or validate her thinking before proceeding.[6] The story she told certainly made divorce seem reasonable, and she had thought through many of the social, emotional, and financial implications of the decision, but it was an enormous step and, not surprisingly, she was somewhat apprehensive. Rather than simply say, "Yeah, divorce the bum!" I took two tacks that would more likely enhance her own self-determination. First, I had her imagine herself five years in the future with two scenarios: what life would be like if she remained married, and what life would be like if she divorced. Drawing on all kinds of experiences, memories, and intuitions that I could never know, she got a strong taste of what both paths seemed to offer for her.[7] The second tack was quite simple: Near the end of the session I said: "Imagine if you were somehow like a 'fly on the wall' and you were invisible, and a woman came in and told me what you've been telling me. Knowing everything you know, what would you think, and how would you advise her?" She was clear in her answer and proceeded accordingly. Drawing her own conclusions from her own (guided) experience allowed her a greater sense of self-empowerment and mastery.

Example Seven

A powerful method of "experiential psychotherapy" has been described by Mahrer (1989). Each treatment session (usually one to two hours) is intended to be a complete experience. Each session moves through four steps: (1) attaining the level of strong, full feeling and accessing inner, "deeper" experiencing; (2) welcoming and appreciating the inner experiencing; (3) feeling the inner experiencing in earlier life scenes so thoroughly as to transform into a "new person"; and (4) experiencing change in being and behavior as the "new person" in the extratherapy world. Giving structure and support for the emergence of strong feelings and fantasies produces, in this model, what Mahrer (p. 101) calls "the distinct possibility that at the end of this session the patient can leave the office as a qualitatively new personality with whole new ways of being and behaving in a world that is seen and lived in completely new ways." In a vivid case report, Mahrer and Roberge (1993) illustrate working with a woman, facilitating her feelingful passage through the four steps with her new experiencing resulting in a commitment to carry forward new behavior in life outside the therapist's office.

Example Eight

A ritual or ceremony can be used to generate a therapeutic experience that helps a patient to consolidate gains and demarcate a before-and-after change of status (Combs and Freedman, 1990; Hudson and O'Hanlon, 1992; White and Epston, 1990). This might involve a powerful but relatively brief "saying good-bye" mental-imagery experience or a more elaborate production such as the case described in Chapter Eight, in which I facilitated a patient's "emotionally divorcing" her abusive father in a ceremony she created. In another case, with the therapist's encouragement a husband and wife together discarded mementos of previous relationships and co-authored and sent a letter to an ex-spouse redefining how they would relate to the third person. Such a process may require considerable preparation and is intended not so much to "resolve" or "cure" as to effect a shift to a different perspective; nor is it intended to replace other work that may be beneficial.

Example Nine

An attractive young woman was on her way out of town, "headed toward a new life," she said. She had been working as an "exotic dancer" at a local adult theater, and she told stories that indicated why she had tired of such an existence. Somehow, she had decided to use her health insurance before leaving town, and she had made an appointment and was in my office. She had no specific goals or agenda; she just wanted to see what the psychiatry department might have to offer that could help her. One session might be useful, I thought, to help prepare her for possible subsequent work and to make a referral. I complimented her on her desire to find a life that would be more satisfying to her. Recognizing that she was intelligent and street smart, I asked if she was bright, and she said, "Yes, why?" I explained that since we would only have one meeting I wanted to say something that would make more sense to a bright person. She nodded, and then I said: "Have you ever seen a really bad bruise? You know, one that aches and turns

yellow and green? I work here in a medical center, so I see
such things. Well, anyway, from what you've told me, I think
that in some ways you've been bruised psychologically, from
what you've been through. But from what you've told me I can
also tell that *nothing is broken, that all the bruises can heal.* Know
what I mean?" She nodded again, and one could almost see
her self-image revising, from "broken" to "bruised," from "ru-
ined" to "repairable." I went on to suggest that she might want
to get into therapy or counseling once she relocated, when she
was ready, and suggested it would be good for her to have
someone she could get to know and depend on over time. I
gave her the names of two counseling centers in the town she
was planning to move to. Almost a year later I got a call from
a therapist in another town. Our patient had changed her plans,
and had relocated in a different area. She was in therapy.

Example Ten

Nelson (1984) has described a method of child discipline in a
book far more humanistic than its title might suggest: *The One
Minute Scolding.* (His ideas are reflected in other "one minute"
books such as Blanchard and Johnson's (1982) best-selling *The
One Minute Manager.*) Nelson presents a structure intended to
provide a complete teaching experience (not punishment) in a
sixty-second framework. His method has several parts: (1) scolding the undesired behavior, (2) a moment of transition, (3) positive affirmation of the child's worth, (4) a quiz, and (5) a hug.
Extraordinarily simple yet grounded in both theory and practice, it provides parent and child with a framework in which
the parent first makes a clear statement of feelings about the
child's behavior. ("I am angry with you. You hit your sister.
That's not the way to deal with your frustration, and I get mad
at you when you forget that rule. You simply may not hit.")
The parent then draws a deep breath and changes feeling tone,
creating a sense of anticipation in the child. The parent then
clearly and lovingly reaffirms the child's worth. ("You're such
a neat fellow. I love you. I know you can do better. Sometimes
you remember to be so loving to your sister. I want to be a

good mother to you. So you don't have to worry. Every time you forget the rule and hit your sister, I'll scold you. That will help you to remember.") A brief but important quiz then follows, to make sure the child has learned. ("Why am I scolding you? Why do I want to help you remember?") Finally, the lesson ends with a hug, a physical and symbolic gesture that signals the end of the "scolding" and further reaffirms the closeness of the relationship. While this thumbnail sketch is quite superficial and the method is drawn from the parent-child realm rather than from psychotherapy proper, it is included because it illustrates how narrative can be shaped quickly as powerful feelings and meanings are expressed, compressed, and constructed.

Example Eleven

Successful one-session treatment for auditory hallucinations is described by Blymyer (1991). Respecting client's beliefs and operating from the assumption that rapid change is possible, an approach is described that includes the following elements: (1) co-defining with the patient a positive future-oriented outcome ("When the voices stop bothering you"); (2) normalizing the experience and joining with the client ("Did you know that all people hear voices all the time?"); (3) relabeling the auditory experience as an "internal voice" and complimenting the client on being sensitive to this "voice"; (4) finding out what the voices say, and looking for interactional complaints that could benefit from intervention; (5) telling stories to illustrate how internal dialogues can change and how they can influence how we feel; (6) asking about exceptions, times the voices are not present or are not bothersome. Assumptive language ("When the voices are no longer bothering you") and questions about how and when change will be noticed set the stage for (7) highlighting exceptions or using predictions tasks generally coupled with directing the client to focus on turning on the voice. For example, a story may be told to clients about a child who learns to turn off a water tap by first learning to turn it on, and the client is instructed to spend fifteen minutes each day working at turning the voice on. Change is anchored when the new behavior is experienced as normal or reality, and the change is also anchored by enlarging upon the new occurrence. Basing his report on a series of ten cases, Blymyer is careful to recognize that speculations about how the successful outcome of rapid treatment for auditory hallucinations come about are just theoretical constructions in their own right. He is also careful to note that resolution of the initial complaint does not necessarily end therapy and that a change (new behavior) may not be fixed and permanent. Resolving a problem in a hopeful and positive context, however, may provide the groundwork for additional useful work.

Example Twelve

In *The Times of Time,* Boscolo and Bertrando (1993) provide a brilliant exposition of the many ways variations in senses of time influence intrapsychic and interpersonal constructions of reality and organize and disorganize individual and family functioning. In one section (pp. 19–29), they present an extraordinary one-visit consultation with Nancy, a severely disturbed twenty-two-year-old woman seen in a psychiatric hospital. Relating empathically to the patient and informed by the temporal differences between Nancy and her delusional alter ego "Mildred" (a fifteen-year-old girl who Nancy felt lived inside of her, enslaving her, burning and cutting her, etc.), Boscolo helps the patient reorganize herself in time. He points both to the past ("You cannot go back in time") and to the future ("So it's possible . . . that when you reach the age of sixty, you will have a fifteen-year-old girl who will tell you what to do or not to do"). He then attempts to help Nancy further collapse the distinction between her "selves" and to develop new and more temporally coordinated positive scenarios, suggesting that Nancy and Mildred have much in common and that they might be able to "start accepting each other" and "find some way to be together. I think they could become good friends or like two sisters, even better, like *twin* sisters" (emphasis in original). We learn that there was a positive outcome. Immediately after the session the anorectic Nancy requested and ate chocolate, saying "Mildred will let me eat, now." She rapidly improved and was soon discharged from the hospital. She reported that Mildred left her soon after she left the hospital, and Nancy was doing fairly well a year later. While this case may have been exceptional, it again points to the powerful effects—even in one session—of helping a patient construct a more functional reality.

Example Thirteen

A full transcript is provided by Yapko (1990b) of a single-session hypnotherapy intervention done with a forty-two-year-old woman named Vicki referred for help in coping with terminal cancer. First interviewing the patient in a "spontaneous" conversational manner, the therapist nicely establishes and builds rapport with the patient while identifying treatment goals, potential pitfalls, and various resources that are then utilized in the second portion of the session, involving more formal induction and trancework. Numerous suggestions for dissociation, time distortion, appetite enhancement, alternation in kinesthetic awareness, and reframing of uncertainty as pleasant are all provided within the patient's frame of reference to facilitate her structuring her experience in ways that minimize her emotional shock and physical discomfort. We learn that these suggestions were very helpful until her physical condition became too severe to self-manage.[8]

Discussion: Once May Be Enough (for Now)

While single-session therapy is obviously neither a panacea nor even appropriate for everyone, clinical experience and some systematic data suggest that when given the choice many patients elect a single treatment session and find it useful, especially if the therapist is open to this possibility and oriented toward maximizing the impact of the session. Therapy should not be "long" or "short." It should be sufficient, adequate, and appropriate, "measured not by its brevity or length, but whether it is efficient and effective in aiding people with their complaints or whether it wastes time" (Fisch, 1982, p. 156). Many people solve psychological problems without professional consultation. For some others, the "light touch" of a single visit may be enough, providing experience, skills, and encouragement to help them get "unstuck" and continue in their life journey.[9] If used appropriately, such "ultra-brief" treatments can promote patients' sense of self-empowerment and autonomy (versus dependency) as well as conserve limited resources for those truly requiring longer treatments.

Powerful experience produces new learning, not just recognition and explanation (Hoyt, 1986; Whitaker and Malone, 1953). Many effective therapies, whatever their length of treatment, help patients access inner strengths and revise the stories that structure their functioning. This appears to hold across the cases presented here. There are various other methods of potential planned SST—such as eye movement desensitization and reprocessing (Butler, 1993; Shapiro, 1989, 1991, in press; Lipke and Botkin, 1992), many of the techniques of neurolinguistic programming (Bandler and Grinder, 1985; Andreas and Andreas, 1989), and the Callahan (1992) "Five-Minute Phobia Cure"—that appear to operate at an energic and/or information-processing level. Another method, based on behavior therapy principles, has been described by Azrin and Nunn (1973) for the elimination of nervous habits and tics. Whatever the putative "mechanism" of change, the patient still winds up with a different construction of reality. Even in the simplest cases of specific skill training and rational problem solving, the patient gets to reexperience himself or herself as competent and thoughtful. Never underestimate the power of the "common factors" of respectful listening, seeking strengths, and practical problem solving (Barber, 1990; Spoerl, 1975; Talmon, 1990, 1993).

Again, it is important to recognize that we are not trying to "cure" patients, nor are we claiming that one session is enough for everyone or that as much can be accomplished in one visit as in many. The choice of a single session (or more, or less) should, whenever possible, be left to the patient to make. "Let's see what we can get done today" is much more "user friendly" and likely to succeed than the resistance-stimulating "We're only going to meet one time." Most effective SST is thus *not* time-limited therapy; it is open-ended. Suggesting the possibility of one session may provide structure and promote change, but it is the patient who may elect to stop (or continue) after one visit.

SST is the modal or most frequent form of psychological treatment. It is probably the oldest, and now appears to be the newest as well. This "discovery" of the potential power of one therapeutic meeting is not just a result of market forces or the development of new treatment methodologies and a shift to a nonpathological model of human functioning. It is very much a result of the public's desire for efficacious and cost-effective psychological help and a recognition that with a little guidance many people can "take the ball and run."[10] While traditional training, certain theoretical obligations, and some fee-for-service arrangements may promote extending treatment, the data suggest that brief, even single-session, therapy will be helpful for many people and that many people want it (Butler, 1992; Goode, 1992; Zimmerman, 1992). With so many people needing our services, it is important to remain open-minded and to look for ways to assist patients as efficiently as possible. We may have to treat them briefly, even if it helps.

Notes

1. This basic pattern, that psychotherapy (not necessarily one session) reduces unnecessary medical visits, is called the "medical utilization offset phenomenon" and is one of the most robust findings in the research literature. It has been replicated approximately sixty times (see Cummings, 1991a; Holden and Blose, 1987; Mumford and others, 1984).

2. The "corrective emotional experience" (Alexander and French, 1946) that may occur when a patient's negative expectations are dramatically disconfirmed can be understood as an event that results in a salutary narrative shift. The old "story" or "beliefs" are seen as no longer tenable.

As discussed at length elsewhere (Hoyt, Rosenbaum, and Talmon, 1992, p. 83), this is what happens in Victor Hugo's *Les Miserables,* the classic example of a corrective emotional experience cited by Franz Alexander. As readers of the novel and viewers of the popular musical version will recall, the Bishop in the story treats the protagonist, Jean Valjean, with unexpected kindness, reawakening in the hero a spirit of goodness. In regular clinical practice such sudden and dramatic shifts may be hard to come by or be less durable, especially with patients who may have strongly held negative views of self and others. Such folks, who are sometimes referred to as "personality disordered" (see Chapter Nineteen), often require more time and support as they revise (learn and test) new schemas and behaviors.

3. The negotiation of achievable goals is a major key to working efficaciously, whatever the length of treatment. It quickly and actively involves the patient; engenders hope and energy by envisioning a better, obtainable future; and helps keep treatment brief by establishing a reachable end point. Haley well describes the importance of framing a problem in such a way that it can be solved: "If therapy is to end properly, it must begin properly—by negotiating a solvable problem. . . . The act of therapy begins with the way the problem is examined" (1977, p. 9; see also especially Haley, 1989). Writers such as de Shazer (1985) and O'Hanlon and Weiner-Davis (1989), among others, have suggested a number of questions that help client and therapist orient toward better times ahead. Some useful ones might include: What's your goal and how will we know when you have reached it? What will be some of the first signs that you are doing better? When X is no longer a problem, how will you be functioning differently? How will we know when we can stop meeting like this? Suppose tonight while you're sleeping a miracle occurs and the problem is gone—how will you notice?

4. A study by Jacobson (1968) at the Beth Israel Hospital in Boston examined the effects of two hour-long evaluation

interviews. It was found that many patients benefited significantly from such a brief psychiatric encounter. In his discussion, Jacobson considers what might be the amount of time for a useful "minimal contact" and suggests, "It may be that one-half hour is too short a time to establish a working relationship with most patients, although it may be sufficient to continue one already established. An hour may not be the optimum time either, and more effective interventions might be made with an even longer initial time span. The factors of duration and frequency of interviews, often practiced as 50-minute rituals, require further scrutiny."

5. Another successful SST approach has been reported by Swinson, Soulios, Cox, and Kuch (1992) who found that patients just beginning to have panic attacks who were instructed to reexpose themselves to the stressful situation until the anxiety decreased did far better on follow-up (in terms of depression, agoraphobic avoidance, and panic frequency) than did patients who were simply reassured.

6. In Friedman's fine book, *The New Language of Change* (1993, p. vi), there is a wonderful *New Yorker* cartoon in which a woman preparing to leave her uncomprehending husband says, "I'm sorry, Herbert, but you're no longer part of the story I want to tell about myself."

7. This was an adaptation of de Shazer's "Miracle Question" (1985) and of its progenitor, Erickson's "Crystal Ball Technique" (1954).

8. Another single-session hypnotherapy was recently reported by Greenleaf (1993) of a young woman troubled with fears and fainting spells. After consultation with her neurologist, the therapist took a future-oriented approach that, within the context of a respectful therapeutic relationship, helped the patient visualize and move into a more successful future. For many other examples of hypnotic and directive brief interventions, of course, the casework of Milton Erickson (Haley, 1973; O'Hanlon and Hexum, 1990; see also Lankton and Erickson, 1994) is a source nonpareil.

9.   Clinicians make frequent use of single-session consultation, speaking with a colleague to get some ideas, techniques, and motivation to carry on work with a particular client. Patients may at times use our services in a similar manner.

10. In the course of our SST study my colleagues, Moshe Talmon, Bob Rosenbaum, and I made a "parallel process" recognition that in many ways typifies a very useful attitude for being brief and effective. Sometimes one or two therapists would observe a case in treatment through a one-way mirror and phone in suggestions to the therapist. This was seldom helpful if the proffered idea was fundamentally different from what the therapist was attempting to do, e.g., suggesting Gestalt-type work when the therapist was taking a psychodynamic tack, or suggesting some kind of dynamic interpretation when the therapist was working strategically to change an interactional pattern. We found it much more helpful if we listened respectfully to our colleagues and tried to assist them in where they were going, not where our pet theories or techniques might suggest. In similar fashion, we find we do better for patients if we help them get to where their informed choices take them.

CHAPTER TEN

Managed Care, HMOs, and the Ericksonian Perspective

I would like to highlight some of the parallels that exist between Ericksonian therapy, as I understand it, and the emerging field of managed mental health care. It has been very helpful to me to recognize these connections, and it is my hope that as they see essential commonalities, therapists working in HMOs and other managed-care settings will become more familiar with the application of Ericksonian approaches and that Erickson-oriented therapists will participate more in professional opportunities within the managed-care movement.

Essential Characteristics of Ericksonian Therapy

What is an "Ericksonian" perspective? What are the defining characteristics that make something Ericksonian? A good summary of the major features (or essences) of an Ericksonian approach is provided by Lankton (1990), who identified seven key aspects:

1. *Nonpathology-based model.* Problems are seen as part of, and a result of, attempts at adaptation. While there can be debate (Fisch, 1990; de Shazer, 1990) about whether Erickson construed problems as essentially intrapsychic or in

Note: Reprinted, with changes, from Hoyt, M. F. "Managed Care, HMOs, and the Ericksonian Perspective." *Ericksonian Monographs,* 1995, *10,* 25–36. Used by permission of the publisher.

    Case Five is included and reprinted, with changes, from Hoyt, M. F., "Two Cases of Brief Therapy in an HMO," in R. A. Wells and V. J. Giannetti (eds.), *Casebook of the Brief Psychotherapies.* Copyright 1993 by Plenum. Used by permission of the publisher.

broader systems terms, symptoms are seen as essentially natural (but limiting) responses of unique individuals, and "Hence, psychotherapy should be formulated to meet the uniqueness of the individual's needs" (Erickson, in Zeig, 1982, p. vii).

2. *Indirection.* This concerns itself with helping an individual or members of a family discover talents and resources, options and answers, seemingly without the aid of the therapist.

3. *Utilization.* This involves using whatever the patient brings to the office (understandings, behaviors, motivations) as part of the treatment.

4. *Action.* Clients are expected and encouraged to quickly get into actions related to the desired goals—this is a basic ingredient of successful brief therapy regardless of theoretical orientation (Budman, Friedman, and Hoyt, 1992).

5. *Strategic.* Therapists are active in setting or initiating the stages of therapy. The therapist takes responsibility for influencing the patient (Haley, 1973; Rosenbaum, 1990).

6. *Future orientation.* The focus is on action and experience in the present and future rather than the past.

7. *Enchantment.* Treatment engages the mind, appeals to the patient, and "captures the ear of the listener" (Gustafson, 1986).

Lankton goes on to emphasize that Ericksonian techniques are custom-fitted to the needs of the particular case, and he notes a number of interventions that are associated with the approach and originated in Erickson's practice: "These include paradoxical assignments, ambiguous function assignments, skill-building assignments, therapeutic metaphors, anecdotes, conscious-unconscious dissociation, hypnotic induction, therapeutic binds, indirect suggestion, and reframing" (p. 366).

All of these interventions—hypnosis and strategic assignments and the like—are valuable ways to get people to have experiences that put them in touch with their latent or overlooked abilities, but they are just methods to an end. For Erickson, I think, the basic problem was not pathology or defect but *rigidity,* the idea that people get "stuck" by failing to use a range of skills, competencies, and learnings that they have but are not applying. The basic principle is thus *utilization,* with treatment being personalized to elicit or capitalize on each individual's useful resources. The essential paradigmatic shift is from deficits to strengths, from problems to solutions, from past to future (Fisch, 1990), utilizing whatever the patient brings in the service of healthful change (de Shazer, 1988). The therapy is "constructive" (Hoyt, 1994c, in press c). As Erickson said: "Patients have problems because their conscious programming has too severely limited their capacities. The solution is to help them break through the limitations of their conscious attitudes to free their unconscious potential for problem solving" (Erickson, Rossi, and Rossi, 1976, p. 18).

The Ericksonian Perspective
in the Context of Managed Care

There is already a vast clinical literature that includes various applications of Ericksonian methods in HMOs (e.g., Budman and Gurman, 1988; Budman, Hoyt, and Friedman, 1992; Chubb, 1983; Friedman and Fanger, 1991; Hoyt, 1993b; Hoyt, Rosenbaum, and Talmon, 1992; Kreilkamp, 1989; Rosenbaum, 1990, 1993; Talmon, 1990). You may already see some of the connections I have in mind—and some others that I don't—but let me suggest a few. It should be obvious, of course, that in the following clinical fragments most of the substance and subtleties of each case—such as tone, timing, nonverbal communication, and much more—can only be implied. All treatments occurred within the context of a large health maintenance organization, the Kaiser Permanente Medical Center in Hayward, California.

Case One

A man in his eighties was referred by his internist. Various oncology treatments had brought about some unwelcome physical changes and had reduced his vigor. Antidepressant

medication had restored some of his energies, but he was demoralized. When my colleague, Norman Weinstein, M.D., and
I met with the patient, we learned that he had been the national
leader of a large Eastern European church.[1] He had escaped
and relocated to the United States just before the crush of
Communist rule and had been a religious prelate in this country as well. He was now semiretired. With recent political developments, he had been invited to return to his native land,
where he had not been for many years, for a triumphant re-
union at which he would be feted and asked to deliver an
important sermon. He was interested and had his wife's support, but he was so discouraged by his appearance and weak-
ened powers that they were sadly and reluctantly preparing to
decline going. Previously a vital and charismatic man, he la-
mented: "They remember a strong man, but look at me."
"Yes, pride is important, especially when you think of how
much it would mean to them to see that you have endured
and still care for them," we reframed. We then switched to
talking with one another about the beauties of Eastern Europe,
the pleasures of speaking one's own language, and the need
for spiritual guidance during times of great change. Our patient's ears pricked up. We then asked our patient if he would,
at a subsequent appointment, provide us with some relevant
scriptural references to use with demoralized medical patients. Not wanting to appear transparent and not wanting to
miss an opportunity for personal growth, we then confessed
that our curiosity was more personal: we needed help coming
to grips with some adversities in our own lives, including
various middle-aged health signals. From his senior perspective, could he offer some guidance? Three more sessions were
held, two weeks apart. In each session he read selected Bible
passages and discussed them with us in detail. Treatment was
effective: we felt encouraged; and the patient made his journey back home. Upon his return he paid us a follow-up visit
in which he reported that the trip had been very satisfying,
successful, and at times quite arduous. His eyes twinkled. He
acknowledged our "good care," as he graciously called it, and
appropriately added, "Thank God I went!"

Case Two

A couple came in with their nineteen-year-old son, a college student who lived at home with them. As they had been for some time, they were all arguing about curfews, discipline, "respecting the rules of the house," and the like. When asked if I had any children, I gestured to a photograph of my son on the desk, "who's still little and dependent, since he's only five." I went on to talk about a bird's nest we had seen and how smart Mother Nature was the way she designed things, like how it worked that a little bird would stay in its nest but when it got big enough to make things crowded in the nest it was big enough to fly on its own, and so its readiness to go was built in and signalled by its size and neither the grown-up birds nor the grown-up bird needed to be told or could help it, since it was natural, and so on. I prattled on for a bit, sort of like an ornithological Lieutenant Columbo, and finally stopped myself. I shifted around in my chair, seemingly pulling myself together and returning to the topic at hand. "It's nice to see such a loving, close family. So, who's going to finally give in?" I asked, and pursued a line of questioning that only escalated the fight and demonstrated the intractability of the conflict. A follow-up phone call six weeks later revealed that a week after the session everyone had agreed that it would be best if the son lived elsewhere. He had moved, and everyone was happy. We'll never know, but the bird's-nest metaphor, with its various embedded suggestions, seemed to prefigure and guide their conflict resolution in a developmentally appropriate direction. The "empty nest syndrome" was better than the "overcrowded nest syndrome."

Case Three

A woman sought therapy to overcome her great anxiety driving across bridges, a problem that can be of considerable inconvenience for someone living in the San Francisco Bay area. The conventional cognitive-behavioral relaxation-and-gradual-exposure treatment was potentiated by a number of Erick-sonian interventions (see Feldman, 1988). Her attention was refocused first through "splitting the symptom" by dividing a bridge into boringly small segments, and later by having her mentally "compress" a bridge trip into "mere seconds" while greatly expanding the attention given to the pleasures beyond the bridges (such as visiting grandchildren and shopping trips). "Pseudo-orientation in time" (Erickson, 1954) was used, having the patient repeatedly visualize and describe aloud various bridges as they would appear from the far side in the near future when she was at ease. Since she wanted the best treat-ment, she was persuaded that more data would be necessary about her reactions at different times and locations, and so she began driving—sometimes quite anxiously—across several bridges at varying times of day and night. This experiment—which was designed to put the cure before the treatment—promoted her desensitizing exposure and convinced her that she could drive with reasonable comfort as long as she could avoid the "ordeal" (Haley, 1984) of rush-hour traffic.

Case Four

Requests for psychological consultation from a medical-surgical ward sometimes occur when interference develops in the patient-caregiver cooperation that good health care requires (see Chapter Eleven). Such was the situation involving a hospitalized medical patient whose many anxious demands for attention had finally overtaxed her nurses' sympathies. They were certainly not neglecting her, but after many visits to her room without seeing any medical urgency they were busy attending to other patients, a situation that resulted in the patient feeling aban-doned and increasingly anxious. She was almost constantly ac-tivating her call light, and the situation was escalating. The level of mutual irritation was temporarily so high that simple reas-surance to the patient and a direct request to the nurses for extraordinary goodwill and increased attention were not likely to succeed. The patient was offered a small dose of tranquilizing medication, which she accepted, and an order was written (with an ostensible medical rationale) for the nurses to check the patient's vital signs every fifteen minutes. Prescribing "kind hand-holding" was not likely to succeed, but this indirection resulted in the patient being repeatedly and gently attended to, including physical contact as her heart sounds, blood pressure, and pulse were taken. This attention, combined with the medication, soothed the patient (Auer, 1988; Goldsmith, 1988). After two hours, peace and cooperation were restored, and the special nursing orders were discontinued. The remainder of the patient's hospital stay was unremarkable.

Case Five

Sue Smith (a pseudonym), a thirty-eight-year-old woman, was brought to our HMO psychiatry department by her parents late one afternoon on a walk-in crisis basis. She and her husband had not been getting along for the past year, with him becoming increasingly angry and critical and her becoming increasingly timid and incompetent. Many of their quarrels focused on how poorly she managed their household and how she "failed to control" their two children. A former alcohol abuser who had been through an outpatient alcohol treatment program and had been abstinent for several years, Sue had recently resumed excessive alcohol consumption to calm and numb herself. The husband had two days before taken the kids and moved out. Sue's parents became alarmed when she did not answer their repeated phone calls, so they went to her home to check. They found her huddled in a corner of the house, quite anxious, fearful, and overwhelmed.

A staff psychologist in our Chemical Dependency Program initially met with the patient. He recommended that she actively participate in the Chemical Dependency Early Recovery Treatment Group, which was scheduled to begin the next week. He also determined that her current level of alcohol abuse did not present any medical risk for detoxification. It was clear that her level of psychosocial dysfunction went beyond her alcohol problem, with her degree of fear and dysphoria making him consider the possible necessity of a short-term psychiatric hospitalization. I was called for consultation.

Entering my colleague's office, I saw a timid, somewhat beaten-down looking woman. The psychologist began to "present" the "case" to me, but I quickly interrupted him and asked the patient why she was there. She hesitated—and I had to ask the other psychologist not to talk for her—and then somewhat haltingly at first, but with increasing fluency, she told her story with some prompting. "I can't do anything right—at least that's what Jim says, and he took the kids," she cried. With lots of active questioning and supportive listening, we soon learned that she felt "stupid," that she had been working as a clerk, and that she desperately wanted to see her kids (ages eight and two). Careful questioning revealed no psychotic thinking and no suicidal ideas, impulses, or history.

I told her that I didn't know yet what would happen with her and the kids, but that "a first step will involve you and your husband. Obviously, you've been having lots of troubles. Maybe we can help you there. Has he said anything about counseling?" She responded, "He said he was leaving until I get help. He said he doesn't want a divorce, but he's had it with all the hassling and the kids running all over me and me being so upset." I then asked where her husband was right then. "Probably at his sister's, with the kids." With her permission, I called the sister. Jim wasn't in, but the sister offered to phone Jim at work and have him call me. About ten minutes later, Jim called. I told him, "Sue is here. She's pretty stressed out, but she's OK, and she wants help getting things back together. Are you interested in counseling to help your marriage and your family? I have an appointment open in two days, at 6 P.M. Do you want it, for you and Sue?"

He accepted the appointment. Sue asked if he would bring the kids over later that day, and he agreed to.

We then asked Sue's parents, who were in the waiting room, to join us. Her father appeared a bit gruff and her mother somewhat anxiously overprotective, although they were both genuinely concerned and distressed by the crisis in the family and the obvious unhappiness of their daughter. I explained to them, with Sue listening, that we had carefully evaluated the situation and had several recommendations: (1) Sue, while "unhappy and demoralized," did not need to be "locked up" in a psychiatric hospital; (2) Sue had agreed to stop all alcohol use and would be following up in our Chemical Dependency Program the next week; and (3) I had spoken with Sue's husband, and she and Jim would be coming in for marital counseling beginning in two days. I conveyed to all present my belief that there was some hard work ahead, and that with everyone's effort we would see what could be done. The parents were relieved, promised to be very available especially during the next few days, and offered a little homily about "everyone having problems" and how sure they were that Sue and Jim could, with counseling, "be as happy as they used to be." I had Sue repeat the plan, reinforced the importance of both her and Jim attending the upcoming session, and reminded her that she could come or call back sooner as needed. They left.

Two days later Sue and Jim were sitting in the waiting room at the appointed hour. Once they were inside my office, I asked Jim what his understanding was about why they were here. He started by saying it was "to learn how to get along better," but he soon refocused his energy on describing his wife's faults. She began to sink visibly. I halted the discussion, noted that "when you point a finger at someone, there are three pointing back at you," and asked him to talk about his role in the problems they had. He acknowledged his being a "perfectionist" and "getting real upset and angry" and asked several specific questions (mostly for his wife's edification) about how to manage the kids, set limits, and so on. Sue entered into the discussion and said that she didn't try to do much disciplining with the kids anymore "because no matter what I do, it isn't good enough, and Jim tells me so right in front of them." This led us into a discussion of what professionals might call *systemic logic* or *circular causality:* "So you're saying that you don't stand up to the kids and then Jim criticizes you and they see they don't have to respect you, and so they act worse and then Jim gets mad and you feel bad and do even less, and then the kids walk over you and Jim blows his top and undermines you, and the madder Jim gets, the sadder you get and the badder the kids

get, and around and around it goes, right? What are you going
to do?" Their mouths dropped open; they stopped arguing and
looked at each other. Jim, to Sue: "He's right. It sounds like
he's been watching in our house!" Sue, to Jim: "We both need
to stop it." Jim, to me: "We'd like help, but we've been doing
this so long I'm not sure we can really change. Can we?" Me,
to them: "It is a mess, but if you're both serious and really
willing to learn and do something different, there's hope. I've
seen bigger messes. I'd say there's more chance of you guys
getting it together and growing up then there is, say, of the
Communist Party getting thrown out of Russia!" They both
seemed to "get it" (fortunately) and laughed.

This launched us into the nuts-and-bolts work of helping
them to improve their communication and parenting, with
both needing to strengthen certain skills and make considerable changes—including Jim struggling to accept Sue and feel
useful without being dominating or undermining and Sue
learning to assert herself without collapsing or engaging in self-
sabotage. Rapid (and accurate) assessment of individual and
family resources indicated that Sue could be maintained as an
outpatient through the family crisis (see Pittman, Flomenhoft,
and DeYoung, 1990). Indeed, hospitalization would have further invalidated her: her self-image ("stupid") and her husband's view of her ("incompetent") might not have recovered
from the stigma of psychiatric hospitalization. For therapy to
be as efficient ("brief") as possible for the Smith family, multiple interventions were used concurrently to impact several
interrelated problems. This is consistent with the idea of Budman and Gurman (1988, p. 6) that treatment be time sensitive
and rationed in a manner likely to "achieve maximum benefit
with the lowest investment of therapist time and patient cost,
both financial and psychological." The effort was first to sta-
bilize and support, and then to engage Sue and Jim in experiences that would help them cope more skillfully and
successfully with their problems in living. From initial contact,
the approach was to respond quickly to avoid further regression, to set clearly defined goals and engage in specific problem
solving, and to foster the patients' sense of hope, competence,

and responsibility for the course and "outcome" of their therapy (and lives).

Case Six

A woman arrived in our emergency room in a somewhat hysterical state, transported by an ambulance from a nearby medical clinic where her family had taken her. When I arrived at the E.R. the physician on duty warned me that "it's going to be a long night." Meaning well, he was anxious to administer some Valium but had held off pending psychiatric consultation. A paramedic was with the patient in an examination room attempting to talk with her. I glanced in and saw that while not as upset as she apparently had been when she first arrived, she was still quite overwrought. The paramedic continued trying to calm her while I sought the husband in the waiting room.

He seemed like a reasonable and sympathetic fellow and related a recent complicated family history of escalating conflict. A sister-in-law had demanded a large personal loan from the patient, which she had refused as both unreasonable and financially impossible. The sister-in-law had, since that time, been making various accusations and vindictively attempting to turn family members against the patient. Described by her husband as "very sensitive" and "close to her family," the patient had found this situation very distressing. A few hours before arriving in our E.R., she had received from her antagonist a threatening letter with an announcement of plans for a lawsuit. At this news, she "snapped." She had been crying uncontrollably, shaking, and unable to walk when her family took her to the medical clinic near their home.

The husband indicated that the patient's father, father-in-law, and mother-in-law were all concerned and present at the E.R. "Will seeing you calm her or just get her more upset?" I asked. He assured me that he could talk with her if given a chance without family interference. I got the paramedic out of the room, thanked him, and brought in the husband. The wife started to get more upset, but I raised my hand and quickly said, "Stop! I have an important question." She hesitated, and

I asked quickly, "Is this your husband? He says he's been married to you for fifteen years. Is that true?" She nodded, and I
continued: "Do you love him? Does he love you? Will you let
him talk with you in a way to help you?" Her emotional "roll"
was disrupted. The yeses tumbled out. I then further distracted
the patient from her upsetness with some banter about the
emergency room plumbing (the husband was a plumber by
trade), got them both laughing, and then asked her, "Is he a
good guy?" When she answered positively, I quickly said to
the husband, "Good. I knew you were the right man for the
case. I'll leave you two alone," and departed, pulling the curtain.

A few minutes later when I checked she was somewhat less
distressed, and they were having a heart-to-heart talk. I chatted
up the E.R. doctor to buy some time. In another fifteen minutes
the husband emerged and asked if the father and in-laws could
see her. He and I got the folks. I let the husband do most of
the talking. When they asked, "Doctor, is she all right?" I said,
"She's OK but is very upset because she thinks you're mad at
her and hate her." They protested and strongly indicated their
love and concern. The husband encouraged them to tell her
so. As we walked into the patient's room I announced, "There
are some people here who love you and want to talk with you.
It's nice to see such a good family," and I left. About fifteen
minutes later I looked in. Something had happened. Tears and
hugs were in evidence all around the room. "I knew this wasn't
a case for a doctor," I remarked. "It's a case for the love of a
family." They appreciated the recognition. A half hour later the
patient and her family, happily reunited, left the E.R. On the
way out the husband shook my hand. "You did a great job," I
said, and thanked him. Like Erickson's famous story of returning the stray horse by simply keeping things on track (Gordon,
1978), the key was remembering to use the available family
resources and to stay out of nature's way.

Solving the so-called presenting complaint, directing treatment so that the patient rapidly gets engaged in therapeutic
activities, using patients' capacities, meeting flexibly within an
intermittent treatment model, and paying keen attention to what
works and to getting the job done are features of both Erick-

sonian and managed-care work. As Dr. Kristina Erickson (1988) has written, careful attention must be paid to the three principles of proper evaluation and creative planning, cultivating and assuring patient commitment, and an emphasis on patient strengths and tailoring treatment to the individual.

Barriers to Ericksonian Brief Therapy

Some of the various general difficulties associated with doing brief therapy include the need to overcome or suspend the self-fulfilling long-term treatment assumptions of much traditional psychotherapy training, the demands for greater therapist alertness and focused activity, potential financial and emotional disincentives, and termination problems with frequent attachment and letting go (see Chapter Seventeen). As noted by Johnson (1988, pp. 411–412), doing so-called Ericksonian strategic or naturalistic therapy has the following added potential disadvantages: (1) unnatural, sometimes nonintuitive behavior is required from the therapist; (2) for many of us, strategic therapy often requires consultative help (Dr. Kristina Erickson's comments [1988, p. 383] about seeing her father spend hours preparing a particular intervention are instructive); (3) there is still little professional support for strategic interventions, which may be seen by the uninitiated as strange or unconventional and disruptive[2] (exactly!); (4) patients give the therapist less credit, which tends to happen with a minimal-intervention approach that empowers patients rather than promoting their dependency and the therapist's authority; and (5) if a therapist does this kind of work long enough he or she begins to have some success with cases other therapists didn't succeed with, the result being that the therapist gets referred more and more "hard" cases while others get or keep the relatively "easy" ones. As the managed-care field evolves I expect that effective therapists will be rewarded with more referrals of all types, however, and the utilization review process will be reduced so that clinicians known for their competencies will be able to proceed without undue interference. Standards of care and accountability are important, lest ineffective or even destructive practices be tolerated in the name of "trusting the unconscious" (Hoyt, 1989a). Still, recently rereading O'Hanlon and Hexum's (1990) wonderful compendium, *An Uncommon Casebook: The Complete Clinical Work of Milton H. Erickson, M.D.*, I chuckled at the thought of Dr. Erickson having to provide *DSM-III-R* diagnoses and explain his treatment plans to justify "preauthorization of services"!

Bridges to the Future

Psychological practice in the years ahead will be increasingly influenced by managed-care forces (Cummings, 1986; Zimet, 1989). Consistent with the principles of therapy in such settings and especially compatible with the HMO ideal of *health* maintenance are cost-effective treatments that strategically amplify and utilize clients' healthful resources and responses. Assisting clients to achieve their self-defined goals through the facilitation of present and future-oriented actions and experience increases the cooperativeness of treatment and, hence, the likelihood of therapeutic efficiency (Erickson, 1988; Lankton, 1990; Zeig, 1990). The characteristics and goals of HMO practice and Ericksonian therapy are highly congruent, including the orientation toward problem solving, the involvement of patients in their own care, the emphasis on a life cycle or developmental model, and the use of interdisciplinary cooperation and treatment planning. HMOs and related managed-care settings should provide fertile grounds for the application of the Ericksonian perspective.

Notes

1. As my colleague Robert Rosenbaum (personal communication) has noted, having others available for consultation and co-therapy can be an advantage of working in an HMO, although attention must be paid to allowing enough time for extended discussion and/or treatment planning.

2. Along related lines, see Sluzki's discussion (1992) of the profound institutional impact that can result when there is a shift to a more collaborative and egalitarian solution-oriented patient-provider relationship.

CHAPTER ELEVEN

Conjoint Patient-Staff Interview
in Hospital Case Management

with Paul K. Opsvig and Norman W. Weinstein

Among the opportunities and challenges of consultation-liaison psychiatry is the call for assistance in the management of "difficult" hospital cases. A patient may refuse to cooperate with necessary medical-surgical procedures and regimens, oftentimes as a response to feelings of helplessness and loss of control and to generalized anxiety (Simmons and others, 1979). When the patient's behavior becomes too disturbing to the treatment staff, a request may be issued for psychiatric consultation.

Such situations may be understood and treated from a social-systems perspective (Glazer and Astrachan, 1978; Firman and Kaplan, 1978) rather than an individual (unilateral) pathology model. The patient's refusal to enact a "good patient" role results in a breakdown in the complementary role relationship system of "patient" and "healer," and the patient's demonstrative challenge to the effectiveness and competency of the medical staff results in his being labeled as "manipulative" or "combative" (Mackenzie, Rosenberg, Bergen, and Tucker, 1978). Once the relationship has gone awry, a volley of apparent and not so obvious mutual antagonisms and misperceptions may develop between patient and staff. The psychiatric consultant

Note: Reprinted, with changes, from Hoyt, M. F., Opsvig, P. K., and Weinstein, N. W. "Conjoint Patient-Staff Interview in Hospital Case Management." *International Journal of Psychiatry in Medicine,* 1981, *11,* 83–87. Copyright 1981 by Baywood Publishing Company, Inc. Used by permission of the coauthors and the publisher.

Paul K. Opsvig, M.D., and Norman W. Weinstein, M.D., are staff psychiatrists at the Kaiser Permanente Medical Center in Hayward, California.

may need to address both sides of this counterproductive reverberation before the system will be able to return to its explicit purpose of effective health care. This communication describes and illustrates with a brief case report an approach we have found useful in the resolution of such conflicts.

Case Report

The patient was a man in his early twenties. He had fractured his right femur, right ulna, and several ribs when, while under the influence of alcohol, he had driven his motorcycle into the rear of a parked vehicle. After a visit to a local emergency room, he was transferred to our hospital, where he was confined to bed and skeletal traction under the care of an orthopedic-surgical team. Almost upon arrival, he began hurling verbal abuse at the nursing staff and was soon banging his encasted arm against the wall while demanding constant attention and increased dosages of pain medication. The staff attempted to "understand" and "humor" him for two days, until he used his cigarette lighter to burn down his traction lines and attempted to get out of bed in order to walk out of the hospital. At this point, a request was issued for psychiatric consultation.

A regular member of the Department of Psychiatry's Crisis and Consultation Team, a clinical psychologist [Hoyt], went to the ward where the patient and staff were, accompanied in this case by a psychiatrist [Opsvig] who was getting acquainted with the consultation service and who could provide clinical backup, including medical and psychiatric skills as needed. Upon entering the ward, the consultants met first with the nursing staff, immediately asking, "What problems are you and the patient having?" (rather than, "What's wrong with the patient?"). This provided a context in which the nurses were able to reveal and ventilate their frustrations and anger about the patient, while indicating their perceptions about his behavior and motivations and describing their responses to him. They were much relieved by the presence of our authority, and after a period of discussion felt encouraged by our offer to "Help you and the patient work together better."

The consultants then left the nursing group and went into

the patient's room. He appeared a medium-sized fellow, flat on his back with his leg up in traction. His hair was somewhat unkempt, but he didn't seem to be the wild man we had just heard about in the corridor. We introduced ourselves and in a friendly way asked him to tell us, "What's happening?" He then proceeded to describe his tale, a mixture of complaints of neglect about the nursing staff, requests for additional pain medication, and some braggadocio about his motorcycle wreck and his attempt to walk out of the hospital. He seemed obviously needy and threatened by his vulnerable state, feelings he attempted to ward off through his tough demeanor. The consultants listened sympathetically, and one then said, "Yeah, it's going to be tough. I guess you'll have to decide if you're tough enough to take it. You know, even Clint Eastwood has to lay back sometimes." This confirmation of his "tough" image seemed reassuring, and the patient began to engage his dependency needs more openly, describing a rather miserable and deprived childhood and recent life situation. After a bit, the consultant interjected, "Well, we could discuss that sometime, but first you'll have to decide whether you can cope with being here for four or six weeks or so. Maybe I could help, if you wanted to get along here." The patient complained of his unhappy lot. The consultant nodded and said, "You're right. You've got two choices, you know. It's *not* going to be fun. While you're here you could either have an absolutely terrible time, or merely a miserable time. It's up to you." While the patient was mulling that over, the second consultant commented to the first, "Maybe it's too much to expect that he can do this. He'll have to decide if he's got it in him, to cope with being here." After some further discussion, the patient saw his situation more realistically, and perhaps stimulated by our comments, he decided to make a "go" of it. A therapeutic alliance was thus established. We then discussed a number of "coping strategies" he could use to get through his time there—visitors, reading, TV, the telephone, a roommate, some sessions of therapy. We also discussed his need for good nursing and hence the importance of his shifting behaviors so as to secure and maintain the nurses' attention and goodwill toward him.

This did not end the consultation, however. The consultant went back to the nursing staff and announced, "Mr. X sees things differently now and would like to work things out with you." The five on-duty nurses that would attend him were then led into the patient's room, and the consultant served as a facilitator and group therapist. The patient apologized to the nurses, they accepted, and an intense, sometimes good-humored discussion ensued. The theme was developed of "Let's face it, we're all in this together, we're really on the same team." The patient expressed his need for attention, and the nurses agreed to look in on him regularly if he'd be "nice." The conjoint interview provided both sides with an opportunity to reassess the other. The consultant was able to observe their actual interaction and to help correct or short-circuit problems. For example, one of the nurses commented, in a pseudo-sympathetic tone, "Oh, it's going to be so hard for you, especially now that the weather's nice." The consultant intervened directly ("Don't rub it in") and commented that remarks like that weren't going to help teamwork. The other nurses agreed, and the patient-staff alliance was strengthened.

The patient's subsequent hospital course was uneventful, from both a medical and case management perspective. The "team" cooperation was generally excellent, and the two or three instances of irritable flare-ups that occurred were minor and handled by the parties involved. The patient requested and received medication as needed, including psychotropics to aid relaxation; he was pleased to have the benefits of sedation during his bed confinement, a use of medication that further strengthened the team's working alliance. The consultant visited the ward regularly and saw the patient occasionally for supportive psychotherapy. The patient resolved to take care of his drinking problem, and he enrolled in the hospital's alcohol treatment program. On the last day of his hospitalization, the nursing staff and patient reconvened with the consultant for a mutually appreciative leave taking. Both sides expressed gratitude for having had the opportunity to talk together. As one nurse put it, "It was really something. We were all face to face. It made us see each other as people."

Discussion

We have described a "problem-solving" approach oriented to-ward meeting the mutual needs of hospital patients and staff. A call for psychiatric assistance in case management often in-dicates that a patient has engendered strong emotional reactions and has disrupted the work roles of the treatment staff. In such instances, separate preparatory consultations with patient and staff will be valuable. For example, in the case reported here, separate interviews allowed each "side" to form a trusting, co-operative alliance with the consultants and to ventilate feelings and misperceptions without adding to the spiral of mutual an-tagonism. The consultants were also able to assess resources in the immediate situation, such as the patient's desire to prove his "manliness," that could be used therapeutically. These pre-paratory interviews thus set the stage for a conjoint patient-staff meeting where actual maladaptive transactions could be ob-served, confronted, and corrected.

This approach emphasized the *liaison* role of the psychiatric consultant, that is, the function of mediator who links up groups for the purpose of effective collaboration (Lipowski, 1974). As such, this approach should be distinguished from a description (Gans, 1979) of a consultee-attended interview in which a co-operative patient is psychiatrically interviewed in the consultee's presence as part of an experiential teaching method. The pres-ent approach, in which the psychiatric consultant intervenes to restructure the patient-staff relationship (Glazer and Strauss, 1964), is an innovation to be considered when communication and cooperation of the patient-staff system have become dys-functional.

CHAPTER TWELVE

❖

Aspects of Termination in a Time-Limited Brief Psychotherapy

So teach us to number our days that we may get us a heart of wisdom.

−Moses (Psalm 90:12)

Therapeutic work is never totally finished or "resolved," of course, just as life must be continually re-solved—a reality Freud (1937) acknowledged in his masterful essay "Analysis Terminable and Interminable." However, much of what has been accomplished in psychotherapy can be either consolidated or compromised in the work of termination. The end phase is not merely a recapitulation and nailing down of earlier work. Rather, all the work of the therapy may be seen as prologue to (and part of) the termination. With the impending loss of the therapeutic relationship the patient's fears and conflicts are restimulated, especially as they pertain to earlier losses and struggles over issues of separation-individuation. Feelings of grief and sadness and possibly guilt and anger will often surface, all signaling the need to mourn the passing of the relationship. The way in which these reemergent issues are handled will do much to determine how closely the ultimate

Note: Reprinted, with changes, from Hoyt, M. F. "Aspects of Termination in a Time-Limited Brief Psychotherapy." *Psychiatry,* 1979, *42,* 208–219. Copyright 1979 by William Alanson White Psychiatric Foundation, Inc. Used by permission of the publisher.

This work, done while Dr. Hoyt was a postdoctoral fellow at the Langley Porter Institute of the University of California, San Francisco, was supported in part by a Clinical Research Center Grant from the National Institute of Mental Health (MH 30899-02) and by funds from the Clinical Innovation and Evaluation Training Program (MH 14609).

goal of therapy, that the patient be able to live independently and well, will be met.

These introductory remarks regarding the importance of termination apply to both long- and short-term psychotherapy. I choose to focus here on some aspects of termination in brief therapy, however, for a number of reasons. First, as Schafer (1973) points out, a great deal of psychotherapy is more or less brief, and more or less comes to an end—the ending having important and variable impact. Secondly, by its very nature, in brief therapy the issue of termination is always present; indeed, as suggested above, it is *the* issue. In light of these considerations, one is surprised by the almost total absence in the literature of extended case material describing termination of brief therapy (an exception is provided by Mann, 1973). There is an obvious need for presentation of detailed clinical reports for the purposes of illustrating various approaches and stimulating further study of the issues under examination.

This chapter describes an approach to using termination in brief psychodynamically-oriented psychotherapy to further mourning and working-through processes. Verbatim excerpts referring explicitly to the work of termination are presented from various sessions of a therapy I conducted with a woman five months after the death of her husband.

The Time-Limited Model
and the Therapeutic Use of Time

An early proponent of the use of time in therapy was Otto Rank, who was probably the first therapist to make regular conscious use of end-setting as a force in treatment.[1] Initially Rank viewed the patient's struggle with separation-individuation as being a fairly literal carryover of the biological birth trauma ([1929] 1973), but in his later, mature work (e.g., *Will Therapy*, 1936) he had revised his thinking to see the struggle around separation from the therapist more metaphorically in terms of a symbolic "rebirth" (Hoyt, 1977). For Rank, end-setting was used in the final phase of therapy to stimulate or "force" confrontation with this dependency issue. The purpose of therapy in this end phase, he contended, was to help the patient finally work through what he saw as essentially a "mother fixation," so that termination work not only meant ending treatment but also involved a positive emphasis on the patient's emerging capacities for independence (see Whitaker and Malone, 1953, especially pp. 212–214). Other writers, such as Alexander (1965) and Masserman (1965), also have emphasized the value of limiting the length of treatment as a means of promoting the patient's work toward self-reliance.[2]

The most extensive discussion of the use of time limit-setting has been presented by Mann (1973), who advocates working within an explicitly brief therapy model. Mann's view is that underlying many neurotic-type difficulties is a concern with time and problems of separation-individuation. To focus on these problems, he contracts to meet with the patient for a set number of times (typically twelve), establishing from the very beginning of therapy the date on which the therapeutic relationship will end. Whatever the manifest content of the ensuing clinical interaction, with the theme of termination always so present, this approach is seen as restimulating conflict situations related to earlier terminations. Mann reports favorable results with this method, although systematic data are not presented. This approach is both theoretically and practically appealing (it avoids drawn-out treatments and permits more patients to be seen per therapist) and is central to the case presented below.

Patients may become especially aware of the passage of time as the end of therapy approaches. How can this be understood? As Hartocollis notes, "Under normal circumstances, time remains implicit and largely unconscious; but it tends to dominate consciousness . . . under stress" (1975, p. 393). In the case of termination, the origins of much of this stress have to do with the patient relinquishing what Kaiser (1965) calls the "illusion of fusion" as the reality of separateness (from the therapist and those figures he or she may represent) becomes more undeniable. This increase in temporal awareness interdigitates nicely with the theoretical understanding (Piaget, [1927] 1969; Hartocollis, 1974) that the child's original sense of time develops out of its perception of the movement of separate (not-me) others in its environment.

A number of writers have observed the importance of engaging the patient's sense of time. For example, Whitaker and Malone contend: "Another important element . . . [is] the patient's concept of time. Any technique which succeeds in equating in the patient all time, whether past or future, with the present time, seems to have validity" (1953, p. 204). Loewald (1972, p. 408) also argues for the essential role of time in the experience of the person. Others, such as May, Angel, and Ellenberger (1958) and Becker (1973), describe the imagination of a future moment of nonbeing as a critical existential crisis for the individual. Goldberg extends this notion: "For psychotherapy to enable an individual to come to terms with the meaning of his existence, he must come to grips with the reality of nonexistence. Psychotherapy is true to this quest insofar as it is a process of termination rather than consolidation of relationship and proliferation of time" (C. Goldberg, 1975, p. 342).

Case Report

The patient was a sixty-nine-year-old widowed woman. An earlier marriage had ended in divorce twenty-five years ago, several years prior to her last marriage. She had never had children. At the time of therapy, the patient was residing with her brother and sister-in-law. She appeared to be about ten years younger than her chronological age and was keen and energetic, despite some physical ailments associated with advanced years. She was fairly articulate, seemed of somewhat above average intelligence, and appeared essentially hysterical in her interpersonal and cognitive style (Horowitz, 1976; Shapiro, 1965).

The patient came self-referred to the Stress Clinic of the Psychotherapy Study Center of the Langley Porter Institute. In an evaluation interview with a staff psychiatric social worker she indicated that two stressful life events had led to her coming to the clinic. Her husband had died five months prior to her seeking therapy. She identified as more disturbing than his death, however, his affair thirteen years earlier with a woman who was then half the age of the patient. The affair had gone on for one and a half years. The patient reported having had some suspicions, but her husband denied any involvement and refused to discuss the matter. When the affair ended, the younger woman had come to the patient's home and had sadistically given her a detailed report of the romance. After listening "in shock" for an hour, the patient had finally ordered the other woman out of her house. She recalled being terribly upset, crying and vomiting. She confronted her husband, but he had again refused to discuss the matter. These events, she reported, had "poisoned" their relationship during the last thirteen years of their marriage. Meaningful communication seldom occurred, and although she still felt "some love for the man," her liking for him was greatly diminished. She had thought of leaving him, and once even did make an attempt for two weeks, but as a woman in her late fifties she had felt restrained by her need for security and had returned. Things had been improving somewhat in the last year or two that he was alive. He had "mellowed," she said, and was more appreciative of her strong nurturing qualities. He suffered an unexpected fatal heart attack while recuperating after an accidental fall from a balcony. She was with him at home during the attack and was with him in the ambulance on the way to the hospital when he died.

She cried painfully as she referred to "the terrible emptiness, the waste of those years." Asked what his affair had meant to her, she replied (showing some keen self-understanding): "It was a crushing blow to my ego, to my self-esteem, and it devalued him in my sight. I was deflated, wiped out. I no longer felt wanted or attractive, as a person or as a woman." She acknowledged always having been "concerned" about the affair but reported that since her husband's death this preoccupation had increased and that she was experiencing "hundreds" of unbidden images per week of him with the other woman and of the woman's subsequent visit and revelations. She had grieved after the bereavement but reported that she was now rather continuously depressed and anxious and felt that "I'm stagnating . . . life has lost purpose and meaning." The affair had become "a block in my head," and she had sought therapy to know why she couldn't get it out of her mind and go on with her life.

Formulation and Treatment Approach

At initial contact the patient was undergoing what Horowitz (1976) calls a "stress response syndrome," characterized by marked cognitive-affective disruptions following a stressful life event. The difficulties of adjusting to her husband's death were compounded by the restimulation of earlier unsettled concerns with loss and betrayal. His final departure was a painful reminder of his infidelity, which had evoked in the patient feelings and self-images of being unattractive and inadequate. Normal mourning had been blocked by ambivalent feelings toward the deceased that the patient had found unacceptable to consciousness (Freud, 1917). Realizing that "my idol had feet of clay" forced her to confront the loss of an idealized romantic fantasy, and she was faced with the problem of relinquishing unfulfilled wishes (Grayson, 1970) of a happy retirement together, an especially difficult situation because the patient had depended on her husband's reactions for much of her self-image and feelings of self-worth (Pincus, 1974). In terms of Mann's model, the basic separation-individuation crisis issue was being expressed through a variety of universal conflict situations, including unresolved mourning, independence versus dependence, and adequate self-esteem versus diminished self-esteem.

The importance of termination work has also been suggested by the Tavistock studies of brief dynamic psychotherapy (Malan, 1963, 1976a, 1976b), underscoring the appropriateness here of a time-limited model. Those studies also found the use of transference interpretations linking therapist to parent to be correlated to favorable outcomes. This approach was modified in the present case, with transference interpretations instead being used to link the therapist and therapy to the deceased husband and the stress of his loss via affair and death. This was done to intensify the work of mourning that would be stimulated by the termination of therapy (Fleming and Altschul, 1963).

My purpose here is to present the work that explicitly involved termination, rather than giving an extended account of the entire therapy. Suffice it to say that much of the therapeutic work involved facilitation of the patient's mourning, with especial attention being focused on her ambivalent feelings toward the deceased husband, her suppression of anger, and her overdependence on him as the source of her own self-esteem. Marked recognition and mobilization of anger toward him were effected, and she was able to "reclaim" and revalue herself. My approach was psychodynamic and personal, in the sense of "talking real" with her (Schafer, 1974). A relationship of genuine mutual liking was formed, which seemed to serve the patient as a substantial corrective emotional experience to the narcissistic blow of the loss of her husband's affections. The value of this symbolic and real relationship also increased her sense of loss at the end of therapy and thus potentiated the impact of the work of termination.

The Explicit Work of Termination

All sessions were video- and audiotape-recorded, with the patient's informed consent. This extra attention may have enhanced the restorative narcissistic value of the therapy, although there was not explicit reference to the recording. A sequence of verbatim excerpts from various sessions will be presented with commentary to illustrate aspects of the termination work.

Session One. As Mann recommends, in the very first session the time-limited contract and the focus of therapy were established. Notice that the focus here is not merely on history but rather that past, present, and future are all called into being and that action through understanding is implied.

Therapist: Let's have an agreement that we might meet, say, a dozen times and keep our focus pretty much on what your husband's passing and what this affair meant in your life, and who you are now and how that is affecting it, and who you can be in the next few years, and not spend a lot of time talking about other problems.

Session Four. Considerable mourning work had transpired. In this session some special therapeutic activity had been directed toward her becoming less overly demanding of self-control so that she might be more comfortable with her feelings of anger and disappointment. Consistent with Hartocollis's suggestion (1976, p. 366) that "if the tension arises from the superego, time is experienced as moving quickly," at the end of the session she commented, "Time just flew by this session. Time can play tricks on you."

Session Five. Approaching the middle of the therapy, near the end of this session I explicitly introduced the topic of termination. The patient had been ill, appropriately postponing this session one meeting. Note her comment regarding time; her acknowledgment of her separateness and her attempt to get extra support from the therapist, but her almost immediate (although unsure) recognition that she should be able to judge her progress for herself; and her rather abrupt departure, with some possible hurt or anger and her again referring to the shortage of time.

T: Is this our fifth or sixth meeting?

P: Fifth, I think—

T: Fifth, that's right, because we skipped on that one. All together we are going to meet twelve times.

P: Oh, my goodness, the time is going fast, isn't it? What do I do then, I graduate? [*Nervous laughter.*]

T: You graduate.

P: This is a silly question, but anyway, I was going to say, "How am I doing?" But how should you know? I'm the one who should know.

T: Uh huh.

P: All right, I'll tell you.

T: You're catching on.

P: I'm catching–[*Long pause.*] Well, that's all I have to say.

T: Well, I will see you Thursday.

P: It was nice seeing you. I enjoyed it. [*Puts coat on.*] I sure hope that I feel better. I haven't got time to be sick now.

T: There is always enough time to do everything that needs to be done.

P: Yeah, that's right–make the effort.

Session Six. No explicit work on termination. It should be noted, however, that the patient began the session by commenting, "Most of my problem has to do with rejection–I look for approval." Also, she revealed that she had left her husband the year after the woman told her about the affair, but that he had let her go, and after two weeks she had returned. Work focused on the anger toward her husband and on a husband-therapist transference interpretation being made about her keeping her feelings to herself after she commented about "using valuable time crying."

Session Seven. I was ten minutes late starting the session. There was only the slightest suggestion of annoyance in her voice, and instead of exploring her anger the therapeutic activity went toward discussing her comments about taking a "postgraduate course," a reference to the fact that therapy was occurring in a university setting. Note the therapist's acknowledgment of her strong self-image before focusing on her feelings about ending. Also notice that she qualifies her comment regarding the speedy passage of time to pertain only to her–a sign of her growing sense of separateness.

P: I'm fine.

T: Good. Sorry I kept you waiting.

P: Oh, that's all right. You know, I'm retired, I'm not going anyplace–never worry about it. I was wondering, I mean, could I take a postgraduate course when I get finished here? [*Laughter.*]

T: How do you mean?

P: I just thought of something funny to say. I really enjoy coming; it's nice. I'm doing fine. I'm not even going to cry today because I don't feel like crying, and I told you last week that it's only when I come here that I've been crying. So how do you like that for progress?

T: Well, it sounds as if you're doing pretty well. You joke about a postgraduate course. I think that you're thinking about the fact that we will be ending pretty soon.

P: Yes, I guess so. Yes, because this is number seven today.

T: Right.

P: So we only have five more to go. Doesn't the time go fast? It has for me. I think God smiled on me the day I called to find out what it was all about.

The day before this seventh session she had met a retired gentleman while walking her dog. She reported being attracted to him and was excited and giggly as she described their encounter and their planned "date" for the zoo the next day. It seems probable that her therapeutic work of mourning had helped her to be responsive to the man's attentions and that she may have been emboldened by her positive relationship with her therapist. Her healthier sense of self plus the interest of the man created a safe enough condition for her to deepen her feelings about termination, a situation that permits what Weiss (1952) calls "crying at the happy ending." Note also the linkage of terminating therapy to the loss of her husband.

T: We are going to have five more meetings. From some of the things you've said, I imagine that you are beginning to have some feelings about the fact that we are going to end, and this is going to be another person that you have come to know and trust, and then it's going to end.

P: [*Bursts into tears.*] It's ridiculous—you'll begin to think I *need* postgraduate work. I don't know why I should cry now. But if

I only cry once a week, that's good, isn't it, while I'm here? I don't know, I don't feel sad. Maybe it's because I've been so happy, that I–I interrupted you; you were telling me that I only have five times more.

T: You said you don't feel sad now.

P: Well, I don't know, I mean I shouldn't feel sad. I don't know why I cried when you said that. You see, I'll have somebody else to talk to, or I'll be able to talk now. Oh, I'm going back East, you know [to see relatives on vacation]–it will be nice seeing all the people that I've known all of my life. But I haven't made any plans for my, anything. I'm no long-range planner, anyhow, Dr. Hoyt. I don't even like to make a date to go out and do something next week–I'd like to say, "Let's do it tomorrow," that's how I am. So when you say, "What am I going to do with my life?" I have no idea. I'm just glad to, if I wake up I'm glad. [*Checks her wristwatch.*]

T: You look at your watch a lot.

P: Well, I'm wondering if it's time. My brother is going to call for me at 10:30. We only have a few minutes more.

T: A minute ago you cried when we talked about separating, and then you kind of quickly talked about going back East.

P: I don't know why.

T: I think that as things come to an end over time we'll miss this relationship, but also it can remind you of other times when you've been involved with someone or cared about someone.

P: Yes, this is true. I'm really happy about things the way they are. [*Goes on to talk about the man she met, alternating between denying her excitement and acknowledging her enjoying his attention.*]

T: It sounds like you're saying that you don't want to become too attached.

P: No, I don't think I do. I don't want any commitment or involvement. I will never live with a man again, never on that kind of basis. I never will. I know this definitely. I never would

do it. I don't mean to say that maybe I wouldn't have a relationship with a man—that's a different thing. But no—no—I never
will. I'm too old, I really am. I don't want to wash anybody's
dirty socks and stuff. [*Laughter.*] But seriously, it's too late for
me, really. I'm going to go now. [*Puts coat on.*]

Session Eight. After talking about her continuing relationship
with her manfriend, the patient described the further surfacing
of feelings about therapy termination. Early in the session she
reported:

P: You know, the other day we were talking about that we
only had a few more visits, and I cried? And you said, "Do
you know why?" and I said, "I don't know why." So that day
I went to the shopping center on the bus, and on the way back
I was thinking about just that and I started to cry on the bus,
not cry like I cry here, but tears came into my eyes. Wasn't
that something? I couldn't understand it. I thought it was rather
interesting. But you did say something about you lose a friend
and you gain a friend, that's true.

Later in the session:

T: I've noticed that the last couple of times we have met
you've been a little anxious to take off early. I know that the
one time your brother was coming to pick you up, but since
we mentioned the fact that we will be ending in a certain number of times [*patient inhales, almost cries for a second*], you've
been wanting to get up and leave a little sooner.
P: [*Checks wristwatch.*] Not necessarily, really. I don't know why
I do that, Dr. Hoyt. [*Laughs nervously.*] I really don't. I'm not
going anywhere, except to shop.

A few minutes later she describes being pleased by "stand-
ing up" for herself recently in her relationship with her brother,
providing an opportunity for exploration of her possible feelings
of anger toward the therapist. Notice the use of a "therapeutic

double-bind" (Bandler and Grinder, 1975), a linguistic structure that results in the patient realizing her difference from the therapist regardless of her answer.

T: Just because I'm the doctor and you're the patient doesn't mean you have to put up with me. There are times when I'm wrong and you want to stand up for yourself.

P: This is so, isn't it? But when you tell me things, I really see that what you said is the truth and I take it from there, and I think about it and it is so. So I haven't been mad at you—*yet.*

T: Yet—oh, I think you have been a couple of times, a little bit.

P: Oh, I wouldn't say that. Not mad, no. Maybe a difference of opinion. No, I don't think so. But that's a nice feeling to be able to say, "I don't think so." You know, that helps: "It's not that way." To me this is a big plus, down the street in the right direction.

Her (characterological) difficulties with expressing anger were explored further at the end of the session. Note that she does express some anger, linked to the termination, albeit via a joking approach.

T: And the fact that you are getting a lot from this relationship may make it difficult for you to let yourself sometimes be annoyed with me or be angry with me.

P: You're right, you see, what you say is the truth. What you say are things I haven't thought about—I think awareness is a great thing to have. . . . Today is Thursday; I will see you on Tuesday. So we will end on the end of the month. What do they say, "Comes in like a lamb, goes out like a lion," or vice versa? That's the month of March.

T: Well, you came in like a lamb.

P: [*Laughs.*] Oh, that's very good, very clever. That was a good note to part on.

Session Nine. The patient was feeling good, and much of the session was devoted to review and working through. There was little explicit reference to termination. At one point I commented that she was "tying up loose ends" and suggested that we keep things open for termination feelings to emerge. Near the end of the session she again remarked, "Doesn't the time go fast?"

Session Ten. The patient was generally feeling good and was happy about the continuing relationship with her manfriend. To explore (and to minimize) the possibility that this other relationship might excessively mute her feelings about our impending termination, I inquired:

T: I imagine your getting involved in that relationship with him has changed your feelings about ending therapy here, having someone else you're talking to.

P: Well, I think they're separate things entirely, really. My relationship with him could never be, say, on a personal basis. He never asks me any questions about anything and I don't tell him, unless there is something I wish to tell him. I could never talk to him the way I talk to you.

Later in the session I interpreted her questions about how I viewed her ("Are we 'research subjects' or 'patients'?") as aspects of "wondering if we'd forget about you." (See Chapter Thirteen for a discussion of the terms *patient* and *client.*) I also suggested that any summary would be premature, that "things will come up in the last two meetings." The following interchange reveals some of her gains: her increased sense of self-reliance, her internalization of favorable aspects of the therapy, her ability to see the therapist as real and separate from M., her husband—all indications of her increasing readiness for termination.

T: What are your feelings about ending, terminating?

P: I really don't know. I don't even feel that it's going to end in that sense. Certainly I'll stop coming, but the experience will be with me forever. It's been an experience. It's been a very, I won't say precious, it's been a very *vital* thing.

T: I understand that you'll take some things away with you, but there is also the reality that we will stop seeing each other, that it will end.

P: I don't know if you mean it this way, but I feel strong enough now that I haven't used you as a crutch. I won't really mind it when you're not there—I'll be able to function in your absence—I won't miss you that way. It's been nice. I'll miss you as a person, but I don't *need* you to help me, and this is a great big plus: I haven't found someone I'm dependent on the way I depended on M.

T: It's good that you see the difference between our relationship and what you had with M. You depended on him so much.

Once again she commented at the session's end, "Doesn't the time fly fast here? At least it does for me." In a sense, these references to time at the end of sessions are a recapitulation of the time-ending aspect of the entire therapy.

Session Eleven. She reiterated her growing readiness for independence:

T: Have you thought much about our finishing?

P: I'll miss this. I've enjoyed it thoroughly. But I can be on my own. I don't *need* you to help me.

Later, the termination and mourning of the therapeutic relationship was again linked to the loss of her husband:

T: Talking about his death and that time seems fitting, since we are almost at the end of our relationship.

There was also an acknowledgment of mutual liking. This

was especially important for the patient because it provided a further valuable satisfaction she could take away from the relationship (Searles, 1975) and allowed her a chance to express her appreciation and have a meaningful adult-to-adult experience that affirmed her human uniqueness and helped signify her readiness for "graduation."

P: I could have been seeing somebody else; perhaps it would have been an entirely different ball game. I would think so, yes. I think we are all responsive to people, some people more than others, receptive, that's true.

T: So we both came out pretty good.

P: Yes, I think so. It was nice. The weeks have gone so fast, really, to me they have. It's been twelve times, and I think it was much better to come twice a week, rather than dragging it all out the while. It's been good for me.

T: It has been very good for me, too. I've not only been helpful, but I have also gained personally from spending time with you.

P: Thank you—thank you.

This is not to suggest that therapy ends here. A bit later she asked me several questions about the characteristics of my other patients. Again, this was linked to her stress event:

T: I thought also when you were asking me if some of my patients are younger it sounded like, "Am I going to go off with a younger woman now?"

P: No I didn't think about that. [*Tears come to her eyes.*]

At session's end she asked if she seemed different. I said she seemed more relaxed and less sad but emphasized her separateness and self-capacities (Hoyt, 1978) by adding, "But I don't know what's in your head. You do."

Session Twelve. Because this was our last meeting, termination was of course central. The patient again expressed her feelings of improvement and confidence in her ability to function independently. She cried when discussing its being our last meeting but checked her wristwatch and stopped herself. There was no overt sense of anger, although as we were discussing her present state a remark was made that perhaps reveals something through countertransference:

T: As you talk you have a real–I'm not sure of the word I want.

P: Positive!

T: Positive! Boy, I wouldn't want to get in an argument with you.

P: [*Laughs.*] I'm a sweet thing, but yes, I *am* a little positive, and this has not been my life all these years. I think if I had been more positive and more accepting and all I might have created a better environment for the possibilities of happiness between M. and me.

Her increasing awareness of her capacity for self-reliance was a central theme all during the therapy, and this was emphasized through the very ending. In leave taking, she thanked me. I accepted her appreciation but indicated that most of the credit went to her, since "You're the one who's changed; you're the one who has done it for yourself."

P: I want you to know that you've given me my life back, to put it that way.

T: I think you *took* it back, and I helped you.

P: OK. Thank you very much for everything.

T: You're very welcome.

On the way out the door she commented that seeing me

again would mean she'd be back for more therapy, which she didn't need or want. "So I'll just have my nice memories."

Outcome and Follow-Up

In the clinical judgment of both therapist and patient, therapy was successful. Her presenting symptoms of depression, anxiety, intrusive thoughts, and feelings of purposelessness and stagnation were no longer present to any significant degree. These improvements were also indicated by change scores on a variety of quantitative rating scales completed independently by therapist and patient at the beginning and end of therapy.[3]

A four-month follow-up interview was conducted by the psychiatric social worker who originally had evaluated the patient. Her clinical impression, also supported by quantitative rating scales, was that the improvements had been maintained. The patient concurred. She reported that her interaction with her manfriend was continuing and had become much more intimate, including a satisfying sexual relationship. She also reported being able to express herself freely with her friend, including having had a couple of fights in which she slammed the door on him. She had gone East on vacation but had been anxious at the site where her husband's ashes were scattered, and she had returned to San Francisco (and her manfriend) a week earlier than planned—perhaps indicating some residual unresolved mourning. She spoke of her therapist fondly and noted, "I thought he would 'cure' me, *do* something to take that block out of my head. That could have been disappointing, except in the meantime I was curing myself." Asked about her sense of time, she replied: "I don't know, I don't think about time. Only today is important. I used to think about age and being at the end of life. Now, if I have another week, great—if not, great. I'm happy to be alive. It's a beautiful world." Asked if she was interested in more therapy, she responded, "No, I'm too busy with what I'm doing." A second follow-up interview, eight months posttherapy, indicated that these gains had been maintained.

Discussion

This case had a most favorable outcome. It seems likely that the psychotherapy, with its emphasis on termination and the work of mourning, contributed to this result. Other factors are implicated, however, and should not be minimized. Most obvious is the new love relationship. It is difficult to estimate to what extent her gains are attributable to her meeting a man-friend. The patient was already showing signs of improvement when this romance first began, and her responses during the termination work of therapy suggested that her new relationship was not an "acting out" that might countertherapeutically protect her from the painful loss and mourning of therapy. Indeed, as was suggested above, the new love interest may have given her the security to further mourn the passing of other relationships. From a "scientific" point of view, of course, things are happily confounded by what Bergin and Strupp (1970), in a felicitous turn of phrase, call "the psychotherapy of everyday life." We should also not discount the favorable outcomes that may result from the "loss" of a significant other with whom one has a heavily conflicted or pathological relationship (Hofling and Joy, 1974), as was the situation here with the patient and her husband.

Still, brief time-limited psychotherapy seems to have been of use with this woman, and there are several points worthy of discussion. First, and most generally, this case may have been especially well suited for a time-limited model, since the basic underlying issue had to do with *loss* per se. My experience has been that the time-limited approach is particularly effective for psychotherapy involving bereavement and other mourning-type cases (see Smith [1967] and Atwood [1974] for descriptions of two other creative applications of "loss-models"). It would still be useful, although perhaps less directly so, with other problems. This is speculative, of course, and indicates the need for further research.

A second point of consideration involves the age of this patient. The successful outcome again demonstrates the value of psychotherapy with older persons. Her age also may be relevant in regard to our emphasis on temporal experience. With advanced age and the realistic awareness of the finitude of life, time may be experienced differently and may in some ways take on more value (Scott-Maxwell, 1968). The utility of a time-limited model thus would make sense both theoretically and practically with geriatric patients. In the case reported here, the patient's references to time occurred almost exclusively within the context of explicit work on termination. Awareness of time during periods of change is not limited to any particular group, of course. As popular songs on the radio tell us, during the personal upheavals of loss and love, time often seems to palpably "stand still," "slip away," "fly by," or "wait for no one."

In this connection, the choice of specifically *twelve* sessions may be commented upon. Mann (1973, p. 15) describes the choice of twelve sessions as being "somewhat arbitrary. Perhaps ten or fourteen would have sufficed equally well." Perhaps, but there is something intuitively appealing about twelve. In our culture, a "dozen" carries some extra meaning, and there is some greater sense of a gestalt being completed with the culmination of a dozen. This may relate to some other frequent measures of time, such as twelve months in a year and twelve hours in the sweep of a clock.[4] It seems that the choice of exactly twelve sessions may somehow capitalize on and heighten the existential impact of termination within the time-limited model.

At the psychodynamic level, the treatment model postulated that the work toward termination would restimulate and thus permit a further "working through" of troubling affects and ideas pertaining to the patient's loss of her husband. This was largely successful in terms of her relationship to her husband—grief, love, anger, and the sadness of mourning and gradual detachment of intense feelings all seemed to occur, and the patient was better able to integrate these experiences into her self-concept. Recognition and acceptance of her anger toward the husband, emphasized by Mann as a key aspect of termination work, was accomplished. There also was some mild expression of anger toward the therapist, but the patient had a tendency to segregate her positive and negative affects, idealizing the therapist while complaining about her husband. It may be that the contractual nature of the twelve-session model plus the relative brevity of treatment simply created too many barriers of rationality. The patient had come to therapy in somewhat of a crisis and quickly received some appreciated support and benefit. In such a situation, with a not-too-disturbed patient, one might well be surprised by a blatant expression of anger toward the helpful therapist. Moreover, it was my tactical choice to foster our positive relationship and allow her to enjoy narcissistic gratification rather than fully explore the possibilities of the negative transference. This maximized the reparative aspect of the therapy; she was able both to recognize and accept her anger toward the husband and to recover some of her damaged self-esteem via our positive alliance. Having my attention (and later, that of her manfriend) may have helped give her something to go on to, thus permitting her to mourn the passing of her husband.

Her characterological tendency to be pleasing and compliant undoubtedly contributed to her being a "good patient." This is not to minimize the value, however, of her experiencing (as in Session Eight) that she could be angry and have differences of opinion without losing the attention or respect of the other person (Whitaker, 1975; Winnicott, 1949). It is important to recall that in the posttherapy follow-up she indicated being able now to express anger openly toward her new lover. This is especially noteworthy in terms of Malan's (1976a, 1976b) dynamic outcome criterion that a successful patient be able to respond differently in a situation similar to that which was pathogenic. The report of this patient regarding her expression of anger would suggest that more than symptom relief occurred in this therapy.

Finally, just a few words about the effect of brief time-limited therapy on the therapist. This modus operandi is effective but demanding. The brief model requires especial alertness. There is a painfulness in the constant awareness of attaching and detaching that the time-limited approach entails, and there is also a range of countertransference reactions to be experienced. As a balance, however, there is also a corresponding quickening to life, and one can only agree with Simos (1977,

p. 342) that "Clinicians are privileged to be able to help people in this process of rebirth and renewal, and become catalysts to their finding ways for more productive and enjoyable living."

Notes

1. In his case study of the Wolf Man, Freud (1918) reported having set a termination date as a way of mobilizing the patient's efforts in therapy.
2. Establishment of time limits may be an aspect of what Whitaker (1968; Warkentin and Whitaker, 1965; Napier and Whitaker, 1978) refers to as the "battle for structure." Once the parameters of treatment are determined, the patient can be squarely confronted with responsibility for the initiative and content of the ensuing work.
3. These scales, the Hopkins Symptom Checklist (Derogatis and others, 1974), the Brief Psychiatric Rating Scale (Overall and Gorham, 1962), the Global Assessment Scale (Endicott, Spitzer, Fleiss, and Cohen, 1976), and the Impact of Event Scale (Horowitz, Wilner, and Alvarez, 1979), were part of a research assessment battery used at the Stress Clinic where the patient was seen.
4. One wonders what effect the popularization of digital clocks may have on children's developing a sense of the cyclical nature of time.

CHAPTER THIRTEEN

◆

"Patient" or "Client": What's in a Name?

Psychotherapists generally refer to the people they work with in therapy as either *patients* or *clients*. The former appellation is usually preferred by those therapists trained in a medical or psychoanalytic setting, whereas the latter is more often used by those who identify themselves more with a nonmedical, "humanistic" orientation. There is nothing inherently correct about the use of either term per se, although each may have certain implications for the conduct of therapy. The purpose of this brief communication is to highlight some of those implications, to enhance awareness of the assumptions that may underlie the choice of language and thus influence therapeutic action and effectiveness. Some other aspects of the use of names in therapy have been discussed by Cath (1975), Selzer (1960), and Mitchell (1976).

Webster's Dictionary (1970) tells us that a *patient* is "1. an individual under or awaiting medical care or treatment, or the recipient of any of various personal services; 2. one that is acted upon," the term being derived from Latin and Greek words having to do with suffering. This, of course, is at the heart of the medical model, the suggestion that suffering is alleviated through the actions of an expert other. There is the connotation of homeostasis and a norm (akin to body temperature or skeletal structure) to which the "sick" patient should be returned.

Note: Reprinted, with changes, from Hoyt, M. F. "'Patient' or 'Client': What's in a Name?" *Psychotherapy: Theory, Research, & Practice,* 1979, *16,* 46–47. Copyright 1979 by American Psychological Association. Used by permission of the publisher.

Grateful acknowledgment is made to Dennis Farrell, Mardi Horowitz, Virginia Patterson, and Jeffry Ordover for their helpful comments.

Certainly the patient must cooperate with the course of treatment, but the implication is that the sufferer must be patient and await the ministrations of the doctor.

But what about the alternative term, *client?* Those who use this term prefer it because it seems more neutral, that is, it avoids the implication of "sickness" and apparently emphasizes the contractual or egalitarian nature of the therapeutic relationship (Rogers, 1951), although it also implies an unfortunate legalistic or business focus. This fits with *Webster's* second definition of the term, "a person under the protection of another: vassal, dependent." Some further etymological research indicates that the term derives from the Latin *clinare,* meaning "to lean" (the words *incline* and *anaclitic* share the same root), and originally referred to a hanger-on or plebeian who lived under the patronage of a patrician in ancient Rome.

Freud (1919a) counseled therapists to provide some limited satisfaction of dependency needs, but he advised that "it must always be done with great caution, and the patient should be educated to liberate and fulfill his own nature, not to resemble ourselves." Greenacre (1954) amplifies this position, and correctly characterizes the therapeutic relationship as "tilted," since it does not usually involve the coequal mutuality typical of friendship or other social situations. Indeed, it is this special nature of the therapeutic situation that helps create some of the symbolic power (transference) that contributes to its effectiveness. Greenacre wisely cautions, however, that "the patient's autonomy [must] be safeguarded and strengthened in the very situation which might seem to favor its depletion" and goes on to suggest that this will be accomplished chiefly by having the psychoanalyst stick to the work of analyzing rather than abandoning a nondirective attitude in favor of serving as guide, model, or teacher.

The basic question of whose efforts are responsible ultimately for the person's care and hoped-for improvement in therapy is central to this discussion. This issue has been well-elaborated elsewhere (Fagan and Shepherd, 1970; Kaiser, 1965; May, 1969; Rank, [1936] 1945; Schafer, 1976). Any term or designation may be useful; what is important is to understand how it helps to define and thus influence, for all persons involved, the nature of their working relationship. In my own practice both terms get used, and I have found it very helpful at times to explore and clarify with people how their choice of terms may indicate assumptions they have about the nature of their difficulties and their expectations regarding our respective parts in their therapy.

It is my hope that by calling attention to this basic semantic question, this note may help others make the arrangement of their therapeutic relationships more conscious and effective. Consider this story recounted by Schloegl (1976, p. 78): "A monk asked of Master Sosan: 'Please sprinkle the compassion of your teaching so that I may be liberated.' 'Who has put you under restraint?' asked the Master. 'No one.' Master Sosan said: 'Why then do you ask to be liberated?' At this, the monk awakened fully."

CHAPTER FOURTEEN

———◆———

"Shrink" or "Expander": An Issue in Forming a Therapeutic Alliance

The terms *shrinks* and *head-shrinking* are sometimes used to refer to psychotherapists and psychotherapy. These slang appellations may be applied casually in an effort to appear cute or clever, without any intended deeper meaning. More careful examination, however, may indicate certain (perhaps unconscious) attitudes or expectations that have implications for the conduct of therapy. The purpose of this chapter is to call attention to some of these implications, especially as they pertain to the issue of the therapeutic alliance, and to suggest some ways of confronting and correcting misunderstandings when they appear lest they impede treatment progress. A related topic, some implications of the terms "patient" or "client" regarding issues of dependency and responsibility, have been discussed in Chapter Thirteen.

As Cath (1975) has pointed out, the term shrink and variants may reveal the expectation or fear that the clinician will somehow shrink, deflate, reduce, or make smaller the recipient of his or her professional services. The idea that there is a correct or normal way to be (akin to normal body temperature or skeletal structure) and that the therapist will attempt to shrink or force the person to fit the mold is a common misconception.

Note: Reprinted, with changes, from Hoyt, M. F. "'Shrink' or 'Expander': An Issue in Forming a Therapeutic Alliance." *Psychotherapy,* 1985, *22,* 813–814. Copyright 1985 by the American Psychological Association. Used by permission of the publisher.

Grateful acknowledgment is made to Jeffry Ordover and Saul Rosenberg for their helpful comments.

Perhaps this is why, in the popular mind, the term shrink is especially associated with psychiatrists and psychoanalysts, who may be seen as upholders and enforcers of conventional values. There is an implicit reference to the shrunken heads produced by witch doctors and primitive healers (Sugar, 1971; Warner, 1982), the emotionally ambivalent suggestion being that psychotherapists have magical powers to help and/or to hurt.

Sometimes the term shrink may be used with mixed affection, the colloquialism expressing a sense of familiarity and intimacy, although it may also be used to convey hostility, as an unprofessional form of address; or it may be used as a way of avoiding acknowledgment, to oneself and friends, that one is a patient or client receiving help with one's personal problems. Other, more specific meanings may relate to a person's particular conflicts and level of psychosocial development. Underlying the usage of the term there is often a connotation of threat to one's narcissism, a suggestion that one's grandiose fantasies and lack of complete self-knowledge and self-control will be exposed. There is, of course, some truth here, since therapy does require the patient or client to be vulnerable (A. Goldberg, 1975). The success of treatment depends on the patient's becoming engaged with the therapist. But this involves a risk, sometimes revealed through use of the term shrink.

Many therapists dislike being called shrinks, since its connotation calls into question their professional intention to be helpers or caretakers. Many go along with its use, however, hoping to appear relaxed or at least not overly sensitive. A few do seem to enjoy the term and may even use it to describe themselves, like Rubin (1974) who entitled his book *Shrink! The Diary of a Psychiatrist*. The term shrink may engender countertransference reactions both because its irreverent humor lets the therapist feel less powerful and pompous and because at times it paradoxically gives the therapist a sense of importance that may exceed and flatter his or her real power to influence patients. Calling a therapist a shrink implies concerns about power: will the shrink be nurturing or critical, helpful or harmful?

How can one bring this conflict to awareness and make use of it? In therapy, patients may refer to a therapist as a shrink

or may comment about needing to get their "heads shrunk."
When this occurs, I explore with them their use of the term,
why they use it when they do, and what their use of the term
may imply about their expectations. In the course of the ensuing
discussion I sometimes offer a comment: "The term shrink suggests that somehow I'm going to make you smaller. The way
I see it, though, is almost the opposite. I think that my job here
is to be an *expander,* to help you grow and expand. The way I
can do that is to help you recognize and understand barriers
you may be creating psychologically that interfere with your
being who you want to be. So I'm an expander, not a shrink."

I have observed repeatedly that patients respond to the term
expander with a marked sense of relief, sometimes accompanied by a good laugh. This occurs (I believe) because I have
addressed and made less threatening their fear of being
"shrunk" or "put down." Instead, I align myself on the side of
growth and accomplishment. (In discussing the assessment of
psychotherapy outcome, Parloff [1970] somewhat irreverently
uses the terms *head-shrinking* and *mind-expanding* to contrast the
treatment goals of symptom amelioration versus personal enhancement and growth.) I am careful, however, not to assume
responsibility for their share of the ensuing process. Sometimes
a further comment is helpful: "I see my role here as to help
you with *informed consent.* That is, I'll help you get more informed about how you see yourself and others and what influences you psychologically, and then you'll be in a better
position to make informed decisions about how you go about
living your life. Therapy can help you to expand your choices."

These early therapist activities serve as part of a therapy induction process (Orne and Wender, 1968) that helps to orient the
patient regarding what to expect and how to use the process of
psychotherapy. Indeed, commenting on the patient's use of the
term shrink serves as a type of transference interpretation, bringing the patient's concerns into the here and now of the budding
therapeutic relationship, providing an initial insight and interpersonal contact. Once engagement with the therapist occurs, an alliance (Gutheil and Havens, 1979; Nadelson, 1980) in the direction
of further psychological exploration and learning is possible.

CHAPTER FIFTEEN

Is Being "In Recovery" Self-Limiting?

Do people "in recovery" ever "recover" and graduate? In my practice as a clinical psychologist I have encountered many people who have benefited by participation in various "recovery" programs (usually based on twelve-step models). Some of these folks have, after a period of involvement, gotten what they came for, resolved their problems, and moved on. Others, however, speak of needing to be always "in recovery," having entered a process that they expect to be lifelong. They do not just mean that life is a long journey of exploration, growth, and development. Rather, they seem to have accepted the idea that they can never be truly "well" or "OK," that they must be constantly "healing" rather than "healed." Their effort seems Sisyphean: they seem to have internalized a belief that perpetuates the shame they seek to heal (Bradshaw, 1988). Aspects of this mentality have been articulated by Kaminer (1992): "It is an odd program in self-esteem that rewards people for calling themselves helpless, childish, addicted, and diseased and punishes them for claiming to be healthy. Admit that you're sick and you're welcomed into the recovering persons' fold; dispute it and you're 'in denial.' Thus the search for identity is perversely resolved: all your bad behaviors and unwanted feelings become conditions of your being" (p. 26).

It is not my purpose to denigrate that which helps. I recognize the advantages of remaining vigilant toward relapse, the utility of establishing a vision of a clear opponent (Miller, 1994),

Note: Reprinted, with changes, from Hoyt, M. F. "Is Being 'In Recovery' Self-Limiting?" *Transactional Analysis Journal,* 1994, *24* (3), 222–223. Copyright 1994 by the International T. A. Association. Used by permission of the publisher.

and the benefits of fellowship and support. I am also aware of the dangers of hubris, the often recurring pattern of alcohol and substance abuse, and the persistent and sometimes chronic nature of personality disorders (Hoyt, 1989b—see Chapter Nineteen). Still, when I ask someone who has been doing well for a long period of time when they will finally feel finished and ready to put a problematic chapter of their life behind them, I am concerned when they sometimes seem surprised that something like that could ever happen. For example, I recently spoke with a woman who was in her eighth year of sobriety and "recovery," with no yearning or likelihood to revert to her former "addictions." She had by all indications completed her "working through" and was on a different path (Blackstone, 1987). When asked why she still thought of herself as "sick" and "addicted," she was at first startled and then said, "I never thought of that. I was told I would have to acknowledge being that way forever to stay sober. But, you know, I used to be a smoker but I don't think of myself as a smoker in recovery or a latent smoker. I don't even think of myself as an ex-smoker. It's just not relevant anymore. It's not part of how I think about myself. I could do the same with alcohol and bad relationships, too. I don't need to keep doubting myself to stay away from them."

She was not "in denial." She owned her past rather than it owning her. "Recovery" had served her to a point, but it was now useful for her to stop using it to define herself. It had become a self-*un*fulfilling prophecy, so to speak, reinforcing an unhealthy image of self. Getting well, being well, and staying well may take a long time but therapy can become unnecessarily interminable if there is no achievable end point.[1] We need to exercise care not to impose an asymptote on a client's potential for "OKness."

Note

1. A person who seems to have "recovered" may sometimes "slip." In such instances it may be useful to reframe the relapse as the client's internal (or unconscious) reminder

that he or she needs to remain vigilant about maintaining healthy progress (Berg, 1994, p. 213). People who may have a persistent biochemical vulnerability to alcohol abuse may be especially wise to abstain from all such consumption.

CHAPTER SIXTEEN

The Four Questions
of Brief Therapy

Don't pass over this page!
                                    –Rabbi Sigmund of Vienna

Therapists who know "The Art of Psychoanalysis" (Haley, 1969) and who attend Brief Therapy Anonymous meetings (Duncan and others, 1992) know what plagues may await those who construct caseloads rather than therapeutic narratives. While the following is loosely and satirically derived from the tradition of the Passover seder, it is hoped that its appeal will be more ecumenical, like Dan Greenberg's *How to Be a Jewish Mother* (1976) and the rye bread ads featuring photographs of smiling African American and Native American children (among others) with the slogan, "You don't have to be Jewish to love Levy's!" As my proto-constructivist grandmother asked, "A Ph.D.? So what kind of disease is philosophy that it needs a doctor?"

Let us remember that there was once a time when all who sought help were made to wait and wait in suffering. Finally, the Br-f Th-r-p-st came and delivered them from this land of misery. Yet even now, when therapists gather to ask, Why is brief therapy different from all other therapies? we hear first from the Simple Therapist: "There is no difference, only non-specific factors, and all must have prizes." Then we hear from the Wicked Therapist Who Doesn't Care: "I suffered long with my therapist. Now my hours are booked, I'm a success, and

Note: Reprinted, with changes, from Hoyt, M. F. "The Four Questions of Brief Therapy." *Journal of Systemic Therapies,* 1994, *13,* 68–69. Copyright 1994 by Guilford Press. Used by permission of the publisher.

they need to suffer, too." The Therapist Who Does Not Know
How to Ask, seeking a guide, listens perplexedly. But finally
there speaks the Wise Therapist, who asks and answers four
times, Why is brief therapy different from all other therapies?

1. Because in brief therapy we and the patient don't loaf. We
    are time sensitive and don't wait for the bread to rise be-
    fore changes are made.
2. Because in brief therapy we dip but little into the salty
    tears of dysphoria, instead drawing from the wells of joy,
    strength, and excitement.
3. Because in brief therapy we do our work together sitting
    up rather than reclining in leisure.
4. Because in brief therapy we but briefly taste the bitterness
    of times past, instead dwelling in the infinite possibilities
    of the present and the hopefulness of the future.

Having thus spoken, the Wise Therapist was again silent.
As were the others.

CHAPTER SEVENTEEN

Therapist Resistances to Short-Term Dynamic Psychotherapy

There is a burgeoning need for clinicians to be willing and able to apply effective short-term therapy methods if the needs of more than a handful of patients are to be served. Long-term treatment, even when effective, requires more time and expense than is feasible for most people. It was Freud ([1937] 1964) himself who recognized this when he described analysis as "interminable" and called for the development of new, more efficient treatment methods based on psychoanalytic principles. Among the various forms of brief therapy that have been developed (see Budman, 1981; Flegenheimer, 1982; Mandel, 1981; Sloane and Staples, 1979), a number of short-term psychodynamic approaches have been well described for use with neurotic-level patients.[1] They all have in common the following characteristics, they are: (1) *short-term,* with early and explicit recognition that treatment is to be of limited duration, often arbitrarily defined as twenty or fewer sessions; (2) *dynamic,* based on the psychoanalytic principles of insightful working through of a focal conflict via interpretation of resistance, transference, and unconscious material; and (3) *therapeutic,* having the goal of both symptom relief and character change, at least in the area of conflict. A number of the technical requirements

Note: Reprinted, with changes, from Hoyt, M. F. "Therapist Resistances to Short-Term Dynamic Psychotherapy." *Journal of the American Academy of Psychoanalysis,* 1985, *13,* 93–112. Copyright 1985 by Guilford Press. Used by permission of the publisher.

Grateful acknowledgment is made to Jeffry Ordover, Saul Rosenberg, Robert Wallerstein, and Norman Weinstein for their helpful comments.

of short-term dynamic psychotherapy are described concisely by Winokur and Dasberg (1983, p. 37): "In addition to the basic psychoanalytic techniques of clarification, confrontation, and interpretation . . . therapists also must learn to attend selectively to issues within a defined focus and neglect other material; to interpret actively and early in the therapy the anxiety-defense-impulse triad in relation to the context of the transference, the current situation, and the link to the past; and to maintain a strong collaborative alliance that provides empathic support to help the patient tolerate anxiety induced by large doses of interpretation."

Evidence (Butcher and Koss, 1978; Malan, 1963, 1976a, 1976b; Marmar, Hoyt, Leong, and Horowitz, 1980; Piper and others, 1984; Sifneos, 1975; Smith and Glass, 1977; Strupp and Hadley, 1979) has accumulated indicating the effectiveness of such approaches in bringing about *focal* changes. The benefits of short-term dynamic therapy, of course, are restricted generally to one psychodynamic sector of a patient's personality and thus are not truly comparable in scope and depth to the positive results (broad identity changes and defensive modifications) that sometimes result from long-term psychoanalysis. Remarkably enough, however, favorable results have been reported, with long-term follow-up, after even a single interview oriented toward increasing patients' sense of personal responsibility and insight into their core conflicts (Bloom, 1981; Malan, Heath, Bacal, and Balfour, 1975; Rockwell and Pinkerton, 1982). Other investigations (Malan, 1963, 1976a, 1976b; Sloane and others, 1975) involving highly experienced psychodynamic clinicians working within a framework of approximately forty sessions have also shown significant and lasting positive effects. Perhaps most impressive, however, is the study of Smith and Glass (1977), who performed a meta-analysis of almost four hundred controlled psychotherapy outcome studies involving more than 25,000 patients and control subjects. Their conclusive finding was that patients who received psychotherapy did better on various outcome measures than 75 percent of those persons who remained untreated, demonstrating the benefits of psychotherapy. Of special interest was the fact that the mean length of these effective treatments was approximately seventeen sessions. As Robert Wallerstein (personal communication) has pointed out, this meta-analysis does not necessarily demonstrate that brief therapy is as effective as longer therapy. The statistical size effects may be comparable, but the criteria are different. Longer-term treatments, when they work, may accomplish more profound changes than are likely to be realized by effective short-term treatments. What is demonstrated is that short-term approaches do often produce significant, measurable benefits for patients.

There has been controversy in the short-term therapy literature about patient selection, therapeutic techniques, and expected outcomes (see Malan, 1976a; Frances and Perry, 1983). Simply stated, the "conservative" position has been that brief treatment generally is appropriate only for the mildly and recently distressed, that techniques should be supportive rather than uncovering or anxiety-producing, and that expected results are basically superficial and symptom suppressive. The "radical" position, on the other hand, is just what the name literally implies: "going to the root"; the radical view is that the skillful clinician working within an explicitly short-term treatment framework can use a full range of psychodynamic methods with a variety of neurotic patients, often achieving some genuine and lasting personality modifications as well as symptomatic relief. While there is more research to be done, the general thrust of the evidence is clear: many patients benefit from brief, focused, psychodynamic therapy.

Sources of Resistance Against
Short-Term Dynamic Psychotherapy

How, then, are we to understand the reluctance of many psychodynamically-oriented therapists to learn and to apply short-term methods as a treatment of choice? (Recent evidence reported by Smith and Glass [1977], Garfield [1978], Koss [1979], and Langsley [1978] suggests that much psychotherapy *is* brief, although this is often not by the choice of the therapist.) For some therapists, lack of awareness of recent clinical and research developments may be the explanation, although the multiplying numbers of publications and workshops on the topic make it unlikely that it is the unavailability of information regarding short-term therapy that has impeded its acceptance. Rather, I would suggest, there are a number of myths, erroneous beliefs, and (perhaps unconscious) "problems about learning" (Ekstein and Wallerstein, 1972) that may make clinicians reluctant or resistant to using short-term dynamic methods. There certainly are also legitimate intellectual reservations to be discussed, although at times they are so permeated with emotion that they qualify as resistances rather than mere disagreements (Winokur and Dasberg, 1983). As seen herein, I have organized these considerations under six broad categories or rubrics. Some of the points pertain especially to psychodynamic therapy, although it will be seen that many of the issues—such as economic incentives and struggles with termination—are factors that all therapists face when considering a short-term treatment approach. Agreeing with Main (1957, p. 130) that "the need for the therapist steadily to examine his motives has long been recognized as a necessary, if painful, safeguard against undue obtrusions from unconscious forces in treatment," I submit that the following factors may serve as obstacles to the open-minded and effective use of short-term dynamic psychotherapy.

The Belief That "More Is Better"

Some therapists hold the belief that short-term therapy is simply "not as good" as long-term or open-ended treatment, despite the fact that there is no research evidence (Butcher and Koss, 1978; Luborsky, Singer, and Luborsky, 1975) that psychoanalysis or long-term psychotherapy necessarily produce more favorable or durable therapeutic outcomes in terms of the resolution of problems that impel most patients toward treatment. And, as noted by Appelbaum (1975), a psychoanalyst impressed by his experiences with brief therapy, even if long-term therapy were to produce some added gains, it would be questionable whether these gains would often be commensurate with the added expenditure of time and money.[2]

As a number of writers (Appelbaum, 1975; C. Goldberg, 1975; Mann, 1973; Wolberg, 1965a) have cautioned, the lack of a time limit may create a situation in which therapy expands endlessly as a resistance to working through, separation, and self-responsibility. Of course, short-term therapy patients, just like those in open-ended treatment, can avoid change by procrastinating and awaiting the end of therapy. In either treatment framework, the effect of using time as a resistance depends on whether the therapist can help the patient to learn about it and give it up. It is actually the case, however, that a time-limited framework often creates a sense of urgency that helps foster a rapid and deep involvement, including the kind of intense encounter that Buber (1973) calls a "meeting." Like the proverbial meeting of strangers on a train, the safety of knowing that the end is clearly defined and in sight sometimes permits short-term therapy patients to become quickly and intensely engaged in treatment (Stierlin, 1968). Observing the operation of "Parkinson's Law" in psychotherapy—work expands or contracts to fill the time available for it—Appelbaum (1975) advocates and illustrates the use of setting the end point at the beginning of brief therapy to stimulate the patient's will (Mann, 1973; Rank, [1936] 1945) and to counteract passive, timeless waiting for change. This method, of forcing the patient to confront issues of separation by setting a termination date, was first reported by Freud ([1918] 1957) in his case of the Wolf Man.

Long-term therapy is based on a number of theoretical assumptions that presuppose that treatment must take a long time to be effective: the belief that pathogenic early experiences inevitably must be slowly and fully uncovered; the belief that rapport and the therapist-patient alliance must form gradually; the belief that the patient must be allowed to regress and that transference takes a long time to develop and should not be interpreted too early; and the belief that the consolidation of gains requires a lengthy period of working through. As Winokur and Dasberg (1983; see also Budman and Gurman, 1983) have noted, these theoretical assumptions—which may become self-fulfilling prophecies—are not necessarily always true, and may at times be held as quasi-intellectual resistances to short-term therapy. An alternative set of assumptions suggests that short-term treatment can be effective: the belief that focused intervention can set into motion a whole system of changes; the belief that selected patients can rapidly form a good working alliance and that early transference interpretations can strengthen the alliance; the belief that generalized regression should be avoided and that regression should be restricted as much as possible to the focal area; and the belief that a time limit increases and intensifies the work accomplished, that gains are consolidated throughout the treatment by repeated interpretation of the central focus in the triangle of past-present-transference, and that reactions to termination can be interpreted throughout the short-term therapy with patients selected to be able to tolerate the anxieties of separation. The differences in these two sets of working assumptions highlight the technical methods that characterize effective short-term work: an explicit understanding that treatment will not be prolonged or "timeless," greater therapist activity and early transference interpretation, selective attention to a central dynamic focus, maintenance of a strong adult-to-adult therapeutic alliance and avoidance of generalized regression, and early attention to termination as part of the working-through process. Therapists accustomed to operating within a long-term treatment context will not be able to adopt these short-term methods effectively without first adjusting or suspending their underlying assumptions and beliefs.

The Myth of the "Pure Gold" of Analysis

Many forget that among the first short-term therapy cases were those of Katarina, Lucy R., and Anna O. reported by Breuer and Freud ([1893–95] 1955) and that Freud continued to occasionally use brief treatments throughout his clinical career (de la Torre, 1978; Sterba, 1951). It is good to be mindful of this, since continued idealization and supposed emulation of training supervisors, mentors, and other ego ideals may serve as a barrier to effective short-term treatments, especially for clinicians who were trained in institutions where psychoanalysis and long-term psychotherapy were held as the most prestigious or "real" treatments in contrast to shorter-term methods that may have been described as useful but essentially "superficial," "palliative," or "supportive." Many therapists and trainees believe that short-term work precludes an analytic or "uncovering" approach. Recent writers (e.g., Malan, Sifneos, Davanloo) have made it abundantly clear that these descriptions are erroneous: short-term dynamic psychotherapy can be highly intensive, exploratory, and anxiety-provoking, and can result in significant and enduring insight and personality change. Short-term dynamic therapy is not mere crisis intervention, which attempts primarily to restore equilibrium without ameliorating the personality pathology that underlies the crisis. As Malan (1963, 1976a, 1976b; see also Frances and Perry, 1983) has documented, favorable outcomes are more likely in short-term dynamic psychotherapy when there has been active, early, and repeated interpretation of the patient's unconscious focal conflict, with special emphasis on the link between therapist (transference) and parental figures and on the patient's reactions to termination.[3] Similarly, Hoyt (1980; Hoyt, Xenakis, Marmar, and Horowitz, 1983) reports data indicating that short-term dynamic therapy sessions are judged to be particularly "good" when the activities of therapist and patient emphasize the patient's expression of thoughts and feelings and the collaborative exploration of the meanings of this expression in terms of the patient's self-concept, reactions to the therapist, and links between past and present. In addition, it might be mentioned here that impressive therapeutic effects also were reported by Alexander and French (1946) in their groundbreaking *Psychoanalytic Therapy*, in which they advocated greater therapist activity and rapid focusing on the patient's core neurotic conflicts, but that those authors were roundly attacked for being revisionistic and challenging to orthodox psychoanalytic technique. It remained for Gill (1954) and Bibring (1954) to publish their seminal papers on psychoanalytically *oriented* psychotherapy before psychotherapeutic techniques based on psychoanalytic principles (interpretation of resistance, transference, and unconscious material) were generally recognized as bonafide and legitimate.

The Confusion of Patients' Interests with Therapists' Interests

Most patients come to therapy hoping for an effective and efficient treatment. In spite of some therapists' emphasis on long-term therapy, relatively few patients request an open-ended "exploratory" approach, even if they are unable to clearly identify a circumscribed symptom or complaint. If told that, say, a dozen sessions of therapy are recommended, patients will often respond, "That many?" *How* the therapist presents the suggestion of a short-term treatment (e.g., optimistically versus apologetically) will do much to affect the patient's expectancies and eventual outcome (Aldrich, 1968; Frank, 1973). If lasting psychotherapeutic gain, rather than the thorough scientific study of the personality, is the primary goal of treatment, much benefit can be derived from a short-term dynamic approach. As Gillieron (1981) has argued, using the metaphor of travel to contrast psychoanalysis and brief therapy, one can get to the same destination by different routes, with different experiences along the way. Psychoanalysis and long-term therapy may provide a valuable and unique perspective, but the traveler-patient may neither want nor need such an extended journey. Patients seeking treatment may stop therapy after only a few sessions. This may involve a "premature termination," or it may indicate that the patient got what was needed. Therapists may be able to see other problems that could be worked on, but these may be beyond what interests the patient. Longer treatments may be required, of course, but my point here is that it may be more the therapist's custom, orientation, or expectations, rather than the patient's, that determine the length of effective treatment. Therapists may have needs to conduct long-term therapy that are not necessarily consonant with the needs of particular patients.

The Demanding Nature of the Therapist's Role

Effective short-term therapy makes demands upon the therapist to be active and intensely alert. Material must be understood, selectively focused, and interpreted quite early in treatment. The mutually intense affective involvement frequently generated by brief treatments may increase the prominence of empathic and intuitive reactions in the therapist (Binder, 1977; Binder, Strupp and Schact, 1983), and a quick perceptiveness and willingness to take risks is required since the therapist must work without the luxury of sitting back for many months until the material clarifies itself through repetition. Kupers (1981, p. 131) emphasizes the importance of a solid psychodynamic understanding for clinicians working under stress: "A therapist well versed in theories and techniques of examining psychological subtleties is that much better prepared to practice therapy with a client who is overwhelmed. . . . The theory and technique often help to prevent the therapist from losing the way in the midst of the pain and chaos." Short-term therapy presents a constant challenge to one's clinical acumen, and thus may be easier for the already experienced clinician than for the relative beginner still developing basic skills and confidence (Mann, 1973). On the other hand, long-term therapists may be hampered by certain working assumptions (discussed above) and by a sense of loss of competence as they experiment with short-term techniques (Winokur and Dasberg, 1983), whereas relative beginners may have fewer ingrained assumptions and greater enthusiasm (Sifneos, 1978) for the comparatively quick results short-term therapy tries to accomplish.

Economic and Other Pressures

I hope and suspect that the therapists are rare who knowingly "string along" patients for monetary or other gain without rendering them commensurate professional service. Various unwitting collusions may occur, however, especially with seductive or dependent patients. It may also be tempting to hold on to those patients who are especially likeable as well as those who have particularly interesting lives and whose psychological problems may bear resemblances to those of their therapists. The economic reality that few patients can afford to pay privately for long-term therapy is a fact that essentially mandates the expansion of short-term therapy (Kovacs, 1982); treatment limitations imposed by outside forces (e.g., insurance companies, peer review) can also be helpful.[4] As Haley (1977) points out, therapists may have a bias against effective brief treatments because they result in a rapid turnover in patients. There is always a temptation to hold on to that which is profitable and dependable, especially in times such as the present when in certain areas there may be a surplus of therapists competing in the marketplace (Klee, 1968). Sometimes it becomes too easy to coast along without examining what purpose is being accomplished by lengthy therapy; therapeutically unnecessary proliferations that can often be detected by careful therapist self-scrutiny. Every therapist, whether working fee-for-service or within some other arrangement, would do well to review periodically what and whose needs ("Money and Other Trade-Offs . . . ," 1979) are getting met by long-continued therapies.

Countertransference and Related Therapist Reactions to Termination

Therapists may also be hesitant to employ brief or time-limited treatment models because such approaches repeatedly confront us with our own difficulties regarding separation and loss. Few people like to say good-bye, and psychotherapists may avoid taking on short-term cases (or may waver in their commitment to ending as the termination date draws near) in an attempt to forestall, dilute, or un-do the impact of leave taking (Small, 1979). A time-limited approach involves a range of possible countertransference reactions. Strong feelings of guilt may be stimulated in the therapist by the patient, who may experience the termination of treatment to be a rejection or abandonment. Well-intended therapists may feel a great temptation to act out "rescue fantasies" (Bellak, 1980; Weddington and Cavenar, 1979). Ideally, these reactions should be understood and worked through during the termination phase for the short-term therapy to be maximally beneficial (Malan, 1976a; Mann, 1973).

The goal of effective short-term dynamic psychotherapy is personality change as well as symptom relief, at least in the area of neurotic conflict. Short-term therapists may sometimes be frustrated by the circumscribed nature of these treatment goals, especially if the patient's gains seem "limited" to a return to function (Goldensohn and Haar, 1974). Symptom relief is no mean feat in itself, and it may be all the patient really desires. Still, it may also be helpful for therapists to recognize that in short-term therapy, much more than in longer-term treatments, change processes may be initiated or set into motion without actually being completely worked through during the course of formal therapy (Horowitz and Hoyt, 1979). It is important to differentiate between treatment goals and life goals (Ticho, 1972), and to recognize that some of the benefits of treatment can be consolidated only later, during the course of living.[5] This may result in patients coming to the end of the agreed-upon treatment period without full resolution of their presenting problems, or perhaps with even a last-minute return or intensification of symptoms. At the end of a well-conducted brief dynamic therapy, both patient and therapist usually are satisfied with a job well done. Sometimes, however, a patient may try to entice or coerce the therapist into continuing therapy, for example, by attempting to provoke guilt with a pleading or demanding, "Don't leave me now!" Therapists with a strong need to be needed will be particularly sensitive to this countertransference pressure, as will those therapists who may feel that they are doing only "Band-Aid" work (Mendelsohn, 1978). Short-term therapy with more disturbed patients will almost inevitably be subject to countertransference difficulties in the termination phase (see Hoyt and Farrell, 1984).

One may sometimes revise a short-term treatment plan with good reason, of course, although experience shows that this is rarely necessary or beneficial. More often, extending treatment beyond the agreed-upon termination point results in an un-doing of the impact of good work. The obsessively perfectionistic temptation to extend treatment "an extra session" (or two, or three . . .) seldom results in anything essential getting completed. Rather, it usually leads into a situation where the failure to abide by the agreement to stop after a certain point in time (usually set as a certain number of sessions or as a calendar

date) casts doubt on the integrity of other agreements, where
there is less and less to talk about, and where therapy finally
ends anticlimactically, in boredom. "Less could have been
more," as the saying goes.[6]

Professional Responsibilities

The series of factors discussed previously is not represented as
complete or all-inclusive but is offered to stimulate thought and
further consideration. It is also not my intention to suggest that
all long-term therapy is inappropriate or indicative of various
resistances to short-term approaches. There are many instances
when patients may realistically want or need a prolonged, open-
ended therapeutic relationship as they undergo self-exploration
and characterological change or to help them weather a difficult
life passage or maintain a tenuous psychosocial adjustment. At
times a therapist might inappropriately employ a short-term approach as a resistance against more open-ended, long-term treatment, e.g., to avoid an extended intimacy or dependency that
makes the therapist uncomfortable, or to satisfy a need for quick
gratification or impatience with the working-through process. It
is good to know one's personal strengths and weaknesses, of
course, but it is important not to impose one's predilections or
preferences in the name of "policy" or "style." As de la Torre
(1978, p. 192) puts it: "Each clinician should become an advocate of what is best for a particular patient at a particular time.
Neither undertreatment or overtreatment should be defended."
Indeed, in my own practice I conduct both short-term and long-
term psychotherapies.

What are the indications for short-term dynamic therapy?
Who really are the patients who can benefit from a short-term
approach, and who isn't served? First, following the principle
of informed consent, as part of a psychiatric and psychodynamic
assessment, I ask patients what bothers them, what they want
and how long they think it will take to accomplish, and explore
with them their ideas and reasons. As part of the assessment
process I ask myself if I can find and convey in a meaningful
way a psychodynamic focus to the patient's problems (Arm-

strong, 1980; Balint, Ornstein, and Balint, 1972; Binder, 1977; Malan, 1976a; Mann, 1973; Ryle, 1979), and I attempt to determine whether he or she is likely to do well in short-term dynamic treatment based on such selection criteria (Clarkin and Frances, 1982; Malan, 1976a; Sifneos, 1972, 1979) as desire for change, psychological-mindedness, capacity for interpersonal relatedness, and responsiveness to trial interpretations. I also try to assess carefully whether the patient has any important contraindications for short-term dynamic therapy, such as significant suicide potential or marked inability to tolerate anxiety, guilt, or depression. "Reality factors" such as patients' ability to pay and how long they plan to be available also need to be considered.

Near the end of the assessment process (which generally takes one session or sometimes two) I tactfully indicate my recommendation regarding possible treatment to the patient. (Again, as Frances and Clarkin [1981a] point out, sometimes no treatment is the best choice. Sometimes, by the nature of the patient's problems, personality, and goals, long-term therapy is the treatment of choice.) Other times, short-term therapy is clearly indicated. Occasionally, both modalities seem possible. When this seems to be the case, I discuss the choice with the patient, oftentimes suggesting that we first try a short-term therapy to see how much can be accomplished. Assuming no contraindications, this is consistent with the advice of Wolberg (1965b, p. 140): "The best strategy, in my opinion, is to assume that every patient, irrespective of diagnosis, will respond to short-term treatment unless he proves himself refractory to it. If the therapist approaches each patient with the idea of doing as much as he can for him, within the space of, say, up to twenty treatment sessions, he will give the patient an opportunity to take advantage of short-term treatment to the limit of his potential. If this fails, he can always then resort to prolonged therapy."

Even if the patient's problems are not resolved in short-term treatment, it may give the patient the opportunity to recognize to what extent he or she is the creator or perpetuator of his or her psychological misery (Schafer, 1973) and may also provide additional useful information that can help in planning subsequent approaches (e.g., long-term individual therapy, family therapy, environmental manipulation, psychopharmacology). Often, however, a short-term approach is effective with appropriately selected patients. As Malan (1976a, p. 352) has demonstrated:

> It needs to be said again and again that the successful use of psychoanalytic methods in brief psychotherapy is a tribute to psychoanalysis, not an attack upon it; especially when, as here, it is shown that the more psychoanalytic the technique [i.e., interpretation of transference, resistance, and unconscious conflict], the more successful the therapy. The only unpalatable fact to emerge is that patients may sometimes appear to recover without going through the deepest psychoanalytic processes; but this is an empirical observation as surprising to us as to everyone else, and it has to be faced.[7]

The social need for efficient mental health treatments is obvious. If psychotherapy is to remain a large and viable profession, especially in these times of limited resources and increased accountability, it is incumbent upon us to develop and apply effective short-term therapy methods (Kovacs, 1982). As Cummings (1977) has shown within the context of the health maintenance organization, application of brief therapy with most patients allows longer-term therapy to be economically feasible for the patients who most need it. Similarly, in the private sector, therapists who prefer to work in an open-ended or long-term framework may increasingly have to supplement their caseload with a number of briefer, more circumscribed cases. It is therefore to be hoped that calling attention to some potential therapist resistances will help clear the way to the wider acceptance and appropriate application of short-term dynamic psychotherapy as an efficient and rewarding form of treatment.

Notes

1. For a general introduction to short-term dynamic therapy, see Burke, White, and Havens (1979), Clarkin and Frances

(1982), Davanloo (1978, 1980), de la Torre (1978), Gustafson (1984), Bauer and Kobos (1984), Lewin (1970), Malan (1976a), Mann (1973), Mann and Goldman (1982), Marmor (1979), Mendelsohn (1978), Sifneos (1972, 1979), Strupp (1980a–d), Strupp and Binder (1984), and Winokur, Messer, and Schact (1981). In addition to these references, specialized short-term dynamic techniques have been described for working with a variety of clinical problems, including dependent personality (Leeman and Mulvey, 1975), borderline personality (Leibovich, 1981; Nurnberg and Suh, 1980), various personality styles (Horowitz and others, 1984a), depression (Rosenberg, 1986; Strupp and others, 1982), narcissistic disturbances (Lazarus, 1982), post traumatic stress disorders (Horowitz, 1976; Horowitz and Kaltreider, 1979), bereavement reactions (Horowitz and others, 1984a), and various sexual dysfunctions (Kaplan, 1979).

2. As Frances and Clarkin (1981a) point out, therapists tend to recommend treatment almost automatically, without careful consideration of its necessity or possible harmful effects. Patients who are negative responders, nonresponders, and spontaneous improvers may be better off without any treatment.

3. Additional empirical support for Malan's findings have been reported by Marziali and Sullivan (1980), who reanalyzed Malan's data with better methodological controls, and by Marziali (1984), who conducted an independent replication study. Another recent study (Piper and others, 1984), however, found little evidence to support the hypothesis of a direct, linear relationship between focal interpretations and favorable outcomes. Horowitz and others (1984b) found the relationship between interpretation and brief therapy outcome to be mediated by patients' motivation and level of self-concept development, with exploratory work being more suitable for highly motivated and/or better-organized patients.

4. Of course, the imposition of a time limit can itself engender resistance (Michael Shiryon, personal communication) since, as described by the principle of "psychological re-

actance" (Brehm and Brehm, 1981), we tend to value that which is taken from us. Therapists may resent being told, in effect, "You have to treat a patient this way, even if it helps him." Patients also may have a variety of reactions to being told that their treatment will be limited in time. Some may be relieved or indifferent, while others may feel "forced" or shunned. Short-term therapists need to attend to these reactions and to convey the belief that there will be adequate time to deal therapeutically with the problems for which the patient has sought treatment.

5. This points to the importance of long-term follow-up if therapeutic outcomes are to be thoroughly evaluated (Bergin, 1971; Butcher and Kolotkin, 1979; Cross, Sheehan, and Khan, 1982). How durable are the effects of treatment? Do patients continue to improve or do the benefits of short-term therapy decay following termination? Do many short-term patients later reenter therapy for the same problems? These uncertainties may make therapists more hesitant to use short-term methods. The solution is not automatically to extend treatment, of course, but to conduct the research necessary to answer these questions.

6. There is also the legitimate and important research question of gauging when less becomes too little, not more. It is not mere expediency or the sheer quantity of patients treated that is important, but the delivery of the best service to the most patients. Inadequate treatment will only waste limited resources, not maximize their utilization. Also, having a successful brief therapy that ends well may encourage a patient to return someday to treatment for another problem. Further treatment does not necessarily indicate a failed or incomplete first therapy. As Freud ([1937] 1964) noted, a resolution of one conflict may have little influence on other conflicts that a patient may have. Certain patients may make very good use of *serial* short-term therapies. A therapist-patient relationship may endure over an extended period, but need not be continuous (Cummings and VandenBos, 1979; Budman and Gurman, 1983; Bennett, 1984).

7.   In a brilliant review and analysis of twenty-five years of brief therapy at the Tavistock Clinic (under the leadership of Balint and Malan), Gustafson (1981, 1984, 1986; see also Strupp, 1975; Frances and Perry, 1983) argues that the success of brief therapy involves more than interpretation of unconscious focal conflict. Gustafson calls attention to the interpersonal relationship between therapist and patient, the provision of a specific kind of interaction that the patient needs. This reformulation derives from both Alexander and French's idea (1946) of the "corrective emotional experience" and the new "control-mastery" theory of Sampson (1976) and Weiss and others (1977). The application of these ideas to short-term therapy has been discussed by Rosenberg, Sampson, Silberschatz, and Weiss (1982). The theoretical arguments go beyond the scope of this paper; the interested reader is referred to those authors for further discussion.

CHAPTER EIGHTEEN

Resolution of a Transference-Countertransference Impasse Using Gestalt Techniques in Supervision

with Robert L. Goulding

Supervision involves one person looking over and instructing the work of another in order to help the latter improve his or her ability and performance. Effective psychotherapy supervision combines didactic (explanatory) and direct experiential work, depending upon the specific needs of the supervisee and the demands of the moment (Erskine, 1982; Zalcman and Cornell, 1983). The supervision situation is, in many ways, akin to the psychotherapy situation and may at times parallel it. Supervisor and supervisee must identify a focus or purpose for their work together (the "contract"), and the supervisor and supervisee then need to address three interrelated questions: (1) Where is the supervisee-therapist "stuck"? (2) What does he or she need to get "unstuck"? (3) How can this be provided or facilitated? The answers to these questions will guide the work of supervision.

Note: Reprinted, with changes, from Hoyt, M. F., and Goulding, R. L. "Resolution of a Transference-Countertransference Impasse Using Gestalt Techniques in Supervision." *Transactional Analysis Journal,* 1989, *19,* 201–211. Copyright 1989 by the International T. A. Association. Used by permission of the publisher.

Robert L. Goulding, M.D., is deceased. He was a clinical teaching member of the International Transactional Analysis Association (ITAA). He was co-director of the Western Institute for Group and Family Therapy in Watsonville, California, and a past president of the American Academy of Psychotherapists.

Countertransference

One way therapists often get stuck is in *countertransference*, which may be defined as the therapist's specific reaction (counter) to the patient's transference. This definition follows Freud's original emphasis ([1910] 1957) on the *reciprocal* nature of the therapist's reaction, and it has the advantage of calling attention to possible information about the patient that may be derived from the specific response stimulated in the therapist.

Other, more general definitions have identified any pathological reaction of the therapist as countertransference. Erskine (1982), for example, uses the term to refer to "all the reactions of the therapist to the client that are the result of the unresolved conflicts within the therapist and may include their [*sic*] beliefs, memories, and future hopes and plans" (p. 318). This broader definition highlights the fact that a therapist's counterproductive reactions may be determined by the carryover of his or her own conflicts, the imposition of the therapist's own transferences on to the dynamics of a particular patient (Robertiello and Schoenewolf, 1987). When considering a therapist's reactions it may be useful to ask, How much of this is appropriate to the present clinical reality, how much is imported by the therapist, and how much is triggered by the patient? The not-so-easy answer may be some admixture of the three, with further examination required to sort out each person's relative contribution to the transaction.

It is important to note that countertransference episodes are not automatically indicative of therapists' personal treatment issues, although therapists who keep getting stuck often or in the same ways are particularly likely to be invested in script-bound behaviors or some unresolved personal problems. As Cornell and Zalcman (1984) wrote, "Only if a trainee's errors continue after options for understanding the clinical problem or for intervening with the client are offered, do we presume that personal issues need to be confronted" (p. 109).

Berne (1972) recognized the bipersonal (two-handed) nature of countertransference. Using the example of a seductive female patient, he wrote: "Countertransference means that not only does the analyst play a role in the patient's script, but she plays a role in his. In that case, both of them are getting scripty responses from each other, and the result is the 'chaotic situation' which analysts speak of as making it impossible for the analysis to proceed to its proper goal" (p. 352).

The "pull" of the patient's transference can stimulate or evoke the therapist's own counterproductive response. A countertransferential reaction may be complementary to the patient's transference (e.g., the therapist feels guilty or becomes overly active in reaction to the patient's demands or neediness) and/or it may involve an isomorphic or "concordant" identification (Racker, 1957) or "mirror" (Kohut, 1976) to the patient's transference (e.g., the therapist feels depressed and helpless in reaction to the patient's depression and helplessness).

A common countertransference problem may occur when a therapist has a strong need to be needed or to be helpful (Hoyt, 1985; Hoyt and Farrell, 1984). When a therapist frequently transacts from a Nurturing Parent ego state, the normal dependency of the therapist-patient relationship may become exaggerated into an unhealthy symbiosis. As Woollams and Brown (1978), stated, "When two persons are related symbiotically, one person expresses a discounted version of feelings, wants, and needs (cathects Child) and the other assumes a discounted caretaking or persecuting position (cathects Parent)" (p. 112). The interpersonal structure for this overassumption of responsibility, a form of co-dependency (Beattie, 1987), is often a combination of both Type II (AA-PC) crossed transaction (see Berne, 1972, pp. 14–17) and therapist-patient symbiosis (see Figure 18.1). The defense mechanisms of projection and projective identification may be used prominently by both participants in attempts to maintain games and scripts by ridding themselves of unwanted ego states or aspects of self (Chang and James, 1987; Moiso, 1985; Novellino, 1984, 1985).

Sometimes a therapist's compulsive "helpfulness" is motivated by the situation described by Masterson (1983, p. 188): "What we do is project the image of our own childhood self on the patient, and then we become the ideal parent to the child, the child that we were; by doing for this child what we

Figure 18.1. Three Models of Common Transference-Countertransference Reactions.

A. Crossed Transaction (from Berne, 1972, pp. 14–17)

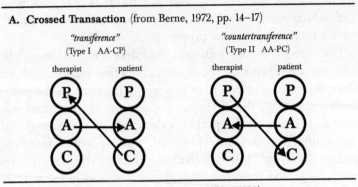

B. Symbiosis (from Woollams & Brown, 1978, p. 108)

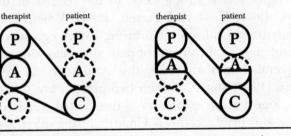

C. Projection-Counteridentification (adapted from Moiso, 1985)

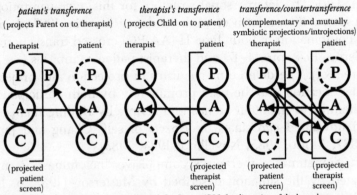

(Dotted lines denote ego states not cathected. See James, 1986, for discussion of the boundary problems of excluded and rigid ego states.)

Source: Reprinted with permission from Hoyt and Goulding (1989).

wanted done for ourselves, we feel better. A tremendous amount of this goes into the motivation to be a therapist to 'help other people.'"

Therapists and supervisors alerted by the unpleasant feelings and lack of change usually associated with such a situation and who are attempting to resolve it will find it helpful to ask, Does this have to do with the therapist, or with the patient, or both? (Goulding, 1978b; Hoyt and Farrell, 1984). If the stuckness has the quality of a *transference-countertransference impasse,* it is likely that the answer will be "both," and the supervisor will be most helpful if he or she can help the therapist-supervisee first recognize and resolve his or her own contribution to the problem. This is illustrated in the following case example.

Case Example

The patient, a forty-year-old man named Anthony, was intelligent, well educated, good looking, creative, articulate, sincere, and a self-described "neurotic mess." He often felt depressed, stuttered, was frustrated by his lack of career development, and frequently numbed and soothed himself in the evening with alcohol and marijuana. He openly stated, "I never wanted to grow up. I hate being an adult, all the responsibility. It's dull and endless. I would love to remain a child." He had developed personality styles (see Chapter Nineteen) that combined pathological narcissism (characterized by unstable self-esteem, a weak "I'm OK," too dependent on situation and other people) and dependency (characterized by helplessness and passivity). Several injunctive decisions were prominent (Goulding and Goulding, 1978, 1979) and had been worked into a life script. For Anthony, these early decisions included Don't Grow Up, Don't Be Important, Don't Make It, Don't Be, and Don't Think.

Six months of therapy had seen him complete part of a significant project in his field of work. He was mostly pleased with the outcome, but he found the Adult demands terribly uncomfortable and had many moments of intense doubt and insecurity along the way. He had a falling out with his best male friend during the work, and his girlfriend had, through an exchange of letters, also made it clear that she was not interested in continuing their relationship. Anthony became more depressed. He barely went to work, socially withdrew, stopped creative activity, thought passively of suicide (a no-suicide contract was made and rechecked as needed [see Drye, Goulding, and Goulding, 1973]), smoked marijuana and drank to escape, and generally felt and acted miserable.

This turn for the worse concerned the therapist, who felt increasingly impotent and stuck. From the beginning of treatment, the therapist had been very attentive and to some extent overly charmed by the patient's friendliness, gratitude, artistry, and emotional sensitivity and vulnerability. The therapist felt a strong empathic contact. There were frequent invitations and temptations for the therapist to be helpful, to make practical suggestions and give advice, to function as a "rewarding unit" (Masterson, 1983, p. 10). In retrospect, this sometimes fostered the collusion of a symbiotic "we" rather than requiring and stroking the patient's own development of greater Adult competency, thus encouraging further entrenchment of the patient's dysfunctional mode of being (Holloway, 1977; Oremland, 1972). The treatment contract was left vague and expressed and enacted more in terms of "needing support" rather than making change. Cogent here is Holloway's observation (1977) that "when the goal is specified by the seeker of change and when the therapist willingly joins the contract, then both can proceed as coequals. This minimizes the likelihood of countertransference interference and enhances working through of transference processes" (p. 174).

As he became more depressed, the patient would literally look to the therapist with pleading eyes. The therapist did not know *what to do for the patient* to pull him out of his funk, a countertransferential assumption of responsibility. Empathy involves resonating with the feelings of another to know his experience, but at this juncture the therapist had become quite overidentified with his patient. In addition to his complementary countertransference (therapist's Nurturing Parent rescuing patient's Helpless Adapted Child), the therapist also projected his own Child feelings of fear and weakness on to the patient.

Although basically psychologically healthy, the therapist experienced the remnants of his own wounded narcissism being activated. The therapist's desire to be "free" and his anxieties about competency and feelings of being overwhelmed were stimulated by counteridentification with the patient and were based on both the immediate therapeutic situation and several large personal and professional responsibilities that the therapist had recently assumed.

All of this had been building gradually and out of awareness. The therapist had the experience of simply being increasingly stuck, of feeling more and more concerned and less and less competent. He was able to recognize the transference-countertransference nature of the bind and presented to his supervisor at his ongoing training group a brief excerpt of a tape recording (made with the patient's consent) of the last therapy session.

Supervision

The work that follows is divided into two phases: the *didactic phase*, in which the therapist–patient process is reported and commented upon; and the *experiential phase*, in which the therapist and supervisor engage in an exchange—in some ways paralleling the therapist–patient relationship—using mental imagery and other Gestalt techniques to quickly produce powerful experiences that result in learning and change.

Didactic Phase. The therapist introduced the vignette saying, "I've got a countertransference problem" and indicated the patient to be a forty-year-old man seen individually. The therapist then played the tape-recorded excerpt, transcribed as follows (with interruptions for comments).

Patient: This week I've felt down, hopeless-type down. I'm very aware that I'm *not* dealing with what I ought to be dealing with, I'm not confronting it. I'm just living it, being a fat, old, depressed, middle-aged man. That's how I see myself. I know that that's probably not your view or someone else's view, but that's the way I decided I am. Like, I get an idea, a positive idea, something that I'll do—and I know all the rules, like, Feelings follow actions; if you do something, then you're going to feel better—but I've even given up on that because that's not working.

Therapist: Do you mean you're doing things but not feeling better?

P: Yeah. Well, not even doing things. It's like, stuck, really stuck. You were talking about tape recording today, and I'm so negative today I don't even know if we can do anything.

T: You've been down for a while.

P: Yeah, I've been down for a long time. And, uh, I'm searching. It's like, I know it's a pattern, this isn't crazy. I know it's within my power to change. And at the same time I don't have the motivation. I know it won't last. I'll just slip back into the crap, so I might as well go on feeling crappy. That's the way I operate. I put diversions in my day to make it through.

T: What do you want?

P: I don't know. I don't even have any goals. I don't know what I want. I'm just tired of being stuck.

T: Do you want to stop feeling so miserable?

P: Well, I'm not sure. I'm not sure. I'm [*sigh*], do I want to stop feeling so miserable? [*Asks self the question.*] That's a very simple question with no simple answer. I don't know. I think I'm still pouting over last summer. I'm still pouting, thinking sort of, if I stay miserable long enough, something will happen. [*Racket*] So I'm not, I don't think that I am ready to stop pouting. Which is pretty fucking stupid!

The supervisor recognized and pointed out the emerging symbiosis (see Woollams and Brown, 1978, pp. 123–124 for a list of ways to recognize symbiotic relationships), the patient's nonautonomous language, his racket (a process to justify "not OK" position—Woollams and Brown, 1978, p. 127), and the polarization of roles into Nurturing Parent and Helpless Adapted

Child. The transcript does not convey as well the therapist's stuckness, the overly concerned tone of voice, lack of spontaneity, and barely restrained urge to rescue the patient. These were commented upon by the supervisor in a constructive manner, and recommendations were made regarding treatment options with emphasis on the importance of stroking (praising, rewarding) the patient's Adult ego state for any positive changes. The supervisor also cautioned against the temptation to rescue the patient and the possible confusion of the patient's needs with the therapist's needs, and he suggested making a diagram (see Figure 18.1B) to keep visible in the therapy room as a reminder to avoid the symbiosis pitfall.

The information was conveyed in a direct Adult-to-Adult manner, and a break was taken in the group supervision session. However, while theoretically accurate and intellectually understandable, the information simply did not click for the supervisee-therapist. He still felt stuck. He knew that he was unsettled and that something else was needed for him to get unstuck.

Experiential Phase. After the break the supervisee-therapist volunteered to be the "client" in some experiential work. He began by saying that he still felt "stuck" and needed to clarify his position. What follows is a transcript of the ensuing work, which took about fifteen minutes. The left column presents the verbatim work, and the right column presents highlighting comments.

Supervision Process

Commentary

Therapist: I've been thinking about him and this symbiosis. As I visualize him I keep—let me put it in poetic language—"falling into the mirror." That is, as I see him I keep seeing how many of his issues are issues that I'm still involved with myself, enough

Therapist states problem, including his role, with allusion to "mirror transference" (Kohut, 1976) and counter-identification aspects.

that when he starts to talk it activates my issues, I lose myself, and it becomes hard for me to pull back.

I want to *clarify* myself more, to get myself more separate, pull myself out of the symbiosis. There are times when I'm sitting with this patient and I can almost see myself in his chair.

Supervision contract stated.

Supervisor: Do you have an idea of how you want to approach this?

Supervisor offers therapist initiative, in effect giving him opportunity to take charge and *clarify* himself.

T: I "understand" it intellectually, drawing little circles and all that, but somehow I want to make it more *real*, reify it.

Therapist indicates limited impact of intellectual explanation and requests more powerful experience to give concepts reality.

I keep coming up with a picture of this fellow sitting in his chair, and I'm sitting in my chair, and it's quiet much like it's quiet in here. And I sense his pain and emptiness. He feels lost . . . and the sense I have, the fantasy that becomes conscious at times, is that I'm his mother and wanting to cradle him and hold him, nurse him, pat him [*gestures with arms as though holding an infant*]. I get stuck in this, I fall into this with this one person.

Experiential process deepens, including emerging parallel process (patient/therapist = therapist/supervisor). Note empathy blending into nursing fantasy.

[*Therapist pauses, focuses attention inward.*] What I'm get-

Security of the supervision situation creates safe space to

ting is a sense of sadness. He's crying and being sad. I then trigger in myself this small, very sad spot. I see myself as this infant, this little baby. And I'm doing it, and it's being stimulated in this situation by, I don't know how to describe it. I feel like I'm activating it. No, I don't feel like I'm activating it. I feel like it's just happening, that I'm falling into it, even though I know I'm somehow activating it. I don't know what to do with this.

S: Well, I do. Take your projection about your client and *be* it: "I'm just a little child wanting someone to hold me in my [*sic*] arms." Just what you said about him, claim for yourself, because that's where you're stuck.

T: Right, yeah.

S: So *do* it, claim it: "I want a mommy who will blah, blah, blah," whatever you said. As you think about him, put it with "I."

play and experiment, "to search for the self," as Winnicott (1971a) says.

Supervisor takes charge and models a way of being with the therapist different from how the therapist is with his patient. The supervisor directs a basic Gestalt exercise, to own one's projections. Note that what appears to be poor grammar ("hold me in my arms") is actually a literal, concrete expression of both sides of the projected fantasy, Child held by Parent.

Intellectually agreeing but not really grasping it yet.

Supervisor continues to direct firmly, not acquiescing to therapist's incomplete response. Getting therapist-supervisees to *do* things rather than just intellectually "know" about them is a common prob-

T: [*Pauses, then says with poignant recognition.*] *I'm* wanting someone to take care of all of these big, adult decisions that need to be made, that are keeping me from being able to play, and not have to worry about things.

S: Be nurtured . . .

T: . . . and be creative and . . .

S: . . . be nurtured.

lem needing to be confronted.

With prompting from supervisor, therapist begins to reclaim projected Child longings.

Supervisor guides therapist to experiment with warded-off experience.

T: [*Pause.*] . . . be nurtured, but it's not so much be nurtured as be *free,* to be able to always do what I want when I want.

S: Say some more about being free and being taken care of.

Supervisor adjusts direction in response to feedback from therapist and continues to facilitate amplification or deepening of therapist's inchoate experience.

T: I would like someone else to take care of business so I can [*pause*], so I can spend more time dreaming.

S: More—carry it to as far a degree as you can let your imagination carry you, about these "being cared fors."

Calls for exaggeration to bring out richness of experience.

T: [*Pause, into reverie.*] I

Slipping into the desired

keep getting little flashes of moments, times when I've been traveling, like I'm walking down a street in Amsterdam, or I'm climbing a mountain somewhere. And they're just little moments, but I feel it's a different part of myself, a very different consciousness that I have.

S: You're leaving the business about being taken care of. Get back to being taken care of—that's where you were a while ago. What were the words you used about how you saw this guy?

T: Empty, collapsing inside . . .

S: So, "I feel empty and collapsing inside."

T: I feel empty, scared. [*Pauses, tunes into body sensation.*] I've got a tingling across my shoulders, like energy.

S: OK, let the tingle go, exaggerate it. [*Therapist does, and sinks into chair.*] You don't look energetic. You said you were feeling energy. Allow yourself to feel the energy that the tingling you said signified.

T: No, that wasn't the right

"free state" he was describing.

Guides and structures, does not let therapist escape contract the way patient escapes responsibility by slipping into fantasy and play. Supervisor prompts for key words to re-evoke state of mind therapist had been projecting.

Guides therapist to experiment.

Supervisor again encourages amplification, now following the therapist's experiencing centered on bodily sensations.

word. I felt like a tingling, but I feel like this guy, like I'm sort of getting weaker and collapsing.

S: Oh, you saw the tingling as getting weaker and collapsing. OK, so get weaker and collapse.

T: [*Slumps in chair.*]

S: And what do you want in that position?

T: To be warmer.

S: Say more.

T: I feel, my hands are real cold, I want to be swaddled, wrapped up.

S: Yep. Can you exaggerate that position some more, that infantile position, both in how your body is and what you're saying inside your head? Play it out. See what you feel as you get more and more.

T: [*Collapses into cuddled-up position, head on armrest of chair, makes small whimpering sounds.*]

S: What are you experiencing?

T: [*Softly.*] Fear and chills.

S: Huh?

T: Chills, cold.

Note adjustment and experiment.

Supervisor validates experience ("Yep") and again encourages exaggeration to enrich awareness.

S: Now, take the opposite position, and get yourself out of there.

Directs dialectic and encourages therapist's self-empowerment.

T: [*Lifts head, sighs, sits up straight.*]

S: Exaggerate it.

T: [*Stretches, flexes shoulders, sits straighter.*]

S: And what are you experiencing?

T: Strength . . .

S: Yeah.

Validates change.

T: . . . . muscles through here [*gestures toward chest*] particularly, power.

S: Stand up, and see what you feel when you stand up.

Amplifies therapist's positive movement, builds on momentum, increases mind-body congruence.

T: [*Stands.*]

S: What do you experience?

T: Not much. I kind of went blank.

S: So go back to the being nothing then. Not nothing, but very small, caved in, and all those other words you had.

Follows the lead and amplifies, suggesting caricature to flood experience. Also note correction of language, more precisely directed toward Don't Grow Up (rather than Don't Be) injunction/script.

T: [*Sits and resumes slumped,*

collapsed position with head down.]

S: And what are you experiencing now?

T: A feeling of disappearance, wanting to hold still and not be.

S: OK. How long do you want us [*sic*] to hold that position? Two minutes, five minutes, five days, five years?

Choice of language ("us") suggests awareness of therapist's quest for symbiotic transference. Question implies initiative belongs to therapist, and referring to protracted time heightens the untenability of the stasis.

T: [*Getting increasingly uncomfortable, physically and psychologically, in collapsed state, speaks softly.*] Me, I don't want to hold it any longer.

Therapist begins to pull out of symbiosis, assert individuality ("Me"). Intensified experience with unpleasant state generates organismic disgust (Simkin, 1976, p. 61).

S: What?

T: No longer for me!

S: OK, then get out of it!

Calls for louder, clearer, more forceful position from therapist.

T: [*Sits right up, laughing with relief and recognition.*]

Protection, permission, potency.

S: What do you experience?

T: I feel more *present*.

Encourages verbalization of experiential recognitions.

S: Yeah.

Positive stroking.

T: I'm [*looks around*], I'm seeing my legs more, I'm in the room more.

S: Yeah, OK. Feel your power?

T: Yeah!

S: OK, now tell this guy what you're going to do with him. There he is out in that chair, even got his back turned to you partially, that's the way he sits, I think.

T: [*Pauses, forms image of patient in chair.*] Anthony, what I'm going to do is be your therapist and not your mother.

S: Yeah! [*Training group claps approval.*]

T: I'm going to assist you and stroke you when you make improvements in your functioning. And I'm going to wait, sometimes patiently and sometimes impatiently, for a while while you're getting yourself together to do that!

S: OK. Satisfied?

T: Yeah! [*Pause.*] That makes very real those circles! [*Happy laugh.*]

S: Yep! [*Laughs.*]

More stroking.

Learning = change as a result of experience. Therapist's experiential work is now linked back to supervision contract, to expedite changes in his work with patient, specifically to resolve symbiotic impasse.

Positive stroking, reinforced by group (Goulding, 1987).

Checks to see if there is more work to do at the present time.

Links experiential and didactic learning. Completing work in an upbeat, winner position adds energy and makes learning more memorable.

Having fun makes for better supervision.

Follow-up

The effects of this supervisory episode were immediate, powerful, and enduring. The therapist felt (self-)empowered and functioned more effectively with his patient in subsequent therapy sessions. He felt freer, in good contact yet more separate, and maintained a supportive attitude that was respectful of the patient's abilities and clearly emphasized the I-Thou nature of their relationship. Anthony responded well and began to reclaim and act upon his autonomy. It is beyond the scope of this chapter, of course, to detail the subsequent course of therapy. What has been illustrated here about supervision is what Whitaker (1983) said well: "Learning only brings recognition; experience produces change" (p. 40).

Discussion

The specific treatment impasse in the case presented here, having to do with a confusion of dependency and responsibility, is only one of many possible countertransference problems that may require skillful supervision to resolve. Indeed, the inevitability of countertransference responses and the potential for problems have long been recognized (Freud [1910] 1957, pp. 144–145; Jung, [1931] 1966, p. 72). Acknowledged and used appropriately, countertransference responses can spotlight therapeutic issues that need attention: "Any feeling, then, of the therapist toward the patient that *could* be labelled countertransference can be used by a properly trained and skilled therapist" (Goulding, 1978a, pp. 185–186). "Furthermore," as Binder, Strupp, and Schacht (1983) noted, "attention to countertransference aspects of the . . . therapy situation is essential to establishing and maintaining a productive alliance with those especially 'difficult' patients whose predominant relationship patterns would otherwise strain the therapist's skill" (p. 622).

In the supervision work described here, by having the supervisee-therapist verbally and nonverbally exaggerate his initially ineffable "stuck" experience, he was able quickly to intensify it sufficiently to recognize and reown his contribution to the therapeutic impasse. A therapist and supervisor who sought to master countertransference by its suppression or affect reduction would be less likely to resolve the therapist's underlying contribution, neither rapidly nor perhaps at all. A direct experiential approach can be especially helpful for cutting through the intellectualizing and "knowing about" rather than "being" that frequently occurs when therapists become patients or trainees (Kaslow, 1984). Techniques that involve enhanced expressiveness through the exaggeration of subtle nonverbal cues may be particularly useful for bringing into awareness transference and countertransference responses based on preverbal experiences.

Patients and therapists will benefit more from a treatment or supervision that provides *experience* as well as *explanation*–power and wisdom combined. The use of treatment approaches in supervision appears consistent with much of TA training practice, as reviewed by Zalcman and Cornell (1983): "Unlike academic training, the resolution of personal therapy issues has been consistently emphasized and frequently integrated into the [TA] supervision session itself" (p. 113). Doing such work requires strong ethical safeguards, of course, including strict confidentiality, no performance-contingent grading or degree granting, scrupulous attention to possible games supervisors and supervisees sometimes play (Hawthorne, 1975; Kadushin, 1968), and clear supervision contracts (Barnes, 1977).

A last point has to do with the possible parallel process (Ekstein and Wallerstein, 1972; Frances and Clarkin, 1981b; Hess, 1980) wherein aspects of the patient-therapist relationship may be repeated in the therapist-supervisor relationship. Elements of this occurred in the supervision described here: the immobile, stuck therapist looked to the supervisor with a passive dependency similar to that with which the patient looked to the therapist. The supervisor also demonstrated effective treatment techniques in his method of supervision, a desirable situation in that a trainee develops partially by modeling and identifying with the supervisor. Simply replacing one identification with another, however–switching from patient to supervisor (mirroring "up" rather than "down," so to speak)–would not result in the change and integration that supervision should involve. In the work presented here, several factors suggest a more substantial working through of the therapist's contribution to the treatment impasse. First, there is the direct impact of the didactic and experiential work, reinforcing earlier personal development and therapy. Second, there is the cognitive reworking that accompanied the experience, partially expressed in this writing. There is also the evidence (with the patient reported upon here as well as with others) that the therapist has subsequently encountered similar situations without significantly and inappropriately yielding to invitations toward symbiosis. Finally, there is the TA/Gestalt method itself: The therapist-supervisee finds the power within himself (not primarily in a supervisor) and is thus directed toward his own unique ability.

CHAPTER NINETEEN

Psychodiagnosis
of Personality Disorders

*What is the hardest of all? That which you hold the most
simple; seeing with your own eyes what is spread out before
you.*

–Johann Wolfgang von Goethe

The term *diagnosis* derives from Greek and Latin words *(via
gnossis)* meaning "the way to know or distinguish." That is precisely what a good, functional diagnosis should do: provide information that helps to point the way. Effective psychotherapeutic treatment planning and implementation considers
what the patient wants in therapy (the "contract") and then addresses three questions: (1) Where is the patient "stuck" (what
is the problem or pathology)? (2) What experience does the
patient need to get "unstuck"? and (3) How can this experience
be facilitated or provided? While "personality restructuring"
would be too vague and ambitious to be considered a good
goal of brief therapy–and would be an endeavor that would
seldom, if ever, be funded under managed care–awareness of
some problematic patient patterns can help the therapist answer
each question efficaciously.

Note: Reprinted, with changes, from Hoyt, M. F. "Psychodiagnosis of Personality Disorders." *Transactional Analysis Journal,* 1989, *19,* 101–113. Copyright
1989 by International T. A. Association. Used by permission of the publisher.

The author gratefully acknowledges Mary and Bob Goulding and the
1986–87 Ongoing Training Group at the Western Institute for Group and
Family Therapy for their assistance. Additional helpful comments were
provided by many of the author's colleagues at the Kaiser Medical Center in
Hayward, California, and by Dennis Farrell, Muriel James, Vann Joines,
Jennifer Lillard, Jeffry Ordover, and Saul Rosenberg.

The purpose of this chapter is to coordinate key transactional analysis (TA) concepts with information about personality derived from psychodynamic clinical theory and descriptive psychiatry in order to enhance therapists' ability to effectively assess, treat, and anticipate difficulties with various types of patients. TA therapists regularly assess and analyze patients' ego states, transactions, stroking patterns, time structuring, rackets and games, injunctions and decisions, drivers, and scripts, although many have been reluctant to formalize their observations into "personality diagnoses" for various reasons, including the lack of clear terminology and a good schema, distaste for labeling and "objectifying" people, fear that diagnoses could fall into the wrong hands, the wish to avoid the possible stigmatizing "You're Not OK" implication of a diagnosis, disenchantment with the medical model, populist and anti-intellectual trends, and the link between diagnosis and psychoanalysis (Brown, 1977; Kadis, 1986).

Although these considerations are not without some merit, I agree with Meehl (1973), who identified and exposed the fallacies in four frequent and erroneous beliefs underlying the antinosological bias of many (not just TA-oriented) psychotherapists: (1) the belief that diagnosis is inherently unreliable; (2) the belief that labeling interferes with understanding; (3) the belief that diagnosis is prognostically worthless; and (4) the belief that diagnosis does not help treatment. Rather, it is possible to form humanistic and confidential diagnostic impressions that help point the way for effective treatment. The importance of a clear understanding was emphasized by Berne (1966) when he said, "Observation is the basis of all good clinical work, and takes precedence even over technique" (pp. 65–66).

Personality as Patterns of Being and Behaving

"Personality represents a *pattern* of deeply embedded and broadly exhibited cognitive, affective, and overt behavioral traits that persist over extended periods of time" (Millon and Everly, 1985, p. 4). The development and maintenance of patterns that limit a person's potential for growth, pleasure, and happiness may be referred to as *psychopathology* (Brown, 1977, p. 1). The value of an accurate diagnosis lies in the way it spotlights observable and predictable patterns of thoughts, feelings, and actions that therapists need to address and help modify in order to be effective.

How does one recognize such patterns? A number of writers have described similar clusters of personality characteristics, referring to them variously as *character* (Reich, 1949), *neurotic styles* (Horowitz and others, 1984b; Shapiro, 1965), *conditioned fixity of character traits* (Corlis and Rabe, 1969), *clinical syndromes* (MacKinnon and Michels, 1971), *personality disorders* (American Psychiatric Association, 1987, 1994), and *personality adaptations* (Joines, 1986, 1988; Ware, 1983). One discerns a "constant attitude" if one looks through the patient's layers of content with the "vertical focus" described by Gustafson (1986, p. 25). Maladaptive when extreme or rigid, Shapiro (1965) defines *style* as "a form or mode of functioning–the way or manner of a given area of behavior–that is identifiable, in an individual, through a range of his specific acts . . . particularly, ways of thinking and perceiving, ways of experiencing emotion; modes of subjective experience in general, and modes of activity that are associated with various pathologies" (p. 1).

Thus each disorder has certain defining characteristics. Although there is considerable overlap between diagnostic categories (Millon, 1988; Morey, 1988), patients receiving the same diagnosis may be expected to operate in similar ways; for example, the hysteric tends to be emotional and avoid Adult thinking, the obsessive thinks rigidly and avoids feelings, and the paranoid is suspicious and avoids vulnerability. An interpersonal loss might devastate a dependent person, whereas a schizoid person might be relatively unruffled. A personal success that might bolster the self-esteem of a narcissist might be negated or discounted by a depressive.

Although details regarding population distribution and longitudinal prognosis are beyond the scope of this chapter, it may be briefly noted that Merikangas and Weissman (1986) reviewed a large number of studies on the epidemiology of personality disorders and concluded: "There is a general agreement that the personality disorders have a chronic course characterized by persistent impairment in social functioning and increased risk of psychiatric symptomatology and diagnoses. . . . [Personality] disorders constitute one of the most important sources of long-term impairment in both treated and untreated populations. Nearly one in every ten adults in the general population, and over one-half of those in treated populations, may be expected to suffer from one of the personality disorders" (p. 274).

It is important to realize that the styles and disorders referred to here are seldom if ever pure types. They are only approximated in reality, and people often manifest a blend of more than one style. Indeed, virtually everyone uses features of several styles to varying degrees, and styles should only be thought of as pathological when one or more become so prominent as to result in subjective distress or interference with successful functioning. Moreover, it should be noted that the terms are not meant to be used pejoratively, and that an individual may exhibit one or another characteristic without being of a certain personality style or disorder (e.g., a person may occasionally use thought to avoid feelings without being a true obsessive personality, and a person can become angry and temporarily see things in all-or-none terms without being a true borderline personality).

Diagnostic categories should be reserved to indicate a predominant way of meeting the world. In this regard, it may be preferable to think of personality styles more as *processes* than as fixed entities (more as verbs than nouns, so to speak) and thus avoid reifying ways of functioning into permanent attributes. There is therapeutic leverage in conceptualizing problems in terms of *how* rather than *who*.

Given these qualifications, the skillful therapist must modify his or her technique according to variations in the patient's personal style of thinking, feeling, and acting. This is one aspect of psychotherapy that makes it an art and an interesting process. The therapist who recognizes certain personality patterns or typical functional styles can tailor treatment to what Ware (1983; Joines, 1986, 1988) calls "doors to therapy": the "open door" of making contact with the patient, the "target door" of intended change, and the "trap door" (pitfall to be avoided) which leads to getting stuck.

Table 19.1 draws on my clinical observations plus the writings of Brown (1977), Horowitz and others (1984b), James (1986), Joines (1986, 1988), MacKinnon and Michels (1971), Millon and Everly (1985), Shapiro (1965), Ware (1983), and the *DSM-III-R* and *DSM-IV,* 1994 (American Psychiatric Association, 1987). It offers guidelines for recognizing treatment issues in relation to differing personality styles and disorders.

How to Read the Table: Characteristics of Personality Disorders

Table 19.1 presents ten personality disorders: Histrionic (Hysterical), Obsessive-Compulsive, Self-Defeating (Masochistic/Depressive), Narcissistic, Borderline, Dependent, Passive-Aggressive, Paranoid, Antisocial (Sociopathic), and Schizoid. For each diagnostic category, information (remember, the map is not the territory!) is provided under a series of rubrics.

The *Watchword* for each diagnosis refers to a word or phrase commonly heard from individuals with the disorder; this word or phrase serves as "a password or sign of recognition . . . a sentiment or motto as embodying a principle or guide to action" (*Webster's Dictionary,* 1951, p. 965).

Presentation and Therapeutic Process presents a brief summary of processes and the mode of presentation typical of each disorder, derived from clinical experience and the literature (and modeled particularly after Horowitz, 1976; Horowitz and others, 1984b). In addition to describing patient presentation, the usually appropriate and effective therapeutic counter is indicated along with likely pitfalls or "trap doors" and the intended patient "target" or desired direction of change (Ware, 1983; Joines, 1986, 1988). These guidelines are necessarily abstract, although therapists may find them instructive regardless of the specific method of intervention employed (e.g., redecision, mobilization of affect, support and advice-giving, reframing, hypnosis, analysis and interpretation).

Table 19.1. Personality Disorders and Some Interrelated Features.

Disorder: HISTRIONIC (Hysterical)

Watchword	"I don't know why, I just feel upset." "I don't want to think about anything that isn't nice."
Presentation and Therapeutic Process	Patient is vague, global, impressionistic, emotional. Therapist is factual, opposes vagueness, strokes thinking. Patient struggles to make connections between feelings and thoughts and actions.
Identity (Self/Other Images)	Child/Parent; Innocent/Seducer; Dumb/Smart; Victim/Abuser
Information Processing, Defenses, Affects	feeling without thinking, repression, denial, magic, regression, dissociation, poor memory, conversion, confusion, fantasy, emotionally labile, underlying anxiety about abandonment and sexual excitement
Interpersonal Relationships	seductive, cute, superficial, eroticized, histrionic, helpless, needy, pseudo-innocent, uproar, suicidal gestures sometimes used for drama and control
Main Injunctive Decisions	Don't Grow Up; Don't Think; Don't Be Important; Don't Be Close
Ego State Boundary Problems	contamination, rigid
Self/Other Existential Position	I'm Not OK, You're OK
Common Reactions to Therapist	dependent, helpless, sexual games, scared, cries, stops thinking, provocative, show me ("No one can help me")
Common Reactions to Patient	paternalistic, overly active, sexual games, critical, do thinking for patient, bored

Table 19.1. Personality Disorders and Some Interrelated Features, *Cont'd.*

Disorder: OBSESSIVE/COMPULSIVE

Watchword	"On the other hand...." "Relatively speaking, it's hard to really know for sure what one should think."
Presentation and Therapeutic Process	Patient shifts topics frequently or is overly detailed, avoids feelings. Therapist holds to main topic, seeks feelings and images, strokes emotional awareness and expression. Patient struggles to stay with topic and feelings.
Identity (Self/Other Images)	Subject/Authority; Controlled/Controller; Victim/Assailant; Servant/Boss
Information Processing, Defenses, Affects	intellectualization, denial, repression, reaction formation, switches meanings, highly structured, overly detailed, rituals and compulsions, worrying, isolation of affect, compartmentalization, thinking used to ward off underlying feelings of anger, sadness, sexual excitement
Interpersonal Relationships	authoritarian, deferent, controlled, critical, distant, formal, orderly, dutiful, structured, mechanical, perfectionistic, cautious, fears making mistakes and so procrastinates
Main Injunctive Decisions	Don't Feel; Don't Enjoy; Don't Be a Child; Don't Be Close
Ego State Boundary Problems	contamination, rigid
Self/Other Existential Position	I'm Not OK, You're OK
Common Reactions to Therapist	deferent, compliant, oppositional ("Yes, but"), competitive, angry
Common Reactions to Patient	bossy, authoritarian, tired, bored, competitive, angry, overly logical and obsessive

Table 19.1. Personality Disorders and Some Interrelated Features, *Cont'd.*

	Disorder: SELF-DEFEATING (Masochistic/Depressive)
Watchword	"Nothing is right." "Snatch defeat from the jaws of victory."
Presentation and Therapeutic Process	Patient is sad and expects/finds the worst. Therapist holds to realistic view, opposes self-defeating thoughts and acts, strokes small positive moves. Patient struggles to see all sides and to seek and accept pleasure.
Identity (Self/Other Images)	Weak/Strong; Bad/Good; Wrong/Critic; Guilty/Judge; Loser/Winner
Information Processing, Defenses, Affects	negativity bias, internalization, rumination, brooding, low energy, passivity, crying, somatization, slowness, denial, guilt, incomplete mourning, anger, choked-off feelings (possible endogenous factors), risk of suicide
Interpersonal Relationships	dull, serious, nothing is right, withdrawal, dissatisfying, joyless, hold at arm's length, masochistic, drab lifestyle
Main Injunctive Decisions	Don't Be; Don't Make It; Don't Be Important; Don't Enjoy; Don't Belong; Don't Be Well; Don't Be Close
Ego State Boundary Problems	contamination, rigid
Self/Other Existential Position	I'm Not OK, You're OK
Common Reactions to Therapist	helpless, invites rejection ("Yes, but"), passivity
Common Reactions to Patient	depressed and drained, hopeless, overly busy, frustrated and angry, advising and exhorting ("Do something!")

Table 19.1. Personality Disorders and Some Interrelated Features, *Cont'd*

Disorder: NARCISSISTIC

Watchword	"I, I, I, me, me, me."
Presentation and Therapeutic Process	Patient is grandiose and arrogant or deflated and despairing. Therapist stabilizes patient's positive self-esteem, relates tactfully, gives small doses of balanced view, strokes "I'm OK" affirmation. Patient struggles to feel OK without exaggeration.
Identity (Self/Other Images)	unstable self-esteem (weak "I'm OK") too dependent on situation and other people; positive views of self/other such as Great/Admirer, Protégé/Mentor are brittle and flip to negative views such as Worthless/Scorner, Fraud/Detective, Defective/Judge, Wounded/Harmer
Information Processing, Defenses, Affects	distorts meanings to aggrandize self, rationalization, externalization, projection, pride/shame, humiliation
Interpersonal Relationships	arrogant, self-centered, shallow, scornful, belittling, attention-seeking, others exist only to admire and please self, exquisitely sensitive to insult and rejection, lacks empathy, energy involved in persona, performs for audience, chameleon
Main Injunctive Decisions	Don't Be Important; Don't Be Who You Are; Don't Be Close; Don't Make It; Don't Grow Up; Don't Be Dependent
Ego State Boundary Problems	contamination, rigid, lesion
Self/Other Existential Position	I'm (Not) OK, You're (Not) OK
Common Reactions to Therapist	idealizes therapist ("We're both great"), mirrors therapist (self-worth as reflection of therapist's reactions), acts superior, detached and scornful alternating with envy, hurt, and rage
Common Reactions to Patient	seduced by admiration, bored, annoyed, critical ("You're a pain in the ass"), rejecting, feels like an object, one-upping patient or showing off in attempt to counter patient's devaluation of therapist

Table 19.1. Personality Disorders and Some Interrelated Features, *Cont'd.*

Disorder: BORDERLINE

Watchword	"Falling apart." "Empty inside." "I don't know why everything always happens to me." "He/she/they/you/everybody is an asshole!"
Presentation and Therapeutic Process	Patient is very upset, unrealistic, overwhelmed. Therapist contacts and stabilizes Adult, supports by setting limits and structure and by stroking sense of self and reality function; confronts transference. Patient struggles to differentiate self and feel OK and to problem-solve.
Identity (Self/Other Images)	unstable or incomplete sense of self that fragments; patient has unintegrated view of world and self that flips from All Good to All Bad, Angel/Devil, Friend/Foe, Love/Hate, Victim/Persecutor, Avenger/Violator, Helpless/Manipulator; patient also sometimes feels literally selfless and empty ("like a black hole")
Information Processing, Defenses, Affects	splitting, projection, externalization, projective identification, denial, regression, rapid shifting, disordered thinking, mini-psychoses, severe acting out, frequent rage and self-disgust, underlying is great psychic pain (terror) and loneliness, disorganization, frequent crises, risk of self-mutilation or suicide
Interpersonal Relationships	tumultuous, chaotic history, impulsive, clinging, little real support, antagonistic, "can't be alone" hostile-dependency, uproar, cycle of merging and losing self/separating with explosion/feeling bereft and terribly alone and lost, sometimes suicidal/reconnecting and merging, losing self/etc.
Main Injunctive Decisions	Don't Be Sane; Don't Be; Don't Grow Up; Don't Think; Don't Make It; Don't Trust; Don't Be Close; Don't Be Well; Don't Be Important
Ego State Boundary Problems	contamination, rigid, lax, lesion
Self/Other Existential Position	I'm Not OK, You're Not OK
Common Reactions to Therapist	demanding, expecting, rejection, helpless, provocative, angry, scornful ("See, I knew you really didn't care"), seductive
Common Reactions to Patient	frightened, overly active, withdraws, antagonistic, rejecting, guilty, feels manipulated, confused, may notice self having unusually intense responses

Table 19.1. Personality Disorders and Some Interrelated Features, *Cont'd.*

Disorder: DEPENDENT

Watchword	"Help me." "What should I do?" "Please do me a favor, if you could."
Presentation and Therapeutic Process	Patient presents as weak, unable, doubts self, relies on help. Therapist expects strength and behavior change (not just talk), does not rescue, strokes patient's efforts. Patient struggles to function effectively and to be "OK."
Identity (Self/Other Images)	Weak/Strong; Small/Big; Child/Parent; Helpless/Rescuer; Needy/Nurturer; Cripple/Caretaker
Information Processing, Defenses, Affects	regression, passivity, externalization of responsibility, confusion, collapse, procrastination, sadness, underlying feelings are fear, weakness, inferiority, suppressed resentment and entitlement
Interpersonal Relationships	clinging, seeks rescuers, inactive and passive, whiny or overly admiring ("Gee, you're good at that") (helps to treat family co-dependents)
Main Injunctive Decisions	Don't Grow Up; Don't Do Well; Don't Make It; Don't Be Important; Don't Think; Don't . . .
Ego State Boundary Problems	contamination, lax
Self/Other Existential Position	I'm Not OK, You're OK
Common Reactions to Therapist	helpless, goes limp, needy, "poor me," wheedling, sycophancy, confused ("Please explain that again")
Common Reactions to Patient	overly active, guilty, angry, rescues, seduced by feeling very important and useful, tired, withdrawal

Table 19.1. Personality Disorders and Some Interrelated Features, *Cont'd.*

Disorder: *PASSIVE-AGGRESSIVE*

Watchword	"I don't know why you're so upset—I didn't do anything." "I'm only trying to help." "Don't blame me (but I got you!)."
Presentation and Therapeutic Processs	Patient presents as a confused misunderstood victim. Therapist nurtures, avoids criticizing, is playful, seeks genuine feelings, strokes direct communications. Patient struggles to act/express more directly, reduce rebellion.
Identity (Self/Other Images)	Victim/Persecutor; David/Goliath; Rebel/Bully; Underdog/Topdog
Information Processing, Defenses, Affects	reaction formation, displacement, denial, projective identification, rationalization, pseudo-sweet with underlying anger, resentment, and hurt feelings
Interpersonal Relationships	frustrating, sarcastic, stubborn, contrary, defiant, pushes away, picky, legalistic, withholding, hurts with passivity, vindictive, procrastinates as way of annoying others
Main Injunctive Decisions	Don't Be Close; Don't Make It; Don't Trust; Don't Feel; Don't Enjoy; Don't Grow Up
Ego State Boundary Problems	contamination, rigid
Self/Other Existential Position	I'm Not OK, You're Not OK
Common Reactions to Therapist	picky, passive, invites criticism, "Yes, but," complaining
Common Reactions to Patient	annoyance, frustration, tired, angry

Table 19.1. Personality Disorders and Some Interrelated Features, *Cont'd.*

Disorder: PARANOID

Watchword	"What did you mean by that?" "You won't get me." "We both know what's really going on." "I can see that you don't believe me either—no one does."
Presentation and Therapeutic Process	Patient is guarded, suspicious, distorts to find expected danger or insult. Therapist nurtures, doesn't attack or criticize, is reliable, gradually seeks feelings and strokes patient's trust and reality testing. Patient struggles to feel safe, make contact, think realistically, expose vulnerable feelings.
Identity (Self/Other Images)	Victim/Attacker; Guard/Enemy; Innocent/Evil; Target/Conspirators
Information Processing, Defenses, Affects	projection, externalization, denial, hypervigilance to avoid surprises or attack, distorts significance of events, rigid, humorless, tense and controlled, underlying feelings are fear and anger (previous hurts), delusions
Interpersonal Relationships	suspicious, guarded, testing, blaming, constricted, structured, distant, touchy, adversarial, accusatory
Main Injunctive Decisions	Don't Trust; Don't Be Close; Don't Feel; Don't Be a Child; Don't Belong; Don't Enjoy
Ego State Boundary Problems	contamination, rigid, lesion
Self/Other Existential Position	I'm OK, You're Not OK
Common Reactions to Therapist	suspicious, withholding, testing, avoidant turning to anger, veiled hostility ("Don't try anything funny")
Common Reactions to Patient	frightened, apologetic or too nice (which invites more suspicion), impatient, guarded, overly logical and argumentative

Table 19.1. Personality Disorders and Some Interrelated Features, *Cont'd.*

Disorder: ANTISOCIAL (Sociopathic)

Watchword	"I just felt like it." "I'm going to get what I can from the suckers." "Get them before they get you." "Well, to be totally honest." or "To tell you the truth."
Presentation and Therapeutic Process	Patient usually presents as victim of behavior/legal problem, acts cool and distant. Therapist sets limits, nurtures, is reliable, gradually seeks and strokes feelings. Patient struggles to feel safe, make real contact, respond to others and tolerate anxiety.
Identity (Self/Other Images)	Deprived/Rich; Smart/Dumb; Entitled/Chump; Tough/Weak
Information Processing, Defenses, Affects	repression, denial, isolation of affect, rationalization, compartmentalization, impulsive, acting out, excitement-seeking, "cool" covers little actual tolerance for anxiety, cynical, resentful, lack of long-range planning or concern for consequences
Interpersonal Relationships	exploitative, manipulative, remorseless, seductive, lying, con artist, uses people, lack of trust in others, restless, thrill-seeking, can be violent or cruel, sadistic, criminal, predatory
Main Injunctive Decisions	Don't Trust; Don't Feel; Don't Belong; Don't Make It; Don't Be
Ego State Boundary Problems	contamination, rigid, lesion
Self/Other Existential Position	I'm OK, You're Not OK
Common Reactions to Therapist	cool and distant, smooth-talking, manipulative, seductive, lying, sneaky, challenging, and threatening, seeks secondary gains (excuses for legal problems, etc.), distrustful
Common Reactions to Patient	wary and distant, seduced, conned, manipulated, victimized, disgusted, disappointed, frightened, enjoy and encourage acting out, feel "cool" and "hip" by association

Table 19.1. Personality Disorders and Some Interrelated Features, *Cont'd.*

Disorder: SCHIZOID [a]

Watchword	"I guess so." "I don't know."
Presentation and Therapeutic Process	Patient is vague with little affect, passive and speechless or rambling without meaning or direction. Therapist structures, seeks and strokes contact, feeling, Adult thinking and acting. Patient struggles to stay in contact and to organize thinking and behavior.
Identity (Self/Other Images)	tends not to have sense of self or feeling of I/Thou relationship, may have unarticulated experience of Small/Big, Lost/Busy, Me/Them
Information Processing, Defenses, Affects	passivity, nonthinking, fantasy, withdrawal (e.g., T.V., science fiction), blank or numb, depressed, flat affect, perseveration, not spontaneous, low energy
Interpersonal Relationships	disconnected, socially isolated, undefined, vague, alienated, detached, withdrawn, "not there," "in a fog," humorless, solitary, loner, monadic, indifferent to others
Main Injunctive Decisions	Don't Make It; Don't Be; Don't Be Close; Don't Grow Up; Don't Enjoy; Don't Feel; Don't Think; Don't Be Important
Ego State Boundary Problems	contamination, lax, lesion
Self/Other Existential Position	I'm Not OK, You're Not OK
Common Reactions to Therapist	passive, not engaged, expects criticism, avoidant, dull, blank, "spaced out"
Common Reactions to Patient	helpless, bored, angry, impatient, "pulling teeth," lose interest

[a] *Schizoid Personality Disorder,* characterized by cognitive-affective blankness and no desire for social relations, should be distinguished from two other personality disorders. *Schizotypical Personality Disorder* is characterized by oddities and eccentricities of thought, perception, speech, and behavior— the individual is "peculiar" and often isolated but does not quite exhibit the frank psychosis required to meet the criteria of schizophrenia. *Avoidant*

Personality Disorder is characterized by terribly painful shyness–the individual yearns for social relations but is socially withdrawn, hypersensitive to
rejection, suffers from low self-esteem, and requires unusually strong guar-
antees of uncritical acceptance before entering into relationships. Individuals with personality styles consistent with any of these three disorders are
usually, for different reasons, socially isolated. The Avoidant Personality is
the most likely to appear in therapy, complaining of loneliness and extreme shyness, with injunctive decisions typically being to not trust, to not
be close, to not belong, to not enjoy, and to not make it.
Source: Reprinted with permission from Hoyt (1989b, pp. 109–113).

    The next three headings–*Identity (Self/Other Images); Infor-
mation Processing, Defenses, Affects;* and *Interpersonal Relationships*–
refer to three closely related aspects of psychological functioning. Several theorists (e.g., Brown, 1977; Horowitz, 1976, 1979;
Horowitz and others, 1984b; Kernberg, 1984; Millon and Everly, 1985; Shapiro, 1965; Strupp and Binder, 1984) have emphasized how a person's view of self and others, ways of
thinking and experiencing emotion, and relationships with others are profoundly intertwined and mutually reinforcing. These
headings are also phenomenologically close; that is, they are
the doors to therapy (Ware, 1983) through which patients enter
when they seek treatment: specific problems with self-esteem,
difficulties with thinking and feeling, and unhappy relationships
with others.

    The open door is where individuals invest their energy (think-
ing, feeling, or behavior) and is thus the avenue of communication
through which the therapist can make contact with them. Affects
(feeling states) may be dysfunctional rackets, but they may also
be useful in stimulating helpful awarenesses and/or problem-
solving behavior (Thomson, 1983). According to Hartmann (1981),
Berne used the term *discounting* to describe the general effect of
all defense mechanisms, although detailed description of specific
modes may provide useful information for recognizing problems
and planning treatment interventions. The terminology of defense
mechanisms originated in psychoanalytic ego psychology (Blanck
and Blanck, 1974; Freud, 1946); within psychoanalysis, Schafer
(1976) has proposed that defenses be recast from "mechanisms"
into more active, autonomous language (e.g., "John is projecting"
rather than "John is using projection").

Awareness of typical defenses (psychological coping methods) associated with different personality disorders allows therapists to recognize where patients get stuck and how various interventions may be perceived and processed. Indeed, it may be helpful for perplexed clinicians to recognize that the frequent use of primitive defenses (e.g., splitting, acting out, hypochondriasis, projective identification, fantasy) qualitatively differentiates personality disorders from more benign personality styles or traits. Additionally, as Horowitz, Rosenbaum, and Wilner (1988) observe, difficult treatment dilemmas and impasses may arise when patients impose mutually contradictory views of self and others on the treatment relationship. For example, the patient may have self-images of one who is both neglected and intruded upon. "If the therapist reacts to reduce a threat embodied in one RRM [role relationship model], the threat contained in another RRM is increased. The result is a double bind affecting both patient and therapist, and contributed to by both" (Horowitz, Rosenbaum, and Wilner, 1988, pp. 241–242). Forming and maintaining a therapeutic alliance with such patients can be particularly problematic.

Main Injunctive Decisions refers to powerful negative messages from parental figures that the growing child may decide to accept and work into a script (Berne, 1972; Goulding and Goulding, 1978, 1979). From the perspective of object-relations theory (Greenberg and Mitchell, 1983), injunctions may be thought of as the "voices" or messages of pathological introjects. (This is why Mary Goulding [1985] titled her book on identifying and detoxifying mental demons, *Who's Been Living in Your Head?*) Injunctions are learned or taken in through spoken precept, actual or misconstrued observation and identification, experience and stroking patterns, or the child's own origination (which ultimately is always the case, since the child chooses how to encode what is accepted). However acquired, injunctive decisions summarize important proscriptions that are limiting even if a person has decided to cope despite accepting the injunctions. These decisions are manifested in the way the patient sees self and others and his or her chosen ways of thinking, feeling, and being with others (including the therapist). Various personality types result from different key injunctive decisions, and identification of these early decisions points to the target doors that are the focus of redecision or other treatment.

Ego State Boundary Problems (James, 1986) refers to specific pathologies occurring when Parent-Adult-Child ego states have boundaries that are frequently *lax, contaminated, rigid,* or have *lesions*–concepts related to the ideas of *ego distortion* and *ego regression* (Blanck and Blanck, 1974). These ego state boundary problems result, respectively, in a floppy lack of control of energy and will, a distortion of Adult functioning by Child and/or Parent ego states, inflexibility and exclusion of one or even two ego states, or emotional sore spots that if irritated can lead to impulsive eruptions of feelings and behavior.

The next heading in Table 19.1, *Self/Other Existential Position* (Joines, 1988), refers to the existential positions (e.g., I'm Not OK, You're OK) assumed by patients with various personality pathologies, positions that keep them stuck until modified (Berne, 1972; Ernst, 1973; Kaplan, Capace, and Clyde, 1984). Each position describes a way of perceiving the self and the world. One can operate out of different positions at different times, and an individual may hold a position and temporarily experience himself or herself in a way that is different from his or her underlying sense of self (e.g., someone operating from an "I'm OK, You're Not OK" position might be basing that attitude on projection or other reality distortion [Chang and James, 1987]). Both ego state boundary problems and various I-Thou perceptions may correlate with different personality disorders.

Finally, *Common Reactions to Therapist* and *Common Reactions to Patient* refer to frequently observed therapist-patient patterns with different personality disorders. The ways in which therapists respond to patients' transferences, cons, rackets, and games are particularly important because to be effective, therapists must stay out of such pitfalls. This is the specific meaning of countertransference: the therapist's reaction or counter induced by the patient's transference or style (e.g., as when a therapist feels guilty or becomes overly active in response to a patient's excessive demands). Therapists have transferences or reactions of their own based on their personality styles, and these must also be taken into account (see James [1977] and Novellino [1984] for useful discussions of self-therapy techniques for therapists). As experienced clinicians recognize, trap doors of reaction and countertransference differ with patients of varying personality types.

Two Examples of Using the Table

A review of two personality disorders illustrates the use of Table 19.1. First, consider the obsessive personality: "On the other hand . . ." and "It's hard to really know for sure what to think" are typical comments as such people intellectualize back and forth over details without much awareness of feelings. Effective therapists need to hold the person to a single topic and to search for and encourage the patient's direct experiencing and expression of feelings. Obsessive individuals tend to see themselves as controlled by authoritarian figures, which can be reenacted in therapy. They cope with psychological stress by intellectualizing, denying, and repressing; rigidly structured thought processes are used to ward off underlying feelings of anger, sadness, and sexual excitement (Hoyt, 1987a). Their relationships reflect this style: controlled, formal, distant, dutiful, and deferent. Key injunctive decisions are often Not to Feel, Not to Be a Child, Not to Enjoy, and Not to Be Close. In terms of typical ego state boundary problems, contamination (Parent into Adult) and rigidity (much Parent, excluded Child) are common. The obsessive often operates from the position of "I'm Not OK, You're OK." In therapy, obsessives tend to be overly compliant as a veil for their competitiveness and anger, and therapists need to be alert to becoming either bored and tired or bossy, competitive, and angry in response to the obsessive's style.

The borderline personality is quite different. Such persons often speak of "falling apart" and "feeling empty inside" and can quickly turn to raging against those whom they perceive as harming or depriving them. They easily become upset and unrealistic, and the effective therapist helps to provide structure and set limits and also strokes the patient's Adult sense of self and problem solving. Individuals using borderline disorder functioning often see themselves as victims, and they struggle to develop a firm, coherent sense of self and to feel OK. At the core of borderline pathology is an incomplete "I" (Farrell and Hoyt, 1983). From session to session they can seem to be almost different people, often bouncing from crisis to crisis; as one woman with severe borderline personality disorder commented, "I don't know who I will be tomorrow." Under stress such people characteristically tend to use the primitive defenses of splitting, projection, and projective identification (wherein the projector plays a hard game of "Gotcha" by continuing to interact with the recipient in order to force him or her to identify with the projection). These individuals may project their anger, berate the recipient until an angry response is provoked, and then triumphantly declare, "See, I knew *you* were angry!" They often shift topics and feelings rapidly, may use irrational thinking, and frequently act out. Hateful rage is a common affect; underlying the anger is great psychic pain and loneliness, with the risk of suicide.

As one might expect, relationships with borderline personalities are tumultuous and chaotic. They often see themselves as victims yet feel that they cannot be alone, thus resulting in hostile-dependent situations with little real support. Many injunctive decisions may be manifested, including Don't Be Sane, Don't Be, Don't Grow Up, Don't Think, Don't Trust, and Don't Make It. Ego state boundary problems of all kinds may exist. Lax boundaries result in poor individuation within the person and poor differentiation from the environment; lesions in the Parent and Child account for the explosiveness and mini-psychoses that all too often occur; Adult functioning is severely contaminated by both Parent and Child.

Individuals with borderline pathology operate from a position of "I'm Not OK, You're Not OK." Their common reactions to therapists, based on a lifetime of unhappy relationships, include helplessness, expectancy of rejection, demandingness, provocation, and anger. Not surprisingly, therapists tend to respond to the strong "pulls" of the borderline patient: fright, overactivity, guilt, antagonism and rejection, and feeling manipulated and confused are all common countertransferential

reactions (Hoyt & Farrell, 1984). It may help therapists to recognize the borderline patient's problematic reactions as desperate "security operations" (to use Sullivan's [1953] term), to see
that the patient is struggling (albeit counterproductively) for
safety and survival. Reframed in this way, one can appreciate
the unpleasant behavior as actually being a drive toward health,
the patient's attempt to get what he or she needs and to take
care of the self. Understood as such, one is then more empathically
aligned with the patient and in a better position to stroke his or
her emerging self and the development of more productive coping methods.

Conclusion

Therapists perplexed by their patients' behavior may find the
information discussed here and summarized in Table 19.1 helpful for sharpening clinical observations and suggesting intercon-
nections between various personality features and therapeutic
issues. It should be kept in mind, however, that this information
is not meant as a guide to total psychological evaluation and
treatment planning, a topic that is beyond the scope of this
chapter. It is important also to consider such variables as
symptom/problem assessment and history, developmental data,
suicide potential, stressors, psychosocial assets and strengths,
medical status, possible alcohol/drug abuse, and the environmental and family situation.

Much of this information can be organized by using the
multiaxial classification scheme of the *DSM-III-R* and *DSM-IV*
(American Psychiatric Association, 1987, 1994). While not perfect, they are better than their predecessors in that they use
relatively atheoretical objective criteria and thus provide a common language for discussion. Axis I refers to acute clinical syndromes (e.g., anxiety reaction, major depression, uncomplicated
bereavement, alcohol intoxication); Axis II refers to more enduring personality disorders and specific developmental disorders (e.g., paranoid personality disorder, mental retardation);
Axis III refers to physical disorders and conditions; Axis IV
refers to severity of psychosocial stressors; and Axis V refers to

highest level of adaptive functioning in the past year.

It is also important to keep in mind that the descriptions in Table 19.1 have been presented in relatively pure or ideal form in order to aid recognition. Most patients manifest only a portion of the descriptors for any one type and may combine characteristics of different styles and have traits or features not usually associated (and listed) with a given disorder. People are never totally, uniformly consistent, and it should be recognized that the information in the table refers to tendencies, not invariable reactions.

Moreover, personality types may vary in how much they interfere with health, growth, and functioning, ranging in impairment from the severe (disorders) through the moderate or somewhat compromising to the benign or harmless (styles, quirks, or flavors). Different types may also to some extent be part of and reinforced by ethnicity (McGoldrick, Pearce, and Giordano, 1982) and need to be appreciated and worked with accordingly. There is always the danger of using diagnoses defensively, to gain distance rather than understanding and better contact; similarly, misused theory can have a chilling effect on a therapist's intuition and creativity (Whitaker, 1976).

A therapist may address a patient's personality problems directly, as the target of change, or may work within the patient's style on more specific problem-solving issues. The focus depends on the contract upon which the patient and therapist agree. In any case, awareness of personality dynamics and likely pitfalls will aid the ensuing work. It should be recognized, as Mary Goulding (personal communication; see also Klein, 1987) has pointed out, that redeciding and working through a primary pathogenic injunctive decision is not a panacea, nor will it erase what has already occurred. Within each personality type environmental opportunities, inherent temperament and talents, plus the individual's main injunctive decisions make for wide variations in performance. Other decisions may need confronting as well (e.g., someone with a Don't Be injunction who redecides to live will have a difficult time having fun if he or she still approaches life with a Don't Enjoy injunctive decision), and to benefit from therapy the person has to find ways to grow and enjoy regardless of what real-life opportunities may already have been lost.

Accurate assessment of personality patterns can enhance clinical effectiveness. As Horowitz and others (1984b, p. 319) have stated: "Personality style is seen as an important factor in understanding symptom formation, therapeutic technique, and syndrome resolution." Knowing what is wrong does not solve it, of course, but it does provide ideas about what needs fixing and where to work. Therapists who recognize certain recurring dysfunctional patterns in their patients—the purpose of personality disorder diagnosis—are in a better position to select and implement treatments designed to correct the problem.

CHAPTER TWENTY

—————◆◆◆—————

Brief Psychotherapies

When a therapist and patient endeavor to get from Point A (the problem that led to therapy) to Point B (the resolution that ends therapy) via a direct, effective, and efficient route, we say that they are deliberately engaging in *brief therapy*. The approach is intended to be quick and helpful, nothing extraneous, no beating around the bush. Another closely related term is *time-limited therapy,* which explicitly emphasizes the temporal boundedness of the treatment. Synonymous with *brief therapy* is the phrase *planned short-term therapy,* meaning literally a "deliberately concise remedy/restoration/improvement." As Bloom (1992a, p. 3) has written: "The word planned is important; these works describe short-term treatment that is intended to accomplish a set of therapeutic objectives within a sharply limited time frame."

This is how de Shazer (1991a, pp. ix–x) describes it: "'Brief therapy' simply means therapy that takes as few sessions as possible, not even one more than is necessary. . . . 'Brief therapy' is a relative term, typically meaning: (a) fewer sessions than standard, and/or (b) a shorter period of time from intake to termination, and/or (c) a lower number of sessions and a lower frequency of sessions from start to finish."

Brevity and *shortness* are watchwords signaling efficiency, the contrast being the more intentionally protracted course of traditional long-term (usually psychodynamic) therapy. Actually, most therapy is de facto brief, by default or design, meaning a few sessions, weeks to months. As Budman and Gurman (1988) and others (Bloom, 1992a; Garfield, 1986; Koss and Butcher,

Note: Reprinted, with changes, from Hoyt, M. F. "Brief Psychotherapies." In A. S. Gurman and S. B. Messer (eds.), *Modern Psychotherapies: Theory and Practice.* Copyright (in press) by Guilford Press. An extended version of this chapter appears in the publication cited above. Used by permission of the publisher.

1986) have noted, numerous studies have reported the average length of treatment to be three to eight sessions, the period of time in which most change occurs even in treatments that are not planned brief therapy (Howard, Kopta, Kraus, and Orlinsky, 1986). The modal or most common length of treatment is actually only one session—even with this "briefest of brief" duration, many successful outcomes are reported (Bloom, 1992b; Talmon, 1990; see Chapters Eight and Nine). Various authors have given different definitions for what constitutes brief therapy. Some have specified a number of sessions, such as five to ten, twelve, or up to twenty; some have emphasized certain types of problems they attempt to address; others have focused more on the idea of the passage of time being a contextual pressure. Budman and Gurman (1988), for example, eschew a specific number of sessions in their definition, instead referring to deliberate or planned brief therapy as "time sensitive" treatment.[1] Focused intentionality is the key. Make everything count; don't be wasteful. Sullivan (1954, p. 224) put it well: "I think the development of psychiatric skill consists in very considerable measure of doing a lot with very little—making a rather precise move which has a high probability of achieving what you're attempting to achieve, with a minimum of time and words."

Planned or intentional brief therapy is predicated on the belief and expectation that change can occur *in the moment,* particularly if theoretical ability, practical skill, and efficacious interest are brought to bear. The work is not superficial or simply technique oriented; it is precise and beneficial, often yielding enduring long-term benefits as well as more immediate gains.

While one can ignore research findings or argue that brief therapy and long-term therapy have different goals, the equivalence of outcomes is compelling. As Bloom (1992a, p. 9) has concluded: "Virtually without exception, these empirical studies of short-term outpatient psychotherapy, or inpatient psychiatric care . . . have found that planned short-term psychotherapies are essentially equally effective and are, in general, as effective as time-unlimited psychotherapy, virtually regardless of diagnosis or duration of treatment (Koss and Butcher, 1986). Indeed, perhaps no other finding has been reported with greater regularity in the mental health literature than the equivalence of effect of time-limited and time-unlimited psychotherapy."

Given the social and professional imperative to provide psychological services to the wide range of persons who might need and benefit from mental health care, the thrust of the accumulated data seems clear. However, before we turn to some of the specific ways that effective brief psychotherapies endeavor to translate complicated understandings into methods likely to yield results sooner rather than later, let us consider some of the overarching principles that guide the practice of brief therapy.

The Fundamental Assumptions and Defining Characteristics of Brief Therapy

The fundamental assumption of all forms of deliberate brief therapy is an attitude and expectation—supported by various theories, methodologies, and findings—that significant and beneficial changes can be brought about relatively quickly. The brief therapist recognizes that there is no time but the present. Historical review may yield some clues about how the patient is "stuck" and what may be needed to get "unstuck," but whatever the therapist's particular theoretical orientation, primary effort is directed to helping the patient recognize options in the present that can result in enhanced coping, new learning, growth, beneficial changes, and improvements. Yapko (1990a) has noted three factors that determine whether a patient will benefit from brief therapy interventions: (1) the person's primary temporal orientation (toward past, present, or future); (2) the general value given to "change," whether he or she is more invested in maintaining tradition or seeking change; and (3) the patient's belief system about what constitutes a complete therapeutic experience.

It is this fundamental assumption, that with skillful facilitation useful changes can be set into motion relatively quickly and that patients can then maintain and often expand the benefits on their own, that underlies the "universal elements" or "common ingredients" of brief treatment that have been synthesized by various authors (Bloom, 1992a; Budman and Gurman, 1988; Friedman and Fanger, 1991; Koss and Butcher, 1986; Wells and Phelps, 1990). As Budman, Friedman, and Hoyt (1992) have written, the most frequently cited generic components of brief treatment are:

1. A rapidly established and generally positive working alliance between therapist and patient
2. Focality, the clear specification of achievable treatment results
3. Clear definition of patient and therapist responsibilities, with a relatively high level of therapist activity and patient participation
4. Emphasis on patient's strengths, competencies, and adaptive capacities
5. Expectation of change, the belief that improvement is within the patient's (immediate) grasp
6. Here-and-now (and next) orientation, the primary focus being on current functioning and patterns in thinking, feeling, and behaving—and their alternatives
7. Time sensitivity

This set of defining characteristics is reflected in the comparison of the dominant values of long-term and short-term treatment presented in the following list:

Long-Term Therapist	Short-Term Therapist
1. Seeks change in basic character.	Prefers pragmatism, parsimony, and least radical intervention; does not believe in the notion of "cure."
2. Believes that significant change is unlikely in everyday life.	Maintains an adult developmental perspective from which significant psychological change is viewed as inevitable.
3. Sees presenting problems as reflecting more basic pathology.	Emphasizes patient's strengths and resources.
4. Wants to "be there" as patient makes significant changes.	Accepts that many changes will occur "after therapy."

(continued)

Long-Term Therapist	Short-Term Therapist
5. Sees therapy as having a "timeless" quality.	Does not accept the timelessness of some models of therapy.
6. Unconsciously recognizes the fiscal convenience of long-term patients.	Fiscal issues are often muted, either by the nature of the practice or the organizational structure.
7. Views therapy as almost always benign and useful.	Views therapy as sometimes useful and sometimes harmful.
8. Views therapy as being the most important part of the patient's life.	Sees being in the world as more important than being in therapy.
9. Views therapist as responsible only for treating a given patient.	Views therapist as having responsibility for treatment of a population.

Source: Budman and Gurman (1992, p. 113). Reprinted by permission of the publisher.

Many of these same value differences are highlighted in Figure 20.1, and can also be detected in many of the "resistances" or contrary attitudes some therapists hold about brief or short-

Figure 20.1.

Source: Drawing by Shanahan; © 1989 by The New Yorker Magazine, Inc. Reprinted by permission of the publisher. All rights reserved.

term therapy (as discussed in detail in Chapter Seventeen):

1. *The belief that "more is better";*
2. *the myth of the "pure gold" of analysis,* the misassumption that change and growth necessarily require "deep" examination and that anything else is dismissable as "superficial" or "merely palliative";
3. *the demand for greater therapist activity,* including the need to be selectively focused, confrontive, directive, and risk taking;
4. *the confusion of patients' interests with therapists' interests,* the tendency of therapists to seek and treat perfectionistically putative "complexes" and "underlying personality issues" rather than attend directly to patients' complaints and stated treatment goals;
5. *financial pressures,* the temptation to hold on to that which is profitable and dependable, as well as other incentives such as the pleasures of intimate conversation and the lure of living vicariously through an extended relationship;
6. *countertransference and termination problems,* including the need to be needed and difficulties saying good-bye;
7. *psychological reactance,* the interesting response of valuing something more if you cannot have it; being told that one has to treat a patient with brief therapy (e.g., because of insurance restrictions or simply because that is what the patient wants) may trigger resentment.

The foregoing notwithstanding, there are certainly times when short-term therapy will not be adequate and appropriate—including instances when a longer process is required for the patient to make desired changes or when ongoing support is required to maintain a tenuous psychosocial adjustment—although the basic attitude of making the most of each session and taking as few sessions as possible will still be valuable. Indeed, if the needs of more than a handful of patients are to be served, the skillful application of brief therapy methods whenever possible will be necessary to make longer-term treatments available for those who truly need them.[2]

To summarize this section before moving on to other topics, it would appear that there are essentially three factors that tend to determine the length of treatment: (1) the theoretical orientation, beliefs, and working assumptions of the therapist; (2) money—how much and for how long the patient can afford to pay;[3] and (3) the patient's problems, situation, personality, psychopathology, and capacities.

Why Do Patients Come to Therapy?

Most patients come to therapy because they hope that working with a psychotherapist will soon relieve some state of unhappiness, distress, or dysfunction that has become so troublesome that professional consultation appears preferable to continuing the status quo.[4] The person feels that something timely has to be done since, as the old adage has it, "If you don't change directions, you'll wind up where you're heading." As Budman and Gurman (1988) have articulated it, there are five common answers to the question, Why now does a patient come for treatment?—five interrelated themes or foci that can often be addressed productively in brief therapy:

1. *Loss,* including bereavement, divorce, certain changes in social status, health problems, and betrayals of trust and confidence
2. *Developmental dyssynchronicities,* life cycle transitions or passages for which the patient is not well prepared and which thus present problems of adjustment, e.g., adolescent emancipation, marriage, starting a family, the empty-nest syndrome, and retirement
3. *Interpersonal conflicts,* problems with significant others such as a spouse, children, authority figures, co-workers, and friends
4. *Specific symptoms,* such as depression, anxiety, or sexual dysfunctions
5. *Personality issues,* characterological issues that come to the fore if the patient makes them the focus of therapy and/or if they impede within- or between-session work to the ex-

tent that they require direct attention for therapy to be successful

Brief therapists generally do not consider assessment to be a separate process to be completed before beginning treatment; rather, they see assessment and treatment as inextricably intertwined. The questions one asks will help to co-create the reality in which therapist and patient work, and the patient's responses to trial interventions will provide useful information about what is likely to be helpful. It is useful to keep in mind the idea that the word *diagnosis* comes from Greek and Latin words meaning "the way of knowing," and this is just what a good functional diagnosis should do: provide information that illuminates a path. Pathologic nosology may contain some important information, but it is seldom enough. Consider, for example, the five axes of the *Diagnostic and Statistic Manual of Mental Disorders, Fourth Edition* (American Psychiatric Association, 1994): Axis I. Clinical Disorders and Other Conditions that May Be a Focus of Clinical Attention; Axis II. Personality Disorders and Other Developmental Deficits; Axis III. General Medical Conditions; Axis IV. Psychosocial and Environmental Problems; and Axis V. Global Assessment of Functioning, usually expressed by a numerical index. Important data may be summarized in the *DSM-IV* (and may be especially useful for communicating with insurance companies and clinical researchers as well as for differentially diagnosing whether medication is likely to be of help), but reviewing the axes also reveals a potentially discouraging orientation toward "disease" and "sickness." As Barten (1971, p. 8) has noted, "Our training predisposes us to describe areas of illness rather than areas of health, and this illness orientation can make the prognosis of a great many people appear rather bleak." Consider what the five *DSM-IV* axes tell us about a person: (Axis I) what's wrong with the patient now, (Axis II) what's been wrong with the patient for a long time, (Axis III) what's wrong with the patient's body, (Axis IV) what's wrong with the patient's social situation, and (Axis V) how well he or she has adapted. Data such as these, including information about potential suicidality and alcohol and substance abuse, can be vital; but we also need to focus on the patient's strengths and capacities, his or her resources and motivations that will be needed for treatment to proceed successfully.

A therapist wishing to do effective brief treatment will need to accomplish a number of tasks early on with a patient:

1. Make contact and establish rapport
2. Define the purpose of the meeting
3. Orient and instruct the patient on how to use therapy
4. Create an opportunity for the patient to express thoughts, feelings, behavior
5. Assess the patient's problems, strengths, motivations, and, expectations
6. Establish realistic (specific and obtainable) treatment goals
7. Make initial treatment interventions, assess effects, and adjust accordingly
8. Assign tasks or "homework" as appropriate
9. Attend to such business matters as future appointments and fees

It is important in the first session to engage the patient and to introduce some novelty. As will be seen in the cases to be presented below as well as those reported in the *The First Session in Brief Therapy* (Budman, Hoyt, and Friedman, 1992), in virtually all successful brief therapies something new happens in the first meeting. More of the same (behavior, outlook, defense, and so on) does not produce change. A *symptom* is an attempted solution to a problem that does not work or that engenders unwanted results (Edelstien, 1990; Fisch, Weakland, and Segal, 1982; Yapko, 1992). Effective therapy involves breaking such a pattern, doing something different. The novelty may come by seeing oneself differently, by practicing a new way of transacting with others, by experiencing unacknowledged feelings, by utilizing strengths and abilities that were previously overlooked. Whatever the means, the brief therapist looks for ways to start or amplify the patient's movement in the desired direction as soon as possible.

Attending carefully to the early identification of specific, achievable goals promotes effective brief work (Cade and O'Hanlon, 1993; de Shazer, 1985, 1988; Goulding and Goulding, 1979; Haley, 1977, 1989, 1990; O'Hanlon and Weiner-Davis, 1989).[5] Operational definitions contribute to treatment accountability, counter the temptation to diffuse/confuse/refuse focality, and help to assure that genuinely obtainable results are not replaced with vague or unrealistic "missions impossible" or "therapeutic perfectionism" (Malan, 1976a). Questions such as the following help to focus treatment and involve the patient:

- What problem are you here to solve?
- If you work hard and make some changes, how will you be functioning differently?
- What are the smallest changes you could make that would tell you're heading in the right direction?
- At those times when the problem isn't so bad or is absent, what are you doing?
- What will tell us we're done?
- How will we know when to stop meeting like this?
- How might therapy help, and how long do you expect it to take?

Treatment revolves around what the patient wants to accomplish plus the answers to three interrelated transtechnical heuristic questions: (1) How is the patient "stuck" (what is the problem or pathology)? (2) What does the patient need to get "unstuck?" and (3) How can I, as therapist, facilitate or provide what is needed? The good brief (or any) therapist is able to reckon from a variety of perspectives lest patients be forced into the Procrustean bed of a pet theory or technique or be dismissed and blamed for being resistant, unmotivated, or ego deficient. As the saying goes, "If all one has is a hammer, everything begins to look like a nail." The importance of having "an array of observing positions" has been well described by Gustafson (1986), who identifies four key paradigms in tracing the history of attempts to answer the question of how patients get stuck and unstuck: "Psychoanalysis sees the hidden demands of the animal in us. The analysis of character sees the 'constant attitude' which protects the animal from without. Interpersonal interviewing sees the interactions which tie us into trouble with other people. Systemic interviewing sees these interactions in the service of stable social relations" (p. 6).[6]

The therapist wishing to be parsimonious (brief and effective) may need to choose which conceptualization(s) will allow for the best chance of a change-producing intervention. Should the approach be toward revealing the intrapsychic domain of warded-off feelings? modifying the patient's typical way of viewing and meeting the world? altering the social skills with which they interact? changing the rules of the labyrinthine games that ensnare patients into maintaining the status quo? or something else? And how to do so? via educational instruction? cognitive-behavioral techniques? psychodynamic interpretations? systemic interviewing and strategic interventions? hypnosis? common-sense appeals or wise exhortations? The brief therapist asks: What would be likely to work with this patient and this therapist at this time?

Interlude: A Brief History of Brief Therapy

People have been having problems and getting help since time immemorial, although the history of psychotherapy, as a practice and a profession, is considered to have begun in earnest about one hundred years ago (Zeig, 1987; Freedheim, 1992). Sigmund Freud, usually thought of as the founder of psychoanalysis, was also the father of brief therapy. Reading his early cases (Breuer and Freud, [1893–95] 1955), one finds him interacting actively with patients and treating them in days, weeks, and months. Psychoanalysis was also a research instrument, however, and treatment became longer and longer as the early pioneers became fascinated with the psychological phenomena that would emerge (such as oedipal fantasies and transference neuroses) if the therapist remained a relatively inactive, and neutral "blank" screen, while the patient freely associated. An early effort to experiment with more active methods in treatment was made by Ferenczi and Rank (1925), but some of their methods were questionable, and the time for revisionism was not right since psychoanalysis was still struggling to establish itself. At the end of his life, Freud (1937) wrote his last great clinical paper, "Analysis Terminable and Interminable," in which he expressed his frustration about the limited therapeutic benefits of psychoanalysis and called for the development of new methods based on the psychoanalytic understanding of transference, resistance, and unconscious material.

World War II intervened, with many consequences for the practice of brief psychotherapy and other kinds of treatment. Prior to the war, psychological treatment usually had been a long-term luxury of the privileged and had fallen under the purview of the psychoanalytic and psychiatric-medical establishment. There were so many GIs needing services, however, that (1) psychologists and clinical social workers finally attained recognition as bonafide psychotherapy providers after long-time relegation to their respective "auxiliary" roles of psychometric testers and home visitors; (2) group therapy became a more common treatment of choice (and necessity) rather than being an isolated and rare specialty; (3) the Veterans Administration (VA) medical system emerged as a training ground for mental health professionals; and, most salient to our present topic, (4) interest was spurred in treatment methods that would help GIs quickly reduce symptoms and return to function either in the combat zones or back in civilian life. Psychoanalytic theory continued to predominate, but "reality factors" were becoming increasingly influential—harbingers of what is today called "accountability."

In 1946, Alexander and French published *Psychoanalytic Therapy: Principles and Applications*. The book was (and is) extraordinary, revisiting and updating many of the ideas of Ferenczi and Rank regarding the use of greater therapist activity. It also suggested that the length and frequency of sessions might be varied, both from case to case and within the same patient's treatment, to avoid excessive dependency in the patient that prolonged therapy and to bring about what Alexander and French referred to as a "corrective emotional experience." Many successful brief therapies were reported. Still, the politics of psychoanalysis were not quite ripe for change, and it remained for two leading psychoanalytic figures of the time, Bibring (1954) and Gill (1954), to publish their seminal papers about modifying the parameters of treatment and calling it psychoanalytically *oriented* therapy (and not psychoanalysis) before attempts at psychodynamic modifications were recognized as legitimate by the mainstream.

By the early 1950s a number of workers were exploring what could be done using psychodynamic principles in more active and shorter treatment. In London, Balint, Ornstein, and Balint (1972) and Malan (1963, 1976a, 1976b) were developing what they referred to as "focal psychotherapy"; in Boston, Sifneos (1972) was beginning to experiment with "short-term anxiety-provoking psychotherapy"; in New York, Wolberg (1965a) was investigating various ways of shortening the length of treatment, including using hypnotherapy to work through patients' resistances more quickly. At the same time, several other important figures were becoming disenchanted with psychoanalytic methods and began to originate other, more active methods for bringing about psychological change more rapidly. Perls, Hefferline, and Goodman (1951) began to develop the theory and techniques of Gestalt therapy; Wolpe (1958; Wolpe and Lazarus, 1966) were developing behavior therapy; Ellis (1962, 1992) began to develop rational emotive therapy, the first systematic form of what is now called cognitive therapy; and Berne (1961, 1972) began to develop transactional analysis. A number of publications began to call professional attention to the expanding field of brief therapy, including important books by Malan (1963), Wolberg (1965a), Bellak and Small (1965), Parad (1965), Barten (1971), and Lewin (1970). Concurrently, the psychiatrist Milton Erickson (1980) was still working in relative obscurity in Phoenix, Arizona, but his uniquely creative uses of hypnosis and strategic interventions to capitalize on patients' existing capacities would soon be recognized (especially with the 1973 publication of Haley's *Uncommon Therapy*) and contributed greatly to both the emerging family therapy movement and various schools of strategic and systemic therapy.

Writing about the expanding spectrum of the brief therapies, Barten (1971) underscored the convergence of a number of historical developments, including a growing professional commitment to providing appropriate mental health services to all segments of the community, an increasing shift from psychoanalysis to more ego-oriented techniques and a recognition of the value of limited therapeutic goals, a diversifying of the roles of mental health professionals, long overdue recognition of the special needs of the disadvantaged,[7] and increased consumer demand for economically feasible services. The community mental health movement of the 1960s and the federal Health Maintenance Organization (HMO) Act of 1973 gave further mandate to brief treatment. Strategic therapists were guided by Haley (1963, 1969, 1973, 1977, 1984), Madanes (1981, 1984), and the work of the Mental Research Institute of Palo Alto (Watzlawick, Beavin, and Jackson, 1967; Watzlawick, Weakland, and Fisch, 1974; Fisch, Weakland, and Segal, 1982) and the Brief Family Therapy Center of Milwaukee (de Shazer, 1982, 1985, 1988), while psychodynamicists wanting to work more concisely drew special inspiration from the work of Sifneos (1972), Mann (1973), Malan (1963, 1976a, 1976b) and Davanloo (1978, 1980). In 1988, a conference entitled "Brief Therapy: Myths, Methods and Metaphors," sponsored by the Milton H. Erickson Foundation, was held in San Francisco, with several thousand mental health professionals attending (Zeig and Gilligan, 1990). The recent enormous acceleration in various forms of managed health care (Austad and Berman, 1991; Austad and Hoyt, 1992; Feldman, 1992; Feldman and Fitzpatrick, 1992; Hoyt and Austad, 1992; VandenBos, Cummings, and DeLeon, 1992), which by 1992 covered approximately 100 million Americans, has given further impetus to the development and expansion of various forms of brief therapy.

Models of Brief Therapy

There are various models or "schools" of brief therapy (see Bloom, 1992a; Budman, 1981; Budman, Hoyt, and Friedman, 1992; Gustafson, 1986; Wells and Giannetti, 1990, 1993; Zeig and Gilligan, 1990). While each case is different and the skillful application of varied psychological principles is part of what makes therapy an interesting and artful endeavor, there are broad general guidelines in theory and practice that distinguish different forms of brief treatment. We will highlight and illustrate a few of them,[8] but the reader should keep in mind three important caveats: (1) no one summary or case presentation can do more than suggest a few broad brush strokes; by necessity, more has been omitted than included under each rubric, and therefore in each section there are references cited to guide those wishing to get started on a fuller study of a particular approach; (2) most therapy is eclectic and integrated, drawing ideas and methods from a range of sources rather than adhering to one particular theory; and (3) to quote Milton H. Erickson, "Each person is a unique individual. Hence, psychotherapy should be formulated to meet the uniqueness of the individual's needs, rather than tailoring the person to fit the Procrustean bed of a hypothetical theory of human behavior" (in Zeig and Gilligan, 1990, p. xix).

Short-Term Psychodynamic Psychotherapy

Beginning with Freud, numerous theoreticians and clinicians have applied the psychoanalytic concepts of the unconscious, resistance, and transference to brief forms of treatment. Building on the principles described in Freud's paper, "Remembering, Repeating, and Working Through" (1914), various short-term dynamic methods have been developed to bring the patient to a greater awareness of his or her maladaptive defenses, wardedoff feelings, and counterproductive relationship patterns.[9] As many reviewers have noted (Bauer and Kobos, 1987; Crits-Cristoph and Barber, 1991; Donovan, 1987; Horner, 1985; Horowitz and others, 1984b; Levenson and Butler, 1994; Malan, 1976a; Marmor, 1979; Peake, Borduin, and Archer, 1988; Rasmussen and Messer, 1986), the emphasis in all of the various short-term dynamic psychotherapies has been on increased therapist activity within a limited (central) focus. There has been a general recognition that relative inactivity on the part of the therapist in the face of increasing resistance leads to prolonged and diffuse treatment. Hence Malan (1980, pp. 13–14), in an allusion to Freud's paper "Turnings in the Way of Psych-oanalysis"

(1919b), refers to Freud's technique of free association as "a wrong turning" that leads to "doubtful therapeutic effectiveness." Brief dynamic therapists endeavor to promote change within a focalized area of conflict via an admixture of de-repression and affective release, corrective emotional experience, relearning, and application of the patient's will. Let us highlight a few of the main short-term psychodynamic approaches in terms of their central characteristics of focus, primary techniques, and length of treatment.

1. *Short-term anxiety-provoking psychotherapy* (Sifneos, 1987, 1992). Primarily for carefully selected patients with oedipal conflicts, anxiety-provoking confrontations and transference interpretations are made by a teacher-therapist endeavoring to produce emotional relearning. Length of treatment varies but is typically about six to fifteen sessions.

2. *Short-term dynamic psychotherapy* (Malan, 1963, 1976a). This method also focuses on issues of oedipal conflict and loss, with the therapist emphasizing interpretive links between transference and past and present issues. Treatment is typically thirty to forty sessions.

3. *Time-limited psychotherapy* (Mann, 1973; Mann and Goldman, 1982). A firm twelve-session treatment framework is established with an emphasis on the patient's sense of self and his or her present and chronically endured pain. The empathic therapist helps the patient master underlying separation issues that become manifest in terms of themes of unresolved mourning, activity versus passivity, independence versus dependence, and adequate versus diminished self-esteem.

4. *Stress response therapy and microanalysis* (Horowitz, 1976, 1979; Horowitz and others, 1984b). The focus is on the patient's "states of mind" (images of self and others and information-processing styles) to help the patient rework and emotionally master a recent stress event, usually over the course of twelve sessions.

5. *Short-term intensive dynamic psychotherapy* (Davanloo, 1978, 1980, 1991; Worchel, 1990). The therapist functions as a

"relentless healer," vigorously confronting and interpreting defenses until there is an "unlocking of the unconscious" and a breakthrough into true feelings. The focus is broad with strong emphasis on characterological defenses as they are manifested within the basic psychoanalytic "triangle of conflict" (impulse-feeling/anxiety/defense) and "triangle of person" (transference/current significant persons/past significant persons), with special attention toward an experience in the transference. Treatment length varies from five to forty sessions, with progress expected to be evident early on.

6. *Time-limited dynamic psychotherapy* (Strupp and Binder, 1984; Butler, Strupp, and Binder, 1992). A "cyclical maladaptive pattern" is identified and interpreted, involving acts of self, expectations of others, acts of others, and self-introjects. The therapist is empathic, appreciating the pull of countertransference as an opportunity to provide a corrective emotional experience. Treatment is usually twenty-five sessions.

There have been many reports of how coming to grips with warded-off conflicts has helped people achieve greater happiness in relationships, success at work, and the ability to say good-bye. While the data are not without complication, the overall direction of the findings has been clear: appropriately selected patients often benefit from brief, focused, psychodynamic therapy.

Short-term dynamic psychotherapy, of course, is not for everyone. It requires a reasonably functional patient with a grip on reality and an ability to tolerate painful emotional material. It is also not a panacea, since there are many biological, social, situational, and existential factors besides intrapsychic dynamics that may require clinical attention. It is also important to remember that for psychodynamic psychotherapy to be effective, regardless of whether it is short-term or more extended, insight must serve as a vehicle and not as a final destination. That is, the real question is not how far back does a problem go, but how much farther will it be carried forward? As one enthusiast of intensive short-term dynamic therapy put it: "Intrinsic in short-term therapy's technique is the appeal to the individual to take action. How to change? The answer is part and parcel of the therapy's technique: the challenge to the defenses and the focus on your buried feelings exhort you to go from a passive to an active stance, to take charge of the way you look at life and deal with your emotions" (Zois, 1992, p. 212). The following case fragment illustrates some aspects of a short-term psychodynamic approach.

The Case of the Forlorn Lover

David was a fifty-two-year-old man who sought therapy a few months after his lover died of AIDS. On the telephone he tensely asked if I was prejudiced against working with homosexuals. When I answered that I wasn't, he said he would see me at the appointment time I had offered.

He arrived a few minutes early, neatly dressed in tie and coat, coming from the job as an office manager that he had held for many years. He spoke slowly with great control—formal, severe, constricted—as he described his dilemma. He had never been close to anyone, he reported. He had grown up in an emotionally cold European household and had then spent many years as a monk in a religious order. Finally, he had left and eventually made his way to San Francisco. He was accepting of his sexual orientation and spent most of his off-work time among gays and lesbians because of greater compatibility and to avoid discrimination. He had adopted a lifestyle of occasional brief sexual encounters until he had met Richard. It was difficult for him even to speak his late friend's name, the loss was so painful. Several times he started to choke up and then put his hand over his face and recomposed himself.

Near the end of our first session I asked him why he had come to therapy; what did he want to accomplish? "The pain is so great I can't stand it, but damn him, he made me feel, and now I don't want to go back to that cold life I had before. I'm lost." He cried a bit, then pulled himself together. He remarked that he found me kind and easy to talk with and that he was relieved that I had directly answered his question about possible anti-gay prejudice since his insurance restricted whom he might be able to see. He asked if he could have an appointment to come back. When I agreed and asked when he would like to return, he indicated that his work schedule would require a two-week interval between sessions. We set an appointment. (This time frame would also allow him to better regulate the intensity of whatever might transpire in our meetings, I thought, but did not share with him.)

Over the next three sessions, David gradually told me more about his relationship with Richard. The telling was slow and painful. Several times, when he felt a wave of emotion, he either closed his eyes and trembled until it passed or set his jaw and actively suppressed his feelings. He was grieving at a pace that seemed tolerable for him while I mostly listened and occasionally asked leading questions. His level of tension and control was remarkable. He would make sure that the sessions stopped exactly on time. When I was a few minutes late to begin, he became especially cold and distant. When I commented that he seemed "somewhat tense," he paused until he was composed and then told me that he was "furious inside." I said I was sorry for the lateness and added an observation:

Therapist: It is remarkable how you are able to keep your feelings in.

Patient: Yes, I can eliminate someone from my emotions. I am well trained not to feel.

T: Yes, but to do that would render me useless to you. And that wouldn't be good for you.

He looked at me and palpably reconnected.

In the next two sessions more details were revealed, hesitatingly, about Richard, including various complaints about his drinking and bouts with irritability. David then became increasingly unforthcoming. I asked why.

P: If I talk more about him and let myself grieve, then the images and memories might fade and I will have nothing left. (*silence*)

T: You're trying to hold on to him in your mind the way some people keep a room exactly like it was the day someone died. It's like a museum, as though time can be frozen . . . but it can't.

P: Oh, God, yes, that's it. (*He cried and then recomposed himself.*)

T: So, what are you going to do?

P: I want to go forward, but I don't know how. Oh, I do, there are other people, but I'm scared.

T: Of what?

P: Of getting hurt again.

T: Then go slow, when you're ready. But life is in front of you.

He continued his mourning process. He also began to experiment over the next several weeks, attending a dance club, having supper with someone, even asserting himself at his workplace and refusing to acquiesce to things he felt were unfair. He was well aware of his pattern of "stuffing" his feelings and still often did so when threatened or hurt, but sometimes—with increasing cognizance—he expressed himself more. He even occasionally smiled, and told stories that revealed a growing tenderness in his relations with others, including a new willingness to forgive and to remain involved with people rather than "eliminating" them if they were sometimes inconsiderate or annoying. He began to exercise and lost a few "extra" pounds that he had been carrying, all in preparation for the possibility of finding a new mate.

Follow-up and comment. This case might best be described as "eclectic-integrated" and falling within the "expressive-supportive" range of brief dynamic therapies (Pinsker, Rosenthal, and McCullough, 1991). Attention was paid to exploring the patient's warded-off feelings, his images of self and others, and ways his defenses and relationship patterns were repeated with the therapist. As one might expect, therapy termination was not easy for David. Relinquishing the therapist reminded him of losing Richard and also meant giving up a person that he had learned to trust and felt at ease talking with, but by the twelfth therapy session he felt strong enough to go forward and so stopped treatment as planned. Consistent with Mann's model (1973), themes of unresolved mourning, activity versus passivity, and independence versus dependence were prominent throughout the therapy and especially during the explicit termination phase. Indeed, there was a countertransference "pull" to extend treatment (Hoyt and Farrell, 1984), but this was not done and we stopped meeting. David's goals for treatment—to get through the pain and to resume moving toward people rather than retreating into isolation—were largely accomplished. He was encouraged to return to therapy as needed, and he agreed to do so.

Transactional Analysis and Redecision Therapy

The transactional analysis (TA) school of therapy was developed by Eric Berne (1961, 1972) out of his desire to help patients more quickly see their autonomous role in their personal difficulties. While TA involves a complicated and comprehensive model of human development, intrapsychic organization, and interpersonal dynamics (see Stewart and Joines, 1987), there are three popular and readily accessible ideas from TA with which Berne is most identified: (1) the "I'm OK, You're OK" matrix of existential positions pertaining to how one regards self and others; (2) the Parent-Adult-Child conceptualization of personality ego states (the progenitor of various "Inner Child" theories); and (3) the "Games People Play" (Berne, 1964a) idea of recognizing many of the ulterior motivations behind dysfunctional relationship patterns.

Combining some of the theory of TA with Gestalt techniques plus many of their own innovations, Robert and Mary Goulding (1978, 1979) developed what they call redecision therapy. As discussed in Chapter Seven, their approach is built on the theory that, as children, people often make key life decisions (such as Don't Feel, Don't Think, or Don't Be Close) in order to survive or adapt to perceived and often veridical parental pressures. In therapy, the patient reenters and reexperiences the pathogenic scene as a child, often via imagery and Gestalt work, and with the encouragement and support of the therapist makes a *re*decision that frees the patient from the pernicious injunction that he or she had earlier accepted and internalized. This approach can be particularly helpful in contexts that require time efficiency in that, unlike many psychodynamic transference-based models, the emphasis is not upon building and examining the therapist-patient relationship. There is implicit the idea of state-dependent learning (and relearning), the work being conducted in the voice of the present tense in order to bring to life how the patient is carrying the conflict. A powerful combination of affect and insight is involved, with support and behavioral anchors maintaining the gains achieved.

R. Goulding (1989; Goulding and Goulding, 1979) describes a thinking structure to guide work in redecision therapy. While many of the important details go beyond the scope of the present discussion, the following are essential aspects of the approach:

1. *Contact,* forming an alliance with the patient
2. *Contract,* constructing the focus or goal of treatment in a way that can be specified and achieved
3. *Con,* emphasizing patients' power and responsibility by confronting their efforts to disown autonomy through various ways they attempt to fool ("con") themselves and therapists into believing that others control their thoughts, feelings, and behavior or with disingenuous claims of "trying" to make changes
4. *Chief bad feelings, thinkings, behaviors, and psychosomatics,* identifying the painful or problematic counterproductive symptoms
5. *Chronic games, belief systems, and fantasies,* clarifying the interpersonal and intrapsychic ways symptoms are maintained
6. *Childhood early decisions,* bringing to vivid awareness a reexperience of childhood feelings via the imaginal reliving of an early pathogenic scene, including recognition of the chief parental messages (injunctions and counterinjunctions), childhood script formation, and stroking (reinforcement) patterns
7. *Impasse resolution,* including redecisions, ego state decontamination and reconstruction (involving the strengthening

of distinctions between Parent, Adult, and Child functions), re-parenting, and other techniques; two-chair Gestalt work is often used to help the patient "extroject" a pathogenic parental introject and then, in powerful dialogue, reclaim a sense of autonomy and self-determination

8. *Maintaining the victory,* including anchoring the patient's new and healthier ways of responding, making changes in stroke (reinforcement) patterns, and forming plans for how to use the redecision in the future.

While this presentation is necessarily brief and schematic, the reader is referred to the Gouldings' work already cited, as well as M. Goulding (1985, 1992), Goulding and Goulding (1989), Kadis (1985), McClendon and Kadis (1983), M. Phillips (1988), and Chapters Seven and Eighteen of this book for numerous clinical applications and examples.

Consistent with the question Eric Berne would ask himself before each session, "What can I do to cure this patient today?" the Gouldings have developed Berne's concept of *contractual therapy* and ask patients, as they begin each treatment session, "What are you willing to change today?" The question focuses therapist and patient on making rapid changes. As the following vignette illustrates, this approach, which combines the theory of injunctions with Gestalt techniques "so that the patient does a great deal of experiential work *and* has a good understanding of his place in his life script, is more likely to change both his behavior and his feelings" (R. Goulding, 1983, p. 634). As M. Goulding (1990) has written, attention to contract plus redecision helps get the important work done fast.

The Case of the Woman Who Stood Up for Herself

Maria, who was twenty-five years old, came to therapy complaining of "insecurity" and "low self-esteem" in her relationships with men as well as in her work performance. She needed to gather her confidence to move on in her adult life. She already had some understanding that many of her insecurities stemmed from her relationship with her verbally abusive, highly critical father. "I know he did this to me," she said, "but what can I do about it?" It appeared that she needed an experience that would separate her from her past, that would "empower" her, a shift out of the "victim" position. She "knew" her father was still living in her head ("It's an old tape"), but so what?

By the end of our first meeting she had achieved several important steps: (1) good contact with the therapist, establishing a sense of safety and working alliance; (2) increased awareness that her pattern of low self-esteem was a carry-over from how her father had treated her; and (3) a greater sense of her present role or personal autonomy, i.e., she could see more clearly that she did the put-downs to herself, that the origin of her problem may have been in childhood with her father but that he was not "making" her feel bad now—*she* was.

As the session drew near an end, the therapist remarked: "So what you want to do, so to speak, is to get his critical voice out of your head, right?" She agreed, and the contract was made specific: to stop putting herself down and, instead, to give herself due credit and not let others demean her.

Conditions were ripe for redecision work. At the second meeting the therapist reiterated the contract to make sure it was still what she wanted. Maria was then asked to give an example of a recent time when she felt lacking in confidence and self-esteem. She did, and was then asked how she felt in that situation and what she had said in her head about herself and the other person. She had felt scared; she had said to herself, "I can't do anything right"; and she had said about the other person, "He is mad and doesn't like you." The therapist then said: "You feel scared, you think you can't do anything right, and he is mad at you. How does that fit in with your childhood? What do you think of?"

Maria recalled a time when she was about six years old. She had spilled juice on the rug in the living room, and her father was chastising her for it. The therapist asked her to stay with the scene, to imagine it vividly, to really get into it. "Let yourself be six years old again and go back there, see the room and the juice on the rug and all the details, and let yourself feel yourself being that scared six-year-old girl." Maria paused, and as she vividly recalled and "got into" the scene, one could see her get smaller and shrink into herself.

The therapist then said to her, "Now sit in this other chair over here (Maria changed seats), and in this chair be your father, looking at the juice on the rug and being furious." With a little prompting, Maria got into the role. The therapist then proceeded to conduct a brief "Parent interview" (McNeel, 1976), asking the "Father" his name and occupation and asking questions to evoke "his" feelings and thoughts about the little girl who in the scene would be cowering in front of him. "He" was angry and didn't like to have to clean up the mess, but as he talked more it became clear that he wasn't all that ferocious and that he actually did love the girl, too.

The therapist had Maria switch back to the six-year-old seat and from there tell her father that she was scared and that she didn't like it when he yelled at her. "I'm only a little kid and I make mistakes, but I'm not bad and you shouldn't yell at me," she spontaneously added. "Yeah," said the therapist. "Good. That's right. Stand up and tell him again. Let him know that he's not going to hurt you, and that you're OK even if you sometimes make mistakes." The little girl stood up for herself.

When she seemed done, the therapist said, "Good job. Notice how strong you feel. Now, as you come back to yourself in the present you'll remember whenever you need to, how it feels to stand up."

Follow-up and comment. The role-playing had a powerful effect. Using the three questions How do you feel? What do you say about yourself? and What do you say about the other person? as a kind of affect bridge back to an early scene often works to rapidly access a pathogenic (perhaps screen) memory, taking a different and quicker route than waiting for a transference neurosis to fully bloom. The two-chair work then allows a reworking or redecision, a new and healthier resolution of the impasse (see Blackstone, 1987). For this patient, this was a turning point, a casting off of the Don't Be a Child and Don't Be Important injunctions she had earlier internalized. Therapy continued for another three visits, the first two occurring weekly and the last one occurring a month later, as the patient made plans and applied (worked through) her "breakthrough" in a variety of current life situations. With support, reminders, and practice, she learned to discount herself less and less. Her treatment goals of enhanced confidence and self-esteem were well met and demonstrated in a variety of contexts.

Cognitive-Behavioral Approaches to Brief Therapy

Cognitive-behavioral approaches to treatment are, by their very nature, almost always brief therapy (Wilson, 1981). They are highly goal directed, offering direct and specific remedies for specific problems. As a group they are characterized by careful and thorough assessment of particular problems and complaints and the active recruitment of the patient's participation and co-operation in treatment. Then, following the basic conception that psychopathology results from and is maintained by dysfunctional cognition and conation, various techniques are applied to alter maladaptive thoughts and behaviors as they are occurring in the present and to prevent their recurrence in the future (Burbach, Borduin, and Peake, 1988).

Cognitive approaches (which typically include behavioral aspects as well), have been categorized by Mahoney and Arnkoff (1978) into three main groups: (1) *cognitive restructuring,* such as Ellis' rational-emotive therapy (1962, 1992) and Beck's cognitive therapy (1976, 1988); (2) *coping skills,* such as Wolpe's systematic desensitization (1958) and Meichenbaum's stress inoculation training (1977, 1985, 1992); and (3) *problem-solving,* such as D'Zurilla and Goldfried's behavioral problem-solving therapy (1973) and Mahoney's personal science approach (1974, 1977). Faulty learning is revised as distortions in cognitive schemata are corrected, relaxation skills and relapse prevention methods are taught, and constructive decision making is increased. In addition to the sources already cited, useful descriptions of cognitive therapy techniques have been provided by Beck, Rush, Shaw, and Emery (1979), Beck and others (1990), McMullin (1986), Meichenbaum (1994), Persons (1989), and Schuyler (1991); the books *Feeling Good: The New Mood Therapy* (Burns, 1980) and *The Feeling Good Handbook* (Burns, 1989) are valuable references for the lay public. Some cognitive-behavioral methods (such as assertiveness training and relaxation programs) are semi-structured and thus can be adapted nicely to cost-effective, short-term psychoeducational group therapy formats (see Chapter Five).

Clear operationalism is one of the hallmarks and advantages of cognitive-behavioral treatments. As Lazarus and Fay (1990, pp. 39–41) wrote:

> Some long-term therapy is not only inefficient (taking longer than necessary because it was insufficiently focused or precise), but even detrimental because of the reinforcement of pathological self-concepts. One of the great advantages of the short-term focus is that if the therapy doesn't work, it will be apparent much sooner. . . . In this regard, to paraphrase an old saying, effective treatment depends far less on the hours you put in, than on what you put into those hours.
>
> We also believe that there are three major impediments to the development and clinical implementation of rapidly effective therapies: (1) the lack of a sufficiently broad technical armamentarium—largely a result of factionalism within our profession; (2) ignorance of, or inadequate attention to, the biological aspects of "psychological" problems; and (3) the concept of resistance and its elaboration, particularly the notion that the locus of resistance is within the patient. . . . Our position is that "resistance" does not rest with the patient, but hinges on the methodology of the therapy as well as the skill and personal qualities of the therapist (cf. de Shazer, 1985).[10] It is *our* responsibility to find the keys to the puzzle.

What is needed, they suggest, is a schema for systematically, comprehensively, and exhaustively assessing a patient's psychological and psychiatric problems as a preparation for the selection of specific effective interventions. They recommend Multimodal Therapy (Lazarus, 1976, 1989). This approach, which they sometimes prefer to call *limited goal therapy,* is not so much a school of therapy as a way of organizing information obtained from the client and then selecting treatments in terms of seven interactive modalities of human personality expressed in the acronym B.A.S.I.C. I.D. The letters stand for Behavior, Affect, Sensation, Imagery, Cognition, Interpersonal, and Drugs (a euphonic choice to complete the acronym, referring more broadly to the biological sector). The Modality Profile displayed in Table 20.1, comprised for a thirty-three-year-old woman who sought therapy for "depression and anxiety," illustrates how the

Table 20.1. Modality Profile.

Modality	Problem	Proposed Treatment
B	"Disorganized/sloppy"	Contingency contracting
	Phobic avoidance	Systematic desensitization
	Leaves things to the last minute	Time management
A	Guilt	Explore antecedents and irrational ideas
	Anxiety related to criticism and rejection	Coping imagery and rational disputation
	Sadness/despondency	Explore faulty thinking and encourage her to seek out positive events
S	Fatigue/lower back pain/tension headaches	Relaxation training/physio-therapy exercises
I	Loneliness images/poor self-image/images of failing	Coping imagery exercises
C	Dichotomous reasoning/too many "shoulds"/over-generalizes	Cognitive restructuring
I	Nontrusting	Risk taking
	Overly competitive	Cooperation training
	Unassertive	Assertiveness training
	Avoids social gatherings	Social skills training
D	Uses alprazolam p.r.n.	Monitor to avoid dependency
	Overweight	Weight control methods (e.g., contingency contracting, self-monitoring, support group)
	Insufficient exercise	Physical fitness program

(A thorough medical examination replete with laboratory tests revealed no diagnosable contributing organic pathology.)

Source: Lazarus and Fay (1990 p. 46), "Brief Therapy: Tautology or Oxymoron?" In J. K. Zeig and S. G. Gilligan (eds.), *Brief Therapy: Myths, Methods, and Metaphors,* © 1990 by Brunner/Mazel, Inc. Reprinted by permission of the publisher.

multimodal framework can be used to identify problems and plan treatments.

Cognitive-behavioral approaches are often useful for the brief therapy of both emotional disorders (anxiety and depression) and marital discord. While there is a complicated range of possible interrelationships between individual and conjoint problems that highlight the need for careful idiographic case conceptualization (see Addis and Jacobson, 1991), the appropriate integration of cognitive and behavioral treatment technologies makes great sense if progress is to be made and maintained without undue delay. Important source material to guide practitioners has been provided by Beach, Sandeen, and O'Leary (1990), Beck (1988), Dattilio and Padesky, 1990, Fay (1990), Jacobson and Margolin (1979), and Stuart (1981). A useful overview is also provided by Robinson (1991), who has summarized typical objectives, techniques, and patient assignments for early, middle, and late phases of treating couples within the parameters of prepaid health care (see Table 20.2).

Table 20.2a. Treating Couples in Prepaid Health Care: Initial Phase.

Objectives	Techniques	Patient Assignments
Assessment of problem	Formal Assessment Objectification Reframing	Relationship Belief Inventory Written statements of their part in problem
Assessment of satisfaction	Formal assessment Long- and short-term focusing	Marital Happiness Scale Dyadic Adjustment Scale
Assessment of communication skills	Observations	Communication practice sessions: objectification, expressing appreciation
Increase in positive exchange	Refocusing attention Noting strengths Increasing rate of caring behaviors Defining collaboration	Sharing romantic or humorous memories "Caring Days" Recalling examples of collaboration

**Table 20.2a. Treating Couples in Prepaid Health Care:
Initial Phase,** *Cont'd.*

Objectives	Techniques	Patient Assignments
Planning and obtainment of commitment to treatment	"As if" participation Discussing model Pros and cons of participation Treatment contract	Listing questions or concerns Discussing beliefs about treatment Planning ways to deal with obstacles to completing treatment

**Table 20.2b. Treating Couples in Prepaid Health Care:
Middle Phase.**

Objectives	Techniques	Patient Assignments
Problem solving	Generating solutions Discussing pros and cons of possible solutions Discovering obstacles	Listing advantages and disadvantages of present solution
Increase of positive exchange	Discussing and identifying shared recreational activities (SRAs)	Scheduling, doing, and evaluating SRAs
Increasing communication skills: validating, listening, making specific positive requests	Instructions, modeling, behavioral rehearsal, feedback Practice sessions	Reading written instructions
Introduction of role of self-talk and self-reinforcement	Instructions, examples	Thought identification

Table 20.2c. Treating Couples in Prepaid Health Care:
Later Phase.

Objectives	Techniques	Patient Assignments
Increasing communication skills: expressing feelings directly, negotiating, problem solving	Instructions, modeling, behavioral rehearsal, feedback	Holding a practice session Keeping a problem-solving notebook
Problem solving and revising	Discussing "good faith" and "quid pro quo" contracts	Writing, implementing, and evaluating contracts
Increasing abilities to monitor self-talk	Practice in problem solving and conflict deescalation situations	Listing thoughts Writing cognitive scripts
Relapse prevention planning	Discussing effective strategies Planning ways to maintain positive exchange rates Planning method to help maintain interaction skill usage Fading treatment	Making individual lists Choosing a monitoring method Deciding on cue to signal the need for a tune-up Planning a booster

Source: Robinson (1991, pp. 176, 179–180), "Providing Couples' Therapy in Prepaid Health Care." In C. S. Austad and W. H. Berman (eds.), *Psychotherapy in Managed Health Care,* © 1991 by American Psychological Association. Reprinted with permission of the publisher.

Brief cognitive-behavioral treatment of the confluence of depression and marital discord is described in the following case report.

The Case of the Martyred Mother

Jackie, a fifty-three-year-old nurse, was referred for therapy after being discharged from a psychiatric hospital, where she had been briefly committed following a threat to kill herself. The patient and her husband, a pleasant and mild-mannered school teacher, were seen together. When asked by the therapist,

"What problem are you trying to solve?" and what each was hoping to get from therapy, Jackie said that she was tired of working all day and then coming home and having to cook and clean and do everything else as well. She and her husband had six children, "all supposedly adults," and three of the children were still living at home and did little or nothing to help. "They ignore me and laugh at me when I want something," she complained. The day of her hospitalization had been her birthday. When 10 P.M. came without a card or birthday greeting from anyone in the house, the identified patient became even more unhappy than usual. An overweight and diabetic woman, she had pulled out a syringe and had threatened to kill herself with a lethal overdose of insulin. Now she admitted that she probably wouldn't have actually injected herself but that she was desperate and had just wanted them to pay attention to her.

Charles, the husband, said that he loved his wife and was greatly concerned, and he admitted that "Yes, maybe I don't do enough." He then began to complain about the children still living at home, particularly one son who was lazy, borrowed money and never returned it, and generally acted the part of a ne'er-do-well. Jackie quickly began to protect the children. She would like the kids out, too, especially the troublesome son, but she wasn't willing to push him or "do any of that tough love stuff," because it had taken a great deal of effort to get him off drugs, and if he went back to the street he would probably quickly resume using and dealing. She reiterated her complaint that the family used her and ignored her and that her depression and suicidal threat were the result of frustration and isolation. When asked, "What's your goal for therapy? How will we know when to stop meeting like this?" Jackie responded: "I'd be happy if they would listen to me and treat me like a person and if I could sometimes get someone to do something for me without having to threaten to kill myself." When Charles then said, "I just want to have peace at home, and I try to do what I can," Jackie quickly became passive and acquiesced. She got quiet and looked obviously more unhappy. The husband tried to comfort her, but she said, "It's okay," and withdrew.

Charles then averred, "This is what always happens. I know it's my fault, too, but I just can't stand any conflict, with Jackie or the kids."

Assessment at the hospital and in the office revealed no evidence for biological depression (she was overweight, but her diabetes was well managed and stable). Her unhappy mental status was a product of intertwined interactional and characterological factors. There was obviously poor communication and a lack of satisfying exchanges, conditions that were promoted by and in turn reinforcing of the patient's schemata of self and others and of future expectations. Her husband was fully part of the equation, too. Evaluation along the lines described in Table 20.2 revealed a variety of problems that might be amenable to improvement through treatments designed to restructure thought processes, enhance coping skills, and promote constructive problem solving. The therapist remarked that improvement was possible but that hard work would be required and that progress might be slow, "but we won't meet any longer than we need to." To enhance motivation and promote cooperation, he added, "It's up to you, of course, but you know what they say: 'If you don't change directions, you'll wind up where you're heading.'" The couple knew they both needed help and agreed to participate in therapy together.

A series of weekly sessions were held. Careful attention was paid to helping each of them see how they thought and acted in ways that did (or did not) promote progress. Assertiveness training was provided. The focus was on helping the couple improve their skills in listening, validating, and making positive requests effectively, with both in-session practice and between-sessions "homework." Shared enjoyable activities were encouraged and prescribed, including an evening out together, a visit with friends, and a daily "report" time when each person talked for a few minutes (sometimes while going for a recommended walk together) about his or her day and feelings while the other listened actively. Progress was achieved, although not always smoothly, with both partners at times needing much encouragement not to give up or return too long to the counterproductive patterns that had led to the crisis that precipitated therapy.

Follow-up and comment. After ten therapy sessions the couple was functioning with much more cooperation and mutual enjoyment. Jackie was not feeling depressed or suicidal, and both partners began to express readiness to "take off the training wheels," as they put it. Two more weekly sessions were held to discuss ways to continue progress and to prevent relapse. What had been learned was reviewed, and strategies were discussed regarding how to recognize and respond to "warning signals" of emerging problems. Two follow-up sessions were then held, a month apart, to monitor progress. The couple was encouraged to continue what they had found effective and to recontact the therapist as needed.

The emphasis in this cognitive-behavioral therapy was on the identification and modification of observable behaviors. The wife already had some awareness of her feelings and the use of suicidality as a way of solving her problems. She and her husband needed to learn more effective and healthy ways of getting their needs met. Informed by cognitive-behavioral and systemic perspectives, an integrated combination of techniques were employed.

At one point in the third session, the therapist made a mistake that could have had major deleterious effects for the therapy. He requested that the difficult son be brought to the next session. A week later the couple came without the son. He had refused to attend but had suggested that his mother ask if her "symptoms" could be manic-depressive illness. A few quick questions and answers ruled out the diagnosis. The therapist then quipped, "What you have is hereditary, though—if you don't work together you can get it from your kids!" The couple appreciated the humor and the message that emphasized family structure and the importance of the marital bond. The therapist also recognized that if the son had come in and if the therapist had tried to get the son out of the house, he probably would have failed, lost his power, and maybe lost his patients, as well. (Recall the husband's initial complaint about the son at home and the wife's refusal to put him out: the therapist might have appeared to be siding with the husband against the wife, who then characteristically might have withdrawn when feeling ganged up on and unappreciated.) One could approach the situation in many different ways, of course, but it was helpful to remember the primary agenda of the patients: greater marital harmony.[11] What might be called resistance could also be seen as the system providing feedback to the therapist about what was ready to happen. Interestingly, several sessions later—after the marital relationship was clearly improved—Jackie began a meeting by announcing that she and Charles had given the at-home children notice that they had to move out within six weeks, a decision the couple (and kids) followed through successfully. To be effective in brief therapy one sometimes needs to go slow and, to avoid stumbling, to take small steps in the right order.

Ericksonian Strategic-Systemic Approaches to Brief Therapy

The term *Ericksonian* is applied to a broad field of creative methods that derive their inspiration from the life and work of the remarkably innovative psychiatrist Milton Erickson. He overcame great personal adversities (such as paralytic polio) to develop a hypnosis-based approach oriented toward growth and problem solving via utilization of whatever assets the patient might bring to therapy. See Erickson's four-volume *Collected Papers* (1980) and his three-volume *Conversations* (Haley, 1985), as well as several excellent books about his concepts and techniques, such as those by Haley (1973), Havens (1989), Lankton and Lankton (1983), O'Hanlon (1987), O'Hanlon and Hexum (1990), Zeig (1982), and Zeig and Lankton (1988). His work has directly or indirectly had a tremendous influence on many schools of therapy, including hypnotherapy, family therapy, and interactional approaches.

It is especially difficult to summarize Ericksonian strategic therapy, since it is so individualistically based on the talents of particular patients and therapists—a situation that also makes systematic research quite problematic. Still, some broad outlines are possible. As Rosenbaum (1990, p. 354) has described it: "Strategic therapy is not a particular approach or theory. . . .

It rather refers, in its broadest sense, to any therapy in which the therapist is willing to take on the responsibility for influencing people and takes an active role in planning a strategy for promoting change."

Haley (1973, p. 17) elaborates: "Therapy can be called strategic if the clinician initiates what happens during therapy and designs a particular approach for each problem. When a therapist and a person with a problem encounter each other, the action that takes place is determined by both of them, but in strategic therapy the initiative is largely taken by the therapist. He must identify solvable problems, set goals, design interventions to achieve those goals, examine the responses he receives to correct his approach, and ultimately examine the outcome of his therapy to see if it has been effective."

What characterizes Ericksonian work? Lankton (1990, p. 364) explains:

> The Ericksonian strategic approach is a method of working with clients emphasizing common, even unconscious natural abilities and talents. Therapy goals are built upon the intelligence and health of individuals. It works to frame change in ways that reduce resistance, reduce dependency upon therapy, bypass the need for insight, and allow clients to take full credit for changes. Most problems are not viewed as internal pathologies but as the natural result of solving developmental demands in ways that do not fully work for the people involved. The Ericksonian strategic approach is distinctive in that it is associated with certain interventions upon which it relies heavily during extramural assignments and therapy sessions. These include skill building homework, paradoxical directives, ambiguous function assignments, indirect suggestions, hypnosis, reframing, metaphors, and therapeutic binds. These are not so much interventions as characteristic parts of the therapist's interactions with clients. As such they are used to motivate clients to actively participate in changing the way they live with themselves and others.

Lankton goes on to underscore that the Ericksonian approach emphasizes creative reorganization of relationships rather than a resistance-stimulating focus on diagnosing pathology. Noting that clients tend to follow suggestions that are most relevant to them, he also emphasizes that strategic therapy is interested in getting patients to take action outside the therapist's office:

> It is from the learning brought by new actions and not from insight or understanding that change develops. Consequently, a client's understanding or insight about a problem is not of central importance. The matter of central importance is the client's participation in new experiences and transactions that congeal developmentally appropriate relational patterns [Lankton, 1990, p. 365].[12]

As discussed in Chapter Ten, Lankton notes seven features that characterize Erickson's work:

1. *Nonpathology-based model.* Problems are seen as part of, and a result of, attempts at adaptation; symptoms are essentially natural (but limiting) responses of unique individuals.
2. *Indirection.* This concerns itself with helping an individual or members of a family discover talents and resources, options, and answers, seemingly without the aid of the therapist.
3. *Utilization.* This involves using whatever the patient brings to the office (understandings, behaviors, motivations) as part of the treatment.
4. *Action.* Clients are expected and encouraged to quickly get into actions related to desired goals—a basic ingredient of most successful brief therapies regardless of theoretical orientation.
5. *Strategic approach.* The therapist takes responsibility for influencing the patient and is active in setting or initiating the stages of therapy.
6. *Future orientation.* The focus is on action and experience in the present and future rather than the past.
7. *Enchantment.* Treatment engages the mind, appeals to the patient, and captures the ear of the listener.

Ericksonian interventions require careful attention to the three principles of proper evaluation and creative planning, cultivating and assuring patient commitment, and an emphasis on patient strengths and tailoring treatment to the individual (K. Erickson, 1988). The importance of *how* rather than *why* is also emphasized by Zeig (1990, p. 376), who stresses the utility of building on positive change and the accessing of the unconscious mind as a health-seeking source of solutions. He, too, values hypnosis and the tailoring and sequencing of treatment to fit the particular patient.

The job of the therapist in Ericksonian psychotherapy can be summarized as a five-step procedure that is conducted more simultaneously than sequentially:

1. Decide what to communicate to the patient.
2. Decide how to communicate it. Usually this entails being indirect, but it could be the presentation of any therapeutic maneuver.
3. Ascertain what the patient values; that is, the position the patient takes.
4. Divide the solution into manageable steps. Each step may be initiated by a therapeutic intervention.
5. Present the intervention within a therapeutic sequence, tailoring the intervention to fit the patient's values. This usually entails a three-step procedure: Moving in small, directed Steps; Intervening; and Following Through. This procedure has been tabbed "SIFT" [Zeig, 1990, p. 373].

An Ericksonian perspective can be appreciated in a wide range of interventions:

1. The indirection of a police officer asking for a cup of coffee as a way of separating a domestically disputing couple (Everstine and Everstine, 1983), or the charming Japanese folk tale (retold by de Shazer, 1991b) of a villager who, unable to warn his neighbors of an impending tidal wave, sets their hillside terraces on fire so that they

will rush up the mountain to battle the flames and thus inadvertently be saved from drowning

2. The use of imagery and hypnosis to construct more useful realities (Andreas and Andreas, 1989; Bandler and Grinder, 1982; Erickson, Rossi, and Rossi, 1976; Lankton and Lankton, 1983; Yapko, 1990b)

3. Instructing and motivating with teaching stories and metaphoric communications (Gordon, 1978; Rosen, 1982)

4. The use of provocation to challenge and motivate patients (Farrelly and Brandsma, 1974), including a last-ditch (and successful) effort to motivate a prideful patient out of a deep funk with humiliating taunts (Haley, 1973)

5. Prescribing ordeals, symptoms, and other paradoxical maneuvers (Weeks, 1991; Haley, 1984; Selvini-Palazzoli, Boscolo, Cecchin, and Prata, 1978) to get patients to abandon undesirable behaviors

6. Assigning ambiguous tasks (such as having an unhappy couple climb a nearby peak) to structure a decision-making experience or elicit an unconscious understanding (Furman and Ahola, 1992; Lankton and Lankton, 1986)

7. Providing directives to alter the conflict-generating rules that govern interactions, as seen in various strategic-systemic therapies such as those developed at the Mental Research Institute of Palo Alto (Watzlawick, Weakland, and Fisch, 1974; Fisch, Weakland, and Segal, 1982), the Family Therapy Institute of Washington, D.C. (Haley, 1977; Madanes, 1981), and the Brief Family Therapy Center of Milwaukee (de Shazer, 1982, 1985, 1988)

The basic principle underlying all of these techniques and methods is *utilization*. The essential paradigmatic shift is from deficits to strengths, from problems to solutions, from past to future (Fisch, 1990; 1994), utilizing whatever the patient brings in the service of healthful change (de Shazer, 1988). For Erickson, the basic problem was not so much one of pathology or defect but *rigidity*, the idea that people get "stuck" by failing to use a range of skills, competencies, and learnings that they have but are not applying. Various interventions are thus designed to get people to have experiences that put them in touch with their latent or overlooked abilities. As Erickson said: "Patients have problems because their conscious programming has too severely limited their capacities. The solution is to help them break through the limitations of their conscious attitudes to free their unconscious potential for problem solving" (Erickson, Rossi, and Rossi, 1976, p. 18).

Even a simple and relatively direct approach can have Ericksonian elements. Remembering how little can actually be conveyed through a single case presentation (including tone, timing, and nonverbal communication), consider the following report (adapted from Hoyt, 1993b; also see Chapter Ten for other examples).

The Case of the Baseball Fan

Sam was a sixty-seven-year-old man when I met him sitting in a wheelchair next to his wife in the waiting room of the HMO Psychiatry Department. He had been referred by his internist: "Post-stroke. Fear of falling." When I introduced myself and shook hands I could see that he was a pleasant and engaging man. He had not shaved in a few days, was casually dressed, and was wearing an Oakland A's baseball cap. His wife immediately began to talk (a lot) and quickly told me that Sam could walk but was afraid to. He had come into the building on his own and then gotten into the wheelchair. The wife was nice and trying to be helpful, but I sensed that it would be useful to have some time with the patient alone, so I asked: "Do you want to walk or ride to my office?" He replied: "I'll take a ride, at least this time."

As I pushed him around the corner and down the corridor, we talked baseball—about a recent trade and how the game had gone that day. His remarks showed a good knowledge of the game and an alert, up-to-date interest. I asked questions, and we connected as we talked. At my office door I stopped and asked him to take a few steps into my office and to use a regular chair, so that I wouldn't have to move the furniture around—an indirect approach that used his natural courtesy to bypass discussion of his need for the wheelchair. He obliged. When we sat down I asked, "So, what's up?" I learned that he was a retired mechanic and printing pressman. He had suffered a stroke three years earlier, with a residual partial paralysis of one arm and leg. He had grown "too damn dependent" on his wife, he said, but could no longer drive and had considerable difficulty walking. "I sure miss Dr. Jarrett," he interjected, referring to his former internist, who had himself retired a few years earlier. When he told me what Dr. Jarrett would have said to get him moving, I "borrowed" the good doctor's mantle of authority and replied: "Took the words right out of my mouth."

Sam went on to tell me that he wanted to go to an upcoming A's game his sons had invited him to, but that he had to first overcome his great fear of falling, since "I get so worried and down that I freeze up." He knew how to fall safely (protecting his head and softening the fall), but he was fearful because "I'm not sure what would happen to me if I fell and no one was around. I might not be able to get back up."

He was a practical man with a predicament. (By coincidence, I had the night before read my four-year-old son a story [Peet, 1972] about an elephant that gets stuck on his back until an ant he befriended rescues him with the help of an ant hoard.) After ascertaining that he was not worried about safety or embarrassment, I suggested: "I'll tell you what. Let's do a little experiment. I'll be you, you be the coach, and teach me how to get up." I then proceeded to sort of throw myself on the floor in front of him. He got right into it, advising me, "No, turn the other way, get up first on three points," and so on. I said, "Let's try it with my arm not working," and held it limply against my side. For the next eight to ten minutes I repeatedly got down on the floor and Sam instructed me on how to get myself up again.

Back in my chair, I asked him if he wanted to "try it" there in my office or wait until he got home—an "illusion of alternatives" (Lankton and Lankton, 1983) with the underlying implication that he would perform the action. He chose to wait until he was home but offered to show me "some exercises I can still do." I watched and then asked him to "stand and do a little walking just so I can see how you do." I opened the office door and we proceeded into the corridor. We slowly made our way up and down the hallway, with my remarking a couple of times, "Good," and "Nice, better than I expected." As we went up and down the hallway I switched back to baseball, asking him about the game he was planning to attend with his sons. "Where are you going to park? Which ramp will you take?" I painted aloud a vivid picture of father and sons entering the baseball stadium as we made our way up and down the hallway a couple of times.

Back in my office he expressed concern about his wife. She was trying to be helpful but was wearing out both herself and Sam with her watchfulness. "Maybe you could talk to her, too," he asked. I said I would be glad to, "and when you begin to do more walking on your own then I'll really be able to convince her to back off." He understood and agreed to practice his falling and getting up, and we playfully bargained about how many times he would do it a day, settling on twice a day to start and then three times per day until I saw him in two weeks.

Before Sam left my office I added: "You know, I think it's really important that you go to that game with your sons if you can. I know you want to, but I think it will be even more important for them. Someday they will look back and remember going to the game with you, you know what I mean?" Sam didn't know exactly how baseball was in my blood, my history of going to games with my father, but he knew I was saying something heartfelt and important. It spoke to him. He said, "I'm sure going to give it my best."

Follow-up and comment. When I next saw Sam he proudly walked into my office, slowly. He told me about going to the game and his plans to go to another one. At his request I then brought his wife into the session, and we talked about ways she could help by doing things and ways she could help by not doing things. He expressed the desire for more activity, and I suggested attending an Older Adults Therapy Group as well as some other outings with neighbors and former co-workers. He followed through on these, and I remain available if and when he may again request to meet with me.

Sam's worries about falling were taken seriously. The approach here was highly pragmatic, with strategies directed toward quickly getting the patient walking. It was helpful and felt natural to temporarily reverse roles, Sam becoming the teacher-coach rather than the humbled stroke patient. This was morale restoring and opened possibilities for change. The hallway walk into the ballpark was hypnotic and future oriented. His desire for assistance in managing his wife was used to further promote treatment compliance. Part of effective brief therapy is deciding what paths *not* to take. Exploring Sam's concerns about failing powers and limited mortality were issues that might be worthwhile (and would be addressed in the Older Adults Group), but first helping Sam regain his confidence in walking and being able to get up when he fell enhanced the quality of his life and put him in a stronger position to realistically appraise his future options. This is what Sam and his wife wanted. Being alert to and using whatever resources are available in the service of the patient's therapeutic needs—including the therapist's own personal experiences with baseball, inverted elephants, and father-son relations[13]—is what I take Erickson and Rossi (1979, p. 276) to mean when they suggest: "To initiate this type of therapy you have to be yourself as a person. You cannot imitate somebody else, but you have to do it in your own way."

An aspect of strategic treatment that has received considerable attention recently is called *solution-focused* (de Shazer, 1985, 1988, 1991b) or *solution-oriented* therapy (O'Hanlon and Wilk, 1987; O'Hanlon and Weiner-Davis, 1989; O'Hanlon and Martin, 1992). The basic premise is deceptively simple: increase what works; decrease what doesn't work. What are the "exceptions" to the problem? What is the patient doing differently at those times when he/she/they are not anxious or depressed or quarrelling? What has worked before? What strengths can the patient apply? What would be a useful solution? How to construct it? Behind these apparently simple questions is a profound paradigmatic shift: competencies, not dysfunctions, are the focus; the quest is to access latent capacities, not latent conflicts. The orientation is toward the future and the full appreciation and utilization of human abilities. Some aspects of this shift are delineated in Table 20.3. The approach is not just technical but, when taken to heart, epitomizes what is best about the Ericksonian perspective: the belief that with skillful facilitation, people have within themselves the resources necessary to achieve their goals.

One of the leading solution-focused therapists, Steve de Shazer (1982, 1985, 1988, 1991b, 1994), prefers minimalist interventions. He sometimes "fast-forwards" to a solution by asking the elegantly goal identifying "Miracle Question": "Suppose tonight while you're sleeping a miracle happens and the problem that brought you here is resolved. . . . How will you know, in the morning, that a miracle has happened?" (1988, pp. 5–6).

Table 20.3. Solution-Building Vocabulary.

In	Out	In	Out
Respect	Judge	Forward	Backward
Empower	Fix	Future	Past
Nurture	Control	Collaborate	Manipulate
Facilitate	Treat	Options	Conflicts
Augment	Reduce	Partner	Expert
Invite	Insist	Horizontal	Hierarchical
Appreciate	Diagnose	Possibility	Limitation
Hope	Fear	Growth	Cure
Latent	Missing	Access	Defense
Assets	Defects	Utilize	Resist
Strength	Weakness	Create	Repair
Health	Pathology	Exception	Rule
Not Yet	Never	Difference	Sameness
Expand	Shrink	Solution	Problem

Source: Hoyt (1994c, p. 4), "Introduction: Competency-Based Future-Oriented Therapy." In M. F. Hoyt (ed.), *Constructive Therapies,* © 1994 by Guilford Press. Reprinted by permission of the publisher.

Patients get enchanted by the question and, with or without prompting, draw upon their own wisdom and experience to create answers that are uniquely theirs and thus more hopeful and likely to occur. Various methods can then be used to promote continued change (Adams, Piercy, and Jurich, 1991; Kral and Kowalski, 1989). As the titles of a number of useful books have it: *In Search of Solutions* (O'Hanlon and Weiner-Davis, 1989), we welcome *Clues* (de Shazer, 1988), and *Keys to Solutions in Brief Therapy* (de Shazer, 1985), since *Becoming Solution-Focused in Brief Therapy* (Walter and Peller, 1992) leads to *Constructive Therapies* (Hoyt, 1994b), *Putting Difference to Work* (de Shazer, 1991b), *Solution Talk* (Furman and Ahola, 1992b), *Therapeutic Conversations* (Gilligan and Price, 1993), and *The New Language of Change* (Friedman, 1993), which may yield *Expanding Therapeutic Possibilities* (Friedman and Fanger, 1991), perhaps even in *Single-Session Therapy* (Talmon, 1990), that will help in *Rewriting Love Stories* (Hudson and O'Hanlon, 1992), *Divorce Busting* (Weiner-Davis, 1992), *Resolving Sexual Abuse* (Dolan, 1991), pursuing *Narrative Means to Therapeutic Ends* (White and Epston, 1990), and *Working with the Problem Drinker* (Berg and Miller, 1992)!

A Long Future for Brief Therapy

Brief therapy has a long history, beginning with Freud, and it appears that it will have a long future as well. The convergence of market forces, the desire of most persons for rapid relief from psychological distress, and the development of new treatment technologies augur well for the continued ascendancy of short-term therapy. Health maintenance organizations (HMOs), the emergence of managed care, and the continuing debate about some form of national health insurance as responses to the runaway costs of health care all suggest the further expansion of brief treatment. What is clear is that consumers, insurers, and health care professionals are all increasingly recognizing the importance of providing psychotherapeutic services that are as efficient as possible. As Shectman (1986) has said, necessity sometimes proves to be the mother of intervention. Brief therapy methods are becoming increasingly attractive, both as treatments of choice and for their value in resource conservation.

We can expect training in brief therapy to expand dramatically in the coming years, stimulated both by the demands of consumers for more efficient mental health services and by the fiscal pressures of managed care (Butler, 1992; Goode, 1992). While there has been some attention paid to aspects of brief therapy teaching and learning—such as potential parallel processes between therapy and training (Dasberg and Winokur, 1984; Frances and Clarkin, 1981a), the use of manuals (Levenson and Butler, 1994), and the impact of training on skills and attitudes (Burlingame and Behrman, 1987; Burlingame, Fuhriman, Paul, and Ogles, 1989; Henry and others, 1993; Levenson and Bolter, 1988)—there has been a dearth of high-quality training for most clinicians. A study by Levenson, Speed, and Budman (1992) of psychologists in California and Massachusetts, for example, found that while most therapists reported a sizeable portion of their clinical work to be short-term treatment, one-third of those doing brief therapy reported having minimal training in brief therapy techniques, and more than 25 percent of all brief treatment hours were being conducted by clinicians with little or no formal training in the special orientation and skills of time-sensitive therapy. Even in managed-care settings such as health maintainence organizations (HMOs), preferred provider organizations (PPOs), and employee assistance programs (EAPs), there has been up to now surprisingly little attention paid to systematic training in brief therapy (Budman and Armstrong, 1992). Combining the fiscal imperative of the managed-care movement with the fact that brief therapy is the treatment of choice for many patients, serving their needs as well as providing the socioeconomic advantage of allowing patients who would otherwise go without to receive the benefits of professional mental health care, we can expect increasing attention to the practice and study of brief psychotherapy in the years ahead.

Coda

The goal of brief psychotherapy, regardless of the specific theoretical approach or technical method, is to help the patient resolve a problem, to get "unstuck" and to move on. Techniques are specific, integrated, and as eclectic as needed. Treatment is focused, the therapist appropriately active, and the patient responsible for making changes. Each session is valuable, and therapy ends as soon as possible. Good outcome, not good process, is most valued. More is not better; *better* is better. The patient carries on, and can return to treatment as needed. The simple truth is that most therapy *is* brief therapy and will be increasingly so; for the sake of our patients and our profession, we should learn to practice it well.

Notes

1. Setting a specific number of sessions may at times be helpful, e.g., to provide structuring (Wells, 1982) or to deliberately stimulate a termination process (Mann, 1973). Attention to temporal parameters is important since Parkinson's Law ("Work expands or contracts to fit the allotted time") may operate in psychotherapy (Applebaum, 1975). Generally, however, the focus should not be on the limit but on the present. If one makes the most of each session, treatment will be efficient and as brief as possible.

2. One can also question if brief therapy is a "resistance" to doing long-term work, e.g., if there is sometimes operating in brief therapists a countertherapeutic desire to avoid extended intimacy, the demands of a prolonged nurturing-dependent relationship, and possible discomfort with "deeper" levels of psychological material. These could all be true in certain instances, of course, although good brief therapists do not turn away from painful subjects if they need to be addressed for useful change to occur. The brief therapist's quest, however, is to help people change in ways that will make the therapist unnecessary as soon as possible; mirroring the finitude of life itself, the goal is termination rather than proliferation (Goldberg, 1975). To point out the strange logic that suspects those who help quickly, Duncan (and others, 1992; see also Haley, 1969) has written a spoof entitled "Brief Therapyism: A Ne-

glected Addiction" in which he confesses, in a tongue-in-cheek way, his weakness for efficient treatment, so typical of those with "Pragmatic Personality Disorder," and reports that he and his Inner Child are "in recovery" and attending daily Brief Therapy Anonymous meetings!

3.   In this regard, Haley (1990, pp. 14–15) has observed: "When we look at the history of therapy, the most important decision ever made was to charge for therapy by the hour. The ideology and practice of therapy was largely determined when therapists chose to sit with a client and be paid for durations of time rather than by results." Recognizing that "therapy will become briefer as insurance companies limit the length of therapy" (p. 14), he foresees changes in the basic financing of therapy and recommends charging a flat fee for relief of a symptom, since such an arrangement would require therapists to hone skills and increase efficiency. Actually, similar arrangements already do exist, in "capitated" HMO plans where the company is "at risk" to provide all needed services in exchange for a set payment (Broskowski, 1991) and in preferred-provider networks where continued referrals will depend upon demonstrated efficacy. Such situations necessitate that treatment be efficient and thus mostly brief. Wells and Phelps (1990) characterize this emerging trend as "Survival of the Shortest."

4.   Throughout this chapter the terms *patient* and *client* are used interchangeably, as they tend to be in the literature. The former term may carry more connotation of distress and a quest for relief (not necessarily in a medical model, although the implication is that of a relatively passive supplicant), while the latter term may seem more "egalitarian" or "businesslike" (but may deny the special quality of suffering that leads people to seek mental health services). It is important to recognize what the choice of either term may imply regarding the model of helping relationship being co-constructed by the patient/client and therapist and to be aware of how these implications may impact on their subsequent work together (see Chapters Thirteen and Fourteen).

5. de Shazer (1991b, p. 112) has described the general characteristics of well-formed goals: (1) small rather than large; (2) salient to clients; (3) described in specific, concrete behavioral terms; (4) achievable within the practical contexts of clients' lives; (5) perceived by the clients as involving their "hard work"; (6) described as the "start of something" and not as the "end of something"; and (7) treated as involving new behavior(s) rather than the absence or cessation of existing behavior(s).

6. Other conceptualizations or models (Kuhn, 1970) are possible, of course. For example, see White and Epston's (1990) very helpful discussion of the different implications for psychotherapy of drawing analogies from positivist physical sciences, biological sciences, or social sciences.

7. Barten (1971, p. 7) went on to say: "Once we redefine our task as the provision of treatment services to patients in all classes with all kinds of problems, traditional, slow-paced techniques become obviously insufficient. . . . Poor and uneducated patients in particular seemed unreached by sophisticated techniques which they found alien and esoteric, assuming they were even available. As a rule, these patients want therapists who are warmly supportive and who provide concrete help rather than an opportunity to examine feelings, though some of them can be taught how to utilize the latter approach." While this statement—like any about an entire group or social class—may be an oversimplification, it is true that much psychotherapy is primarily oriented toward the lifestyles, values, and problems of the middle and upper classes. The complicated issues of culture, class, ethnicity, and race go far beyond the scope of this discussion, of course, and the reader is referred to Kupers (1981), McGoldrick, Pearce, and Giordano (1982), Lorion and Felner (1986), Mays and Albee (1992), and Gonzales, Biever, and Gardner (1994) for useful overviews. One needs to appreciate cultural differences and work respectfully, especially if one hopes in brief therapy to form a rapid working alliance and access patients' various resources for their therapeutic benefits. It should

also be recognized that while psychotherapy can play a valuable role—and especially brief therapy, with its emphasis on efficiency and specific goals—problems that fundamentally result from pernicious social and economic conditions may require redress at political and socioeconomic levels.

8. The present author was the therapist in each case to be reported, and all treatments occurred within the context of a staff-model health-maintenance organization.

9. Freud was not opposed to such developments, although he made it abundantly clear that one should not confuse such alloys with the "pure gold" of analysis. In 1910 (pp. 111–120) he wrote: "In practice, it is true, there is nothing to be said against a psychotherapist combining a certain amount of analysis with some suggestive influence in order to achieve a perceptible result in a shorter time. . . . But one has a right to insist that he himself should be in no doubt about what he is doing and should know that his method is not that of true psychoanalysis." In his later paper, "Analysis Terminable and Interminable" (1937) he further cautioned that the introduction of nonanalytic elements would interfere with or even eliminate the possibility of completing a formal psychoanalysis in a given case.

10. Also see de Shazer's (1984) discussion of "The Death of Resistance." In this regard, another interesting perspective is provided by Furman and Ahola (1992a, p. 8): "In our view, therapists are like pickpockets on a nudist camp. Some of them see front pockets and some see back pockets, depending on their particular specialisation. The therapist has to actually sew pockets on to the clients in order to start stealing. Fortunately, clients are very generous and they will let the therapist sew almost any type of pocket on them in order to let the therapist do the job. If, however, the client shows signs of discomfort in the process of sewing, this is aptly called resistance."

11. While a cognitive-behavioral model may be particularly useful in brief couples therapy because it lends itself readily to specifying particular actions to be changed (thus

avoiding broad generalizations that can easily lead to conflict escalation), it is also important to have an overarching integrated view that includes interpersonal, developmental, and existential perspectives (Budman and Gurman, 1988). As Gurman (1992, p. 199) has written: "We detail the areas of assessment that we find important to be aware of in most, if not all, couples therapy: presenting problems, attempted solutions, and the consequences of change; individual and couple assets and strengths; communication and problem-solving skills and styles; styles of influence; relational boundaries; life-cycle status and accomplishment; affection and attachment; marital (couple) relationship history; sexuality and sexual functioning; relationship commitment; spousal and substance abuse. . . . Keep in mind that 'assessment' does not end at the end of the first session."

12. Since the strategic therapist assumes responsibility for using the treatment session to "make something happen," key significance is not placed on the session *per se* but on what results *from* the session. Whereas traditional psychodynamic therapists largely judge the "good session" (Hoyt, 1980; Hoyt, Xenakis, Marmar, and Horowitz, 1983) by the depth of feeling and meaningfulness of what occurs in the consulting room, strategic therapists are more directly concerned about what happens after the session and will thus need to see its impact (outcome: change and durability) before assessing the "goodness" of a session.

13. I love the story my father told me (recounted in Hoyt, 1993b) about the time he was at a baseball game at Wrigley Field in Chicago and a drunken and belligerent fan in the bleachers was verbally abusing one of the players. The man let it be known that he was packing a gun, and it became alarmingly possible that he might use it. My father, who was a salesman by trade and something of a strategic therapist, got involved. Dad was also a gun fancier, and he got the irate fan engaged in a discussion about the type of gun, showed some interest, and wound up bargaining and buying the gun on the spot. (The police

never came.) When I asked my father what he had done with the weapon, he said he had taken it the next day to a shop and sold it, for a profit. When I asked why he had done that, he replied, "Hey, you've got to get paid for this kind of work!"

References

---◆---

Abrams, H. S. "Harvard Community Health Plan's Mental-Health Redesign Project: A Management and Clinical Partnership." *Psychiatric Quarterly,* 1993, *84*(1), 13–31.

Adams, J. F., Piercy, F. P., and Jurich, J. A. "Effects of Solution Focused Therapy's 'Formula First Session Task' on Compliance and Outcome in Family Therapy." *Journal of Marital and Family Therapy,* 1991, *17,* 277–290.

Addis, M. E., and Jacobson, N. S. "Integration of Cognitive Therapy and Behavioral Marital Therapy for Depression." *Journal of Psychotherapy Integration,* 1991, *4,* 249–264.

Adler, A. *Individual Psychology.* Patterson, N.J.: Littlefield, Adams, 1963.

Aldrich, C. K. "Brief Psychotherapy: A Reappraisal of Some Theoretical Assumptions." *American Journal of Psychiatry,* 1968, *125,* 585–592.

Alexander, F. "Psychoanalytic Contributions to Short-Term Psychotherapy." In L. R. Wolberg (ed.), *Short-Term Psychotherapy.* Philadelphia: Grune & Stratton, 1965.

Alexander, F., and French, T. M. *Psychoanalytic Therapy: Principles and Applications.* New York: Ronald Press, 1946.

Allgeyer, J. M. "Using Groups in a Crisis-Oriented Outpatient Setting." *International Journal of Group Psychotherapy,* 1973, *23,* 217–222.

Alonzo, A., and Rutan, J. S. "Shame and Guilt in Psychotherapy Supervision." *Psychotherapy,* 1988, *25,* 576–581.

Altman, L., and Goldstein, J. M. "Impact of HMO Model Type on Mental Health Service Delivery: Variation in Treatment and Approaches." *Administration in Mental Health,* 1988, *15,* 246–261.

American Psychiatric Association. *Diagnostic and Statistical Manual of Mental Disorders.* (3rd ed., rev.) Washington, D.C.: American Psychiatric Association, 1987.

American Psychiatric Association. *Diagnostic and Statistical Manual of Mental Disorders.* (4th ed.) Washington, D.C.: American Psychiatric Association, 1994.

Anderson, R. O. "Shifting from External to Internal Provision of Mental Health Services in a Health Maintenance Organization." *Hospital and Community Psychiatry,* 1981, *32,* 31.

Andreas, C., and Andreas, S. *Heart of the Mind.* Moab, Utah: Real People Press, 1989.

Appelbaum, S. A. "Parkinson's Law in Psychotherapy." *International Journal of Psychoanalytic Psychotherapy,* 1975, *4,* 426–436.

Appelbaum, S. A., and Holzman, P. S. "'End-Setting' as a Therapeutic Event." *Psychiatry,* 1967, *30,* 276–282.

Arendt, H. *The Life of the Mind.* Orlando, Fla.: Harcourt Brace Jovanovich, 1978.

Armstrong, S. "Dual Focus in Brief Dynamic Psychotherapy." *Psychotherapy and Psychosomatics,* 1980, *33,* 147–154.

Ashe, A., and Rampersad, A. *Days of Grace: A Memoir.* New York: Ballantine, 1993.

Atwood, G. "The Loss of a Loved Parent and the Origin of Salvation Fantasies." *Psychotherapy: Theory, Research and Practice,* 1974, *11,* 256–258.

Auer, J. "Ericksonian Hypnosis and Psychotherapy in Clinical Settings." *Ericksonian Monographs,* 1988, *4,* 100–109.

Austad, C. S. "A Comparison: Psychotherapists in Independent Practice and Managed Health Care." Symposium presented at the annual convention of the American Psychological Association, New Orleans, Louisiana, August 1989.

Austad, C. S., and Berman, W. H. (eds.). *Psychotherapy in Managed Health Care: The Optimal Use of Time and Resources.* Washington, D.C.: American Psychological Association, 1991.

Austad, C. S., DeStefano, L., and Kisch, J. "The Health Maintenance Organization. II. Implications for Psychotherapy." *Psychotherapy,* 1988, *25,* 449–454.

Austad, C. S., and Henault, K. "Group Psychotherapy with Elderly Women." *HMO Practice,* 1989, *3,* 70–71.

Austad, C. S., and Hoyt, M. F. "The Managed Care Movement and the Future of Psychotherapy." *Psychotherapy,* 1992, *29,* 109–118.

Austad, C. S., Sherman, W. O., and Holstein, L. "Psychotherapists in the HMO." *HMO Practice,* 1993, *7*(3), 122–126.

Austin, L., and Inderbitzin, L. "Brief Psychotherapy in Late Adolescence: A Psychodynamic and Developmental Approach." *American Journal of Psychotherapy,* 1983, *37,* 202–209.

Azrin, N. H., and Nunn, R. G. "Habit-Reversal: A Method of Eliminating Nervous Habits and Tics." *Behavior Research and Therapy,* 1973, *11,* 619–628.

Baekeland, F., and Lundwall, L. "Dropping Out of Treatment: A Critical Review." *Psychological Bulletin,* 1975, *82,* 738–783.

Balint, M., Ornstein, P. H., and Balint, E. *Focal Psychotherapy.* London: Tavistock, 1972.

Bandler, R., and Grinder, J. *The Structure of Magic.* Vol. 1. Palo Alto, Calif.: Science & Behavior Books, 1975.

Bandler, R., and Grinder, J. *Reframing.* Moab, Utah: Real People Press, 1982.

Bandler, R., and Grinder, J. *Using Your Brain—For a Change.* Moab, Utah: Real People Press, 1985.

Barber, J. "Miracle Cures? Therapeutic Consequences of Clinical Demonstrations." In J. K. Zeig and S. G. Gilligan (eds.), *Brief Therapy: Myths, Methods, and Metaphors.* New York: Brunner/Mazel, 1990.

Barnes, G. "Techniques of Contractual Supervision." In M. James (ed.), *Techniques in Transactional Analysis for Psychotherapists and Counselors.* Reading, Mass.: Addison-Wesley, 1977.

Barten, H. H. "The 15-Minute Hour: A Brief Therapy in a Military Setting." *American Journal of Psychiatry,* 1965, *122,* 565–567.

Barten, H. H. (ed.). *Brief Therapies.* New York: Behavioral Publications, 1971.

Bateson, G. *Mind and Nature: A Necessary Unity.* New York: Dutton, 1979.

Bauer, G. P., and Kobos, J. C. "Short-Term Dynamic Psychotherapy: Reflections on the Past and Current Practice." *Psychotherapy,* 1984, *21,* 153–170.

Bauer, G. P., and Kobos, J. C. *Brief Therapy: Short-Term Psychodynamic Intervention.* New York: Jason Aronson, 1987.

Beach, S. R., Sandeen, E. E., and O'Leary, K. D. *Depression in Marriage: A Model for Etiology and Treatment.* New York: Guilford, 1990.

Beattie, M. *Codependent No More.* New York: Harper/Hazelden, 1987.

Beck, A. T. *Cognitive Therapy and the Emotional Disorders.* Madison, Conn.: International Universities Press, 1976.

Beck, A. T. *Love Is Never Enough.* New York: HarperCollins, 1988.

Beck, A. T., Rush, A. J., Shaw, B. F., and Emery, G. *Cognitive Therapy of Depression.* New York: Guilford, 1979.

Beck, A. T., and others. *Cognitive Therapy of Personality Disorders.* New York: Guilford, 1990.

Becker, E. *The Denial of Death.* New York: Free Press, 1973.

Bellak, L. "Brief and Emergency Psychotherapy." In T. B. Karasu and L. Bellak (eds.), *Specialized Techniques in Individual Psychotherapy.* New York: Brunner/Mazel, 1980.

Bellak, L., and Small, L. *Emergency Therapy and Brief Psychotherapy.* Philadelphia: Grune & Stratton, 1965.

Bennett, M. J. "Focal Psychotherapy—Terminable and Interminable." *American Journal of Psychotherapy,* 1983, *37,* 365–375.

Bennett, M. J. "Brief Psychotherapy and Adult Development." *Psychotherapy,* 1984, *21,* 171–177.

Bennett, M. J. "Maximizing the Yield of Brief Therapy, II." *HMO Mental Health Newsletter,* 1986, *1,* 1–4.

Bennett, M. J. "The Greening of the HMO: Implications for Prepaid Psychiatry." *American Journal of Psychiatry,* 1988, *145,* 1544–1549.

Bennett, M. J. "The Importance of Teaching the Principles of Managed Care." *Behavioral Healthcare Tomorrow,* 1994, *2* (3), 28–32.

Bennett, M. J., and Wisneski, M. J. "Continuous Psychotherapy Within an HMO." *American Journal of Psychiatry,* 1979, *136,* 1283–1287.

Berenbaum, H. "Massed Time-Limit Psychotherapy." *Psychotherapy: Theory, Research, and Practice,* 1969, *6,* 54–56.

Berg, I. K. *Family-Based Services: A Solution-Focused Approach.* New York: W.W. Norton, 1994.

Berg, I. K., and Miller, S. D. *Working with the Problem Drinker.* New York: W.W. Norton, 1992.

Bergin, A. E. "The Evaluation of Therapeutic Outcomes." In A. E. Bergin and S. L. Garfield (eds.), *Handbook of Psychotherapy and Behavior Change.* New York: Wiley, 1971.

Bergin, A. E., and Lambert, M. J. "The Evaluation of Therapeutic Outcomes." In A. E. Bergin and S. L. Garfield (eds.), *Handbook of Psychotherapy and Behavior Change.* (2nd ed.) New York: Wiley, 1978.

Bergin, A. E., and Strupp, H. H. "New Directions in Psychotherapy Research." *Journal of Abnormal Psychology,* 1970, *76,* 13–26.

Berkman, A. S., Bassos, C. A., and Post, L. "Managed Mental Health Care and Independent Practice: A Challenge to Psychology." *Psychotherapy,* 1988, *25,* 434–440.

Berman, W. H. "The Practice of Psychotherapy in Managed Health Care." *Psychotherapy in Private Practice,* 1992, *11* (2), 39–46.

Berne, E. *Transactional Analysis in Psychotherapy.* New York: Grove Press, 1961.

Berne, E. *Games People Play.* New York: Grove Press, 1964.

Berne, E. *Principles of Group Treatment.* New York: Oxford University Press, 1966.

Berne, E. *What Do You Say After You Say Hello?* New York: Grove Press, 1972.

Berwick, D. M. "Continuous Improvement as an Ideal in Health Care." *New England Journal of Medicine,* 1989, *320,* 53–56.

Berwick, D. M., Baker, M. W., and Kramer, E. "The State of Quality Management in HMOs." *HMO Practice,* 1992, *6,* 26–32.

Bibring, E. "Psychoanalysis and the Dynamic Psychotherapies." *Journal of the American Psychoanalytic Association,* 1954, *2,* 745–770.

Binder, J. L. "Modes of Focusing in Psychoanalytic Short-Term Therapy." *Psychotherapy: Theory, Research, and Practice,* 1977, *14,* 232–241.

Binder, J. L., Strupp, H. H., and Schacht, T. E. "Countertransference in Time-Limited Dynamic Psychotherapy." *Contemporary Psychoanalysis,* 1983, *19,* 605–623.

Bion, W. R. "Notes on Memory and Desire." *Psychoanalytic Forum,* 1967, *2,* 271–280.

Bion, W. R. "Attention and Interpretation." In W. R. Bion, *Seven Servants.* New York: Jason Aronson, 1977.

Bittker, T. E. "The Industrialization of American Psychiatry." *American Journal of Psychiatry,* 1985, *21,* 171–177.

Bittker, T. E., and George, J. "Psychiatric Service Options Within a Health Maintenance Organization." *Journal of Clinical Psychiatry,* 1980, *41,* 192–195.

Bittker, T. E., and Idzorek, S. "The Evolution of Psychiatric Services in a Health Maintenance Organization." *American Journal of Psychiatry,* 1978, *135,* 339–342.

Blackstone, P. "Loving Too Much—Disease or Decision?" *Transactional Analysis Journal,* 1987, *17,* 185–190.

Blackwell, B., and Schmidt, G. "The Educational Implications of Managed Mental Health Care." *Hospital Community Psychiatry,* 1992, *43,* 962–964.

Blanchard, K., and Johnson, S. *The One Minute Manager.* New York: William Morrow, 1982.

Blanck, G., and Blanck, R. *Ego Psychology: Theory and Practice.* New York: Columbia University Press, 1974.

Bloom, B. L. "Focused Single-Session Therapy: Initial Development and Evaluation." In S. H. Budman (ed.), *Forms of Brief Therapy.* New York: Guilford Press, 1981.

Bloom, B. L. *Planned Short-Term Psychotherapy.* Needham Heights, Mass.: Allyn & Bacon, 1992a.

Bloom, B. L. "Bloom's Focused Single-Session Therapy." In B. L. Bloom, *Planned Short-Term Psychotherapy.* Needham Heights, Mass.: Allyn & Bacon, 1992b.

Blymyer, D. "The Rapid Resolution of Auditory Hallucinations." *Journal of Strategic and Systemic Therapies,* 1991, *10* (2), 1–5.

Boaz, J. T. *Delivering Mental Healthcare: A Guide for HMOs.* Chicago: Pluribus Press, 1988.

Bonaparte, M. "Time and the Unconscious." *International Journal of Psycho-Analysis,* 1941, *21,* 427–468.

Bonstedt, T. "Managing Psychiatric Exclusions." In J. L. Feldman and R. J. Fitzpatrick (eds.), *Managed Mental Health Care: Administrative and Clinical Issues.* Washington, D.C.: American Psychiatric Press, 1992.

Bonstedt, T., and Baird, S. H. "Providing Cost Effective Psychotherapy in a Health Maintenance Organization." *Hospital and Community Psychiatry,* 1979, *30,* 129–135.

Boorstin, D. J. *The Discoverers.* New York: Random House, 1985.

Boscolo, L., and Bertrando, P. *The Times of Time.* New York: W.W. Norton, 1993.

Bowles, J., and Hammond, J. *Beyond Quality.* New York: Berkley Books, 1991.

Bradshaw, J. *Healing the Shame That Binds You.* Deerfield Beach, Fla.: Health Communications, Inc., 1988.

Brehm, S., and Brehm, J. *Psychological Reactance.* (2nd. ed.) San Diego, Calif.: Academic Press, 1981.

Breuer, J., and Freud, S. "Studies in Hysteria." In J. Strachey (ed.), *The Standard Edition of the Complete Psychological Works of Sigmund Freud.* Vol. 2. London: Hogarth Press, 1955. (Originally published 1893–1895.)

Brodaty, H. "Techniques in Brief Psychotherapy." *Australian and New Zealand Journal of Psychiatry,* 1983, *17,* 109–115.

Brooks, J. B. "Preventive Psychotherapy on Medical Wards." Paper presented at the annual convention of the American Psychological Association, Anaheim, California, August 1983.

Broskowski, A. "Current Mental Health Care Environments: Why Managed Care Is Necessary." *Professional Psychology: Research and Practice,* 1991, *22,* 6–14.

Brown, M. *Psychodiagnosis in Brief.* Dexter, Mich.: Huron Valley Institute, 1977.

Browning, C. H., and Browning, B. J. *How to Partner with Managed Care.* Los Alamitos, Calif.: Duncliff's International, 1993.

Buber, M. (ed.). *Meetings.* LaSalle, Ill.: Open Court, 1973.

Budman, S. H. (ed.). Forms of Brief Therapy. New York: Guilford, 1981.

Budman, S. H. "Psychotherapeutic Services in an HMO: Zen and the Art of Mental Health Maintenance." *Professional Psychology: Research and Practice*, 1985, *16*, 798–809.

Budman, S. H. "Manual for Time-Limited Group Psychotherapy for Patients with Personality Disorders." Unpublished. Boston: Harvard Community Health Plan, 1989.

Budman, S. H. "The Myth of Termination in Brief Therapy: Or, It Ain't Over Until It's Over." In J. K. Zeig and S. G. Gilligan (eds.), *Brief Therapy: Myths, Methods, and Metaphors*. New York: Brunner/Mazel, 1990.

Budman, S. H., and Armstrong, E. "Training for Managed-Care Settings: How to Make it Happen." *Psychotherapy*, 1992, *29*, 416–421.

Budman, S. H., and Bennett, M. J. "Short-Term Group Psychotherapy." In H. I. Kaplan and B. J. Sadock (eds.), *Comprehensive Group Psychotherapy*. (2nd ed.) Baltimore, Md.: Williams & Wilkins, 1983.

Budman, S. H., Bennett, M. J., and Wisneski, M. J. "An Adult Developmental Model of Short-Term Group Psychotherapy." In S. H. Budman (ed.), *Forms of Brief Therapy*. New York: Guilford, 1981.

Budman, S. H., Demby, A., and Feldstein, M. "A Controlled Study of Psychotherapeutic Intervention and Medical Utilization." *Medical Care*, 1984a, *22*, 216–222.

Budman, S. H., Demby, A., and Feldstein, M. "Insight into Reduced Use of Medical Services After Psychotherapy." *Professional Psychology: Research and Practice*, 1984b, *15*, 353–361.

Budman, S. H., Demby, A., and Randall, M. "Psychotherapeutic Outcome and Reduction in Medical Utilization: A Cautionary Tale." *Professional Psychology: Research and Practice*, 1982, *13*, 200–207.

Budman, S. H., Feldman, J., and Bennett, M. J. "Adult Mental Health Services in a Health Maintenance Organization." *American Journal of Psychiatry*, 1979, *136*, 392–395.

Budman, S. H., Friedman, S., and Hoyt, M. F. "Last Words on First Sessions." In S. H. Budman, M. F. Hoyt, and S. Friedman (eds.),

The First Session in Brief Therapy. New York: Guilford, 1992.

Budman, S. H., and Gurman, A. S. "The Practice of Brief Therapy." *Professional Psychology,* 1983, *14,* 277–292.

Budman, S. H., and Gurman, A. S. *Theory and Practice of Brief Therapy.* New York: Guilford, 1988.

Budman, S. H., and Gurman, A. S. "A Time-Sensitive Model of Brief Therapy: The I-D-E Approach." In S. H. Budman, M. F. Hoyt, and S. Friedman (eds.), *The First Session in Brief Therapy.* New York: Guilford, 1992.

Budman, S. H., Hoyt, M. F., and Friedman, S. (eds.). *The First Session in Brief Therapy.* New York: Guilford, 1992.

Budman, S. H., and others. "Experiential Pre-Group Preparation and Screening." *Group,* 1981, *5,* 19–26.

Budman, S. H., and others. "Preliminary Findings on a New Instrument to Measure Cohesion in Group Psychotherapy." *International Journal of Group Psychotherapy,* 1987, *37,* 75–94.

Budman, S. H., and others. "Comparative Outcome in Time-Limited Individual and Group Psychotherapy." *International Journal of Group Psychotherapy,* 1988, *38,* 63–85.

Burbach, D. J., Borduin, C. M., and Peake, T. H. "Cognitive Approaches to Brief Psychotherapy." In T. H. Peake, C. M. Borduin, and R. P. Archer (eds.), *Brief Psychotherapies: Changing Frames of Mind.* Newbury Park, Calif.: Sage, 1988.

Burke, J. D., Jr., White, H. S., and Havens, L. L. "Which Short-Term Therapy?" *Archives of General Psychiatry,* 1979, *36,* 177–186.

Burlingame, G. M., and Behrman, J. A. "Clinician Attitudes Toward Time-Limited and Time-Unlimited Therapy." *Professional Psychology: Research and Practice,* 1987, *18,* 61–65.

Burlingame, G. M., Fuhriman, A., Paul, S., and Ogles, B. M. "Implementing a Time-Limited Therapy Program: Differential Effects of Training and Experience." *Psychotherapy,* 1989, *26,* 303–312.

Burns, D. D. *Feeling Good: The New Mood Therapy.* New York: Signet, 1980.

Burns, D. D. *The Feeling Good Handbook.* New York: Plume, 1989.

Butcher, J. N., and Kolotkin, R. L. "Evaluation of Outcome in Brief Psychotherapy." *Psychiatric Clinics of North America,* 1979, *2,* 157–169.

Butcher, J. N., and Koss, M. P. "Research on Brief and Crisis-Oriented Psychotherapies." In S. L. Garfield and A. E. Bergin (eds.), *Handbook of Psychotherapy and Behavior Change: An Empirical Analysis.* (2nd ed.) New York: Wiley, 1978.

Butler, K. "Hard Times Shrink Psychotherapy." *San Francisco Chronicle,* Apr. 15, 1992, pp. 1, A6.

Butler, K. "The Enigma of EMDR. Too Good to Be True?" *Family Therapy Networker,* 1993, *17* (6), 18–31.

Butler, S. F., Strupp, H. H., and Binder, J. L. "Time-Limited Dynamic Psychotherapy." In S. H. Budman, M. F. Hoyt, and S. Friedman (eds.), *The First Session in Brief Therapy.* New York: Guilford, 1992.

Cade, B., and O'Hanlon, W. H. *A Brief Guide to Brief Therapy.* New York: W.W. Norton, 1993.

Callahan, R. J. *The Five-Minute Phobia Cure: How to Do It.* Indian Wells, Calif.: R. J. Callahan, 1992. Videotape.

Cameron, J. R., Hansen, R., and Rosen, D. "Preventing Behavioral Problems in Infants." In J. H. Johnson (ed.), *Advances in Child Health Psychiatry.* Gainesville: University of Florida Press, 1990.

Cameron, J. R., and Rice, D. "Developing Anticipatory Guidance Programs Based on Early Assessment of Infant Temperament: Two Tests of a Prevention Model." *Journal of Pediatric Psychology,* 1986, *81,* 823–828.

Caplan, G. *Principles of Preventive Psychiatry.* New York: Basic Books, 1964.

Carter, E. and McGoldrick, M. *The Family Life Cycle.* New York: Gardner Press, 1980.

Castelnuovo-Tedesco, P. *The Twenty-Minute Hour: A Guide to Brief Psychotherapy.* Washington, D.C.: American Psychiatric Press, 1986.

Castaneda, C. *Journey to Ixtlan.* New York: Simon & Schuster, 1972.

Castaneda, C. *The Power of Silence.* New York: Simon & Schuster, 1987.

Cath, S. H. "Narcissism and the Use of the Word 'Shrink.'" *Bulletin of the Menninger Clinic,* 1975, *39,* 209–221.

Cavafy, C. P. "Che Fece . . . Il Gran Rifiuto." In E. Keeley and P. Sherrard (eds.), *Voices of Modern Greece.* Princeton, N. J.: Princeton University Press, 1981.

Cermak, L., and Craik, F.I.M. (eds.). *Levels of Processing in Human Memory.* New York: Wiley, 1979.

Chang, V., and James, M. "Anxiety and Projection in Relation to Games and Scripts." *Transactional Analysis Journal,* 1987, *17,* 178–184.

Cheifetz, D. I., and Salloway, J. C. "Mental Health Services in Health Maintenance Organizations: Implications for Psychology." *Professional Psychology: Research and Practice,* 1984, *15,* 152–164.

Chestnut, W. J., Wilson, S., Wright, R. H., and Zemlich, M. J. "Problems, Protests, and Proposals." *Professional Psychology: Research and Practice,* 1987, *18,* 107–112.

Chubb, H. "Interactional Brief Therapy: Child Problems in an HMO Clinic." *Journal of Strategic and Systemic Therapy,* 1983, *2,* 70–76.

Clarkin, J. F., and Frances, A. "Selection Criteria for the Brief Psychotherapies." *American Journal of Psychotherapy,* 1982, *36,* 166–180.

Clarkin, J. F., Frances, A., Taintor, Z., and Warburg, M. "Training in Brief Therapy: A Survey of Psychiatric Residency Programs." *American Journal of Psychiatry,* 1980, *136,* 392–395.

Combs, G., and Freedman, J. *Symbol, Story and Ceremony: Using Metaphor in Individual and Family Therapy.* New York: W.W. Norton, 1990.

Cooper, L. F., and Erickson, M. H. *Time Distortion in Hypnosis.* (2nd ed.) Baltimore, Md.: Williams & Wilkins, 1959.

Corlis, R. B., and Rabe, P. *Psychotherapy from the Center: A Humanistic View of Change and of Growth.* Scranton, Pa.: International Textbook Company, 1969.

Cornell, W. F., and Zalcman, M. J. "Teaching Transactional Analysts to Think Theoretically." *Transactional Analysis Journal,* 1984, *14,* 105–113.

Cottle, T. J., and Klineberg, S. L. *The Present of Things Future: Explorations of Time in Human Experience.* New York: Macmillan, 1974.

Crits-Cristoph, P., and Barber, J. P. (eds.). *Handbook of Short-Term*

Dynamic Psychotherapy. New York: Basic Books, 1991.

Cross, D. G., Sheehan, P. W., and Khan, J. A. "Short- and Long-Term Followup of Clients Receiving Insight-Oriented Therapy and Behavior Therapy." *Journal of Consulting and Clinical Psychology,* 1982, *50,* 103–112.

Cumberlage, G. (ed.). *The Oxford Dictionary of Quotations.* (2nd ed.) London: Oxford University Press, 1953.

cummings, e. e. "stand with your lover on the ending earth." In *Complete Poems 1913–1962.* Orlando, Fla.: Harcourt Brace Jovanovich, 1972. (Originally published 1958.)

Cummings, N. A. "Prolonged (Ideal) Versus Short-Term (Realistic) Psychotherapy." *Professional Psychology,* 1977, *4,* 491–501.

Cummings, N. A. "The Dismantling of Our Health Care System: Strategies for the Survival of Psychological Practice." *American Psychologist,* 1986, *41,* 426–431.

Cummings, N. A. "Emergence of the Mental Health Complex: Adaptive and Maladaptive Responses." *Professional Psychology: Research and Practice,* 1988, *19,* 308–315.

Cummings, N. A. "Brief Intermittent Psychotherapy Throughout the Life Cycle." In J. K. Zeig and S. G. Gilligan (eds.), *Brief Therapy: Myths, Methods, and Metaphors.* New York: Brunner/Mazel, 1990.

Cummings, N. A. "The Somatizing Patient." In C. S. Austad and W. H. Berman (eds.), *Psychotherapy in Managed Health Care: The Optimal Use of Time and Resources.* Washington, D.C.: American Psychological Association, 1991a.

Cummings, N. A. "Ten Ways to Spot Mismanaged Mental Health Care." *Psychotherapy in Private Practice,* 1991b, *9* (3), 79–83.

Cummings, N. A., and Follette, W. T. "Brief Psychotherapy and Medical Utilization." In H. Dorken and others (eds.), *The Professional Psychologist Today.* San Francisco: Jossey-Bass, 1976.

Cummings, N. A., and VandenBos, G. "The General Practice of Psychology." *Professional Psychology: Research and Practice,* 1979, *10,* 430–440.

Dasberg, H., and Winokur, M. "Teaching and Learning Short-Term Dynamic Psychotherapy: Parallel Processes." *Psychotherapy,* 1984, *21,* 184–188.

Dattilio, F. M., and Padesky, C. A. *Cognitive Therapy with Couples.* Sarasota, Fla.: Professional Resource Exchange, 1990.

Davanloo, H. (ed.). *Basic Principles and Techniques in Short-Term Dynamic Psychotherapy.* New York: Spectrum, 1978.

Davanloo, H. (ed.). *Short-Term Dynamic Psychotherapy.* New York: Jason Aronson, 1980.

Davanloo, H. "Intensive Short-Term Psychotherapy with Highly Resistant Patients. Part 1: Handling Resistance." *International Journal of Short-Term Psychotherapy,* 1986, *1,* 107–133.

Davanloo, H. *Unlocking the Unconscious: Selected Papers.* West Sussex, England: Wiley Ltd., 1991.

de la Torre, J. "Brief Encounters: General and Technical Psychoanalytic Considerations." *Psychiatry,* 1978, *41,* 184–193.

DeLeon, P. H., Uyeda, M. K., and Welch, B. L. "Psychology and HMOs: New Partnership or New Adversary?" *American Psychologist,* 1985, *40,* 1122–1124.

Deming, W. E. *Out of the Crisis.* Cambridge, Mass.: M.I.T. Press, 1986.

Derogatis, L. E., and others. "The Hopkins Symptom Checklist (HSCL): A Self-Report Symptom Inventory." *Behavioral Science,* 1974, *19,* 1–15.

de Shazer, S. *Patterns of Brief Family Therapy.* New York: Guilford, 1982.

de Shazer, S. "The Death of Resistance." *Family Process,* 1984, *23,* 79–83.

de Shazer, S. *Keys to Solution in Brief Therapy.* New York: W.W. Norton, 1985.

de Shazer, S. *Clues: Investigating Solutions in Brief Therapy.* New York: W.W. Norton, 1988.

de Shazer, S. "Erickson's Systemic Perspective." *Ericksonian Monographs,* 1990, *7,* 6–8.

de Shazer, S. "Forward." In Y. M. Dolan, *Resolving Sexual Abuse.* New York: W.W. Norton, 1991a.

de Shazer, S. *Putting Difference to Work.* New York: W.W. Norton, 1991b.

de Shazer, S. *Words Were Originally Magic.* New York: W.W. Norton, 1994.

Dies, R. R. "Leadership in Short-Term Group Therapy: Manipulator or Facilitator?" *International Journal of Psychotherapy*, 1985, *35*, 435–455.

Dolan, Y. M. *Resolving Sexual Abuse*. New York: W.W. Norton, 1991.

Donabedian, A. "The Quality of Medical Care." *Science*, 1978, *200*, 856–864.

Donabedian, A. "Quality and Cost: Choices and Responsibilities." *Inquiry*, 1988, *25*, 90–99.

Donovan, J. M. "Brief Dynamic Psychotherapy: Toward a More Comprehensive Model." *Psychiatry*, 1987, *50*, 167–183.

Donovan, J. M., Bennett, M. J., and McElroy, C. M. "The Crisis Group: Its Rationale, Format and Outcome." In S. Budman (ed.), *Forms of Brief Therapy*. New York: Guilford, 1981.

Doob, L. *Patterning of Time*. New Haven, Conn.: Yale University Press, 1971.

Dorken, H., and others (eds.). *The Professional Psychologist Today*. San Francisco: Jossey-Bass, 1976.

Dreiblatt, I. S., and Weatherly, D. "An Evaluation of the Efficiency of Brief Contact Therapy with Hospitalized Psychiatric Patients." *Journal of Consulting Psychology*, 1965, *29*, 513–519.

Drucker, P. F. *Innovation and Entrepreneurship: Practice and Principles*. New York: Harper & Row, 1991.

Drye, R. C., Goulding, R. L., and Goulding, M. M. "No-Suicide Decisions: Patient Monitoring of Suicidal Risk." *American Journal of Psychiatry*, 1973, *130*, 171–174.

Duncan, B., and others. "Brief Therapyism: A Neglected Addiction." *Journal of Strategic and Systemic Therapies*, 1992, *10*, 32–42.

Dunne, J. S. *Time and Myth*. Notre Dame, Ind.: University of Notre Dame, 1973.

Dylan, B. *The Times They Are A-Changin'*. New York: Columbia, 1963. Record album.

D'Zurilla, T. J., and Goldfried, M. R. "Cognitive Processes, Problem Solving, and Effective Behavior." In M. R. Goldfried and M. Merbaum (eds.), *Behavior Change Through Self-Control*. Troy, Mo.: Holt, Rinehart, & Winston, 1973.

Edelstien, M. G. *Symptom Analysis: A Method of Brief Therapy*. New York: W.W. Norton, 1990.

Ekstein, R., and Wallerstein, R. S. *The Teaching and Learning of Psychotherapy.* (2nd ed.) Madison, Conn.: International Universities Press, 1972.

Eliot, T. S. *Four Quartets.* Orlando, Fla.: Harcourt Brace Jovanovich, 1943.

Ellis, A. *Reason and Emotion in Psychotherapy.* New York: Stuart, 1962.

Ellis, A. "Brief Therapy: The Rational-Emotive Method." In S. H. Budman, M. F. Hoyt, and S. Friedman (eds.), *The First Session in Brief Therapy.* New York: Guilford, 1992.

Emery, G., and Campbell, J. *Rapid Relief from Emotional Distress.* New York: Rawson Associates, 1986.

Endicott, J., Spitzer, R. L., Fleiss, J. L., and Cohen, J. "The Global Assessment Scale." *Archives of General Psychiatry,* 1976, *33,* 766–771.

Erickson, E. H. *Identity and the Life Cycle.* Madison, Conn.: International Universities Press, 1959.

Erickson, K. K. "One Method for Designing Short-Term Intervention-Oriented Ericksonian Therapy." In J. K. Zeig and S. R. Lankton (eds.), *Developing Ericksonian Therapy: State of the Art.* New York: Brunner/Mazel, 1988.

Erickson, M. H. "Pseudo-Orientation in Time as a Hypnotherapeutic Procedure." *Journal of Clinical and Experimental Hypnosis,* 1954, *2,* 261–283.

Erickson, M. H. *Collected Papers.* Vols. 1–4. (E. Rossi, ed.) New York: Irvington, 1980.

Erickson, M. H., and Rossi, E. *Hypnotherapy: An Exploratory Casebook.* New York: Irvington, 1979.

Erickson, M. H., Rossi, E., and Rossi, S. *Hypnotic Realities.* New York: Irvington, 1976.

Erikson, E. H. *Childhood and Society.* New York: W.W. Norton, 1963.

Erikson, E. H. *Identity, Youth, and Crisis.* New York: W.W. Norton, 1968.

Ernst, F. H., Jr. "Psychological Rackets in the OK Corral." *Transactional Analysis Journal,* 1973, *3* (2), 19–25.

Erskine, R. G. "Supervision of Psychotherapy: Models for Professional Development." *Transactional Analysis Journal,* 1982, *12,* 314–321.

Everstine, D. S., and Everstine, L. *People in Crisis: Strategic Therapeutic Interventions.* New York: Brunner/Mazel, 1983.

Fagan, J., and Shepherd, I. L. (eds.). *Gestalt Therapy Now.* Palo Alto, Calif.: Science & Behavior Books, 1970.

Fanshel, D. *Playback: A Marriage in Jeopardy Examined.* New York: Columbia University Press, 1971.

Farrell, D., and Hoyt, M. F. "On Speaking of Oneself by Name." *International Journal of Psychoanalytic Psychotherapy,* 1983, *9,* 603–619.

Farrelly, F., and Brandsma, J. *Provocative Therapy.* Cupertino, Calif.: Meta Publications, 1974.

Fay, A. *PQR: Prescription for a Quality Relationship.* New York: Simon & Schuster, 1990.

Feldman, J. B. "The Utilization of Cognition in Psychotherapy: A Comparison of Ericksonian and Cognitive Therapies." *Ericksonian Monographs,* 1988, *4,* 57–73.

Feldman, J. L. "The Managed Care Setting and the Patient-Therapist Relationship." In J. L. Feldman and R. J. Fitzpatrick (eds.), *Managed Mental Health Care: Administrative and Clinical Issues.* Washington, D.C.: American Psychiatric Press, 1992.

Feldman, J. L., and Fitzpatrick, R. J. (eds.). *Managed Mental Health Care: Administrative and Clinical Issues.* Washington, D.C.: American Psychiatric Press, 1992.

Feldman, S. (ed.). *Managed Mental Health Services.* Springfield, Ill.: C. C. Thomas, 1992.

Ferenczi, S., and Rank, O. The Development of Psychoanalysis. New York: Nervous and Mental Disease Publication Company, 1925.

Firman, G. J., and Kaplan, M. P. "Staff 'Splitting' on Medical-Surgical Wards." *Psychiatry,* 1978, *41,* 289–295.

Fisch, R. "Erickson's Impact on Brief Psychotherapy." In J. K. Zeig (ed.), *Ericksonian Approaches to Hypnosis and Psychotherapy.* New York: Brunner/Mazel, 1982.

Fisch, R. "The Broader Implications of Milton H. Erickson's Work." *Ericksonian Monographs,* 1990, *7,* 1–5.

Fisch, R. "Basic Elements in the Brief Therapies." In M. F. Hoyt (ed.), *Constructive Therapies.* New York: Guilford, 1994.

Fisch, R., Weakland, J. H., and Segal, L. *The Tactics of Change:*

Doing Therapy Briefly. San Francisco: Jossey-Bass, 1982.

Flegenheimer, W. V. *Techniques of Brief Psychotherapy.* New York: Jason Aronson, 1982.

Fleming, J., and Altschul, S. "Activation of Mourning and Growth by Psychoanalysis." *International Journal of Psycho-Analysis,* 1963, *44,* 419–431.

Folkers, C., and Steefel, N. M. "Group Psychotherapy in HMO Settings." In C. S. Austad and W. H. Berman (eds.), *Psychotherapy in Managed Health Care: The Optimal Use of Time and Resources.* Washington, D.C.: American Psychological Association, 1991.

Follette, W. T., and Cummings, N. A. "Psychiatric Services and Medical Utilization in a Prepaid Health Plan Setting." *Medical Care,* 1967, *5,* 25–35.

Fraisse, P. *The Psychology of Time.* New York: HarperCollins, 1963.

Frances, A., and Clarkin, J. F. "No Treatment as the Prescription of Choice." *Archives of General Psychiatry,* 1981a, *38,* 542–545.

Frances, A., and Clarkin, J. F. "Parallel Techniques in Supervision and Treatment." *Psychiatric Quarterly,* 1981b, *53,* 242–248.

Frances, A., Clarkin, J., and Perry, S. *Differential Therapeutics in Psychiatry: The Art and Science of Treatment Selection.* New York: Brunner/Mazel, 1984.

Frances, A., and Perry, S. "Transference Interpretations in Focal Therapy." *American Journal of Psychiatry,* 1983, *140,* 405–409.

Frank, J. D. *Persuasion and Healing.* New York: Shocken, 1973.

Fraser, J. T. (ed.). *The Voices of Time.* New York: George Braziller, 1966.

Fraser, J. T. (ed.). *Of Time, Passion, and Knowledge.* New York: George Braziller, 1975.

Freedheim, D. K. (ed.). *History of Psychotherapy: A Century of Change.* Washington, D.C.: American Psychological Association, 1992.

Freeman, M. A., and Leggett, J. R. "How to Participate in Managed Behavioral Healthcare Systems." San Francisco: Institute for Behavioral Healthcare Conference, 1992.

Freud, A. *The Ego and the Mechanisms of Defence.* London: Hogarth Press, 1946.

Freud, S. "The Future Prospects of Psycho-Analytic Therapy."

In J. Strachey (ed.), *The Standard Edition of the Complete Psychological Works of Sigmund Freud.* Vol. 11. London: Hogarth Press, 1953–1974. (Originally published 1910.)

Freud, S. "Remembering, Repeating, and Working Through." In J. Strachey (ed.), *The Standard Edition of the Complete Psychological Works of Sigmund Freud.* Vol. 12. London: Hogarth Press, 1953–1974. (Originally published 1914.)

Freud, S. "On Transience." In J. Strachey (ed.), *The Standard Edition of the Complete Psychological Works of Sigmund Freud.* Vol. 14. London: Hogarth Press, 1953–1974. (Originally published 1916.)

Freud, S. "Mourning and Melancholia." In J. Strachey (ed.), *The Standard Edition of the Complete Psychological Works of Sigmund Freud.* Vol. 14. London: Hogarth Press, 1953–1974. (Originally published 1917.)

Freud, S. "From the History of an Infantile Neurosis." In J. Strachey (ed.), *The Standard Edition of the Complete Psychological Works of Sigmund Freud.* Vol. 17. London: Hogarth Press, 1953–1974. (Originally published 1918.)

Freud, S. "Lines of Advance in Psycho-Analytic Therapy." In J. Strachey (ed.), *The Standard Edition of the Complete Psychological Works of Sigmund Freud.* Vol. 17. London: Hogarth Press, 1953–1974. (Originally published 1919a.)

Freud, S. "Turnings in the Ways of Psycho-analysis." In J. Strachey (ed.), *The Standard Edition of the Complete Psychological Works of Sigmund Freud.* Vol. 17. London: Hogarth Press, 1953–1974. (Originally published 1919b.)

Freud, S. "Group Psychology and the Analysis of the Ego." In J. Strachey (ed.), *The Standard Edition of the Complete Psychological Works of Sigmund Freud.* Vol. 18. London: Hogarth Press, 1953–1974. (Originally published 1921.)

Freud, S. "The Unconscious: New Introductory Lectures." In J. Strachey (ed.), *The Standard Edition of the Complete Psychological Works of Sigmund Freud.* Vol. 22. London: Hogarth Press, 1953–1974. (Originally published 1933.)

Freud, S. "Analysis Terminable and Interminable." In J. Strachey (ed.), *The Standard Edition of the Complete Psychological Works of Sigmund Freud.* Vol. 23. London: Hogarth Press, 1953–1974. (Originally published 1937.)

Friedman, S. "Child Mental Health in an HMO: A Family Systems Approach." *HMO Practice,* 1988, *3,* 52–59.

Friedman, S. (ed.). *The New Language of Change: Constructive Collaboration in Psychotherapy.* New York: Guilford, 1993.

Friedman, S., and Fanger, M. T. *Expanding Therapeutic Possibilities: Getting Results in Brief Psychotherapy.* New York: Lexington Books/Macmillan, 1991.

Frieswyk, S. H., and others. "Therapeutic Alliance: Its Place as a Process and Outcome Variable in Dynamic Psychotherapy Research." *Journal of Consulting and Clinical Psychology,* 1986, *54,* 32–38.

Furman, B., and Ahola, T. *Pickpockets on a Nudist Camp: The Systemic Revolution in Psychotherapy.* Adelaide, Australia: Dulwich Centre Publications, 1992a.

Furman, B., and Ahola, T. *Solution Talk: Hosting Therapeutic Conversations.* New York: W.W. Norton, 1992b.

Gans, J. S. "The Consultee-Attended Interview: An Approach to Liaison Psychiatry." *General Hospital Psychiatry,* 1979, *1,* 24–30.

Garfield, S. L. "Research on Client Variables in Psychotherapy." In S. L. Garfield and A. E. Bergin (eds.), *Handbook of Psychotherapy and Behavior Change: An Empirical Analysis.* (2nd ed.) New York: Wiley, 1978.

Garfield, S. L. "Research on Client Variables in Psychotherapy." In S. L. Garfield and A. E. Bergin (eds.), *Handbook of Psychotherapy and Behavior Change: An Empirical Analysis.* (3rd ed.) New York: Wiley, 1986.

Garfield, S. L., and Bergin, A. E. "Introduction and Historical Overview." In S. L. Garfield and A. E. Bergin (eds.), *Handbook of Psychotherapy and Behavior Change: An Empirical Analysis.* (3rd ed.) New York: Wiley, 1986.

Garfield, S. L., and Wolpin, M. "Expectations Regarding Psychotherapy." *Journal of Nervous and Mental Disease,* 1963, *137,* 353–362.

Garvin, C. D. "Short-Term Group Therapy." In R. A. Wells and V. J. Giannetti (eds.), *Handbook of the Brief Psychotherapies.* New York: Plenum, 1990.

German, M. "Effective Case Management in Managed Mental

Health Care: Conditions, Methods and Outcomes." *HMO Practice*, 1994, *8*, 34–40.

Giles, T. R. *Managed Mental Health Care: A Guide for Practitioners, Employers, and Hospital Administrators.* Needham Heights, Mass.: Allyn & Bacon, 1993.

Gill, M. M. "Psychoanalysis and Exploratory Psychotherapy." *Journal of the American Psychoanalytic Association*, 1954, *2*, 771–797.

Gillieron, E. "Psychoanalysis and Brief Psychotherapy: Some New Considerations on the Psychotherapeutic Process." *Psychotherapy and Psychosomatics*, 1981, *35*, 244–256.

Gilligan, S., and Price, R. (eds.). *Therapeutic Conversations.* New York: W.W. Norton, 1993.

Glazer, B. G., and Strauss, A. L. "Awareness Contexts and Social Interaction." *American Sociological Review*, 1964, *29*, 669–679.

Glazer, W. M., and Astrachan, B. M. "A Social Systems Approach to Consultation-Liaison Psychiatry." *International Journal of Psychiatry in Medicine*, 1978, *9*, 33–47.

Goldberg, A. "Narcissism and the Readiness for Psychotherapy Termination." *Archives of General Psychiatry*, 1975, *32*, 659–699.

Goldberg, C. "Termination–A Meaningful Pseudodilemma in Psychotherapy." *Psychotherapy: Theory, Research & Practice*, 1975, *12*, 341–343.

Goldensohn, S. S. "Cost, Utilization, and Utilization Review of Mental Health Services in a Prepaid Group Practice Plan." *American Journal of Psychiatry*, 1977, *134*, 1222–1226.

Goldensohn, S. S., and Haar, E. "Transference and Countertransference in a Third-Party Payment System (HMO)." *American Journal of Psychiatry*, 1974, *131*, 256–260.

Goldman, W. "Mental Health and Substance Abuse Services in HMOs." *Administration in Mental Health*, 1988, *15*, 189–200.

Goldsmith, S. "The Application of Ericksonian Principles to the Use of Medication." *Ericksonian Monographs*, 1988, *4*, 91–99.

Gomes-Schwartz, B. "Effective Ingredients in Psychotherapy: Prediction of Outcome from Process Variables." *Journal of Consulting and Clinical Psychology*, 1978, *46*, 1023–1035.

Gonzales, R. C., Biever, J. L., and Gardner, G. T. "The Multicultural Perspective in Therapy: A Social Constructionist Approach." *Psychotherapy*, 1994, *31*, 515–524.

Goode, E. E. "Therapy for the '90s." *U.S. News & World Report,* Jan. 13, 1992, pp. 55–56.

Goodman, M., Brown J., and Deitz, P. *Managing Managed Care: A Mental Health Practitioner's Survival Guide.* Washington, D.C.: American Psychiatric Press, 1992.

Gordon, D. *Therapeutic Metaphors.* Cupertino, Calif.: Meta Publications, 1978.

Gorman, B. S., and Wesman, A. E. *The Personal Experience of Time.* New York: Plenum, 1977.

Gottlieb, M. C. "Practicing Ethically with Managed Care Patients." *Innovations in Clinical Practice: A Sourcebook,* 1992, *11,* 481-493.

Gould, S. J. *The Panda's Thumb: More Reflections in Natural History.* New York: W.W. Norton, 1980.

Goulding, M. M. *Who's Been Living in Your Head?* (2nd ed.) Watsonville, Calif.: Western Institute for Group and Family Therapy Press, 1985.

Goulding, M. M. "Getting the Important Work Done Fast: Contract Plus Redecision." In J. K. Zeig and S. G. Gilligan (eds.), *Brief Therapy: Myths, Methods, and Metaphors.* New York: Brunner/Mazel, 1990.

Goulding, M. M. *Sweet Love Remembered: Bob Goulding and Redecision Therapy.* San Francisco: Transactional Analysis Press, 1992.

Goulding, M. M., and Goulding, R. L. *Changing Lives Through Redecision Therapy.* New York: Brunner/Mazel, 1979.

Goulding, M. M., and Goulding, R. L. *Not to Worry!* New York: William Morrow, 1989.

Goulding, M. M., Goulding, R. L., and Silverthorn, A. I. "Integrators/Innkeepers/Therapists/Trainers/Theoreticians." *Voices,* 1983, *18,* 64–72.

Goulding, R. L. "The Formation and Beginning Process of Transactional Analysis Groups." In R. L. Goulding and M. M. Goulding, *The Power Is in the Patient.* (P. McCormick, ed.) San Francisco: Transactional Analysis Press, 1978a.

Goulding, R. L. "The Training of Psychotherapists in Transactional Analysis." In R. L. Goulding and M. M. Goulding, *The Power Is in the Patient.* (P. McCormick, ed.) San Francisco: Transactional Analysis Press, 1978b.

Goulding, R. L. "Gestalt Therapy and Transactional Analysis." In C. Hatcher and P. Himelstein (eds.), *Handbook of Gestalt Therapy*. New York: Jason Aronson, 1983.

Goulding, R. L. "Group Therapy: Mainline or Sideline?" In J. K. Zeig (ed.), *The Evolution of Psychotherapy*. New York: Brunner/Mazel, 1987.

Goulding, R. L. "Teaching Transactional Analysis and Redecision Therapy." *Journal of Independent Social Work*, 1989, *3*, 71–86.

Goulding, R. L., and Goulding, M. M. *The Power Is in the Patient*. (P. McCormick, ed.) San Francisco: Transactional Analysis Press, 1978.

Goulding, R. L., and Goulding, M. M. *Redecision Therapy*. San Francisco: International Transactional Analysis Association, 1988. Videotape.

Grayson, H. "Grief Reactions to the Relinquishing of Unfulfilled Wishes." *American Journal of Psychotherapy*, 1970, *24*, 287–295.

Greenacre, P. "The Role of Transference." *Journal of the American Psychoanalytic Association*, 1954, *2*, 671–684.

Greenberg, D. *How to Be a Jewish Mother*. Los Angeles: Price Stern Sloan, 1976.

Greenberg, J. R., and Mitchell, S. A. *Object Relations in Psychoanalytic Theory*. Cambridge, Mass.: Harvard University Press, 1983.

Greenleaf, E. "Case Report: Isabel." *The Milton H. Erickson Foundation Newsletter*, 1993, *13*(3), 12.

Grudin, R. *Time and the Art of Living*. New York: Ticknor & Fields, 1982.

Guerin, P. J., Jr. (ed.). *Family Therapy: Theory and Practice*. New York: Gardner Press, 1976.

Gurman, A. S. "Integrative Marital Therapy: A Time-Sensitive Model for Working with Couples." In S. H. Budman, M. F. Hoyt, and S. Friedman (eds.) *The First Session in Brief Therapy*. New York: Guilford, 1992.

Gurman, A. S., and Kniskern, D. P. (eds.). *Handbook of Family Therapy*. New York: Brunner/Mazel, 1981.

Gustafson, J. P. "The Complex Secret of Brief Psychotherapy

in the Works of Malan and Balint." In S. H. Budman (ed.), *Forms of Brief Therapy.* New York: Guilford Press, 1981.

Gustafson, J. P. "An Integration of Brief Dynamic Psychotherapy." *American Journal of Psychiatry,* 1984, *141,* 935–944.

Gustafson, J. P. *The Complex Secret of Brief Psychotherapy.* New York: W.W. Norton, 1986.

Gustafson, J. P. "The Neighboring Field of Brief Individual Psychotherapy." *Journal of Marital and Family Therapy,* 1987, *13,* 409–422.

Gustafson, J. P., and Dichter, H. "Winnicott and Sullivan in the Brief Psychotherapy Clinic. Part 1: Possible Activity and Passivity." *Contemporary Psychoanalysis,* 1983, *19,* 624–637.

Gutheil, T. G., and Havens, L. L. "The Therapeutic Alliance: Contemporary Meanings and Confusions." *International Review of Psycho-Analysis,* 1979, *6,* 467–481.

Haas, L. J., and Cummings, N. A. "Managed Outpatient Mental Health Plans: Clinical, Ethical, and Practical Guidelines for Participation." *Professional Psychology: Research and Practice,* 1991, *22,* 45–51. Reprinted in R. L. Lowman and R. J. Resnick (eds.), *The Mental Health Professional's Guide to Managed Care.* Washington, D.C.: American Psychological Association, 1994.

Haley, J. *Strategies of Psychotherapy.* New York: Grune & Stratton, 1963.

Haley, J. "The Art of Psychoanalysis." In *The Power Tactics of Jesus Christ and Other Essays.* New York: Avon, 1969.

Haley, J. *Uncommon Therapy: The Psychiatric Techniques of Milton H. Erickson, M.D.* New York: W.W. Norton, 1973.

Haley, J. *Problem-Solving Therapy.* San Francisco: Jossey-Bass, 1977.

Haley, J. *Ordeal Therapy: Unusual Ways to Change Behavior.* San Francisco: Jossey-Bass, 1984.

Haley, J. *The First Therapy Session: How to Interview Clients and Identify Problems Successfully.* San Francisco: Jossey-Bass, 1989. Audiotape.

Haley, J. "Why Not Long-Term Therapy?" In J. K. Zeig and S. G. Gilligan (eds.), *Brief Therapy: Myths, Methods, and Metaphors.* New York: Brunner/Mazel, 1990.

Haley, J. (ed.). *Conversations with Milton H. Erickson, M.D.* Vols. 1–3. New York: Triangle Press/W.W. Norton, 1985.

Hartley, D. E., and Strupp, H. H. "The Therapeutic Alliance: Its Relationship to Outcome in Brief Psychotherapy." In M. Masling (ed.), *Empirical Studies of Psychoanalytic Theories.* Hillsdale, N.J.: Analytic Press, 1983.

Hartmann, F. "A Systematization of the Defense Modes for Structural Analysis." *Transactional Analysis Journal,* 1981, *11,* 150–158.

Hartocollis, P. "Origins of Time: A Reconstruction of the Ontogenetic Development of the Sense of Time Based on Object-Relations Theory." *Psychoanalytic Quarterly,* 1974, *43,* 243–261.

Hartocollis, P. "Time and Affect in Psychopathology." *Journal of the American Psychoanalytic Association,* 1975, *23,* 383–395.

Hartocollis, P. "On the Experience of Time and Its Dynamics, with Special Reference to Affects." *Journal of the American Psychoanalytic Association,* 1976, *24,* 363–382.

Hartocollis, P. *Time and Timelessness.* Madison, Conn.: International Universities Press, 1983.

Hatcher, S. L., Huebner, D. A., and Zakin, D. F. "Following the Trail of the Focus in Time-Limited Psychotherapy." *Psychotherapy,* 1986, *23,* 513–520.

Havens, R. A. (ed.). *The Wisdom of Milton H. Erickson.* Vols. 1–2. New York: Paragon House, 1989.

Hawthorne, L. "Games Supervisors Play." *Social Work,* 1975, *20,* 179–183.

Heidegger, M. (1927). *Being and Time.* New York: HarperCollins, 1962.

Henry, W. P., and others. "The Effects of Training in Time-Limited Dynamic Psychotherapy: Mediators of Therapists' Response to Training." *Journal of Consulting and Clinical Psychology,* 1993, *61,* 441–447.

Herman, R. E. *Keeping Good People.* New York: McGraw-Hill, 1991.

Hess, A. K. (ed.). *Psychotherapy Supervision: Theory, Research, and Practice.* New York: Wiley, 1980.

Hesse, H. *The Glass Bead Game.* (R. Winston and C. Winston, trans.) Troy, Mo.: Holt, Rinehart & Winston, 1969. (Originally published 1943.)

Hofling, C. K., and Joy, M. "Favorable Responses to the Loss of a Significant Figure: A Preliminary Report." *Bulletin of the Menninger Clinic,* 1974, *38,* 527–537.

Holden, H. D., and Blose, J. O. "Changes in Health Care Costs and Utilization Associated with Mental Health Treatment." *Hospital and Community Psychiatry,* 1987, *38,* 1070–1075.

Holloway, W. H. "Transactional Analysis: An Integrative View." In G. Barnes (ed.), *Transactional Analysis After Eric Berne: Teachings and Practices of Three TA Schools.* New York: HarperCollins, 1977.

Horner, A. J. (ed.). *Treating the Oedipal Patient in Brief Psychotherapy.* New York: Jason Aronson, 1985.

Horowitz, L. M., and others. "Inventory of Interpersonal Problems: Psychometric Properties and Clinical Applications." *Journal of Consulting and Clinical Psychology,* 1988, *56,* 885–892.

Horowitz, M. J. *Stress Response Syndromes.* New York: Jason Aronson, 1976.

Horowitz, M. J. *States of Mind.* New York: Plenum, 1979.

Horowitz, M. J., and Hoyt, M. F. "Book Notice of Malan's 'The Frontier of Brief Psychotherapy.'" *Journal of the American Psychoanalytic Association,* 1979, *27,* 279–285.

Horowitz, M. J., and Kaltreider, N. B. "Brief Therapy of the Stress Response Syndrome." *Psychiatric Clinics of North America,* 1979, *2,* 365–377.

Horowitz, M. J., Rosenbaum, R., and Wilner, N. "Role Relationship Dilemmas: A Potential New Process Variable." *Psychotherapy,* 1988, *25,* 241–248.

Horowitz, M. J., Wilner, N., and Alvarez, W. "Impact of Event Scale: A Measure of Subjective Stress." *Psychosomatic Medicine,* 1979, *41,* 209–218.

Horowitz, M. J., and others. "Brief Psychotherapy of Bereavement Reactions." *Archives of General Psychiatry,* 1984a, *41,* 438–448.

Horowitz, M. J., and others. *Personality Styles and Brief Psychotherapy.* New York: Basic Books, 1984b.

Howard, K. I., Kopta, S. M., Kraus, M. S., and Orlinsky, D. E.

"The Dose-Effect Relationship in Psychotherapy." *American Psychologist,* 1986, *41,* 159–164.

Hoyt, M. F. "Primal Scene and Self Creation." *Voices,* 1977, *13,* 24–28.

Hoyt, M. F. "Secrets in Psychotherapy: Theoretical and Practical Considerations." *International Review of Psycho-Analysis,* 1978, *5,* 231–241.

Hoyt, M. F. "Aspects of Termination in a Time-Limited Brief Psychotherapy." *Psychiatry,* 1979a, *42,* 208–219.

Hoyt, M. F. "'Patient' or 'Client': What's in a Name?" *Psychotherapy: Theory, Research & Practice,* 1979b, *16,* 46–47.

Hoyt, M. F. "Therapist and Patient Actions in 'Good' Psychotherapy Sessions." *Archives of General Psychiatry,* 1980, *37,* 159–161.

Hoyt, M. F. "Concerning Remorse: With Special Attention to Its Defensive Function." *Journal of the American Academy of Psychoanalysis,* 1983, *11,* 435–444.

Hoyt, M. F. "'Shrink' or 'Expander': An Issue in Forming a Therapeutic Alliance." *Psychotherapy,* 1985a, *22,* 813–814.

Hoyt, M. F. "Therapist Resistances to Short-Term Dynamic Psychotherapy." *Journal of the American Academy of Psychoanalysis,* 1985b, *13,* 93–112.

Hoyt, M. F. "Mental-Imagery Methods in Short-Term Dynamic Psychotherapy." In M. Wolpin, J. Shorr, and L. Krueger (eds.), *Imagery 4.* New York: Plenum, 1986.

Hoyt, M. F. "Notes on Psychotherapy with Obsessed Patients." *The Psychotherapy Patient,* 1987a, *3,* 13–21.

Hoyt, M. F. "Resistances to Brief Therapy." *American Psychologist,* 1987b, *42,* 408–409.

Hoyt, M. F. "Review of *The Complex Secret of Brief Psychotherapy,* by J. P. Gustafson." *American Journal of Psychiatry,* 1988, *145,* 374–375.

Hoyt, M. F. Letter to the Editor. *The Milton H. Erickson Foundation Newsletter,* 1989a, *9*(1), 5.

Hoyt, M. F. "Psychodiagnosis of Personality Disorders: A Guide for the Perplexed." *Transactional Analysis Journal,* 1989b, *19,* 101–113.

Hoyt, M. F. "On Time in Brief Therapy." In R. A. Wells and

V. J. Giannetti (eds.), *Handbook of the Brief Psychotherapies*. New York: Plenum, 1990.

Hoyt, M. F. "Teaching and Learning Short-Term Psychotherapy Within an HMO." In C. S. Austad and W. H. Berman (eds.), *Psychotherapy in Managed Health Care: The Optimal Use of Time and Resources*. Washington, D.C.: American Psychological Association, 1991.

Hoyt, M. F. "Discussion of the Effects of Managed Care on Psychotherapy." *Psychotherapy in Private Practice*, 1992a, *11*, 79–84.

Hoyt, M. F. "Psychotherapy in HMOs: Some Information for Private Practitioners." *Psychotherapy in Private Practice*, 1992b, *11* (2), 47–54.

Hoyt, M. F. "Group Psychotherapy in an HMO." *HMO Practice*, 1993a, *7*, 129–132.

Hoyt, M. F. "Two Cases of Brief Therapy in an HMO." In R. A. Wells and V. J. Giannetti (eds.), *Casebook of the Brief Psychotherapies*. New York: Plenum, 1993b.

Hoyt, M. F. "Characteristics of Psychotherapy Under Managed Health Care." *Behavioral Healthcare Tomorrow*, 1994a, *3* (5), 59–62.

Hoyt, M. F. (ed.). *Constructive Therapies*. New York: Guilford, 1994b.

Hoyt, M. F. "Introduction: Competency-Based Future-Oriented Therapy." In M. F. Hoyt (ed.), *Constructive Therapies*. New York: Guilford, 1994c.

Hoyt, M. F. "Is Being 'in Recovery' Self-Limiting?" *Transactional Analysis Journal*, 1994d, *24* (3), 223–224.

Hoyt, M. F. "On the Importance of Keeping It Simple and Taking the Patient Seriously: A Conversation with Steve de Shazer and John Weakland." In M. F. Hoyt (ed.), *Constructive Therapies*. New York: Guilford, 1994e.

Hoyt, M. F. "Promoting HMO Values and a Culture of Quality: Doing the Right Thing in a Staff-Model HMO Mental-Health Department." *HMO Practice*, 1994f, *8*, 122–126.

Hoyt, M. F. "Single Session Solutions." In M. F. Hoyt (ed.), *Constructive Therapies*. New York: Guilford, 1994g.

Hoyt, M. F. "The Four Questions of Brief Therapy." *Journal of Systemic Therapies*, 1994h, *13*, 68–69.

Hoyt, M. F. "Managed Care, HMOs, and the Ericksonian Perspective." *Ericksonian Monographs,* 1995, *10,* 25–36.

Hoyt, M. F. "Brief Psychotherapies." In A. S. Gurman and S. B. Messer (eds.), *Modern Psychotherapies: Theories and Practice.* New York: Guilford, in press a.

Hoyt, M. F. "A Golfer's Guide to Brief Therapy (with Footnotes for Baseball Fans)." In M. F. Hoyt (ed.), *Constructive Therapies 2.* New York: Guilford, in press b.

Hoyt, M. F. (ed.) *Constructive Therapies 2.* New York: Guilford, in press c.

Hoyt, M. F., and Austad, C. S. "Psychotherapy in a Staff-Model HMO: Providing and Assuring Quality Care in the Future." *Psychotherapy,* 1992, *29,* 119–129.

Hoyt, M. F., and Farrell, D. "Countertransference Difficulties in a Time-Limited Psychotherapy." *International Journal of Psychoanalytic Psychotherapy,* 1984, *10,* 191–203.

Hoyt, M. F., and Goulding, R. L. "Resolution of a Transference-Countertransference Impasse Using Gestalt Techniques in Supervision." *Transactional Analysis Journal,* 1989, *19,* 201–211.

Hoyt, M. F., and Janis, I. L. "Increasing Adherence to a Stressful Decision via a Motivational Balance-Sheet Procedure: A Field Experiment." *Journal of Personality and Social Psychology,* 1975, *31,* 833–839. Reprinted in I. L. Janis (ed.), *Counseling on Personal Decisions: Theory and Research in Short-Term Helping Relationships.* New Haven: Yale University Press, 1982.

Hoyt, M. F., Opsvig, P., and Weinstein, N. W. "Conjoint Patient-Staff Interview in Hospital Case Management." *International Journal of Psychiatry in Medicine,* 1981, *11,* 83–87.

Hoyt, M. F., Rosenbaum, R. L., and Talmon, M. "Planned Single-Session Psychotherapy." In S. H. Budman, M. F. Hoyt, and S. Friedman (eds.), *The First Session in Brief Therapy.* New York: Guilford, 1992.

Hoyt, M. F., and Talmon, M. "Single-Session Therapy in Action: A Case Example." In M. Talmon, *Single-Session Therapy: Maximizing the Effect of the First (and Often Only) Therapeutic Encounter.* San Francisco: Jossey-Bass, 1990.

Hoyt, M. F., Xenakis, S. N., Marmar, C. R., and Horowitz, M. J. "Therapists' Actions That Influence Their Perceptions of 'Good' Psychotherapy Sessions." *Journal of Nervous and Mental Diseases,* 1983, *171,* 400–404.

Hudson, P., and O'Hanlon, W. H. *Rewriting Love Stories: Brief Marital Therapy.* New York: W.W. Norton, 1992.

Imber, S. D., and Evanczuk, K. J. "Brief Crisis Therapy Groups." In R. A. Wells and V. J. Giannetti (eds.), *Handbook of the Brief Psychotherapies.* New York: Plenum, 1990.

Jacobson, G. "The Briefest Psychiatric Encounter: Acute Effects of Evaluation." *Archives of General Psychiatry,* 1968, *18,* 718–724.

Jacobson, N. S., and Margolin, G. *Marital Therapy: Strategies Based on Social Learning and Behavior Exchange Principles.* New York: Brunner/Mazel, 1979.

James, M. "Self-Therapy Techniques for Therapists." In M. James (ed.), *Techniques in Transactional Analysis for Psychotherapists and Counselors.* Reading, Mass.: Addison-Wesley, 1977.

James, M. *It's Never Too Late to Be Happy.* Reading, Mass.: Addison-Wesley, 1985.

James, M. "Diagnosis and Treatment of Ego State Boundary Problems." *Transactional Analysis Journal,* 1986, *16,* 188–196.

James, W. *The Principles of Psychology.* Vol. 2. Troy, Mo.: Holt, Rinehart & Winston, 1890.

Johnson, H., and Gelso, C. "The Effectiveness of Time Limits in Counseling and Psychotherapy." *The Counseling Psychologist,* 1980, *9,* 70–83.

Johnson, L. D. "Naturalistic Techniques with the 'Difficult' Patient." In J. K. Zeig and S. R. Lankton (eds.), *Developing Ericksonian Therapy: State of the Art.* New York: Brunner/Mazel, 1988.

Joines, V. "Using Redecision Therapy with Different Personality Adaptations." *Transactional Analysis Journal,* 1986, *16,* 152–160.

Joines, V. "Diagnosis and Treatment Planning Using a Transactional Analysis Framework." *Transactional Analysis Journal,* 1988, *18,* 185–190.

Joint Commission for the Accreditation of Healthcare Organizations (JCAHO). *Definitions of Dimensions of Performance.* Chicago, Ill.: JCAHO, 1993.

June, L. N., and Smith, E. J. "A Comparison of Client and Counselor Expectancies Regarding the Duration of Counseling." *Journal of Counseling Psychology,* 1983, *30,* 596–599.

Jung, C. G. "Problems of Modern Psychotherapy." In *Collected Works of C. G. Jung, Vol. 16: The Practice of Psychotherapy.* Princeton, N.J.: Bollingen/Princeton University Press, 1966. (Originally published 1931.)

Kadis, L. B. (ed.). *Redecision Therapy: Expanded Perspectives.* Watsonville, Calif.: Western Institute for Group and Family Therapy Press, 1985.

Kadis, L. B. "Diagnosis and Treatment Planning." Paper presented at the International Transactional Analysis Association (ITAA) Twenty-Fourth Annual Summer Conference, San Francisco, 1986.

Kadushin, A. "Games People Play in Supervision." *Social Work,* 1968, *13,* 23–32.

Kaiser, H. "The Problem of Responsibility in Psychotherapy." In L. B. Fierman (ed.), *Effective Psychotherapy: The Contribution of Hellmuth Kaiser.* New York: Free Press, 1965.

Kaminer, W. *I'm Dysfunctional, You're Dysfunctional: The Recovery Movement and Other Self-Help Fashions.* New York: Vintage, 1992.

Kaplan, H. S. *Disorders of Sexual Desire.* New York: Simon & Schuster, 1979.

Kaplan, J. G. "Efficacy: The Real Bottom Line in Health Care." *HMO Practice,* 1989, *3,* 108–110.

Kaplan, K. J., Capace, N., and Clyde, J. D. "A Bidimensional Distancing Approach to TA: A Suggested Revision of the OK Corral." *Transactional Analysis Journal,* 1984, *14,* 114–119.

Karon, B. P. "Problems of Psychotherapy Under Managed Health Care." *Psychotherapy in Private Practice,* 1992, *11,* 55–63.

Kaslow, F. W. (ed.). *Psychotherapy with Psychotherapists.* New York: Haworth Press, 1984.

Keeney, B. P. *Aesthetics of Change.* New York: Guilford, 1983.

Kellner, R., Neidhardt, J., Krakow, B., and Pathak, D. "Changes in Chronic Nightmares After One Session of Desensitization or Rehearsal Instruction." *American Journal of Psychiatry,* 1992, *149,* 659–663.

Kempler, H. L. "Couple Therapy in a Health Maintenance Organization." *Psychotherapy,* 1985, *22,* 219–223.

Kernberg, O. *Severe Personality Disorders*. New Haven, Conn.: Yale University Press, 1984.

Kiesler, C. A., and Morton, T. L. "Psychology and Public Policy in the 'Health Care Revolution.'" *American Psychologist*, 1988, *43*, 993–1003.

Kiesler, D. J. "Some Myths of Psychotherapy Research and the Search for a Paradigm." *Psychological Bulletin*, 1966, *65*, 110–136.

Kisch, J. "Utilization of Mental Health Services: Attrition Versus Aggregation." *HMO Practice*, 1992, *6*, 33–38.

Kisch, J., and Austad, C. S. "The Health Maintenance Organization. 1. Historical Perspective and Current Status." *Psychotherapy*, 1988, *25*, 441–448.

Kisch, J., and Makover, R. "Psychotherapy in the HMO: Clinical Perspectives." *HMO Practice*, 1990, *4*, 24–29.

Klee, G. D. "Research in Psychotherapy: A Backward Leap into the Future." *American Journal of Psychotherapy*, 1968, *22*, 674–683.

Klein, M. "How to Be Happy Though Human." *Transactional Analysis Journal*, 1987, *17*, 152–162.

Klein, R. H. "Some Principles of Short-Term Group Therapy." *International Journal of Group Psychotherapy*, 1985, *35*, 309–321.

Kogan, L. S. "The Short-Term Case in a Family Agency." *Social Casework*, 1957, *38*, 231–238, 296–302, 366–374.

Kohut, H. *The Analysis of the Self.* Madison, Conn.: International Universities Press, 1976.

Koss, M. P. "Length of Psychotherapy for Clients Seen in Private Practice." *Journal of Consulting and Clinical Psychology*, 1979, *47*, 210–212.

Koss, M. P., and Butcher, J. N. "Research on Brief Psychotherapy." In S. L. Garfield and A. E. Bergin (eds.), *Handbook of Psychotherapy and Behavior Change: An Empirical Analysis.* (3rd ed.) New York: Wiley, 1986.

Koss, M. P., Butcher, J. N., and Strupp, H. H. "Brief Psychotherapy Methods in Clinical Research." *Journal of Clinical and Consulting Psychology*, 1986, *54*, 60–67.

Kovacs, A. L. "Survival in the 1980s: On the Theory and Practice of Brief Psychotherapy." *Psychotherapy: Theory, Research and Practice*, 1982, *19*, 142–159.

Kral, R., and Kowalski, K. "After the Miracle: The Second Stage in Solution-Focused Brief Therapy." *Journal of Strategic and Systemic Therapies,* 1989, *8,* 73–76.

Kramon, G. "Why Kaiser Is Still the King." *New York Times,* July 2, 1989, Business Section, p. 1.

Kreilkamp, T. *Time-Limited Intermittent Therapy with Children and Families.* New York: Brunner/Mazel, 1989.

Kuhn, T. S. *The Structure of Scientific Revolutions.* (2nd ed.) Chicago: University of Chicago Press, 1970.

Kupers, T. *Public Therapy.* New York: Free Press/Macmillan, 1981.

Lamb, W. "Sources and Solutions to Affective Responses Observed in the Integration of Therapies." *Journal of Integrative and Eclectic Psychotherapy,* 1988, 7(1), 37–41.

Lambert, M. J. "Implications of Psychotherapy Outcome Research for Eclectic Psychotherapy." In J. Norcross (ed.), *Handbook of Eclectic Psychotherapy.* New York: Brunner/Mazel, 1986.

Lange, M. A., and others. "Providers' Views of HMO Mental Health Services." *Psychotherapy,* 1988, *25,* 455–462.

Langman-Dorwart, N., and Harris, E. A. "Working with Managed Care: An Overview of Marketing, Strategic, and Legal Issues." Workshop presented at the Harvard Community Health Plan Annual Mental Health Conference, Boston, March 1992.

Langs, R. *The Therapeutic Environment.* New York: Jason Aronson, 1979.

Langsley, D. G. "Comparing Clinic and Private Practice of Psychiatry." *American Journal of Psychiatry,* 1978, *135,* 702–706.

Lankton, S. R. "Ericksonian Strategic Therapy." In J. K. Zeig and W. M. Munion (eds.), *What Is Psychotherapy? Contemporary Perspectives.* San Francisco: Jossey-Bass, 1990.

Lankton, S. R., and Erickson, K. K. "The Essence of a Single-Session Success." *Ericksonian Monographs,* 1994, *9,* 1–164.

Lankton, S. R, and Lankton, C. H. *The Answer Within: A Clinical Framework for Ericksonian Hypnotherapy.* New York: Brunner/Mazel, 1983.

Lankton, S. R., and Lankton, C. H. *Enchantment and Intervention in Family Therapy.* New York: Brunner/Mazel, 1986.

Lazarus, A. A. *Multimodal Behavior Therapy.* New York: Springer, 1976.

Lazarus, A. A. "The Need for Technical Eclecticism: Science, Breadth, Depth, and Specificity." In J. K. Zeig (ed.), *The Evolution of Psychotherapy.* New York: Brunner/Mazel, 1987.

Lazarus, A. A. *The Practice of Multimodal Therapy.* Baltimore, Md.: Johns Hopkins University Press, 1989.

Lazarus, A. A., and Fay, A. "Brief Psychotherapy: Tautology or Oxymoron?" In J. K. Zeig and S. G. Gilligan (eds.), *Brief Therapy: Myths, Methods, and Metaphors.* New York: Brunner/Mazel, 1990.

Lazarus, L. W. "Brief Psychotherapy of Narcissistic Disturbances." *Psychotherapy: Theory, Research and Practice,* 1982, *19,* 228–236.

Leary, T. F. *Interpersonal Diagnosis of Personality.* New York: Ronald Press, 1957.

Leeman, C. P, and Mulvey, C. H. "Brief Psychotherapy of the Dependent Personality: Specific Techniques." *Psychotherapy and Psychosomatics,* 1975, *25,* 36–42.

Leibovich, M. A. "Short-Term Psychotherapy for the Borderline Personality Disorder." *Psychotherapy and Psychosomatics,* 1981, *35,* 257–264.

Leon, I. G. "Short-Term Psychotherapy for Perinatal Loss." *Psychotherapy,* 1987, *24,* 186–195.

Lesse, S. "Future Oriented Psychotherapy–A Prophylactic Technique." *American Journal of Psychotherapy,* 1971, *25,* 180–193.

Levenson, H., and Bolter, K. "Short-Term Psychotherapy Values and Attitudes: Changes with Training." Paper presented at the annual convention of the American Psychological Association, Atlanta, Georgia, August 1988.

Levenson, H., and Butler, S. F. "Brief Dynamic Individual Psychotherapy." *Textbook of Psychiatry.* (2nd ed.) Washington, D.C.: American Psychiatric Press, 1994.

Levenson, H., Speed, J., and Budman, S. H. "Therapists' Training and Skill in Brief Therapy: A Survey." Paper presented at the annual meeting of the Society for Psychotherapy Research, Berkeley, California, June 1992.

Lewin, K. K. *Brief Psychotherapy: Brief Encounters.* St. Louis, Mo.: Warren H. Green, 1970.

Lipke, H. J., and Botkin, A. L. "Case Studies of EMDR with Chronic Post-Traumatic Stress Disorder." *Psychotherapy,* 1992, *29,* 591–595.

Lipowski, Z. J. "Consultation-Liaison Psychiatry: An Overview." *American Journal of Psychiatry,* 1974, *131,* 623–630.

Loewald, H. W. "The Experience of Time." *Psychoanalytic Study of the Child,* 1972, *27,* 401–410.

Lomas, J., and others. "Opinion Leaders vs. Audit and Feedback to Implement Practice Guidelines." *Journal of the American Medical Association,* 1991, *265,* 2202–2207.

Lonergan, E. C. *Group Intervention: How to Begin and Maintain Groups in Medical and Psychiatric Settings.* New York: Aronson, 1981.

Lonergan, E. C. "Utilizing Group Process in Crisis Waiting-List Groups." *International Journal of Group Psychotherapy,* 1985, *35,* 355–372.

Lorion, R. P., and Felner, R. D. "Research on Psychotherapy with the Disadvantaged." In S. L. Garfield and A. E. Bergin (eds.), *Handbook of Psychotherapy and Behavior Change: An Empirical Analysis.* (3rd ed.) New York: Wiley, 1986.

Lowman, R. L., and Resnick, R. J. (eds.). *The Mental Health Professional's Guide to Managed Care.* Washington, D.C.: American Psychological Association, 1994.

Luborsky, L., Singer, B., and Luborsky, L. "Comparative Studies of Psychotherapies: Is It True That 'Everyone Has Won and All Must Have Prizes'?" *Archives of General Psychiatry,* 1975, *32,* 995–1008.

McClendon, R., and Kadis, L. B. *Chocolate Pudding and Other Approaches to Intensive Multiple-Family Therapy.* Palo Alto, Calif.: Science and Behavior Books, 1983.

McGoldrick, M., Pearce, J. K., and Giordano, J. (eds.). *Ethnicity and Family Therapy.* New York: Guilford Press, 1982.

McKay, M., and Paleg, K. (eds.). *Focal Group Psychotherapy.* Oakland, Calif.: New Harbinger Publications, 1992.

MacKenzie, K. R. *Time-Limited Group Psychotherapy.* Washington, D.C.: American Psychiatric Press, 1990.

MacKenzie, K. R. (ed.). *Effective Use of Group Therapy in Managed Care.* Washington, D.C.: American Psychiatric Press, 1994.

Mackenzie, T. B., Rosenberg, S. D., Bergen, B. J., and Tucker, G. J. "The Manipulative Patient: An Interactional Approach." *Psychiatry,* 1978, *41,* 264–271.

MacKinnon, R. A., and Michels, R. *The Psychiatric Interview in Clinical Practice.* Philadelphia: Saunders, 1971.

McMullin, R. E. *Handbook of Cognitive Therapy Techniques.* New York: W.W. Norton, 1986.

McNeel, J. "The Parent Interview." *Transactional Analysis Journal,* 1976, *6,* 61–68.

Madanes, C. *Strategic Family Therapy.* San Francisco: Jossey-Bass, 1981.

Madanes, C. *Behind the One-Way Mirror.* San Francisco: Jossey-Bass, 1984.

Mahoney, M. J. *Cognition and Behavior Modification.* New York: Ballinger, 1974.

Mahoney, M. J. "Personal Science: A Cognitive Learning Therapy." In A. Ellis and R. Grieger (eds.), *Handbook of Rationale-Emotive Therapy.* New York: Springer, 1977.

Mahoney, M. J., and Arnkoff, D. "Cognitive and Self-Control Therapies." In S. L. Garfield and A. E. Bergin (eds.), *Handbook of Psychotherapy and Behavior Change.* (2nd ed.) New York: Wiley, 1978.

Mahrer, A. R. *How to Do Experiential Psychotherapy: A Manual for Practitioners.* Ottawa, Canada: University of Ottawa Press, 1989.

Mahrer, A. R., and Roberge, M. "Single-Session Experiential Therapy with Any Person Whatsoever." In R. A. Wells and V. J. Giannetti (eds.), *Casebook of the Brief Psychotherapies.* New York: Plenum, 1993.

Main, T. F. "The Ailment." *British Journal of Medical Psychology,* 1957, *30,* 129–145.

Malan, D. H. *A Study of Brief Psychotherapy.* London: Tavistock, 1963.

Malan, D. H. *The Frontier of Brief Psychotherapy.* New York: Plenum, 1976a.

Malan, D. H. *Toward the Validation of Dynamic Psychotherapy.* New York: Plenum, 1976b.

Malan, D. H. "The Most Important Development in Psychotherapy Since the Discovery of the Unconscious." In H. Davanloo (ed.), *Short-Term Dynamic Psychotherapy.* New York: Jason Aronson, 1980.

Malan, D., Heath, E., Bacal, H., and Balfour, F. "Psychodynamic Changes in Untreated Neurotic Patients. II. Apparently Genuine Improvements." *Archives of General Psychiatry,* 1975, *32,* 110–126.

Malinak, D. P., Hoyt, M. F., and Patterson, V. "Reactions to the Death of a Parent in Adult Life: A Preliminary Study." *American Journal of Psychiatry,* 1979, *136,* 1152–1156.

Mandel, H. P. *Short-Term Psychotherapy and Brief Treatment Techniques: An Annotated Bibliography 1920–1980.* New York: Plenum, 1981.

Mann, J. *Time-Limited Psychotherapy,* Cambridge, Mass.: Harvard University Press, 1973.

Mann, J. "The Management of Countertransference in Time-Limited Psychotherapy: The Role of the Central Issue." *International Journal of Psychoanalytic Psychotherapy,* 1984, *10,* 205–214.

Mann, J., and Goldman, R. *A Casebook in Time-Limited Psychotherapy.* New York: McGraw-Hill, 1982.

Marmar, C. R., Hoyt, M. F., Leong, A., and Horowitz, M. J. "Relating the Process to the Outcome of Brief Psychotherapy for Post-Traumatic Stress Disorders." Paper presented at meetings of the Society for Psychotherapy Research, Pacific Grove, California, June 1980.

Marmor, J. "Short-Term Dynamic Psychotherapy." *American Journal of Psychiatry,* 1979, *136,* 149–155.

Martin, C. "Who Will Fill the Primary Care Psychosocial Service Gap? A Proposal to Add a Psychosocial Clinician." *NWP Journal of Clinical Practice,* 1994, *1* (2), 7–18.

Marziali, E. A. "Prediction of Outcome of Brief Psychotherapy from Therapist Interpretive Interventions." *Archives of General Psychiatry,* 1984, *41,* 301–304.

Marziali, E. A., and Sullivan, J. M. "Methodological Issues in the Content Analysis of Brief Psychotherapy." *British Journal of Medical Psychology,* 1980, *53,* 19–27.

Masserman, J. H. "Historical-Comparative and Experimental

Roots of Short-Term Therapy." In L. R. Wolberg (ed.), *Short-Term Psychotherapy*. Philadelphia: Grune & Stratton, 1965.

Masterson, J. F. *Countertransference and Psychotherapeutic Technique*. New York: Brunner/Mazel, 1983.

May, R. *Love and Will*. New York: Dell, 1969.

May, R., Angel, E., and Ellenberger, H. F. (eds.). *Existence*. New York: Simon & Schuster, 1958.

Mays, V. M., and Albee, G. W. "Psychotherapy and Ethnic Minorities." In D. K. Freedheim (ed.), *History of Psychotherapy: A Century of Change*. Washington D.C.: American Psychological Association, 1992.

Meehl, P. E. "Why I Do Not Attend Case Conferences." In *Psychodiagnosis: Selected Papers*. Minneapolis: University of Minnesota Press, 1973.

Meichenbaum, D. *Cognitive Behavior Modification*. New York: Plenum, 1977.

Meichenbaum, D. *Stress Inoculation Training*. New York: Pergamon, 1985.

Meichenbaum, D. "Stress Innoculation Training: A Twenty-Year Update." In R. L. Woofold and P. M. Lehrer (eds.), *Principles and Practices of Stress Management*. New York: Guilford, 1992.

Meichenbaum, D. *A Clinical Handbook/Practical Therapist Manual for Assessing and Treating Adults with Post-Traumatic Stress Disorder (PTSD)*. Waterloo, Ontario, Canada: Institute Press, University of Waterloo, 1994.

Meier, G. "HMO Experiences with Mental Health Services to the Long-Term Emotionally Disabled." *Inquiry*, 1981, *18*, 125.

Melges, F. T. "Future Oriented Psychotherapy." *American Journal of Psychotherapy*, 1972, *26*, 22–33.

Melges, F. T. *Time and the Inner Future: A Temporal Approach to Psychiatric Disorders*. New York: Wiley, 1982.

Meltzoff, J., and Kornreich, M. *Research in Psychotherapy*. New York: Atherton Press, 1970.

Mendelsohn, R. "Critical Factors in Short-Term Psychotherapy: A Summary." *Bulletin of the Menninger Clinic*, 1978, *42*, 133–149.

Meresman, J. F. "Developmental Crises in an HMO: Treatment Throughout the Life Cycle." Paper presented at the annual convention of the American Psychological Association, Anaheim, California, August 1983.

Merikangas, K. R., and Weissman, M. M. "Epidemiology of DSM-III Axis II Personality Disorders." *Psychiatry Update: American Psychiatric Association Annual Review,* 1986, *5,* 258–278.

Miller, S. D. "Some Questions (Not Answers) for the Brief Treatment of People with Drug and Alcohol Problems." In M. F. Hoyt (ed.), *Constructive Therapies.* New York: Guilford, 1994.

Millon, T. "Personologic Psychotherapy: Ten Commandments for a Posteclectic Approach to Integrative Treatment." *Psychotherapy,* 1988, *25,* 209–219.

Millon, T., and Everly, G. S., Jr. *Personality and Its Disorders: A Biosocial Learning Approach.* New York: Wiley, 1985.

Minkowski, E. *Lived Time: Phenomenological and Psychopathological Studies.* Evanston, Ill.: Northwestern University Press, 1970. (Originally published 1933.)

Minsky, T. "Prisoners of Psychotherapy." *New York,* 1987, *20,* 34–40.

Mitchell, K. R. "Clinical Relevance of the Boundary Functions of Language." *Bulletin of the Menninger Clinic,* 1976, *40,* 641–654.

Moiso, C. "Ego States and Transference." *Transactional Analysis Journal,* 1985, *15,* 194–201.

"Money and Other Trade-Offs in Psychotherapy." *Voices: Journal of the American Academy of Psychotherapists,* 1979, *14,* (entire issue 4).

Moreno, J. D. "The HMO Pediatrician as Patient Advocate." Pediatric Annals, 1989, *18,* 269–271.

Morey, L. C. "Personality Disorders in DSM-III and DSM-III-R: Convergence, Coverage, and Internal Consistency." *American Journal of Psychiatry,* 1988, *145,* 573–577.

Morrill, R. G. "The Future for Mental Health in Primary Health Care Programs." *American Journal of Psychiatry,* 1978, *135,* 1351–1355.

Mumford, E., and others. "A New Look at Evidence About Reduced Cost of Medical Utilization Following Mental-Health Treatment." *American Journal of Psychiatry,* 1984, *141,* 1145–1158.

Nadelson, T. "Engagement Before Alliance." *Psychotherapy and Psychosomatics,* 1980, *33,* 76–86.

Nannum, A. "Time in Psychoanalytical Technique." *Journal of the American Psychoanalytical Association,* 1972, *20,* 736–750.

Napier, A. Y., and Whitaker, C. A. *The Family Crucible.* New York: HarperCollins, 1978.

Naranjo, C. "Present-Centeredness: Technique, Prescription, and Ideal." In J. Fagan and I. L. Shepherd (eds.), *Gestalt Therapy Now.* Palo Alto, Calif.: Science and Behavior Books, 1970.

Nelson, G. *The One Minute Scolding.* Boston: Shambhala, 1984.

Nelson, J. "The History and Spirit of the HMO Movement." *HMO Practice,* 1987, *1,* 75–85.

Neugarten, B. L., and Datan, N. "The Middle Years." In S. Arieti (ed.), *American Handbook of Psychiatry,* Vol. 1. (2nd ed.) New York: Basic Books, 1974.

Newman, F. L., and Howard, K. I. "Therapeutic Effort, Treatment Outcome, and National Health Policy." *American Psychologist,* 1986, *41,* 181–187.

Newman, R., and Bricklin, P. M. "Parameters of Managed Mental Health Care: Legal, Ethical, and Professional Guidelines." *Professional Psychology: Research and Practice,* 1991, *22,* 26–35. Reprinted in R. L. Lowman and R. J. Resnick (eds.), *The Mental Health Professional's Guide to Managed Care.* Washington, D.C.: American Psychological Association, 1994.

Novellino, M. "Self-Analysis of Countertransference in Integrative Transactional Analysis." *Transactional Analysis Journal,* 1984, *14,* 63–67.

Novellino, M. "Redecision Analysis of Transference: A TA Approach to Transference Neurosis." *Transactional Analysis Journal,* 1985, *15,* 202–206.

Nurnberg, H. G., and Suh, R. "Limits: Short-Term Treatment of Hospitalized Borderline Patients." *Comparative Psychiatry,* 1980, *21,* 70–80.

O'Hanlon, W. H. *Taproots: Underlying Principles of Milton H. Erickson's Therapy and Hypnosis.* New York: W.W. Norton, 1987.

O'Hanlon, W. H., and Hexum, A. L. *An Uncommon Casebook: The Complete Clinical Work of Milton H. Erickson, M.D.* New York: W.W. Norton, 1990.

O'Hanlon, W. H., and Martin, M. *Solution-Oriented Hypnosis: An Ericksonian Approach.* New York: W.W. Norton, 1992.

O'Hanlon, W. H., and Weiner-Davis, M. *In Search of Solutions: A New Direction in Psychotherapy.* New York: W.W. Norton, 1989.

O'Hanlon, W. H., and Wilk, J. *Shifting Contexts: The Generation of Effective Psychotherapy.* New York: Guilford, 1987.

Oremland, J. D. "Transference Cure and Flight into Health." *International Journal of Psychoanalytic Psychotherapy,* 1972, *1,* 61–75.

Orne, M. T., and Wender, P. H. "Anticipatory Socialization for Psychotherapy: Method and Rationale." *American Journal of Psychiatry,* 1968, *124,* 1203–1212.

Ornstein, R. E. *On the Experience of Time.* New York: Penguin, 1969.

Overall, J. E., and Gorham, D. R. "The Brief Psychiatric Rating Scale." *Psychological Reports,* 1962, *10,* 799–812.

Parad, H. J. (ed.). *Crisis Intervention: Selected Readings.* New York: Family Service Association of America, 1965.

Parloff, M. B. "Assessing the Effects of Headshrinking and Mind-Expanding." *International Journal of Group Psychotherapy,* 1970, *20,* 14–24.

Patrick, D. L., Coleman, J. V., Eagle, J., and Nelson, E. "Chronic Emotional Patients and Their Families in an HMO." *Inquiry,* 1978, *15,* 166–173.

Peake, T. H., Borduin, C. M., and Archer, R. P. (eds.) *Brief Psychotherapies: Changing Frames of Mind.* Newbury Park, Calif.: Sage Publications, 1988.

Peet, B. *The Ant and the Elephant.* Boston: Houghton Mifflin, 1972.

Pekarik, G., and Wierzbicki, M. "The Relationship Between Clients' Expected and Actual Treatment Duration." *Psychotherapy,* 1986, *23* (4), 532–534.

Pepe, P. *The Wit and Wisdom of Yogi Berra.* Westport, Conn.: Meekler Books/St. Martin's Press, 1988.

Perls, F. S. *Gestalt Therapy Verbatim.* Lafayette, Calif.: Real People Press, 1969.

Perls, F. S., Hefferline, R. F., and Goodman, P. *Gestalt Therapy.* New York: Julian Press, 1951.

Perry, S. W. "The Choice of Duration and Frequency for Outpatient Psychotherapy." *Annual Review of Psychiatry,* 1987, *6,* 398–414.

Persons, J. B. *Cognitive Therapy in Practice: A Case Formulation Approach.* New York: W.W. Norton, 1989.

Phillips, E. L. "Length of Psychotherapy and Outcome: Observations Stimulated by Howard, Kopta, Krause, and Orlinsky." *American Psychologist,* 1988, *43,* 669–670.

Phillips, M. "Changing Early Life Decisions Using Ericksonian Hypnosis." *Ericksonian Monographs,* 1988, *4,* 74–87.

Piaget, J. *The Child's Conception of Time.* New York: Basic Books, 1969. (Originally published 1946.)

Pincus, L. *Death and the Family.* New York: Pantheon, 1974.

Pinsker, H., Rosenthal, R., and McCullough, L. "Dynamic Supportive Psychotherapy." In P. Crits-Christoph and J. P. Barber (eds.), *Handbook of Short-Term Dynamic Psychotherapy.* New York: Basic Books, 1991.

Piper, W. E. "Brief Group Psychotherapy." *Psychiatric Annals,* 1991, *21,* 419–422.

Piper, W. E., Debanne, E. G., Bienvenu, J. P., and Garant, J. "A Comparative Study of Four Forms of Psychotherapy." *Journal of Consulting and Clinical Psychology,* 1984, *52,* 268–279.

Piper, W. E., and Perrault, E. L. "Pretherapy Preparation for Group Members." *International Journal of Group Psychotherapy,* 1989, *39,* 17–34.

Piper, W. E., and others. "Relationships Between the Focus of Therapist Interpretations and Outcome in Short-Term Individual Psychotherapy." Paper presented at meetings of the Society for Psychotherapy Research, Lake Louise, Canada, June 1984.

Pittman, F. S., III, Flomenhoft, K., and DeYoung, C. D. "Family Crisis Therapy." In R. A. Wells and V. J. Giannetti (eds.), *Handbook of the Brief Psychotherapies.* New York: Plenum, 1990.

Poey, K. "Guidelines for the Practice of Brief, Dynamic Group Therapy." *International Journal of Group Psychotherapy,* 1985, *35,* 331–354.

Pollack, G. H. "On Time and Anniversaries." In M. Kanzer (ed.), *The Unconscious Today.* Madison, Conn.: International Universities Press, 1971.

Polster, E., and Polster, M. "Therapy Without Resistance." In A. Burton (ed.), *What Makes Behavior Change Possible?* New York: Brunner/Mazel, 1976.

Poynter, W. L. *The Preferred Provider's Handbook: Building a Successful Private Therapy Practice in the Managed Care Marketplace.* New York: Brunner/Mazel, 1994.

Practice Directorate. "Federal Report Inconclusive on Effect of Physician-HMO Pay Incentives on Quality of Care." *Practitioner Focus,* 1988a, *2*(3), 6–7.

Practice Directorate. "Practice Directorate Argues for Better Mental Health Coverage and HMO Reform in Federal Health Plan." *Practitioner Focus,* 1988b, *2* (3), 10–11.

Practice Directorate. "HMO Bonus Plans Can Threaten Quality: GAO." *Practitioner Focus,* 1989, *3* (1), 4.

Priestly, J. B. *Man and Time.* New York: Dell, 1968.

Psychotherapy Finances. *Managed Care Handbook.* Jupiter, Fla.: Ridgewood Financial Institute, 1994.

Racker, H. "The Meaning and Uses of Countertransference." *Psychoanalytic Quarterly,* 1957, *16,* 330–357.

Rank, O. *Will Therapy.* New York: Knopf, 1945. (Originally published 1936.)

Rank, O. *The Myth of the Birth of the Hero.* New York: Knopf, 1964. (Originally published 1914.)

Rank, O. *The Trauma of Birth.* New York: HarperCollins, 1973. (Originally published 1929.)

Rasmussen, A., and Messer, S. B. "A Comparison and Critique of Mann's Time-Limited Psychotherapy and Davanloo's Short-Term Dynamic Psychotherapy." *Bulletin of the Menninger Clinic,* 1986, *50,* 163–184.

Reich, W. *Character Analysis.* New York: Farrar, Straus & Giroux, 1949.

Reider, N. "A Type of Transference to Institutions." *Journal of Hillside Hospital,* 1953, *2,* 23–29.

Relman, A. S. "Reforming the Health Care System." *New England Journal of Medicine,* 1990, *323,* 991–992.

Robertiello, R. C., and Schoenewolf, G. *101 Common Therapeutic Blunders.* New York: Jason Aronson, 1987.

Robinson, P. J. "Providing Couples' Therapy in Prepaid Health

Care." In C. S. Austad and W. H. Berman (eds.), *Psychotherapy in Managed Health Care: The Optimal Use of Time and Resources.* Washington, D.C.: American Psychological Association, 1991.

Rockwell, W.J.K., and Pinkerton, R. S. "Single-Session Psychotherapy." *American Journal of Psychotherapy,* 1982, *36,* 32–40.

Rogers, C. R. *Client-Centered Therapy.* Boston: Houghton Mifflin, 1951.

Roller, B., and Nelson, V. *The Art of Co-Therapy.* New York: Guilford, 1991.

Roller, B., Schnell, C., and Welsch, M. "Organization and Development of Group Psychotherapy Programs in Health Maintenance Organizations." In *Proceedings.* Detroit, Mich.: Group Health Institute, 1982 (Mimeographed).

Rosen, S. *My Voice Will Go with You: The Teaching Tales of Milton H. Erickson.* New York: W.W. Norton, 1982.

Rosenbaum, M. (ed.). *Handbook of Short-Term Therapy Groups.* New York: McGraw-Hill, 1983.

Rosenbaum, R. "Life-Cycle Psychotherapies and Health Maintenance Organizations." Paper presented at the American Psychological Association Convention, Anaheim, California, August 1983.

Rosenbaum, R. "Feelings Toward Integration: A Matter of Style and Identity." *Journal of Integrative and Eclectic Psychotherapy,* 1988a, *7*(1), 52–60.

Rosenbaum, R. "Musical Perspectives on Termination." Symposium presented at the Fourth Annual National Convention of the Society for the Exploration of Psychotherapy Integration, Boston, 1988b.

Rosenbaum, R. "Strategic Psychotherapy." In R. A. Wells and V. J. Giannetti (eds.), *Handbook of the Brief Psychotherapies.* New York: Plenum, 1990.

Rosenbaum, R. "Heavy Ideals: Strategic Single-Session Hypnotherapy." In R. A. Wells and V. J. Giannetti (eds.), *Casebook of the Brief Psychotherapies.* New York: Plenum, 1993.

Rosenbaum, R., Hoyt, M. F., and Talmon, M. "The Challenge of Single-Session Therapies: Creating Pivotal Moments." In R. A. Wells and V. J. Giannetti (eds.), *Handbook of the Brief Psychotherapies.* New York: Plenum, 1990.

Rosenberg, S. E. "Short-Term Dynamic Psychotherapy for Depression." In E. Beckham and W. Lieder (eds.), *Depression: Treatment, Assessment, and Research*. Belmont, Calif.: Dorsey Press, 1986.

Rosenberg, S. E., Sampson, H., Silberschatz, G., and Weiss, J. "Assessing the Process and Outcome of Brief Dynamic Therapy." Paper presented at the annual meeting of the Society for Psychotherapy Research, Smugglers' Notch, Vermont, June 1982.

Rubin, S. S. "Ego-Focused Psychotherapy: A Psychodynamic Framework for a Technical Eclecticism." *Psychotherapy*, 1986, *23*, 385–389.

Rubin, T. *Shrink! The Diary of a Psychiatrist*. New York: Popular Library, 1974.

Ryle, A. "The Focus of Brief Interpretive Psychotherapy: Dilemmas, Traps and Snags as Target Problems." *British Journal of Psychiatry*, 1979, *134*, 46–54.

Sabin, J. E. "Clinical Skills for the 1990s: Six Lessons from HMO Practice." *Hospital and Community Psychiatry*, 1991, *42*, 601–608.

Sabin, J. E. "The Therapeutic Alliance in Managed Care Mental Health Practice." *Journal of Psychotherapy Practice and Research*, 1992, *1*, 29–36.

Sabin, J. E., and Borus, J. F. "Mental Health Teaching and Research in Managed Care." In J. L. Feldman and R. J. Fitzpatrick (eds.), *Managed Mental Health Care: Administrative and Clinical Issues*. Washington, D.C.: American Psychiatric Press, 1992.

Sampson, H. "A Critique of Certain Traditional Concepts in the Psychoanalytic Theory of Therapy." *Bulletin of the Menninger Clinic*, 1976, *10* (3), 255–262.

Sarason, S. B., Sarason, E. K., and Cowden, P. "Aging and the Nature of Work." *American Psychologist*, 1975, *30*, 584–592.

Savitz, S. A. "Measuring Quality of Care and Quality Maintenance." In J. L. Feldman and R. J. Fitzpatrick (eds.), *Managed Mental Health Care: Administrative and Clinical Issues*. Washington, D.C.: American Psychiatric Press, 1992.

Schafer, R. "The Termination of Brief Psychoanalytic Psychotherapy." *International Journal of Psychoanalytic Psychotherapy,* 1973, *2,* 135–148.

Schafer, R. "Talking to Patients in Psychotherapy." *Bulletin of the Menninger Clinic,* 1974, *38,* 503–515.

Schafer, R. *A New Language for Psychoanalysis.* New Haven, Conn.: Yale University Press, 1976.

Schilder, P. "Psychopathology of Time." *Journal of Nervous and Mental Diseases,* 1936, *83,* 530–546.

Schloegl, I. *The Wisdom of the Zen Masters.* New York: New Directions, 1976.

Schneider-Braus, K. "A Practical Guide to HMO Psychiatry." *Hospital and Community Psychiatry,* 1987, *38,* 876–879.

Schneider-Braus, K. "Managing a Mental Health Department in a Staff Model HMO." In J. L. Feldman and R. J. Fitzpatrick (eds.), *Managed Mental Health Care: Administrative and Clinical Issues.* Washington, D.C.: American Psychiatric Press, 1992.

Schuyler, D. *A Practical Guide to Cognitive Therapy.* New York: W.W. Norton, 1991.

Schwartz, A. J., and Bernard, H. S. "Comparison of Patient and Therapist Evaluations of Time-Limited Psychotherapy." *Psychotherapy: Theory, Research and Practice,* 1981, *18,* 101–108.

Scott-Maxwell, F. *The Measure of My Days.* New York: Knopf, 1968.

Searles, H. F. "The Patient as Therapist to His Analyst." In P. L. Giovacchini (ed.), *Tactics and Techniques in Psychoanalytic Psychotherapy,* Vol. 2: *Countertransference.* New York: Jason Aronson, 1975.

Seeman, M. V. "Time and Schizophrenia." *Psychiatry,* 1976, *39,* 189–195.

Selvini-Palazzoli, M., Boscolo, L., Cecchin, G., and Prata, G. *Paradox and Counterparadox.* New York: Jason Aronson, 1978.

Selzer, M. L. "The Use of First Names in Psychotherapy." *Archives of General Psychiatry,* 1960, *3,* 215–218.

Shadle, M., and Christianson, J. B. "The Organization of Mental Health Care Delivery in HMOs." *Administration in Mental Health,* 1988, *15,* 201–225.

Shapiro, D. *Neurotic Styles.* New York: Basic Books, 1965.

Shapiro, D. A., and Shapiro, D. "Meta-Analysis of Comparative Therapy Outcome Studies: A Replication and Refinement." *Psychological Bulletin,* 1982, *92,* 581–604.

Shapiro, F. "Efficacy of Eye Movement Desensitization Procedure in the Treatment of Traumatic Memories." *Journal of Traumatic Stress Studies,* 1989, *2,* 199–233.

Shapiro, F. "Eye Movement Desensitization and Reprocessing Procedure: From EMD to EMD/R–A New Treatment Model for Anxiety and Related Traumata." *The Behavior Therapist,* 1991, *128,* 133–135.

Shapiro, F. *Eye Movement Desensitization and Reprocessing: Basic Principles, Protocols and Procedures.* New York: Guilford, in press.

Shapiro, J., Sank, L. I., Shaffer, C. S., and Donovan, D. C. "Cost Effectiveness of Individual vs. Group Cognitive Behavior Therapy for Problems of Depression and Anxiety in an HMO Population." *Journal of Clinical Psychology,* 1982, *38,* 674–677.

Sharfstein, S. S. "Managed Mental Health Care." *Review of Psychiatry,* 1992, *11,* 570–584.

Shectman, F. "Time and the Practice of Psychotherapy." *Psychotherapy,* 1986, *23* (4), 521–525.

Sheehy, G. *Passages: Predictable Crises in Adult Life.* New York: Dutton, 1976.

Shorr, J. E. *Psycho-Imagination Therapy: The Integration of Phenomenology and Imagination.* New York: Intercontinental Medical Book Corporation, 1972.

Shorr, J. E. *Psychotherapy Through Imagery.* New York: Intercontinental Medical Book Corporation, 1974.

Shulman, M. E. "Cost Containment in Clinical Psychology: Critique of Biodyne and the HMOs." *Professional Psychology: Research and Practice,* 1988, *19,* 298–307.

Sifneos, P. E. *Short-Term Psychotherapy and Emotional Crisis.* Cambridge, Mass.: Harvard University Press, 1972.

Sifneos, P. E. "Criteria for Psychotherapeutic Outcome." *Psychotherapy and Psychosomatics,* 1975, *26,* 49–58.

Sifneos, P. E. "The Teaching and Supervision of STAPP." In H. Davanloo (ed.), *Basic Principles and Techniques in Short-Term Dynamic Psychotherapy.* New York: Spectrum, 1978.

Sifneos, P. E. *Short-Term Dynamic Psychotherapy*. New York: Plenum, 1979.

Sifneos, P. E. "Short-Term Anxiety-Provoking Psychotherapy." In S. H. Budman (ed.), *Forms of Brief Therapy*. New York: Guilford, 1981.

Sifneos, P. E. *Short-Term Dynamic Psychotherapy: Evaluation and Technique.* (Rev. ed.) New York: Plenum, 1987.

Sifneos, P. E. *Short-Term Anxiety-Provoking Psychotherapy: A Treatment Manual*. New York: Plenum, 1992.

Simkin, J. S. *Gestalt Therapy Mini-Lectures*. Millbrae, Calif.: Celestial Arts, 1976.

Simmons, R. D., and others. "Pain Medication Contracts for Problem Patients." *Psychosomatics,* 1979, *20,* 118, 123, 127.

Simos, B. G. "Grief Therapy to Facilitate Healthy Restitution." *Social Casework,* 1977, 58, 337–342.

Singer, J. L. *Imagination and Daydream Methods in Psychotherapy and Behavior Change*. San Diego, Calif.: Academic Press, 1974.

Singh, R. N. "Brief Interviews: Approaches, Techniques, and Effectiveness." *Social Casework,* 1982, 63, 599–606.

Sloane, R. B., and Staples, F. R. (eds.). "Symposium on Brief Psychotherapy." *Psychiatric Clinics of North America,* 1979, *2,* (entire issue).

Sloane, R. B., and others. *Psychotherapy Versus Behavior Therapy.* Cambridge, Mass.: Harvard University Press, 1975.

Sluzki, C. E. "Forward." In B. Furman and T. Ahola, *Solution Talk: Hosting Therapeutic Conversations*. New York: W.W. Norton, 1992.

Small, L. *The Briefer Psychotherapies.* New York: Brunner/Mazel, 1979.

Small, R. F. "Managed Care: A Guide for Psychotherapists." *Innovations in Clinical Practice: A Sourcebook,* 1992, *11* 241–250.

Smith, M. L., and Glass, G. V. "Meta-Analysis of Psychotherapy Outcome Studies." *American Psychologist,* 1977, *32,* 752–760.

Smith, M. L., Glass, G. V., and Miller, T. I. *The Benefits of Psychotherapy.* Baltimore, Md.: Johns Hopkins University Press, 1980.

Smith, W. L. "Death and Transfiguration: A Psychotherapeutic Technique for Resolving Impasse Resistance." *Psychotherapy: Theory, Research and Practice,* 1967, *4,* 162–163.

Spitz, R. A. "On Anticipation, Duration, and Meaning." *Journal of the American Psychoanalytic Association,* 1972, *20,* 721–735.

Spoerl, O. H. "Treatment Patterns in Prepaid Psychiatric Care." *American Journal of Psychiatry,* 1974, *131,* 56–59.

Spoerl, O. H. "Single-Session Psychotherapy." *Diseases of the Nervous System,* 1975, *36,* 283–285.

Sterba, R. "A Case of Brief Psychotherapy by Sigmund Freud." *Psychoanalytic Review,* 1951, *38,* 75–80.

Sterman, P. "Promoting the Culture of Quality." Paper presented at the Group Health Association of America Conference, Lake Tahoe, Nevada, January 1993.

Stewart, I., and Joines, V. *TA Today.* Chapel Hill, N.C.: Lifespace Publishing, 1987.

Stierlin, H. "Short-Term Versus Long-Term Psychotherapy in the Light of a General Theory of Human Relationships." *British Journal of Medical Psychology,* 1968, *41,* 357–367.

Strosahl, K. D. "Cognitive and Behavioral Treatment of the Personality Disordered Patient." In C. S. Austad and W. H. Berman (eds.), *Psychotherapy in Managed Health Care: The Optimal Use of Time and Resources.* Washington, D.C.: American Psychological Association, 1991.

Strosahl, K. D. "New Dimensions in Behavioral Health/Primary Care Integration." *HMO Practice,* 1994, *8,* 176–179.

Strosahl, K. D., and Quirk, M. "The Trouble with Carve Outs." *Business and Health,* 1994, July, p. 52.

Strupp, H. H. "Psychoanalysis, 'Focal Psychotherapy,' and the Nature of the Therapeutic Influence." *Archives of General Psychiatry,* 1975, *32,* 127–135.

Strupp, H. H. "Success and Failure in Time-Limited Psychotherapy." *Archives of General Psychiatry,* 1980a–d, *37,* 595–603(a), 708–716(b), 831–841(c), 947–954(d).

Strupp, H. H., and Binder, J. L. *Psychotherapy in a New Key: A Guide to Time-Limited Dynamic Psychotherapy.* New York: Basic Books, 1984.

Strupp, H. H., and Hadley, S. W. "Specific Versus Nonspecific Factors in Psychotherapy." *Archives of General Psychiatry,* 1979, *36,* 1125–1136.

Strupp, H. H., and others. "Short-Term Dynamic Psychotherapies for the Depressed Patient." In A. J. Rush (ed.), *Short-Term Psychotherapy for Depression*. New York: Guilford, 1982.

Stuart, R. B. *Helping Couples Change: A Social Learning Approach to Marital Therapy*. New York: Guilford, 1981.

Sugar, O. "Head Shrinking." *Journal of the American Medical Association*, 1971, *216*, 117–120.

Sullivan, H. S. *The Interpersonal Theory of Psychiatry*. New York: W.W. Norton, 1953.

Sullivan, H. S. *The Psychiatric Interview*. New York: W.W. Norton, 1954.

Suzuki, D. T. *Zen Buddhism*. New York: Doubleday, 1956.

Swinson, R. P., Soulios, C., Cox, B. J., and Kuch, K. "Brief Treatment of Emergency Room Patients with Panic Attacks." *American Journal of Psychiatry*, 1992, *149*, 944–946.

Szasz, T. *The Manufacture of Madness*. New York: HarperCollins, 1970.

Szilagyi, P. G., and others. "The Effect of Independent Practice Association Plans on Use of Pediatric Ambulatory Medical Care in One Group Practice." *Journal of the American Medical Association*, 1990, *263*, 2198–2203.

Talmon, M. *Single Session Therapy: Maximizing the Effect of the First (and Often Only) Therapeutic Encounter*. San Francisco: Jossey-Bass, 1990.

Talmon, M. *Single Session Solutions*. Reading, Mass.: Addison-Wesley, 1993.

Talmon, M., Hoyt, M. F., and Rosenbaum, R. "Effective Single-Session Therapy: Step-by-Step Guidelines." In M. Talmon, *Single-Session Therapy: Maximizing the Effect of the First (and Often Only) Therapeutic Encounter*. San Francisco: Jossey-Bass, 1990.

Talmon, M., Rosenbaum, R., Hoyt, M. F., and Short, L. *Single Session Therapy*. Kansas City, Mo.: Golden Triad Films, 1990. Videotape.

Tart, C. T. (ed.). *Altered States of Consciousness*. New York: Wiley, 1969.

Thomson, O. "Fear, Anger, and Sadness." *Transactional Analysis Journal*, 1983, *13*, 20–24.

Ticho, E. A. "Termination of Psychoanalysis: Treatment Goals,

Life Goals." *Psychoanalytic Quarterly*, 1972, *41*, 315–333.

Torphy, D. E., Campbell, K., and Davis, S. D. "Effects of a Faculty Prepaid Group Practice in a Pediatric Primary Care Clinic." *Journal of Medical Education*, 1988, *63*, 839–847.

Tulkin, S. R., and Frank, G. W. "The Changing Role of Psychologists in Health Maintenance Organizations." *American Psychologist*, 1985, *40*, 1125–1130.

Tulkin, S. R., and Weinstein, N. W. "A Systems Approach to Preventive Health Care." Paper presented at the annual convention of the American Psychological Association, Montreal, August 1980.

Valdez, R. B., and others. "Prepaid Group Practice Effects on the Utilization of Medical Services and Health Outcomes for Children: Results from a Controlled Trial." *Pediatrics*, 1989, *83*, 168–180.

VandenBos, G. R., Cummings, N. A., and DeLeon, P. H. "A Century of Psychotherapy: Economic and Environmental Influences." In D. K. Freedheim (ed.), *History of Psychotherapy: A Century of Change*. Washington, D.C.: American Psychological Association, 1992.

Volkan, V. D. "'Re-Grief' Therapy." In B. Schoenberg (ed.), *Bereavement: Its Psychosocial Aspects*. New York: Columbia University Press, 1975.

von Franz, M. L. *Time: Rhythm and Repose*. New York: Thames & Hudson, 1978.

Wallace, M., and Rabin, A. I. "Temporal Experience." *Psychological Bulletin*, 1960, *57*, 213–226.

Walter, J. L., and Peller, J. E. *Becoming Solution-Focused in Brief Therapy*. New York: W.W. Norton, 1992.

Walter, J. L., and Peller, J. E. "'On Track' in Solution-Focused Brief Therapy." In M. F. Hoyt (ed.), *Constructive Therapies*. New York: Guilford, 1994.

Ware, P. "Personality Adaptations (Doors to Therapy)." *Transactional Analysis Journal*, 1983, *13*, 11–19.

Warkentin, J., and Whitaker, C. A. "Time-Limited Therapy for an Agency Case." In A. Burton (ed.), *Modern Psychotherapeutic Practice: Innovations in Technique*. Palo Alto, Calif.: Science and Behavior Books, 1965.

Warner, S. L. "What Is a Headshrinker?" *American Journal of Psychotherapy,* 1982, *36,* 256–263.

Watzlawick, P., Beavin, J. H., and Jackson, D. D. *Pragmatics of Human Communication: A Study of Interactional Patterns, Pathologies, and Paradoxes.* New York, W.W. Norton, 1967.

Watzlawick, P., Weakland, J. H., and Fisch, R. *Change: Principles of Problem Formation and Problem Resolution.* New York: W.W. Norton, 1974.

Webster's New Collegiate Dictionary. Springfield, Mass.: Merriam-Webster, 1951.

Webster's Seventh New Collegiate Dictionary. Springfield, Mass.: Merriam-Webster, 1970.

Weddington, W. W., Jr., and Cavenar, J. O., Jr. "Termination Initiated by the Therapist: A Countertransference Storm." *American Journal of Psychiatry,* 1979, *136,* 1302–1305.

Weeks, G. R. (ed.). *Promoting Change Through Paradoxical Therapy.* New York: Brunner/Mazel, 1991.

Weiner-Davis, M. *Divorce Busting.* New York: Fireside/Simon & Schuster, 1992.

Weiner-Davis, M., de Shazer, S., and Gingerich, W. J. "Building on Pretreatment Change to Construct the Therapeutic Solution: An Exploratory Study." *Journal of Marital Family Therapy,* 1987, *13,* 359–363.

Weiss, J. "Crying at the Happy Ending." *Psychoanalytic Review,* 1952, *39,* 338.

Weiss, J., and others. *Research on the Psychoanalytic Process, 1 and 2.* Bulletin San Francisco: Department of Psychiatry, Mt. Zion Hospital and Medical Center, 1977.

Wells, R. A. *Planned Short-Term Treatment.* New York: Free Press/Macmillan, 1982.

Wells, R. A., and Giannetti, V. J. (eds.). *Handbook of the Brief Psychotherapies.* New York: Plenum, 1990.

Wells, R. A., and Giannetti, V. J. (eds.). *Casebook of the Brief Psychotherapies.* New York: Plenum, 1993.

Wells, R. A., and Phelps, P. A. "The Brief Psychotherapies: A Selective Review." In R. A. Wells and V. J. Giannetti (eds.), *Handbook of the Brief Psychotherapies.* New York: Plenum, 1990.

Westen, D. "What Changes in Short-Term Dynamic Psychotherapy?" *Psychotherapy,* 1986, *23,* 501–512.

Whitaker, C. A. Interview. In J. Haley and L. Hoffman (eds.), *Techniques of Family Therapy.* New York: Basic Books, 1968.

Whitaker, C. A. "Psychotherapy of the Absurd with a Special Emphasis on the Psychotherapy of Aggression." *Family Process,* 1975, *4,* 1–16.

Whitaker, C. A. "The Hindrance of Theory in Clinical Work." In P. J. Guerin, Jr. (ed.), *Family Therapy: Theory and Practice.* New York: Gardner Press, 1976.

Whitaker, C. A. "Comment." *Voices,* 1983, *19,* 40.

Whitaker, C. A., and Malone, T. P. *The Roots of Psychotherapy.* New York: Blakiston, 1953.

White, M., and Epston, D. *Narrative Means to Therapeutic Ends.* New York: W.W. Norton, 1990.

Wierzbicki, M., and Pekarik, G. "A Meta-Analysis of Psychotherapy Dropout." *Professional Psychology: Research and Practice,* 1993, *24* (2), 190–195.

Wilson, G. T. "Behavior Therapy as a Short-Term Therapeutic Approach." In S. H. Budman (ed.), *Forms of Brief Therapy.* New York: Guilford, 1981.

Winegar, N. *The Clinician's Guide to Managed Mental Health Care.* Binghamton, N.Y.: Haworth Press, 1992.

Winegar, N., and Bistline, J. L. *Marketing Mental Health Services to Managed Care.* Binghamton, N.Y.: Haworth Press, 1994.

Winnicott, D. W. "Hate in the Countertransference." *International Journal of Psycho-Analysis,* 1949, *30,* 69–74.

Winnicott, D. W. *Playing and Reality.* London: Tavistock, 1971a.

Winnicott, D. W. *Therapeutic Consultations in Child Psychiatry.* New York: Basic Books, 1971b.

Winokur, M., and Dasberg, H. "Teaching and Learning Short-Term Dynamic Psychotherapy." *Bulletin of the Menninger Clinic,* 1983, *47* (1), 36–52.

Winokur, M., Messer, S. B., and Schact, T. "Contributions to the Theory and Practice of Short-Term Dynamic Psychotherapy." *Bulletin of the Menninger Clinic,* 1981, *45,* 125–142.

Wolberg, L. R. (ed.). *Short-Term Psychotherapy.* Philadelphia: Grune & Stratton, 1965a.

Wolberg, L. R. "The Technic of Short-Term Psychotherapy." In L. R. Wolberg (ed.), *Short-Term Psychotherapy*. Philadelphia: Grune & Stratton, 1965b.

Wolberg, L. R. "Catalyzing the Therapeutic Process: The Use of Hypnosis." In L. R. Wolberg, *Handbook of Short-Term Psychotherapy*. New York: Thieme-Stratton, 1980.

Wolberg, L. R. "The Evolution of Psychotherapy: Future Trends." In J. K. Zeig (ed.), *The Evolution of Psychotherapy*. New York: Brunner/Mazel, 1987.

Wolinsky, S. *Trances People Live*. Norfolk, Conn.: Bramble Books, 1991.

Wolpe, J. *Psychotherapy by Reciprocal Inhibition*. Palo Alto, Calif.: Stanford University Press, 1958.

Wolpe, J. *The Practice of Behavior Therapy*. (2nd ed.) Elmsford, N.Y.: Pergamon, 1973.

Wolpe, J., and Lazarus, A. A. *Behavior Therapy Techniques*. New York: Pergamon Press, 1966.

Woollams, S., and Brown, M. *Transactional Analysis*. Ann Arbor, Mich.: Huron Valley Institute Press, 1978.

Worchel, J. "Short-Term Dynamic Psychotherapy." In R. A. Wells and V. J. Giannetti (eds.), *Handbook of the Brief Psychotherapies*. New York: Plenum, 1990.

Wright, R. H. "The Cons of Psychotherapy in Managed Health Care." *Psychotherapy in Private Practice*, 1992, *11*(2), 71–78.

Yalom, I. D. *Theory and Practice of Group Psychotherapy*. (3rd ed.) New York: Basic Books, 1985.

Yapko, M. D. "Brief Therapy Tactics in Longer-Term Psychotherapies." In J. K. Zeig and S. G. Gilligan (eds.), *Brief Therapy: Myths, Methods, and Metaphors*. New York: Brunner/Mazel, 1990a.

Yapko, M. D. "The Case of Vicki: Hypnosis for Coping with Terminal Cancer." In *Trancework*. (2nd ed.) New York: Brunner/Mazel, 1990b.

Yapko, M. D. "Therapy with Direction." In S. H. Budman, M. F. Hoyt, and S. Friedman (eds.), *The First Session in Brief Therapy*. New York: Guilford, 1992.

Zalcman, M. J., and Cornell, W. F. "A Bilateral Model for Clinical Supervision." *Transactional Analysis Journal*, 1983, *13*, 112–123, 195–197.

Zeig, J. K. *A Teaching Seminar with Milton H. Erickson.* New York: Brunner/Mazel, 1980.

Zeig, J. K. (ed.). *Ericksonian Approaches to Hypnosis and Psychotherapy.* New York: Brunner/Mazel, 1982.

Zeig, J. K. (ed.). *The Evolution of Psychotherapy.* New York: Brunner/Mazel, 1987.

Zeig, J. K. "Ericksonian Psychotherapy." In J. K. Zeig and W. M. Munion (eds.), *What Is Psychotherapy? Contemporary Perspectives.* San Francisco: Jossey-Bass, 1990.

Zeig, J. K., and Gilligan, S. G. (eds.) *Brief Therapy: Myths, Methods, and Metaphors.* New York: Brunner/Mazel, 1990.

Zeig, J. K., and Lankton, S. R. (eds.). *Developing Ericksonian Therapy: State of the Art.* New York: Brunner/Mazel, 1988.

Zeigarnik, B. "On Finished and Unfinished Tasks." In W. D. Ellis, *A Source Book of Gestalt Psychology.* Orlando, Fla.: Harcourt Brace Jovanovich, 1938. Summarized in J. W. Atkinson, *An Introduction to Motivation.* New York: Van Nostrand Reinhold, 1964.

Zimet, C. N. "Developmental Task and Crisis Groups: The Application of Group Psychotherapy to Maturational Processes." *Psychotherapy: Theory, Research and Practice,* 1979, *16,* 2–8.

Zimet, C. N. "The Mental Health Care Revolution: Will Psychology Survive?" *American Psychologist,* 1989, *44,* 703–708.

Zimmerman, J. "Fast Freud." *Pacific Sun,* Mar. 6, 1992 pp. 1, 11–14.

Zirkle, G. "Five-Minute Psychotherapy." *American Journal of Psychiatry,* 1961, *118,* 544–546.

Zois, C. *Think Like a Shrink.* New York: Warner, 1992.

For Further Reading

———◆◆◆———

The following additional bibliographic resources have been divided into two sections: A. *Brief/Short-Term Therapy* and B. *Managed Care/HMO Practice*. Many of these items could be placed in either section and are obviously relevant to both.

A. Brief/Short-Term Therapy

Alford, B. A., Freeman, A., Beck, A. T., and Wright, F. D. "Brief Focused Cognitive Therapy of Panic Disorder." *Psychotherapy,* 1990, *27,* 230–234.

Barlow, D. H. "Long-Term Outcome for Patients with Panic Disorder Treated with Cognitive-Behavioral Therapy." *Journal of Clinical Psychiatry,* 1990, *51,* 17–23.

Barlow, D. H., and Craske, M. G. *Mastery of Your Anxiety and Panic.* Albany, N.Y.: Graywind Publications, 1989.

Barlow, D. H., Craske, M. G., Cerny, J. A., and Klosko, J. S. "Behavioral Treatment of Panic Disorder." *Behavior Therapy,* 1989, *20,* 261–282.

Bateson, G. *Steps to an Ecology of Mind.* New York: Aronson, 1972.

Beck, A. T., Steer, R. A., and Garbin, M. G. "Psychometric Properties of the Beck Depression Inventory: Twenty-Five Years of Evaluation." *Clinical Psychology Review,* 1988, *8,* 77–100.

Beckfield, D. F. *Master Your Panic and Take Back Your Life! Twelve*

Treatment Sessions to Overcome High Anxiety. San Luis Obispo, Calif.: Impact Publishers, 1994.

Bellak, L., and Siegal, H. *Handbook of Intensive Brief and Emergency Psychotherapy.* Larchmont, N.Y.: C.P.S., Inc., 1983.

Bergman, J. S. *Fishing for Barracuda: Pragmatics of Brief Systemic Therapy.* New York: W.W. Norton, 1985.

Binder, J. L., Henry, W. P., and Strupp, H. H. "An Appraisal of Selection Criteria for Dynamic Psychotherapies and Implications for Setting Time Limits." *Psychiatry,* 1987, *50,* 154–166.

Bolter, K., Levenson, H., and Alvarez, W. "Differences in Values Between Short-Term and Long-Term Therapists." *Professional Psychology: Research and Practice,* 1990, *21,* 285–290.

Brandt, L. M. "A Short-Term Group Therapy Model for Treatment of Adult Female Survivors of Childhood Incest." *Group,* 1989, *13,* 74–82.

Buchele, B. J. "Innovative Uses of Psychodynamic Group Psychotherapy." *Bulletin of the Menninger Clinic,* 1994, 58, 215–223.

Budman, S. H., and Hoyt, M. F. "Active Interventions in Brief Therapy and Control Mastery Theory: A Case Study." In R. A. Wells and V. J. Giannetti (eds.), *Casebook of the Brief Psychotherapies.* New York: Plenum, 1993.

Cameron-Bandler, L. *Solutions: Practical and Effective Antidotes for Sexual and Relationship Problems.* San Rafael, Calif.: Future-Pace, 1985.

Conte, H. R., Plutchik, R., Wild, K., and Karasu, T. B. "Combined Psychotherapy and Psychopharmacology for Depression." *Archives of General Psychiatry,* 1986, *43,* 471–479.

Covey, S. R. *The Seven Habits of Highly Effective People.* New York: Fireside/Simon & Schuster, 1989.

Crandell, J. S. "Brief Treatment for Adult Children of Alcoholics: Accessing Resources for Self-Care." *Psychotherapy,* 1989, *26,* 510–513.

Crits-Christoph, P., Cooper, A., and Luborsky, L. "The Accuracy of Therapists' Interpretations and the Outcome of Dynamic Psychotherapy." *Journal of Consulting and Clinical Psychology,* 1988, *56,* 490–495.

Dass, R., and Gorman, P. *How Can I Help?* New York: Knopf, 1985.

de Shazer, S., and others. "Brief Therapy: Focused Solution Development." *Family Process,* 1986, *25,* 207–222.

Dolan, Y. M. *A Path with a Heart: Ericksonian Utilization with Resistant and Chronic Clients.* New York: Brunner/Mazel, 1985.

Dulcan, M. K. "Brief Psychotherapy with Children and Their Families: The State of the Art." *Journal of the American Academy of Child Psychiatry,* 1984, *23,* 544–551.

Duncan, B. L., Solovey, A. D., and Rusk, G. S. *Changing the Rules: A Client-Directed Approach to Therapy.* New York: Guilford, 1992.

Durrant, M., and White, C. (eds.). *Ideas for Therapy with Sexual Abuse.* Adelaide, Australia: Dulwich Centre Publications, 1990.

Elkin, I., Parloff, M. B., Hadley, S. W., and Autry, J. H. "NIMH Treatment of Depression Collaborative Research Program." *Archives of General Psychiatry,* 1985, *42,* 305–316.

Ellis, A. *Reason and Emotion in Psychotherapy.* New York: Stuart, 1962.

Epston, D. *Collected Papers.* Adelaide, South Australia: Dulwich Centre Publications, 1989.

Epston, D., and White, M. *Experience, Contradiction, Narrative and Imagination: Selected Papers of David Epston and Michael White 1989–1991.* Adelaide, South Australia: Dulwich Centre Publications, 1992.

Fishman, H. C. *Treating Troubled Adolescents: A Family Therapy Approach.* New York: Basic Books, 1988.

Garfield, S. L. *The Practice of Brief Psychotherapy.* New York: Pergamon Press, 1989.

Gergen, K. J. "Therapeutic Professions and the Diffusion of Deficit." *Journal of Mind and Behavior,* 1990, *11,* 353–368.

Gergen, K. J. *The Saturated Self.* New York: Basic Books, 1991.

Gilligan, S. *Therapeutic Trances: The Cooperation Principle in Ericksonian Hypnotherapy.* New York: Brunner/Mazel, 1987.

Greenberg, D. *How to Make Yourself Miserable.* New York: Random House, 1987.

Greenberg, D., and O'Malley, S. *How to Avoid Love and Marriage.* New York: Freuendlich Books, 1983.

Greenwald, H. *Direct Decision Therapy.* New York: Wyden, 1973.

Greenwald, H. (ed.). *Active Psychotherapy.* New York: Aronson, 1974.

Grinder, J., and Bandler, R. *The Structure of Magic.* Vol. 2. Palo Alto, Calif.: Science and Behavior Books, 1976.

Grove, D. R., and Haley, J. *Conversations on Therapy: Popular Problems and Uncommon Solutions.* New York: W.W. Norton, 1993.

Gustafson, J. P. *Self-Delight in a Harsh World: The Main Stories of Individual, Marital, and Family Psychotherapy.* New York: W.W. Norton, 1992.

Haley, J. "How to Be a Therapy Supervisor Without Knowing How to Change Anyone." *Journal of Systemic Therapies,* 1993, *12* (4), 41–52.

Haley, J. *Jay Haley on Milton H. Erickson.* New York: Brunner/Mazel, 1994.

Hall, M. J., Arnold, W. N., and Crosby, R. M. "Back to Basics: The Importance of Focus Selection." *Psychotherapy,* 1991, *27,* 578–584.

Herr, S. J., and Weakland, J. H. *Counseling Elders and Their Families: Practical Techniques for Applied Gerontology.* New York: Springer, 1979.

Hoglend, D., and others. "Some Criteria for Brief Dynamic Psychotherapy: Reliability, Factor Structure and Long-Term Validity." *Psychotherapy and Psychosomatics,* 1992, *57,* 67–74.

Hopkins, T. *How to Master the Art of Selling.* New York: Warner Books, 1982.

Hopwood, L., and Taylor, M. "Solution-Focused Brief Therapy for Chronic Problems." *Innovations in Clinical Practice: A Source Book,* 1993, *12,* 85–97.

Huber, C., and Backlund, B. *The Twenty-Minute Counselor: Transforming Brief Conversations Into Effective Helping Experiences.* New York: Continuum, 1991.

Hudson, P. *Making Friends with Your Unconscious Mind: The User Friendly Guide.* Omaha, Nebr.: The Center Press, 1993.

Jacobson, N. S. (ed.). *Psychotherapists in Clinical Practice: Cognitive and Behavioral Perspectives.* New York: Guilford, 1987.

Karpel, M. A. *Evaluating Couples: A Handbook for Practitioners.* New York, W.W. Norton, 1994.

Keeney, B. P. *Improvisational Therapy.* St. Paul, Minn.: Systemic Therapy Press, 1990.

Kiser, D. J., Piercy, F. P., and Lipchik, E. "The Integration of Emotion in Solution-Focused Therapy." *Journal of Marital and Family Therapy,* 1993, *19* (3), 233–242.

Kreisman, J. J., and Straus, H. *I Hate You—Don't Leave Me: Understanding the Borderline Personality.* New York: Avon Books, 1989.

Leibenluft, E., Tasman, A., and Green, S. A. (eds.). *Less Time to Do More: Psychotherapy on the Short-Term Inpatient Unit.* Washington, D.C.: American Psychiatric Press, 1993.

Linehan, M. M. *Skills Training Manual for Treating Borderline Personality Disorder.* New York: Guilford, 1993.

Linehan, M. M. *Treating Borderline Personality Disorder.* New York: Guilford, 1993.

Lipchik, E. "The Rush to Be Brief." *Family Therapy Networker,* 1994, *18* (2), 34–39.

Lipchik, E., and de Shazer, S. "Purposeful Sequences for Beginning the Solution-Focused Interview." In E. Lipchik (ed.), *Interviewing.* Rockville, Md.: Aspen, 1988.

Luborsky, L., Crits-Christoph, P., Mintz, J., and Auerbach, A. *Who Will Benefit from Psychotherapy? Predicting Therapeutic Outcomes.* New York: Basic Books, 1988.

Lyddon, W. J. First- and Second-Order Change: Implications of Rationalist and Constructivist Cognitive Therapies. *Journal of Counseling and Development,* 1990, *69,* 122–127.

McFarland, B. *Brief Therapy and Eating Disorders: A Practical Guide to Solution-Focused Work with Clients.* San Francisco: Jossey-Bass, 1995.

MacKenzie, K. R. "Recent Developments in Brief Psychotherapy." *Hospital and Community Psychiatry,* 1988, *39,* 742–752.

McNamee, S., and Gergen, K. J. (eds.). *Therapy as Social Construction.* Newbury Park, Calif.: Sage, 1992.

Madanes, C. *Sex, Love, and Violence.* New York: W.W. Norton, 1990.

Madanes, C. "Strategic Humanism." *Journal of Systemic Therapies,* 1993, *12* (4), 69–75.

Magnavita, J. J. "The Evolution of Short-Term Dynamic Psychotherapy: Treatment of the Future?" *Professional Psychology: Research and Practice,* 1993, *24,* 360–365.

Mahoney, M. J. *Human Change Processes: The Scientific Foundations of Psychotherapy.* New York: Basic Books, 1991.

Mathews, B. "Planned Short-Term Therapy Utilizing the Techniques of Jay Haley and Milton Erickson: A Guide for the Practitioner." *Psychotherapy in Private Practice,* 1988, *6,* 103–118.

Meichenbaum, D., and Fitzpatrick, D. "A Constructivist Narrative Perspective on Stress and Coping: Stress Inoculation Applications." In L. Goldberger and S. Breznitz (eds.), *Handbook of Stress.* New York: Free Press, 1993.

Meichenbaum, D., and Fong, G. "How Individuals Control Their Own Minds: A Constructivist Narrative Perspective." In D. M. Wegner and J. W. Pennebaker (eds.), *Handbook of Mental Control.* Englewood Cliffs, N.J.: Prentice-Hall, 1993.

Meichenbaum, D., and Turk, D. *Facilitating Treatment Adherence: A Practitioner's Guidebook.* New York: Plenum, 1987.

Miller, S. D. "The Symptoms of Solution." *Journal of Strategic and Systemic Therapies,* 1992, *11,* 1–11.

Miller, S. D., and Berg, I. K. *The "Miracle" Method: A Radically New Approach to Problem Drinking.* New York: W.W. Norton, 1995.

Minuchin, S., and Fishman, H. C. *Family Therapy Techniques.* Cambridge, Mass.: Harvard University Press, 1981.

Minuchin, S., and Nichols, M. P. *Family Healing: Strategies for Hope and Understanding.* New York: Free Press/Macmillan, 1993.

Morawetz, A., and Walker, G. *Brief Therapy with Single-Parent Families.* New York: Brunner/Mazel, 1989.

Neill, J., and Kniskern, D. (eds.). *From Psyche to System: The Evolving Therapy of Carl Whitaker.* New York: Guilford, 1982.

Nelson, G., and Walsh-Bowers, R. "Psychology and Psychiatric Survivors." *American Psychologist,* 1994, *49,* 895–896.

Nylund, D., and Corsiglia, V. "Becoming Solution (Focused) Forced in Brief Therapy: Something Important We Already Knew." *Journal of Systemic Therapies,* 1994, *13* (1), 1–8.

O'Conner, J. J. "Strategic Individual Psychotherapy with Bulimic Women." *Psychotherapy,* 1984, *21,* 491–499.

O'Hanlon, W. H. "Not Strategic, Not Systemic: Still Clueless After All These Years." *Journal of Strategic and Systemic Therapies,* 1991, *10,* 105–109.

O'Hanlon, W. H. "The Third Wave." *Family Therapy Networker,* 1994, *18* (6), 18–26, 28–29.

O'Hanlon, W. H., and Beadle, S. *A Field Guide to Possibilityland: Possibility Therapy Methods.* Omaha, Nebr.: The Center Press, 1994.

O'Hanlon, W. H., and Hudson, P. *Love Is a Verb.* New York: W.W. Norton, 1995.

Omer, H. *Critical Interventions in Psychotherapy.* New York, W.W. Norton, 1994.

Organista, K. C., Munoz, R. F., and Gonzalez, G. "Cognitive Behavioral Therapy for Depression in Low Income and Minority Medical Outpatients: Description of a Program and Exploratory Analyses." *Cognitive Therapy and Research,* 1994, *18,* 241–259.

Papp, P. "The Greek Chorus and Other Techniques of Paradoxical Therapy." *Family Process,* 1980, *19,* 45–57.

Penn, P. "Feed-Forward: Future Questions, Future Maps." *Family Process,* 1985, *24,* 289–310.

Persons, J. B. "Psychotherapy Outcome Studies Do Not Accurately Represent Current Models of Psychotherapy: A Proposed Remedy." *American Psychologist,* 1991, *46,* 99–106.

Persons, J. B., Burns, D. D., and Perloff, J. M. "Predictors of Dropout and Outcome in Cognitive Therapy for Depression in a Private Practice Setting." *Cognitive Therapy and Research,* 1988, *12,* 557–575.

Phillips, E. L. *A Guide for Therapists and Patients to Short-Term Psychotherapy.* Springfield, Ill.: Charles C. Thomas, 1985.

Pinkerton, R. S., and Rockwell, W. J. K. "Termination in Brief Psychotherapy: The Case for an Eclectic Approach." *Psychotherapy,* 1990, *27,* 362–365.

Prochaska, J., and DiClemente, C., and Norcoss, J. "In Search of How People Change: Application to Addictive Behaviors." *American Psychologist,* 1992, *47* (9), 1102–1114.

Quackenbush, R. L. "The Prescription of Self-Help Books by Psychologists: A Bibliography of Selected Bibliotherapy Resources." *Psychotherapy,* 1991, *28,* 671–677.

Quick, E. "The Strategic Therapy Planning Worksheet." *Journal of Systemic Therapies,* 1990, *9,* 29–33.

Quick, E. "Strategic/Solution-Focused Therapy: A Combined Approach." *Journal of Strategic and Systemic Therapies,* 1994, *13,* 74–75.

Quick, E. "From Unattainable Goals to Achievable Solutions." *Journal of Systemic Therapies,* 1994, *13*(2), 59–64.

Quintana, S. M. "Toward an Expanded and Updated Conceptualization of Termination: Implications for Short-Term, Individual Psychotherapy." *Professional Psychology: Research and Practice,* 1993, *24,* 426–432.

Rabkin, R. *Strategic Psychotherapy.* New York: Basic Books, 1977.

Rasmussen, P. T., and Tomm, K. "Guided Letter Writing: A Long Brief Therapy Method Whereby Clients Carry Out Their Own Treatment." *Journal of Strategic and Systemic Therapies,* 1992, *11,* 1–18.

Ray, W. A., and Keeney, B. P. *Resource Focused Therapy.* New York: Brunner/Mazel, 1993.

Rosenberg, R. C. "The Therapeutic Alliance and the Psychiatric Emergency Room Crisis as Opportunity." *Psychiatric Annals,* 1994, *24,* 610–614.

Rouse, J. D. "Borderline and Other Dramatic Personality Disorders in the Psychiatric Emergency Service." *Psychiatric Annals,* 1994, *24,* 598–602.

Ryle, A. *Cognitive-Analytic Therapy: Active Participation in Change.* New York: Wiley, 1990.

Sanders, M. R., and Dadds, M. R. *Behavioral Family Intervention.* Boston: Allyn & Bacon/Longwood, 1993.

Saposnek, D. T. "Aikido: A Model for Brief Strategic Therapy." In R. S. Heckler (ed.), *Aikido and the New Warrior.* Berkeley, Calif.: North Atlantic Books, 1980.

Selekman, M. D. *Pathways to Change: Brief Therapy Solutions with Difficult Adolescents.* New York: Guilford, 1993.

Sherman, R., and Fredman, N. *Handbook of Structured Techniques in Marriage and Family Therapy.* New York: Brunner/Mazel, 1986.

Sherman, R., Oresky, P., and Rountree, Y. *Solving Problems in Couples and Family Therapy.* New York: Brunner/Mazel, 1991.

Shutty, M. S., Jr., and Sheras, P. "Brief Strategic Psychotherapy with Chronic Pain Patients: Reframing and Problem Resolution." *Psychotherapy*, 1991, *28*, 636–642.

Slaikeu, K. A. *Crisis Intervention: A Handbook for Practice and Research.* (2nd ed.) Boston: Allyn & Bacon/Longwood, 1990.

Smith, G. B., Schwebel, A. I., Dunn, R. L., and McIver, S. D. "The Role of Psychologists in the Treatment, Management, and Prevention of Chronic Mental Illness." *American Psychologist*, 1993, *48*, 966–971.

Sperry, L. "Contemporary Approaches to Brief Psychotherapy: A Comparative Analysis." *Individual Psychology: The Journal of Adlerian Therapy, Research and Practice*, 1989, *45*, 3–25.

Steenbarger, B. N. "Duration and Outcome in Psychotherapy: An Integrative Review." *Professional Psychology: Research and Practice*, 1994, *25*, 111–119.

Straker, M. "Brief Psychotherapy in an Outpatient Clinic: Evolution and Evaluation." *American Journal of Psychiatry*, 1968, *124*, 1219–1226.

Strayhorn, J. M. *The Competent Child: An Approach to Psychotherapy and Preventive Mental Health.* New York: Guilford, 1988.

Strupp, H. H. "Can the Practitioner Learn from the Researcher?" *American Psychologist*, 1989, *44*, 717–724.

Suzuki, S. *Zen Mind, Beginner's Mind.* New York: Weatherhill, 1970.

Tannen, D. *You Just Don't Understand: Women and Men in Conversation.* New York: Ballantine Books, 1990.

Tomm, K. "Interventive Interviewing, I: Strategizing as a Fourth Guideline for the Therapist." *Family Process*, 1987, *26*, 3–13.

Tomm, K. "Interventive Interviewing, II: Reflexive Questioning as a Means to Enable Self-Healing." *Family Process*, 1987, *26*, 167–183.

Tomm, K. "Interventive Interviewing, III: Intending to Ask Lineal, Circular, Strategic and Reflexive Questions." *Family Process*, 1988, *27*, 1–16.

Tomm, K. "Externalizing the Problem and Internalizing Personal Agency." *Journal of Strategic and Systemic Therapies*, 1989, *8*, 54–59.

Turecki, S. *The Difficult Child.* New York: Bantam, 1985.

Ursano, R. J., and Dressler, D. M. "Brief versus Long-Term Psychotherapy: A Treatment Decision." *Journal of Nervous and Mental Disease,* 1974, *159,* 164–171.

Ursano, R. J., and Dressler, D. M. "Brief versus Long-Term Psychotherapy: Clinician Attitudes and Organization Design." *Comprehensive Psychiatry,* 1977, *18,* 55–60.

Ursano, R. J., and Hales, R. E. "A Review of Brief Individual Psychotherapies." *American Journal of Psychiatry,* 1986, *143,* 1507–1517.

Weakland, J. H., and Fisch, R. "Brief Therapy–MRI Style." In S. H. Budman, M. F. Hoyt, and S. Friedman (eds.), *The First Session in Brief Therapy.* New York: Guilford, 1992.

Weakland, J. H., Fisch, R., Watzlawick, P., and Bodin, A. M. "Brief Therapy: Focused Problem Resolution." *Family Process,* 1974, *13,* 141–168.

Weeks, G. R., and L'Abate, L. *Paradoxical Psychotherapy: Theory and Practice with Individuals, Couples, and Families.* New York: Brunner/Mazel, 1982.

Whitaker, C. A. *Midnight Musings of a Family Therapist.* New York: W.W. Norton, 1989.

White, M. *Selected Papers.* Adelaide, South Australia: Dulwich Centre Publications, 1989.

Wile, D. B. "Kohut, Kernberg, and Accusatory Interpretations." *Psychotherapy,* 1984, *21,* 353–364.

Wolin, S., and Wolin, S. *The Resilient Self: How Survivors of Troubled Families Rise Above Adversity.* New York: Random House, 1993.

Yapko, M. D. (ed.). *Brief Therapy Approaches to Treating Anxiety and Depression.* New York: Brunner/Mazel, 1989.

Zeig, J. K. (ed.). *The Evolution of Psychotherapy–The Second Conference.* New York: Brunner/Mazel, 1992.

Zeig, J. K. (ed.). *Ericksonian Methods: The Essence of the Story.* New York: Brunner/Mazel, 1994.

B. Managed Care/HMO Practice

Abrahamson, D. J. "A Scientist-Practitioner Organization Responds to the Challenges of Managed Mental Health Care." *Psychotherapy in Private Practice,* 1992, *11* (2), 21–28.

Alden, M. *Managed Mental Health Care Training Series Module 1: Treatment Planning.* Salt Lake City, Utah: Psych-Resources Network (c/o Dr. Curtis Reisinger, Intermountain Health Care, Inc.), 1993. Videotape.

Anthony, W. H., and others. "Clinical Care Update: The Chronically Mentally Ill. Case Management: More Than a Response to a Dysfunctional System." *Community Mental Health Journal,* 1988, *24,* 219–228.

Austad, C. S. "Managed Health Care and Its Effects on the Practice and Evolution of Psychotherapy: Pros and Cons." *Psychotherapy in Private Practice,* 1992, *11* (2), 11–14.

Austad, C. S. "Health Care Reform, Managed Mental Health Care, and Short-Term Psychotherapy." *Innovations in Clinical Practice,* 1993, *13,* 241–256.

Austad, C. S., Kisch, J., and Destafano, L. "The Health Maintenance Organization, II: Implications for Psychotherapy." *Psychotherapy,* 1988, *25,* 449–454.

Austad, C. S., and Sherman, W. O. "The Psychotherapist and Managed Care: How Will Practice Be Affected?" *Psychotherapy in Private Practice,* 1992, *11*(2), 1–10.

Austad, C. S., Sherman, W. O., Morgan, T., and Holstein, L. "The Psychotherapist and the Managed Care Setting." *Professional Psychology: Research and Practice,* 1992, *23,* 329–332.

Bak, J. S., Weiner, R. H., and Jackson, L. J. "Managed Mental Health Care: Should Independent Private Practitioners Capitulate or Mobilize?" *The Independent Practitioner,* 1992, *12,* 31–35, 75–80, 159–164.

Bennett, A., and Adams, O. *Looking North for Health: What We Can Learn from Canada's Health Care System.* San Francisco: Jossey-Bass, 1993.

Bennett, M. J. "Quality Assurance Activities for Mental Health Services in Health Maintenance Organizations." In G. A. Striker and A. R. Rodriguez (eds.), *Handbook of Quality Assurance in Mental Health.* New York: Plenum, 1988.

Boland, P. (ed.). *Making Managed Healthcare Work: A Practical Guide to Strategies and Solutions.* Gaithersburg, Md.: Aspen, 1993.

Borenstein, D. "Managed Care: A Means of Rationing Psychiatric Treatment." *Hospital and Community Psychiatry*, 1990, *41*, 1095–1098.

Brown, F. "Resisting the Pull of the Health Insurance Tarbaby: An Organizational Model for Surviving Managed Care." *Clinical Social Work Journal*, 1994, *22*, 59–71.

Buchele, B. J. "Innovative Uses of Psychodynamic Group Psychotherapy." *Bulletin of the Menninger Clinic*, 1994, *58*, 215–223.

Budman, S. H., and Clifford, M. "Short-Term Group Therapy for Couples in an HMO." *Professional Psychology: Research and Practice*, 1979, *10*, 419–429.

Burton, W. N., Hoy, D. A., Bonin, R. L., and Gladstone, L. "Quality and Cost-Effective Management of Mental Health Care." *Journal of Occupational Medicine*, 1989, *31*, 363–367.

Califano, J. A., Jr. *America's Health Care Revolution: Who Lives? Who Dies? Who Pays?* New York: Random House, 1986.

Chodoff, P. "Effects of the New Economic Climate on Psychotherapeutic Practice." *American Journal of Psychiatry*, 1987, *144*, 1293–1297.

Coleman, J. V., Patrick, D. L., Eagle, J., and Hermalin, J. A. "Collaboration, Consultation and Referral in an Integrated Health–Mental Health Program at an HMO." *Social Work in Health Care*, 1979, *5*, 83–96.

Cummings, N. A. "The Anatomy of Psychotherapy Under National Health Insurance." *American Psychologist*, 1977, *32*, 711–718.

Cummings, N. A. "Psychologists Can Manage Mental Health Care: An Alternative to Having It Manage Us." *Psychotherapy in Private Practice*, 1992, *11* (2), 65–70.

Cummings, N. A., and Duhl, L. J. "The New Delivery System." In L. J. Duhl and N. A. Cummings (eds.), *The Future of Mental Health Services: Coping with Crisis*. New York: Springer, 1987.

Curtiss, F. "How Managed Care Works." *Personnel Journal*, 1989, *68*, 38–53.

Donovan, J. M., Steinberg, S. M., and Sabin, J. E. "A Successful Fellowship Program in an HMO Setting." *Hospital and Community Psychiatry*, 1991, *42*, 952–953.

Donovan, J. M., Steinberg, S. M., and Sabin, J. E. "Managed Mental Health Care: An Academic Seminar." *Psychotherapy*, 1994, *31*, 201–207.

Dorken, H. "Psychotherapy in the Marketplace: CHAMPUS 1986." *Psychotherapy,* 1988, *25,* 387–392.

Dorken, H. "The CHAMPUS Reform Initiative in Hawaii: Reestablishing a Medical Monopoly." *Professional Psychology: Research and Practice,* 1994, *25,* 102–105.

Dorken, H., and Cummings, N. A. "Psychotherapy Research on Medicaid in Hawaii." *Psychotherapy,* 1988, *25,* 365–369.

Dorken, H., and others. "Impact of Law and Regulation on Professional Practice and Use of Mental Health Services: An Empirical Analysis." *Professional Psychology: Research and Practice,* 1993, *24,* 256–265.

Dorwart, R. A. "Managed Mental Health Care: Myths and Realities in the 1990s." *Hospital and Community Psychiatry,* 1990, *41,* 1087–1091.

Dorwart, R. A., and Schlesinger, M. "Privatization of Psychiatric Services." *American Journal of Psychiatry,* 1988, *145,* 543–553.

Eckert, P. A. "Cost Control Through Quality Improvement: The New Challenge for Psychology." *Professional Psychology: Research and Practice,* 1994, *25,* 3–8.

Eisenberg, L. "Health Care: For Patients or for Profits?" *American Journal of Psychiatry,* 1986, *143,* 1015–1019.

Endicott, J., Herz, M. I., and Gibbon, M. "Brief versus Standard Hospitalization: The Differential Costs." *American Journal of Psychiatry,* 1978, *135,* 707–712.

Enthoven, A., and Kronick, R. "A Consumer-Choice Health Plan for the 1990s: Universal Health Insurance in a System Designed to Promote Quality and Economy." *New England Journal of Medicine,* 1989, *320,* 29–37 (Part 1), 94–101 (Part 2).

Flinn, D. E., McMahon, T. C., and Collins, M. F. "Health Maintenance Organizations and Their Implications for Psychiatry." *Hospital and Community Psychiatry,* 1987, *38,* 255–263.

Fox, P. D., and Wasserman, J. "Academic Medical Centers and Managed Care: Uneasy Partners." *Group Practice Journal,* 1993, Sept./Oct., 46–47.

Frank, R. G., Sullivan, M. J., and DeLeon, P. H. "Health Care Reform in the States." *American Psychologist,* 1994, *49,* 855–867.

Gabbard, G. O., and others. "A Psychodynamic Perspective on

the Clinical Impact of Insurance Review." *American Journal of Psychiatry*, 1991, *148*, 318–323.

Geraty, R., and others. "The Impact of Managed Behavioral Healthcare on the Costs of Psychiatric and Chemical Dependency Treatment." *Behavioral Healthcare Tomorrow*, 1994, *3* (2), 18–30.

German, M. "Effective Case Management in Managed Mental Health Care: Conditions, Methods and Outcomes." *HMO Practice*, 1994, *8*, 34–40.

Gerson, S. N. "When Should Managed Care Firms Terminate Private Benefits for Chronically Mentally Ill Patients?" *Behavioral Healthcare Tomorrow*, 1994, *3* (2), 31–35.

Goldman, H. H., and Taube, C. A. "High Users of Outpatient Mental Health Services, II: Implications for Practice and Policy." *American Journal of Psychiatry*, 1988, *145*, 24–28.

Goldstein, L. S. "Genuine Managed Care in Psychiatry: A Proposed Practice Model." *General Hospital Psychiatry*, 1989, *11*, 271–277.

Good, P. R. "Brief Therapy in the Age of Regapeutics." *American Journal of Orthopsychiatry*, 1987, *57*, 6–11.

Gorski, T. T. "Integrating Relapse Prevention Into Managed Chemical Dependency Services." *Behavioral Healthcare Tomorrow*, 1993, *2* (3), 20–34.

Granat, J. P. and Lightman, R. *How to Survive and Profit in a Managed Care Environment: A Guide for Mental Health Professionals, Clinics, Hospitals, and Drug and Alcohol Treatment Facilities*. Fort Lee, N.J.: Skyline Press, 1992. Videotape.

Hall, R.C.W. "Legal Precedents Affecting Managed Care: The Physician's Responsibilities to Patients." *Psychosomatics*, 1994, *35*, 105–117.

Hall, R.C.W. "Social and Legal Implications of Managed Care in Psychiatry." *Psychosomatics*, 1994, *35*, 150–158.

Hendricks, R. *A Model for National Health Care: The History of Kaiser Permanente*. New Brunswick, N.J.: Rutgers University Press, 1993.

Herron, W. G. "Managed Mental Health Care Redux." *Professional Psychology: Research and Practice*, 1992, *23*, 163–164.

Herron, W. G., Javier, R. A., Primavera, L. H., and Schultz,

C. L. "The Cost of Psychotherapy." *Professional Psychology: Research and Practice,* 1994, *25,* 106–110.

Herron, W. G., and others. "Session Effects, Comparability, and Managed Care in the Psychotherapies." *Psychotherapy,* 1994, *31,* 279–285.

Hoge, M. A., and others. "Defining Managed Care in Public-Sector Psychiatry." *Hospital and Community Psychiatry,* 1994, *45,* 1085–1089.

Hudson, P., and Applegarth, R. "The Bottom Line: A Primer on Managing Managed Care." *Family Therapy Networker,* 1994, *18*(4), 73–74.

Inglehart, J. K. "HMOs (for-profit and not-for-profit) on the Move." *New England Journal of Medicine,* 1984, *310,* 1203–1208.

Johnson, L. D. *Psychotherapy in the Age of Accountability.* New York, W.W. Norton, in press.

Kisch, J. "Psychotherapy: Dilemmas of Practice in Managed Care." *Psychotherapy in Private Practice,* 1992, *11*(2), 33–38.

LaCourt, M. "The HMO Crisis: Danger/Opportunity." *Family Systems Medicine,* 1988, *6,* 80–93.

Lehman, A. F. "Capitation Payment and Mental Health Care: A Review of the Opportunities and Risks." *Hospital and Community Psychiatry,* 1987, *38,* 31–38.

Lowman, R. L. "Managing Mental Care Wisely: More Is not Necessarily Better." *Professional Psychology: Research and Practice,* 1991, *23,* 164–166.

Lowman, R. L., and Resnick, R. J. (eds.). *The Mental Health Professional's Guide to Managed Care.* Washington, D.C.: American Psychological Association, 1994.

McDermott, K. C. "Healthcare Reform: Past and Future." *Oncology Nursing Forum,* 1994, *21,* 827–832.

Manning, W. G., Wells, K. B., and Benjamin, B. "Use of Outpatient Mental Health Services Over Time in a Health Maintenance Organization and Fee-for-Service Plans." *American Journal of Psychiatry,* 1987, *144,* 283–287.

Marshall, J. "HMOs and Psychiatry: Could There Be a Silver Lining?" *International Journal of Law and Psychiatry,* 1987, *10,* 35–43.

Mechanic, D. "Strategies for Integrating Public Mental Health

Services." *Hospital and Community Psychiatry*, 1991, *42*, 797–801.

Mechanic, D., and Aiken, L. H. "Improving the Care of Patients with Chronic Mental Illness." *New England Journal of Medicine*, 1987, *317*, 1634–1638.

Melnick, S. D., and Lyter, L. L. "The Negative Impacts of Increased Concurrent Review on Psychiatric Inpatient Care." *Hospital and Community Psychiatry*, 1987, *38*, 300–303.

Minkoff, K. "The Future of Community Psychiatry: Public-Sector Managed Care." *Community Psychiatrist*, 1993, *7*, 1–2, 7.

Moldawsky, S. "Is Solo Practice Really Dead?" *American Psychologist*, 1990, *45*, 544–546.

Nahmias, V. R. "Training for a Managed Care Setting." *Psychotherapy in Private Practice*, 1992, *11*(2), 15–20.

Nylund, D., and Thomas, J. "The Economics of Narrative." *Family Therapy Networker*, 1994, *18* (6), 38–39.

Olfson, M. and Pincus, H. A. "Outpatient Psychotherapy in the United States, I: Volume, Costs, and User Characteristics." *American Journal of Psychiatry*, 1994, *151*, 1281–1288.

Olfson, M. and Pincus, H. A. "Outpatient Psychotherapy in the United States, II: Patterns of Utilization." *American Journal of Psychiatry*, 1994, *151*, 1289–1294.

Pallak, M. S. "National Outcomes Management Survey: Summary Report." *Behavioral Healthcare Tomorrow*, 1994, Sept./Oct., 63–69.

Patterson, D. "Managed Care: An Approach to Rational Psychiatric Treatment." *Hospital and Community Psychiatry*, 1990, *41*, 1092–1095.

Peake, T. H., and Ball, J. D. "Brief Psychotherapy: Planned Therapeutic Change for Changing Times." *Psychotherapy in Private Practice*, 1987, *5*, 53–63.

Pepe, M. M., and Wu, J. "The Economics of Mental Health Care." *Psychotherapy*, 1988, *25*, 352–355.

Psychiatric Times. "Special Report: Hospital Psychiatry." *Psychiatric Times*, 1994, *11* (12), 18–23.

Quirk, M., and others. "Quality and Customers: Type 2 Change in Mental Health Delivery Within Health Care Reform." *Journal of Mental Health Administration*, in press.

Richardson, L. M., and Austad, C. S. "Realities of Mental

Health Practice in Managed-Care Settings." *Professional Psychology: Research and Practice,* 1991, *22,* 52–59.

Rush, D., and Cagney, T. "Clinician Update: The Nuts and Bolts of Managing Managed Care." *Behavioral Healthcare Tomorrow,* 1993, *2* (3), 38–39.

Sabin, J. E., Steinberg, S. M., and Donovan, J. M. "Mental Health Education in an HMO." *HMO Practice,* 1988, *2,* 143–146.

Schlesinger, H. J., and others. "Mental Health Treatment and Medical Care Utilization in a Fee-for-Service System: Outpatient Mental Health Treatment Following the Onset of a Chronic Disease." *American Journal of Public Health,* 1983, *73,* 422–429.

Schreter, R. K. "Ten Trends in Managed Care and Their Impact on the Biopsychosocial Model." *Hospital and Community Psychiatry,* 1993, *44,* 325–327.

Schreter, R. K., Sharfstein, S. S., and Schreter, C. A. (eds.). *Allies and Adversaries, The Impact of Managed Care on Mental Health Services.* Washington, D.C.: American Psychiatric Press, 1994.

Sederer, L. I., and St. Clair, R. L. "Managed Health Care and the Massachusetts Experience." *American Journal of Psychiatry,* 1989, *146,* 1142–1148.

Sharfstein, S. "Medicaid Cutbacks and Block Grants: Crisis or Opportunity for Community Mental Health?" *American Journal of Psychiatry,* 1982, *139,* 466–470.

Sharfstein, S., and Beigel, A. "Less Is More? Today's Economics and Its Challenge to Psychiatry." *American Journal of Psychiatry,* 1984, *141,* 1403–1408.

Sharfstein, S., and Beigel, A. *The New Economics and Psychiatric Care.* Washington, D.C.: American Psychiatric Press, 1985.

Sharfstein, S. S., and others. "Impact of Benefit Limits and Managed Care on Discharge Plans and Outcome: A Research Design and Preliminary Results." *Psychiatric Hospital,* 1990, *21,* 177–182.

Sherman, C. F. "Changing Practice Models in Managed Health Care." *Psychotherapy in Private Practice,* 1992, *11* (2), 29–32.

Shore, M. F., and Cohen, M. D. "The Robert Wood Johnson Program on Chronic Mental Illness: An Overview." *Hospital and Community Psychiatry,* 1990, *41,* 1212–1216.

Siddall, L., Haffey, N., and Feinman, J. "Intermittent Brief Psychotherapy in an HMO Setting." *American Journal of Psychotherapy,* 1988, *42,* 96–106.

Simon, G. E., and others. "Predictors of Outpatient Mental Health Utilization by Primary Care Patients in a Health Maintenance Organization." *American Journal of Psychiatry,* 1994, *151,* 908–913.

Smillie, J. *Can Physicians Manage the Quality and Costs of Health Care? The Story of the Permanente Medical Group.* New York: McGraw-Hill, 1991.

Stern, S. "Managed Care, Brief Therapy, and Therapeutic Integrity." *Psychotherapy,* 1993, *30,* 162–175.

Talbott, J. A. "Commentary: The Emerging Crisis in Chronic Care." *Hospital and Community Psychiatry,* 1981, *32,* 447–454.

Taube, C. A., Goldman, H. H., Burns, B. J., and Kessler, L. G. "High Users of Outpatient Mental Health Services, I: Definition and Characteristics." *American Journal of Psychiatry,* 1988, *145,* 19–24.

Wedding, D., Ritchie, P., Kitchen, A., and Binner, P. "Mental Health Services in a Single-Payer System: Lessons from Canada and Principles for an American Plan." *Professional Psychology: Research and Practice,* 1993, *24,* 387–393.

Welch, B. "The Best Care: Integrated, Not Managed." *The APA Monitor,* 1992, *23*(8), 30.

Wells, K. B., and others. "Detection of Depressive Disorder for Patients Receiving Prepaid or Fee-for-Service Care." *Journal of the American Medical Association,* 1989, *262,* 3298–3302.

White House Domestic Policy Council. *Health Security: The Official Text.* New York: Touchstone/Simon & Schuster, 1993.

Williams, S. J., Diehr, D., Drucker, W. L., and Richardson, W. C. "Mental Health Services: Utilization by Low-Income Enrollees in a Prepaid Group Practice Plan and in an Independent Practice Plan." *Medical Care,* 1979, *17,* 139–151.

Wise, E. A. "Issues in Psychotherapy with EAP Clients." *Psychotherapy,* 1988, *25,* 415–419.

Wylie, M. S. "Toeing the Bottom Line." *Family Therapy Networker,* 1992, *16*(2), 30–39, 74–75.

Wylie, M. S. "Endangered Species: The Managed Care Revolution." *Family Therapy Networker,* 1994, *18* (2), 20–23.

Yoken, C., and Berman, J. S. "Third-Party Payment and the Outcome of Psychotherapy." *Journal of Consulting and Clinical Psychology,* 1987, *55,* 571–576.

Zuckerman, R. "Iatrogenic Factors in 'Managed' Psychotherapy." *American Journal of Psychotherapy,* 1989, *43,* 118–131.

Directories for Training, Publications, Professional Associations, and Managed-Care Organizations

❖

Professionals wanting to increase their knowledge of the rapidly expanding fields of brief therapy and managed mental health care have a number of valuable resources available to them, including those organized below under the following headings: A. Training Institutes and Conferences, B. Publications and Newsletters, C. Professional Associations, and D. Managed-Care Organizations. These are provided for convenience. The list is not exhaustive, and no specific endorsement is implied or intended.

A. Training Institutes and Conferences

1. Institute for Behavioral
   Healthcare
   4370 Alpine Road, Suite 108
   Portola Valley, CA 94028
   (415) 851-8411

2. New England Educational
   Institute
   92 Elm Street
   Pittsfield, MA 01201
   (413) 499-1489

3. Institute for Advanced Clinical
   Training, Inc.
   P.O. Box 326
   Villanova, PA 19085
   (215) 790-1414

4. The Milton H. Erickson
   Foundation, Inc.
   3606 North 24th Street
   Phoenix, AZ 85016-6500
   (602) 956-6196

407

5. Innovative Training Systems
   24 Loring Street
   Newton Centre, MA 02159
   (617) 332-6028

6. Brief Family Therapy Center
   P.O. Box 1373
   Milwaukee, WI 53213-0736
   (414) 785-9001

7. The Hudson Center for Brief
   Therapy
   11926 Arbor Street
   Omaha, NE 68144
   (402) 330-1144

8. Mental Research Institute
   555 Middlefield Road
   Palo Alto, CA 94301
   (415) 321-3055

9. Family Therapy Institute of
   Washington, D.C.
   5850 Hubbard Drive
   Rockville, MD 20852
   (301) 984-5730

10. Consultations
    1620 W. Thome
    Chicago, IL 60660
    (312) 338-7230

11. Brief Therapy Training
    Network
    P.O. Box 578264
    Chicago, IL 60657-8264
    (312) 404-5130

12. The Brief Therapy Center
    166 East 5900 South
    Suite B108
    Salt Lake City, UT 84107
    (801) 261-1412

13. Foundation for Behavioral
    Health
    360 Oyster Point Blvd.
    Suite 200
    South San Francisco, CA
    94080
    (415) 871-1291

B. Publications and Newsletters
(see also bibliographies in References and For Further Reading
sections)

1. *Behavioral Healthcare Tomorrow*
   1110 Mar West Street, Suite E
   Tiburon, CA 94920-1879
   (415) 435-9821

2. *Psychotherapy Finances*
   1016 Clemons Street, Suite 407
   Juniper, FL 33477
   (407) 747-1960

3. *Open Minds: The Behavioral*
   Health Industry Analyst
   4465 Old Harrisburg Road
   Gettysburg, PA 17325
   (717) 334-1329

4. *NFSCSW Managed Care News*
   P.O. Box 3740
   Arlington, VA 22203
   (708) 998-1680

5. *HMO Practice*
   Health Care Plan
   900 Guaranty Building
   Buffalo, NY 14202
   (716) 857-6361

6. *EAP Digest*
   Performance Resource Press
   1863 Technology Drive
   Troy, MI 48083-4244
   (810) 588-7733

C. Professional Associations

1. American Psychological
   Association
   APA Practice Directorate
   750 First Street NE
   Washington, DC 20002-4242
   (202) 336-5500

2. National Registry of Providers
   in Psychology
   1730 Rhode Island Avenue
   Washington, DC
   (202) 833-2377

3. National Association
   of Social Workers
   7981 Eastern Avenue
   Silver Spring, MD 20910
   (800) 638-8799

4. American Board of Examiners
   in Clinical Social Work
   8484 Georgia Avenue
   Suite 800
   Silver Spring, MD 20910-5604
   (304) 587-8783

5. American Psychiatric
   Association
   Managed Care Committee
   1400 K Street NW
   Washington, DC 20036
   (202) 682-6000

6. American Association of
   Marriage and Family
   Therapists
   1100 17th Street NW
   Washington, DC 20036-4601
   (202) 452-0109

7. American Mental Health
   Counselors Association
   5999 Stevenson Avenue
   Alexandria, VA 22304
   (800) 326-2642

8. American Nursing Association
   2420 Pershing Road
   Kansas City, MO 64108
   (816) 474-5720

D. Managed-Care Organizations

1. Group Health Association of
   America (GHAA)
   1929 20th Street NW
   Suite 600
   Washington, DC 20036-3403
   (202) 364-2002

2. American Association
   of Preferred Provider
   Organizations
   401 North Michigan Avenue
   Chicago, IL 60611
   (312) 245-1555

3. Employee Assistance
   Professionals Association
   (EAPA)
   4601 North Fairfax Drive
   Suite 1001
   Arlington, VA 22203
   (703) 522-6272

4. Utilization Review
   Accreditation Commission
   (URAC)
   1130 Connecticut Avenue NW
   Suite 450
   Washington, DC 20036
   (202) 296-0120

5. Joint Commission on
   Accreditation of Healthcare
   Organizations (JCAHO)
   1 Renaissance Boulevard
   Oakbrook Terrace, IL 60181
   (708) 916-5600

6. National Directory
   of Managed Care Companies
   and EAPs
   Professional Health Plan
   5856 College Avenue
   Suite 206
   Oakland, CA 94618
   (800) 428-7559

Author Index

411

Subject Index